D0881314

STUDIES IN ENGLISH LINGUISTICS
FOR RANDOLPH QUIRK

STUDIES IN ENGLISH LINGUISTICS

FOR RANDOLPH QUIRK

EDITED BY SIDNEY GREENBAUM
GEOFFREY LEECH & JAN SVARTVIK

LONGMAN
LONDON AND NEW YORK

LONGMAN GROUP LIMITED LONDON

Associated companies, branches and representatives throughout the world
Published in the United States of America by Longman Inc, New York
© **Longman Group Ltd 1979**

First published 1980
ISBN 0 582 55079 3

British Library Cataloguing in Publication Data
Studies in English linguistics.
I. English language – Addresses, essays, lectures
I. Quirk, Randolph   II. Greenbaum, Sidney
III. Leech, Geoffrey Neil   IV. Svartvik, Jan
420   PE 1072   79–41023
ISBN 0 582 55079 3

Typeset by CCC, printed and bound in Great Britain by
William Clowes (Beccles) Limited, Beccles and London

PREFACE

In this book, a number of Randolph Quirk's friends have joined together in paying tribute to his outstanding contribution to the study of the English language over the past thirty years. These friends are scholars with whom he has been associated, several as collaborators or as former students.

Studies in English Linguistics covers a broad range of research in modern English, and thus mirrors, in part, the breadth of scholarship of the man whose work it celebrates. The contributions are arranged in thematic groupings. Papers 1–2 concern theoretical aspects of language as exemplified in present-day English. Papers 3–8 are descriptive studies in modern English grammar. The theme of the English verb (in papers 5–8) links this group with the next (papers 9–11), in which aspects of English semantics, specifically of modal semantics, are treated. In papers 12–18, the unifying theme is the study of text and discourse, with particular concern for the role of intonation (papers 13 and 14) and the use of corpus data (papers 15–18). Papers 19–21 have the common theme of literary stylistics, and papers 22–24 that of attitudes to language. In the final two papers, the connecting topics are lexicology and phonology, seen from a typological viewpoint in 25, and from a historical viewpoint in 26. These groupings do not, of course, form watertight compartments: it would be contrary to the spirit of this book to imply that one domain of language can be studied in isolation from another, and many of the essays, in various ways, bear witness to this interconnectivity.

Through its spectrum-like arrangement, the book aims to capture a Quirkian sense of the unity underlying diversities of model, method, and topic in contemporary research on English. It can only, however, be a partial reflection of the enormous range of Randolph Quirk's own contributions to English linguistics, and of the peculiar quality of the mind we see in them: a mind which tirelessly explores and exposes the interconnections between linguistic phenomena; which focuses meticulously on the observed data of language, and at the same time places such data in their context within the language as a whole, seen, for all its multiplicity, as a single system.

Beginning with a bibliography of Randolph Quirk's major academic publications, the book testifies to the influence of his thought in the many references to, and discussions of, his work that it contains. But one major area of his research has been largely neglected, for reasons of space and coherence: this is the area of historical and medieval studies in which the name of Randolph Quirk was renowned long before the Survey of English Usage and the *Grammar of Contemporary English* were heard of. This neglect of the diachronic dimension of his scholarship, though a practical necessity, is regrettable: it should not be forgotten here that as Quain Professor at University College London, he has held for 12 years the oldest chair of English in the United Kingdom, and is rightful heir to a distinguished tradition of historical scholarship. Yet the point may be put more positively: it is fitting that through him, the College which first recognized English as a worthy subject for academic study has become a focal, metropolitan, centre for the study of English as an international language in the present-day world. In Randolph Quirk, the humanistic spirit of philology has been revitalized and happily united with the more scientific spirit of modern linguistics.

As editors, we thank our contributors for their generous participation in this volume. Valerie Adams, who undertook the daunting task of compiling a bibliography of Randolph Quirk's scholarly publications (even though this excluded untold lesser, or at least less academic, writings), has deserved our sympathy as well as our gratitude. Our final acknowledgment goes to Peggy Drinkwater, whose vigilance and editorial guidance saw this volume through the press. Her long and valued publishing association with RQ, as well as with the present editors, deserves commemoration on this page in type as large as she will allow.

SG   GL   JS

CONTENTS

CONTENTS

SEMANTICS OF ENGLISH MODALS

TEXT AND DISCOURSE

STYLISTICS

[viii]

CONTENTS

ACKNOWLEDGMENTS

We are grateful to the following for permission to reproduce copyright material:

The author's agent and Macmillan Publishing Co. Inc. for the poem 'Who Goes With Fergus' by W. B. Yeats from *The Collected Poems of William Butler Yeats*, Copyright 1906 by Macmillan Publishing Co. Inc., renewed 1934 by W. B. Yeats, by permission of Michael Yeats, Anne Yeats and Macmillan London Ltd.

SELECT LIST OF PUBLICATIONS BY RANDOLPH QUIRK COMPILED BY VALERIE ADAMS

1950 1 'On the problem of morphological suture in Old English'. *Modern Language Review* 45.1–5. [Revised and reprinted in 53 as 'On the problem of inflexional juncture in Old English'.]

1951 2 'Expletive or existential *there*'. *London Mediæval Studies* 2.32

3 'Puns to sell'. *Studia Neophilologica* 23.81–6

4 'Textual notes on Hrafnkelssaga'. *London Mediæval Studies* 2.1–31

1953 5 (with P. G. Foote) Edition of *Gunnlaugssaga Ormstungu*. London: Viking Society for Northern Research. [Reprinted 1974 with revised pagination and addenda.]

6 'Langland's use of *kind wit* and *inwit*'. *Journal of English and Germanic Philology* 52.182–8. [Reprinted in 53.]

7 (with Sherman M. Kuhn) 'Some recent interpretations of Old English digraph spellings'. *Language* 29.143–56. [Reprinted in 53.]

1954 8 *The concessive relation in Old English poetry*. New Haven: Yale University Press. London: Oxford University Press. Second edition 1973. Hamden, Conn: Archon Books, Shoestring Press Inc

9 'Vis imaginativa'. *Journal of English and Germanic Philology* 53.81–3. [Reprinted in 53.]

1955 10 'Colloquial English and communication'. *Studies in Communication* contributed to the Communication Research Centre, University College London, with an introduction by B. Ifor Evans. 169–82. [Revised and reprinted as 'Speech and communication' in 67.]

11 'Dasent, Morris, and aspects of translation'. *Saga-Book* 14.64–77. [Revised and reprinted in 72.]

12 'The language of the Leechbook'. *Bald's Leechbook: British Museum Royal Manuscript 12 D.xvii*, ed C. E. Wright. Copenhagen: Rosenkilde and Bagger. London: George Allen and Unwin. Baltimore: The Johns Hopkins Press

13 'Linguistics'. Chapter 2, *The Year's Work in English Studies* 36.27–43

14 (with C. L. Wrenn) *An Old English Grammar*. London: Methuen. Second edition 1957

15 (with Sherman M. Kuhn) 'The Old English digraphs: a reply'. *Language* 31.390–401. [Reprinted in 53.]

16 (with A. H. Smith) 'Some problems of verbal communication'. *Transactions of the Yorkshire Dialect Society* 9.10–20

1956 17 'Linguistics'. Chapter 2, *The Year's Work in English Studies* 37.33–53

1957 18 'Linguistics'. Chapter 2, *The Year's Work in English Studies* 38.32–54

19 'Relative clauses in educated spoken English'. *English Studies* 38.97–109. [Reprinted in 53.]

20 (with P. G. Foote) *The Saga of Gunnlaug Serpent-Tongue*. London: Nelson

1958 21 '"Dialects" within Standard English'. *Transactions of the Yorkshire Dialect Society* 10.29–42

22 'From descriptive to prescriptive: an example'. *English Language Teaching* 12.9–13. [Revised and reprinted in 53, and in *ELT Selections*, ed W. R. Lee. London: Oxford University Press 1967.91–4.]

23 (with J. Warburg) 'James Eyre: annotator'. *English Studies* 39.241–8. [Reprinted, slightly shortened, in 72, as 'A glimpse of eighteenth-century prescriptivism'.]

24 'Substitutions and syntactical research'. *Archivum Linguisticum* 10.37–42. [Reprinted, with slight alterations, in 53. Based upon a paper read at the Eighth International Congress of Linguists at Oslo, August 1957, a shortened version of which was published in the *Proceedings* of the Congress, 1958.817–8, as 'Some limitations of the substitution test'.]

1959 25 'Charles Dickens and appropriate language'. Inaugural lecture. Durham: Durham University Press. [Reprinted in part in *Charles Dickens*, ed Stephen Wall. Harmondsworth: Penguin 1970. 409–22. Revised and conflated with 31 in 72.]

26 'English language and the structural approach'. Chapter 2 (6–35) of 27

27 (edited and introduced in collaboration with A. H. Smith) *The*

Teaching of English. London: Secker and Warburg. London: Oxford University Press 1964

1960 28 'Towards a description of English usage'. *Transactions of the Philological Society* 40–61. [Revised and reprinted as 'The survey of English usage' in 53.]

1961 29 (with A. P. Duckworth) 'Co-existing negative preterite forms of *dare'. Language and society: essays presented to Arthur M. Jensen.* Copenhagen: Berling. 135–40. [Reprinted in 53.]

30 'Research problems'. *English teaching abroad and the British Universities,* ed H. G. Wayment. London: Methuen. 51–7. [Reprinted as 'Research problems and the teaching of English' in 53.]

31 'Some observations on the language of Dickens'. *Review of English Studies* 2.19–28. [Revised and conflated with 25 in 72.]

32 'The study of the mother tongue'. Inaugural lecture. London: H. K. Lewis. [Reprinted in 72, and in *Five inaugural lectures,* ed P. Strevens. London: Oxford University Press 1966.51–76.]

33 'The survey of English usage'. *The Linguistic Reporter* (Washington DC) 3, No 2.3–7

1962 34 *The use of English.* (with supplements by A. C. Gimson and J. Warburg). London: Longman 1962. New York: St Martin's Press 1963. Second edition 1968

1963 35 'English teaching in India'. *Educational Forum* (Delhi) 8.1–4

36 'Poetic language and Old English metre'. *Early English and Norse Studies* presented to Hugh Smith, ed A. Brown and P. G. Foote. London: Methuen. 150–71. [Reprinted in 53.]

1964 37 'Change in language'. *The Study of Current English* 19.6–15

38 (with A. H. Marckwardt) *A common language: British and American English.* The British Broadcasting Corporation, and The United States Government

39 (with J. Mulholland) 'Complex prepositions and related sequences'. *English Studies presented to R. W. Zandvoort.* Supplement to *English Studies* 45.64–73. [Reprinted in 53.]

40 'The English language problem'. *Bulletin of the National Association for the Teaching of English* 1.7–12

41 'The examining of English'. [Appendix D of *The examining of English language.* The eighth report of the Secondary School Examinations Council.] London: HMSO. 64–9

42 (with J. Svartvik, A. P. Duckworth, J. P. L. Rusiecki, A. J. T. Colin) 'Studies in the correspondence of prosodic to grammatical features in English'. *Proceedings of the Ninth International Congress of Linguistics.* The Hague: Mouton. 679–91. [Reprinted in 53.]

43 'The survey of English usage'. *The Rising Generation.* (Tokyo) 110.139–41

44 (with D. Crystal) *Systems of prosodic and paralinguistic features in English*. The Hague: Mouton

1965 45 'Descriptive statement and serial relationship'. *Language* 41.205–217. [Reprinted in 53.]

1966 46 'Acceptability in language'. *Proceedings of the University of Newcastle upon Tyne Philosophical Society* I. 79–92. [Reprinted in 53.]

47 (with J. Svartvik) *Investigating linguistic acceptability*. The Hague: Mouton

48 'On English usage'. *Journal of the Royal Society of Arts* 114.837–51. [Revised and reprinted as 'On knowing English' in 67.]

49 (with D. Crystal) 'On scales of contrast in connected English speech'. *In Memory of J. R. Firth*, ed C. E. Bazell, J. C. Catford, M. A. K. Halliday, R. H. Robins. London: Longman. 359–69. [Revised and reprinted in 53.]

50 'Types of deviance in English sentences'. *A common purpose*, ed J. R. Squire. Champaign, Illinois: National Council for the Teaching of English. 46–60

1967 51 'Our knowledge of English'. *The Incorporated Linguist* 6.1–6. [Reprinted in 72.]

1968 52 'On conceptions of good grammar'. *Essays by divers hands*, edited by Lady Birkenhead. 115–27. [Reprinted in 67.]

53 *Essays on the English language–medieval and modern*. London: Longman. Bloomington: Indiana University Press

1969 54 (with D. Davy) 'An acceptability experiment with spoken output'. *Journal of Linguistics* 5.109–20

55 'English today: a world view'. *TESOL Quarterly* 3.23–9. [Reprinted in 67.]

1970 56 'Aspect and variant inflection in English verbs'. *Language* 46.300–311

57 (with W.-D. Bald). 'A case study of multiple meaning'. *Essays and Studies* N.S. 23.101–19

58 (with S. Greenbaum) *Elicitation experiments in English: linguistic studies in use and attitude*. London: Longman. Coral Gables, Florida: University of Miami Press; distributor, Austin, Texas: University of Texas Press

59 'English and the native speaker'. *Modern English lexicology*, ed S. S. Khidekel. Leningrad: Prosveshchenie. 56–62

60 'English in twenty years'. *The Incorporated Linguist* 9.67–70. [Reprinted in 67.]

61 'Taking a deep smell'. *Journal of Linguistics* 6.119–24

62 (with J. Svartvik) 'Types and uses of non-finite clause in Chaucer'. *English Studies* 51.393–411

1971 63 'Conceptions of grammar'. *Didaskolos* 3.563–76

64 (with R. M. Kempson) 'Controlled activation of latent contrast'. *Language* 47.548-72

65 'Linguistics, usage and the user'. *Linguistics at large*, ed N. Minnis. London: Gollancz. 295-313. [Reprinted in 67.]

66 'Shakespeare and the English language'. *A new companion to Shakespeare studies*, ed K. Muir and S. Schoenbaum. Cambridge: Cambridge University Press. 68-72. [Reprinted, with minor alterations, in 72.]

1972 67 *The English language and images of matter*. London: Oxford University Press

68 (with S. Greenbaum, G. Leech and J. Svartvik) *A grammar of contemporary English*. London: Longman. Eighth impression (corrected) 1979

69 *Speech Therapy Services*. Report of the Committee of Inquiry. London: HMSO

1973 70 'The social impact of dictionaries in the UK'. *Lexicography in English*, ed R. I. McDavid Jr and A. R. Duckert. Annals of the New York Academy of Sciences 211.76-88

71 (with S. Greenbaum) *A university grammar of English*. London: Longman. Ninth impression (corrected) 1979. [*A concise grammar of contemporary English*. New York: Harcourt Brace Jovanovich.]

1974 72 *The linguist and the English language*. London: Edward Arnold

1975 73 (with V. Adams and D. Davy) *Old English literature: a practical introduction*. London: Edward Arnold

1976 74 'Albert Henry Marckwardt'. *English Language Teaching* 30.168-9

1977 75 (with R. A. Close and A. C. Gimson) 'English as a language of international communication'. *IATEFL Newsletter* 47.9-14

76 'Setting new word records'. *Visible Language* 11.63-74

77 'A tough object to trace'. *Journal of Linguistics* 13.99-102

78 (with S. Greenbaum and Y. Ikegami) *A university grammar of English*. Tokyo: Kinokuniya

1978 79 'Aspects of English as an international language'. *Sproglæreren* 9.20-34

80 'Focus, scope, and lyrical beginnings'. *Language and Style* 11.30-9

81 'Grammatical and pragmatic aspects of countability'. *Die Neueren Sprachen* 77.317-25

82 (with P. Collier and D. M. Neale) 'The Hornby Educational Trust: the first ten years'. *In honour of A. S. Hornby*, ed P. Strevens. London: Oxford University Press. 3-7

1979 83 (with J. Svartvik) 'A corpus of modern English'. *Empirische Textwissenschaft: Aufbau und Auswertung von Text-Corpora*, ed H. Bergenholtz and B. Schaeder. Königstein: Scriptor. 204-18

84 'Language and nationhood'. *The Crown and the Thistle*, ed Colin Maclean. Edinburgh: Scottish Academic Press 56-70

85 'Trends in contemporary English'. *NHK Journal* (Tokyo), 4 (1979) 56–71

1980 86 (with J. Svartvik) *A corpus of English conversation.* Lund Studies in English, vol 56. Lund: Gleerups/Liber

87 'The grammar of "Nuclear English"'. *English for cross-cultural communication*, ed L. E. Smith. London: The Macmillan Press

88 (with B. Kachru) Introduction. *English for cross-cultural communication*, ed L. E. Smith. London: The Macmillan Press

89 'Sound barriers and Gangbangsprache'. *The state of the language*, ed L. Michaels and C. Ricks. Los Angeles and Berkeley; London: University of California Press 3–14

90 (with J. Rusiecki) 'Supplementary corpus by elicitation'. *Language form and Linguistic variation*, ed John M. Anderson. Amsterdam: John Benjamins

ON OPACITY
NOAM CHOMSKY

In this paper I will assume the general framework of the Extended Standard Theory of generative grammar, and more specifically, the version of this theory presented in Chomsky and Lasnik 1977.[1] The basic structure of grammar is assumed to have the following form:

[1] 1 Base rules
2 Transformational rules
3a Deletion rules   3b Construal rules
4a Filters   4b Interpretive rules
5a Phonology and stylistic rules   5b Conditions on binding

The rule systems 1, 2 constitute the syntax. The rules 3a–5a assign phonetic representation to syntactically-derived structures, and the rules 3b–5b assign them logical form (LF). I assume also the trace theory of movement rules, and the general properties of 1–5 as in the reference cited. I will be concerned here particularly with the construal rules and conditions on binding.

Rules of construal associate antecedents and anaphors, let us say, by the device of coindexing. Some familiar properties of this association are illustrated in [2]:

[2]a the men saw each other
 b *each other saw the men

---

1 This paper forms part of a more extensive study of properties of binding, now in preparation.

    c the candidates want [each other to win]
    d the candidates believe [each other to be crooks]
    e *the candidates believe [each other are crooks]
    f *the candidates want [me to vote for each other]
    g *the candidates believe [the electorate to prefer each other]
    h the candidates hurled insults at each other

Examples (*a*), (*b*) illustrate the command requirement for bound anaphora. In examples (*c–g*), we can take the brackets to be clause-brackets labelled $\bar{\text{S}}$. As (*c*), (*d*) indicate, the antecedent of *each other* may be outside of its clause, and as (*h*) shows, it need not be the nearest plural NP. Examples (*e*), (*f*), (*g*) illustrate what have been called the Specified Subject Condition (SSC) and Propositional Island Condition (PIC – alternatively, the 'Tensed-S condition') in Chomsky 1975 and 1977, and elsewhere. As discussed in these references and elsewhere (*cf* Fiengo 1977), the same conditions apply to movement rules. We may unify these observations by regarding the conditions in question not as conditions on certain rules (transformations, construal rules) but as conditions on LF, that is, binding conditions falling under 5*b* of [1]. An inappropriate application of a movement rule then will produce a phrase-trace relation that violates the conditions on binding, where we think of this relation as a special case of bound anaphora. See the references cited for discussion; also Freidin 1978.

In Chomsky and Lasnik 1977, note 30, it is suggested that what are called there 'structures of obligatory control' might also be brought within this framework. I would now like to spell out that proposal more carefully.

Consider the sentences [3]:

[3]*a* it is unclear who to visit
    b John asked Bill who to visit
    c John told Bill who to visit

Each of the sentences of [3] contains an embedded indirect question, which we may take to have the form [4] after the application of syntactic rules:

[4] ... [$_{\bar{\text{S}}}$[$_{\text{COMP}}$ *wh*-phrase + WH][$_{\text{S}}$ PRO to visit *t*]]

where ... is the matrix phrase, PRO is base-generated empty NP (*ie*, [$_{\text{NP}}$ *e*]), and *t* is the trace of the *wh*-phrase, *ie*, [$_{\text{NP}}$ *e*] coindexed with the *wh*-phrase by the conventions associated with transformational rules.

Some general properties of the structures [3–4] are familiar. Thus, in [3*a*] PRO is arbitrary in interpretation, whereas in (*b*) it is controlled by the matrix subject *John* and in (*c*) by the matrix object *Bill*. To survey the relevant properties more systematically, consider the structures [5]:

[5]*a* ... [$_\alpha$ who [$_\beta$ NP visited *t*]]   ('it is unclear who Bill visited')
    b ... [$_\alpha$ who [$_\beta$ *t* visited NP]]   ('it is unclear who visited Bill')
    c ... [$_\alpha$ who [$_\beta$ NP$_1$ to visit NP$_2$]]   ('it is unclear who to visit')

[2]

In [5], *t* is the trace of *who* and we may take . . . to be as in [3].

It is clear, in the first place, that *wh*-movement takes place in α in each case. Therefore, in the framework assumed here, $\alpha = \bar{S}$ and $\beta = S$. In cases (*a*) and (*b*), $NP \neq PRO$; that is, construal is impossible. For example, we cannot have such sentences as 'John asked Bill who visited', meaning that John asked Bill which person he, John, visited or which person visited him, John; even though *ask* assigns control by its subject (*John*, in this case), as we see from [3*b*]. Furthermore, in case [5*c*], NP_2 cannot be PRO with NP_1 = trace. Thus 'it is unclear who to visit' cannot mean that it is unclear who is to visit some unspecified person.

These are among the most elementary and general properties of indirect questions. It is evident at once that these are essentially the same properties as illustrated in [2]. That is, the basic properties of construal, as in [3], are the same as those that we observe in the case of bound anaphora and movement rules. The command property carries over without comment. Let us now consider a formulation of SSC and PIC that will bring all of these cases together.

Assume that the basic expansion of $\bar{S}$ and S in rules [1] is [6]:

[6] [$_{\bar{S}}$ COMP [$_S$ NP Tense VP]]

Cf Emonds 1976. Thus Tense c-commands both the subject and predicate of S, where we understand C-COMMAND in the sense of Reinhart, 1976: α c-commands β if $\alpha \neq \beta$ and α does not dominate β, and the first branching node dominating α dominates β, *ie*, β is IN CONSTRUCTION WITH α in the sense of Klima 1964. We say in this case that β is in the DOMAIN of α. Furthermore, the subject c-commands every constituent of S. These notions can be extended to deal with bound anaphora in noun phrases, as in 'they saw pictures of each other', *"they saw my pictures of each other' (*cf* Chomsky 1975, 1977).

To assign control in such structures as [3–5], we formulate the general rule of CONTROL [7]:

[7] An occurrence of PRO in an embedded clause α is coindexed with some lexical NP in the matrix clause in which α is immediately embedded, or is assigned the index *arb* (interpreted as 'arbitrary in reference') if there is no such lexical NP; choice of NP is determined by the matrix verb, as illustrated in [3].

Notice that the rule [7] is no doubt redundant. Thus the fact that PRO finds its antecedent in the matrix clause follows from properties of command; the fact that the clause must IMMEDIATELY dominate α follows from the property of subjacency, which holds of all antecedent-anaphor relations where the anaphor is null (*ie*, movement rules with trace, and control); the fact that the antecedent must be outside the clause in which PRO appears follows from the same 'irreflexivity' principle that prevents formation of 'John killed t' from 'PRO kill John' by an NP-movement rule. Thus in the correct theory of universal grammar, towards which research is striving (and perhaps progressing), the rule [7] should be analogous to the rule [8] for reciprocals:

[8] Coindex *each other* with some NP (*ie*, assign *each other* an antecedent)

A person learning English must learn the language-specific fact that *each other* is a reciprocal, and therefore requires an antecedent. It seems doubtful that anything else must be learned; *ie*, perhaps the other properties of reciprocals, as illustrated in [2], follow by principles of universal grammar. The same should be true of Control. Nevertheless, I will leave the rule of Control in the improperly redundant form [7].

Consider now a structure of the form [9]:

[9] $\ldots [_\beta \ldots \alpha \ldots] \ldots$

We can now formulate SSC and PIC as in [10]:

[10] If α in [9] is an anaphor in the domain of the tense or the subject of β, then α cannot be free in β (where $\beta = \text{NP}$ or $\bar{\text{S}}$).[2]

Among the anaphors we include reciprocals, PRO, trace, and bound pronouns (as in 'John lost *his* way', 'John hurt *him*self'; *cf* Helke 1971), but not lexical NPs.

What do we mean by 'free' in [10]? Let us say that an anaphor α is BOUND in β if there is a category c-commanding it and coindexed with it in β; otherwise it is FREE in β. Note that NP_{arb} is always free.

It follows from [10] that an anaphor in $\bar{\text{S}}$ cannot be free in $\bar{\text{S}}$ unless it is the subject of an infinitive, and that an anaphor in NP cannot be free in NP if it is in the domain of a possessive 'subject' of NP. Note that [10] expresses SSC and PIC.

The condition [10] suggests the familiar phenomenon of opacity.[3] Thus the domain of modal operators or verbs of propositional attitude is opaque in the sense that a variable within such a domain cannot be bound outside it (under the opaque or *de dicto* interpretation). Given the analogy, we may refer to [10] as 'the opacity condition'. In effect, Tense and Subject are 'operators' that make certain domains opaque.

It can easily be seen that this formulation covers the standard cases.[4] In the reciprocal construction [2] the reciprocal phrase is free in the opaque domain $\bar{\text{S}}$ (the embedded clause) in the starred examples (*e–g*). For the same reason, movement is blocked from a tensed clause or any position other than

---

2 it is also necessary to stipulate that β is minimal, *ie*, the smallest such domain, for reasons that I will not elaborate on here.
3 This is why the term was used in Chomsky and Lasnik 1977, note 13.
4 It must be modified slightly to accommodate disjoint reference; *cf* Chomsky 1978, Appendix.

the subject of an infinitive, since a trace will be left that is free in an opaque domain (though bound outside it, namely by its antecedent, the moved phrase). The same reasoning extends to the structures of obligatory control illustrated in [3–5]. The embedded NP cannot be either controlled or assigned *arb* in [5*a*] (because it would then be free in the domain of Tense) or [5*b*] (because it would then be free in the domain of the subject). And in [5*c*], only NP_1 can be assigned control or the index *arb* without violating opacity.

Given this formulation of the opacity condition, we can regard movement as free (but governed by subjacency), and can give the rules for anaphors in the optimal form [8] – with [7], presumably a rule of core grammar, yet to be improved to this state. Many of the general properties of anaphor–antecedent relations follow, though some still remain to be explained. Note that the same mechanisms apply without change to embedded infinitives as in 'John persuaded Bill [to leave]', 'John promised Bill [to leave]', *'John persuaded Bill [that will leave]' (meaning, that Bill will leave), *'John persuaded Bill [to leave]' (meaning that someone is to leave Bill). These results follow if we take the embedded infinitive to be a clause, thus adopting what seems the simplest base structure: clauses can be finite or infinitival and all rules, including rules expanding NP, are optional.   The opacity condition as given here differs in several important respects from earlier formulations of PIC and SSC. First, it is a general condition on LF rather than a condition on some collection of rules of grammar, including transformations, control, bound anaphora, etc. Second, the opacity condition is not given as a 'constraint on variables' relating two positions involved in some rule, but rather as a condition on the anaphor. This change allows us to incorporate the case of arbitrary reference. It is evident that arbitrary reference has essentially the properties of bound anaphora – it is restricted to the subject of an infinitive – but under earlier formulations of SSC and PIC it was not covered; there is no constraint on variables, since only one position is involved in the rule, namely, the position of the uncontrolled NP. Third, it is now unnecessary to introduce the notion 'specified' in the analogue to SSC. There are other technical problems in the formulation of SSC that are also avoided under this formulation.

The COMP position of a tensed sentence has sometimes been called an 'escape hatch' for movement, and various stipulations have been given in earlier formulations of PIC to allow for this property. More generally, the trace t can be free in $\bar{S}$ in either of the two constructions [11], [12]:

[11] who do they think [$_{\bar{S}}$[$_{COMP}$ t] [Bill will see t']]
[12] who do they believe [$_{\bar{S}}$ t to be incompetent]

Nothing further need be said about [12]. Consider [11]. Here, t' is not free in $\bar{S}$, since it is bound by t; and t, though free in $\bar{S}$, is not in an opaque domain. Thus no condition at all blocks [11]; no special stipulation is

[5]

required to permit cyclic *wh*-movement, just as none is required to permit the analogous cyclic N P-movement, as in familiar analyses of such sentences as 'John seems to be likely to leave'.

AMBIGUITY AND WORD MEANING
RUTH KEMPSON

The analysis of varying lexical meaning in terms of homonymous lexical items, each having a constant meaning, conflicts with an analysis of lexical meaning in terms of polysemy, which allows the meaning an individual item has to vacillate from context to context. This paper reconsiders the status of this distinction.[1] The initial problem in assessing the homonymy–polysemy distinction is to decide whether one has to allow for vacillation of meaning within a single lexical item according to context. If polysemy is maximalized, the number of lexical items for each phonological word is restricted, but the interaction between context and interpretation of the lexical item needs systematic specification. If, however, homonymy is maximalized, the lexicon becomes very much larger. The theoretical concept of homonymy I assume is clear enough. However, the concept of polysemy is not. As a preliminary definition of polysemy, one might propose that a polysemous item is one whose semantic representation involves a disjunction between all the interpretations that the lexical item may bear, each listed with the context which determines the particular interpretation.

Though the phenomena of homonymy and polysemy are traditionally distinguished, it is not immediately obvious that there is a critical theoretical

---

1 I shall assume throughout that the description of word meaning is a viable linguistic exercise, though this is doubted by some. Whether this should be in terms of componential analysis or meaning postulates, I leave open. Any use of semantic components is for exegetical reasons only.

distinction between a set of homonymous lexical items and a single polysemous item whose characterization contains a disjunction of pairs of interpretation-plus-context. For if the contexts controlling the interpretation of a lexical item are mutually exclusive, then both the polysemy and the homonymy analyses predict that a lexical item has an agreed specific number of separate interpretations. However, these analyses lead to different predictions about sentence ambiguity if the contexts in which the interpretations occur are not mutually exclusive. The homonymy formulation implies that in environments where two interpretations of the word in question are possible, the resulting sentence will be ambiguous with only two distinct interpretations. But if the suggested definition of polysemy is correct, then the problem that arises is that the truth conditions of a disjunction are met if both elements of the disjunction are true. In other words, where the linguistic context in which the polysemous item occurs is compatible with more than one interpretation of that item, and those interpretations are not themselves mutually exclusive, then there is predicted to be a third possible understanding of the sentence in which both interpretations are simultaneously asserted. Consider in this connection [1-6].

[1] He ran onto the field.
[2] He ran the race for Hampshire.
[3] The ball ran onto the field.
[4] The car is running well.
[5] The road runs from Manchester to Birmingham.
[6] He ran the motorshow.

Since all of these examples seem to be non-metaphorical (none of them having the duality of interpretation between literal and metaphorical readings characteristic of examples of metaphor), each of them provides a potentially distinct lexical item. Since it is the context which determines the sense of *run* in [1], [3-6], both the homonymy and the polysemy formalizations would predict that these sentences are unambiguous. However [2] has two interpretations, with *run* having either its central sense denoting a particular kind of motion on legs, or a transferred causative sense implying an action of organizing. The range of subjects which these two senses of the verb can occur with is very similar, animate in the central sense, human in the transferred causative sense. [2] therefore provides a test case. What is significant is that it does not have a third interpretation in which the subject can be understood as both taking part in and organizing the race. And this prediction of two interpretations but not three is an automatic consequence only of the formulation of varying lexical meaning in terms of discrete lexical items. Since *run* is a typical case of lexical extensions of meaning, this evidence suggests that it is homonymy which should be maximalized, and not polysemy. This is not say that there are no cases of lexical items which

[8]

need a disjunct semantic representation, but the examples where such a characterization is required are not ones which are generally thought to be cases of polysemy. One such example is *book*, which can simultaneously be interpreted in terms of the physical properties of the object it denotes (when it behaves like a concrete noun) and in terms of the contents of that object (when it behaves like an abstract noun). Thus the sentence *My book is three hundred pages long and is quite incomprehensible* contains one use of the lexical item *book* but this is simultaneously interpreted in terms of physical properties and in terms of the content of the object denoted. Indeed the interpretation of concrete nouns in general displays this type of vacillation. The detailed solution to the characterization of this fluctuation remains somewhat unclear, but one aspect of the problem is not in doubt: the duality must be predicted by general rule and not listed individually for each lexical item. Despite the attributes of polysemy, it will therefore not meet the defining condition of polysemy suggested earlier that it be a disjunction within a single lexical entry.

It must be pointed out that in drawing the conclusion that homonymy should be maximalized, there appears to be a conflict with Lyons (1977), who argues that it is polysemy that should be maximalized, and that there are no cases of 'absolute homonymy'. Lyons argues that the only cases of absolute homonymy are those cases where there is syntactic equivalence as well as morphological and phonological equivalence, and that in any case where the condition of syntactic equivalence is not met, we have neither homonymy nor polysemy but 'lexemic distinctness' (560–1). Demanding such a strong condition both on homonymy and polysemy however makes the conflict more apparent than real. For suppose we take *run* as our paradigm example again. In nearly all the cases [1–6], it can be argued that the items *run* are syntactically distinct, and hence 'lexemically distinct'. The only two cases which are at all unclear are the relationship between [3] and [5], and the two interpretations of [2], together with [6]. But we have already seen that there is evidence to suggest that the *run* of [2] and [6] should not be seen as a single lexical item because even though both its interpretations are compatible with the same type of noun phrase as subject, it is not possible for these interpretations to be simultaneous, as a single disjunct entry in the lexicon would suggest. And the distinction between the *run* in [3] and the *run* in [5] is a type of case over which there can be no dispute; the context will always determine which interpretation will be possible. It thus appears that Lyons' claim of the need to maximalize polysemy involves such a restrictive account of both polysemy and homonymy that it becomes equivalent to the view that it is homonymy that should be maximalized, given a somewhat less stringent view of homonymy. In what follows, therefore, I shall assume that polysemy should be invoked only if two differing compatible interpretations of a lexical item are simultaneously possible given a single context which itself allows both interpretations. In all other cases of the same phonological form and varying meaning, the analysis I suggest should be in terms of homonymy, not of polysemy.

We are now in a position to consider a general problem about ambiguity which bears directly on the homonymy-polysemy problem. It was pointed out in Zwicky and Sadock 1975 that any proposed cases of sentence ambiguity where the sentence in question is claimed to have two interpretations, one entailing the other, defy any of the standard test procedures for ambiguity. In Kempson 1979, however, it is suggested that wherever such an ambiguity is claimed, the sentence is invariably unambiguous with respect to the proposed distinction but has only the more general of the two interpretations as its semantic representation. The central argument of Kempson 1979 is that under the counterfactual assumption that there is no ambiguity in natural languages, the only cases which result in implausible analyses are cases of true ambiguity such as *John saw her duck*. Under such a counterfactual assumption, there are two alternative analyses accounting for the properties of an ambiguous sentence-string, both of them implausible. On the one hand, the analyst could propose an extremely restricted semantic representation corresponding only to the inferences which are common to both interpretations; which in the case of *John saw her duck* are *There is someone called John, She exists*, and *John saw something*. Such an analysis is transparently inadequate. On the other hand, the analyst could propose a single semantic representation consisting of a disjunction of the (two) possible interpretations. This is no more plausible, since the same problem arises as in the account of polysemy as a disjunctive lexical entry: the truth conditions of a disjunction include as one of its conditions that the disjunction be true if both disjuncts are true. If we assume a fairly standard pragmatic account of language use with maxims of truth and relevance (*cf* Grice 1975), then the analyst is faced with the prediction that any utterance of a sentence which contains a disjunction of truth conditions will not be violating the maxim of truthfulness if the utterer of the sentence intends both items to be taken as true. In other words, a single representation for an ambiguous sentence in the form of a disjunction would predict incorrectly that an utterance of *John saw her duck* could carry the simultaneous interpretation that John saw her lower her head in the appropriate way and that John saw the duck that she had. But it cannot; and this is unlike the clear cases of disjunctive truth conditions such as coordination across *or*.[2] Hence the need to invoke ambiguity. In contrast to sentences such as *John saw her duck*, for all apparent cases of sentential ambiguity where there is a logical dependence between the proposed interpretations (as in negative sentences and some opaque contexts), the two alternative analyses under this counterfactual assumption of no

---

2 That *or* is often said to be ambiguous between an inclusive and an exclusive interpretation is not relevant, since both senses involve a disjunctive statement. That *or* is unambiguous has in any case been argued by Barrett and Stenner 1971 and Gazdar 1977.

ambiguity are not implausible. Hence the proposal in Kempson 1979 that all such cases should be analysed as unambiguous.

The argument extends straightforwardly to lexical ambiguity. The proposal is that lexical ambiguity is excluded in those cases where the lexical ambiguity is reflected in a corresponding sentential ambiguity of which one interpretation entails the other. In accordance with the ambiguity constraint outlined above, any such cases are predicted to have only the more general of the two interpretations in question. The fact that lexical ambiguity does not stand in a one-to-one correspondence with sentential ambiguity is relevant at this point: cases of homonymy where the linguistic context determines which specific lexical item among the homonyms is the only possible one will not be relevant to the ambiguity restriction since the sentence-string itself will not be ambiguous (as is [1], [3–6] above). But in cases such as [7] the linguistic context is under-specified semantically, allowing *run* to be attributed either to animate objects (with legs) or to inanimate objects such as balls (*cf* [1] and [3] above).

[7] It ran across the field.

For syntactic reasons, it appears that *run* in [3] is distinct from *run* in [1] since only the former use demands a prepositional phrase of locational direction. *Make him run* is a straightforwardly interpretable imperative, whereas *Make the ball run*, which contains the same sense of *run* as [3], is surely only interpretable as metaphorical and is not strictly grammatical. Yet a sentence such as [7], which allows interpretations parallel to [1] and [3] in virtue of having a pronominal subject, will be predicted to be unambiguous if the proposed semantic representations involving homonymy of *run* are logically dependent. The prediction here depends on the status of the so-called selectional restrictions. If they are part of the intrinsic semantic specification of the verb and hence of any sentence in which the item in question occurs (as argued in Kempson 1977: 112–17), then a sentence such as [7] is allowed to be ambiguous. The specification of the distinct lexical items *run* will include a specification of the animacy and the inanimacy of the subject respectively, and accordingly the semantic representation of the sentence will include a specification of the animacy or inanimacy of the subject, depending on the precise homonym *run* that the sentence contains. The two interpretations of the sentence will therefore be logically independent. If selectional specifications are not part of the semantic representation of either lexical items or sentences (but only conditions of wellformedness on such representations – *cf* Bierwisch 1967), then such a sentence is predicted to be unambiguous, with only the more general interpretation of *run* (as in [3]). Since the analysis of selectional restrictions proposed in Kempson 1977 is somewhat contentious, I leave this question open.

The example of lexical ambiguity discussed by Zwicky and Sadock is *dog*, which they claim is ambiguous between a general interpretation and a sex-restricted interpretation antonymous to *bitch*. Should this example stand as a counter-example to the ambiguity restriction? There is reason to think that it should not, relating to the counterfactual-premise argument outlined above. It was argued (*p* 10) that the implausibility of assigning any ambiguous sentence-string a single disjunctive representation led irrevocably to the conclusion that some sentence-strings be ambiguous, having more than one distinct semantic representation. However there is one further move in this argument which a protagonist might make, which is relevant to our assessment of the problem-case of *dog*. Suppose that another operator be admitted into the metalanguage: '∨̄' (corresponding to the exclusive sense of *or*). This would allow unambiguous sentences to have a single non-disjunctive semantic representation; sentences such as *He went to the party with John or Bill* to have a single disjunctive representation involving disjuncts joined by '∨' (the logical operator corresponding to the inclusive sense of *or*); and sentences such as the so-called ambiguous sentences to have a single disjunctive representation involving disjuncts joined by '∨̄'. Hence, it might be argued, each sentence-string in any natural language can be assigned a single semantic representation. That this argument is easy to demolish is not relevant here. It is not however coincidental that an impossible move under such an analysis is to analyse *dog* as involving lexical disjunction across '∨̄'. For such a representation would predict that a sentence containing *dog* could never be true under the interpretation denoting male dogs, since 'P ∨̄ Q' is false if both P and Q are true. Not only this, but it would predict that the only possible interpretation would be one in which the object denoted is canine but not a male canine. In other words, such an analysis predicts that the only possible interpretation is one in which the object denoted is a female dog! So the disjunction involved if it be one, cannot be disjunction across '∨̄'. But it is only the cases which (at least superficially) allow the characterization by '∨̄' which constitute the true cases of ambiguity. Thus this argument forces the conclusion that *dog* is not ambiguous between two separate items *dog*$_1$ denoting male canines, and *dog*$_2$ denoting canines.

So how shall *dog* be characterized? According to the ambiguity restriction against sentential ambiguity between two logically dependent interpretations, it seems that *dog* must be entered in the lexicon as unambiguous, denoting merely the entire class of canines. Two problems immediately arise. Firstly, how can its use denoting male canines be explained? Secondly, such an analysis incorrectly predicts that [8] is contradictory.

[8] That's not a dog: it's a bitch.

At least two alternatives suggest themselves. A pragmatic account of the extended use of such an item might be put forward, and this account would include an explanation of how [8], despite its contradictory semantic properties, is re-analysed pragmatically as non-contradictory. A second alternative is to suggest that it is not *dog* that is ambiguous but negation: it can either be understood as a denial-of-truth operator, or as a denial-of-relevance operator. Under this analysis, it is negation as a denial-of-relevance operator which is predominant in the natural (non-contradictory) interpretation of [8]. A separate alternative is to admit that the lexicon must contain some account of the duality in the use of *dog* and to invoke the concept of polysemy. So one might argue, the vacillation of meaning of *dog* is not sufficient to cause sentential ambiguity and should be analysed as a polysemous item with a single disjunctive lexical entry.

There are problems with each of these three solutions. The invocation of pragmatic principles in the face of a semantic characterization of [8] as contradictory is extremely suspicious, given that the pragmatic interpretation that has to be invoked involves an assertion of precisely the positive congener of the negative sentence in [8] with only one further inference added, that of femininity. It might be argued that such a principle is needed in any case for quantified sentences such as [9].

[9] She hasn't got two books in her hand: she's got three.

But the exceptionless and particular nature of this phenomenon in the case of quantified expressions suggests that the generalization, whether semantic or pragmatic, should be stated specifically for quantified expressions, and not extended to the extensions of meaning that arise in cases such as *dog*. The invocation of ambiguity of negation is no more satisfactory: if negative sentences are said to be ambiguous between an interpretation of denial of truth and an interpretation of denial of relevance, one would predict an exceptionless paradigm of cases parallel to [8]. But [10–12] are contradictory.[3]

[10] She isn't a woman: she's a grandmother.
[11] He didn't go to the station: he ran to the station.
[12] That isn't a hat: it's my best hat.

In general it is not possible to simultaneously deny a positive sentence and to assert a sentence which entails that positive sentence without asserting a contradiction, despite the prediction involved in setting up a denial-of-relevance operator.

So we come to the third alternative: that *dog* is a single polysemous item, which according to the initial characterization of polysemy would be an item entered in the lexicon as a disjunct lexical item (involving the operator corresponding to the inclusive sense of *or* – 'v'). The problem with this

3 These are of course not contradictory with an item such as *merely* added, since then the sentence implies that its subject is not only implied to have the properties in question, but additional ones too.

proposal lies in the particular disjunction which has to be entered in the lexicon. If we set up a lexical entry for *dog*:[4]

[CANINE] v ([CANINE] & [MALE])

then this is not significantly distinct from a lexical entry containing merely '[CANINE]'. The reason is this.[5] The only possible way of testing such a definition by attempting to falsify it would be to show that the item *dog* does not denote the class of canines. For if it could be shown that *dog* did not denote the class of male canines, nothing would follow: the definition implicitly claims merely that the interpretation of *dog* is either '[CANINE] & [MALE]' or '[CANINE]', and it would not be falsified. Thus the definition is falsified only if it can be shown that *dog* does not denote canines. But it follows that the disjunct suggested is not distinct from the entry:

dog: [CANINE]

There is one further possibility before relinquishing the polysemy solution – to reconsider the definition of polysemy. As a preliminary to doing so, it should be recalled that it was claimed above that the only motivation for involving polysemy lay in cases where, should the context be compatible with the two interpretations in question and the two interpretations themselves not be mutually exclusive, it is possible to have an interpretation in which they are simultaneously present. The vacillation in interpretation of concrete nouns such as *book* meets such a condition. The case of *dog* also meets this criterion, since if the sex-restricted interpretation is invoked, then the more general interpretation must be simultaneously present. Now there is an additional property of the vacillating interpretation of concrete nouns that is relevant here. It was pointed out above (*p* 9) that the problem is not specific to particular lexical items, but applies generally. This phenomenon would not therefore be reflected in the form of a disjunction within a single lexical entry. In the light of this, consider the following restriction on polysemy: the only cases of polysemy which arise in natural language are those which can be predicted by general rule. According to this restriction, polysemy is not characterized by disjunction in a single lexical entry, but is only invoked in cases where the extension of meaning in question can be predicted by rule formulation from individual non-disjunctive lexical items. This is indeed true of the concrete/abstract vacillation that arises with concrete nouns. Furthermore, one immediate advantage of this characterization of polysemy in terms of semantic rules is that it correctly allows for lexical items such as *or* that require a disjunct semantic representation but are not examples of polysemy.

4 Square brackets and capital letters are used as a notation for semantic components.
5 This argument is due to A. Cormack.

The case of *dog* would fall within this characterization of polysemy if the variation in its meaning could be predicted by a general principle. And it can. The phenomenon is by no means restricted to *dog*, or even to pairs of items one of which is marked for sex. Consider [13–17].

[13] That's not a duck: it's a drake.
[14] That's not a cow: it's a bull.
[15] That's not a cow: it's a calf.
[16] That's not a line: it's a curve.
[17] That's not a rectangle: it's a square.

A preliminary statement of the general principle relating the two interpretations of lexical items such as *dog* might be:

If a lexical item L_1 has as its extension[6] a set S_1 which includes the set S_2 which a second lexical item L_2 has as its extension, then the lexical item L_1 may be used to denote that subset of S_1 which excludes S_2.

However the principle in this form is far from exceptionless. We have already seen some examples which seem unavoidably contradictory ([10–12] above), and [18–20] provide further examples.

[18] That's not a book: it's a novel.
[19] That's not a room: it's a lounge.
[20] That's not a musical instrument: it's a clarinet.

There is however a general property which distinguishes [13–17] from [10–12] and [18–20]. In these latter examples, the contrastive items involved are members of multiple sets. For example, together with *book*, the general term, we have not only *novel*, but *textbook*, *biography*, *autobiography*, etc. Analogously for the items in [10–12] and [19–20]. The determining factor in whether a lexical item denoting a set of objects has a more specific use to denote a subset of that set seems to be that along any one dimension of contrast, there must be only one lexically designated subset. If there is more than one lexical item denoting a subset of the general term along any single parameter, then the more specific use of the general term is excluded. Hence [10–12] and [18–20] seem contradictory, but [8] and [13–17] do not. Accordingly the general principle requires the following revision:

If a lexical item L_1 has as its extension a set S_1 which includes the set S_2 which a second lexical item L_2 has as its extension, and S_2 is the only lexically designated subset of the extension of L_1 along any one dimension of contrast, then the lexical item L_1 may be used to denote that subset of S_1 which excludes S_2.

Informally, this principle is a restatement of the well-known semantic

---

6 *Extension* is being used here in its logical sense to mean the set of objects which a lexical item denotes.

markedness problem: if for some general term, representing a lexical field, there is a gap in the sub-parts of that lexical field, with only one more narrowly specified lexical item, then the gap may be filled by a more specific use of the general term. The need for the revised, more precise, statement of this general principle can be demonstrated by the items *sheep* and *cow* (*cf* [14-15] above). *Sheep*, the cover term, has both sexes lexically specified, as *ewe* and as *ram*, and according to the principle does not therefore have a special use denoting either only male sheep or only female sheep. *Cow*, the cover term, has only one sex separately lexically specified, *viz bull*, and *cow* is therefore predicted to have a use denoting solely female cows. It is not however relevant to this particular extension of use that *cow* also has an extended use contrasting with *calf*, since this second contrast is along a different parameter, that of age. Furthermore, the existence of the item *heifer* is also compatible with the principle as stated: since heifers are female cows before they have had a calf, they form a subset of the sexually relevant subset of cows in general, and therefore the item *heifer* does not stand in direct contrast to *bull*. In the case of the item *dog* itself, the only subset of the cover term is *bitch*, and hence the principle predicts correctly that *dog* has an extended use to denote those dogs not included in the set denoted by *bitch* - *viz* male dogs. Thus it seems that we have a general principle whereby the item *dog* can be correctly predicted to have the sex-restricted interpretation that it does, and it will therefore no longer provide a problem for the constraint against proposing logically dependent sentential ambiguities.

In sum, my overall proposal has been fourfold. First, I argued that variation in the meaning of a word which is not merely due to indeterminacy or under-specification of its meaning,[7] should in general be characterized in terms of discrete, homonymous lexical items. Second, I have argued for a constraint on sentential ambiguity, that it should not be invoked in cases where one interpretation of a sentence entails the other interpretation. Third, I have argued that a case such as *dog* which appears to lead to violations of this constraint in being itself a traditional example of (logically dependent) homonymy should, rather, be analysed as a single polysemous item. Finally, I have proposed a restriction on polysemy, that it be invoked only when the vacillation of meaning in question can be predicted by general rule. If this analysis of polysemy is correct, then cases such as *I bought a dog* no longer stand as counter-examples to the proposed restriction on ambiguity that no sentence be assigned two distinct semantic representations if one interpretation of the sentence is logically dependent on the other.[8]

7 *Cf* Kempson 1977 Ch 8 for a discussion of ambiguity and vagueness.
8 This paper is a by-product of a seminar on ambiguity given in the autumn of 1977. I am grateful to all those who took part, and also to C. Bazell, D. Bennett, A. Cormack, G. Gazdar, D. Wilson and the editors of this book, for their criticisms of an earlier draft of this paper.

THE TREATMENT OF
CLAUSE AND SENTENCE IN
A GRAMMAR OF
CONTEMPORARY ENGLISH
SIDNEY GREENBAUM

Every grammatical description presupposes some descriptive framework, however rudimentary, which reflects the goal of the description and the theoretical inclinations of the authors. In GCE, our goal has been to describe the surface structure of the English Language systematically and comprehensively and to relate the structure to meanings and situational uses. That goal has precluded reliance on any one linguistic theory, since no theories are yet capable of permitting a comprehensive description and some are not interested in language use. We have drawn for our framework eclectically on the grammatical tradition and on various current linguistic theories. Our terminology matches our eclecticism, though occasionally it is original to GCE or is based on previous work by the authors.

Readers of GCE may be misled by terms that they are familiar with from other sources. Terms are often capricious: identical terms may mask different approaches, whereas different terms may be synonymous. I propose to examine some sets of terms in GCE applied to clauses and sentences.[1] Some indicate syntagmatic relations of linking, such as SYNDETIC/ASYNDETIC, or of inclusion, such as SUPERORDINATE/SUBORDINATE and SENTENCE/(MAIN) CLAUSE. Others indicate paradigmatic relations. They include terms for sentence types, such as SIMPLE SENTENCE/

---

[1] My reflections on the use of the terminology in GCE are my own responsibility. They do not commit my co-authors.

COMPLEX SENTENCE/COMPOUND SENTENCE, and clause types, such as INDEPENDENT/ DEPENDENT and FINITE/NON-FINITE/VERBLESS.

Following the grammatical tradition (*eg* Poutsma 1928–9:545, and Jespersen 1924:103), GCE distinguishes between CLAUSE and SENTENCE in that the higher-ranked unit SENTENCE contains the lower-ranked unit CLAUSE. GCE does not attempt a definition of SENTENCE, an omission that I shall discuss later. It defines CLAUSE with respect to its internal structure (GCE:7.1): a unit that can be analysed into the functional elements subject (S), verb (V), direct object (Od), indirect object (Oi), subject complement (Cs), object complement (Co), and adverbial (A). If a functional element of a clause is realized by a clause, that included clause is a SUBORDINATE CLAUSE and the clause as a whole is the SUPERORDINATE CLAUSE (GCE:11.2). Thus, in the superordinate clause

I know *that he has bought a new car*

the direct object *that he has bought a new car* is a subordinate clause, and in the superordinate clause

When you next see them, you should mention my name

the adverbial *when you next see them* is a subordinate clause. SUPERORDINATE and SUBORDINATE are relative terms; a subordinate clause may in turn be superordinate. For example, in

He said that he heard that they sold their house

the clause *that he heard that they sold their house* is subordinate (as direct object) to its superordinate clause (*He said that he heard that they sold their house*), but at the same time it is superordinate to the subordinate clause (again, direct object) *that they sold their house*. Each clause can in turn be analysed into functional elements, as indicated in the diagram below (where *conj* is the abbreviation for conjunction).

We need the category of superordinate clause (in addition to such categories as main clause and sentence) because many rules refer to the superordinate clause regardless of whether or not it is itself subordinate. For example, the 'understood' subject of a non-finite or verbless adverbial clause is assumed to be identical in reference to the subject of the superordinate clause (GCE:11.44). Thus, in

I know that *before leaving they will clear up the mess*

the understood subject of the non-finite *before leaving* is identical with the *they* of the superordinate clause and not with the *I* of the sentence. Similarly, the rules of tense and pronoun shift in indirect speech relate to the superordinate clause (GCE:11.73–7):

It worries me *that she complained that she was tired*

[18]

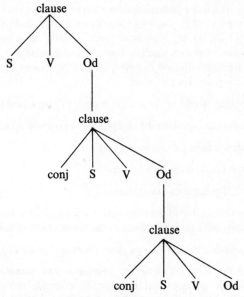

Fig 1 Subordination within subordination

And the numerous rules for verb complementation must make reference to the verb of the superordinate clause; for example, the subjunctive *be* depends on *move* (GCE: 12.47) in the superordinate infinitive clause in

She wanted *to move that the meeting be adjourned*

In the examples we have been discussing, the subordinate clauses have been functioning within superordinate clauses. But a subordinate clause can also function within a phrase. A typical example (GCE: 13.1) is the relative clause:

The girl *who waved to you* is Mary Smith

The relative clause *who waved to you* is not subordinate to the clause *The girl who waved to you is Mary Smith*, since it does not function directly within that clause; rather, it functions as a postmodifier within the noun phrase *the girl who waved to you*, and it is the noun phrase that functions as an element (subject) within the clause. This analysis is consistent with treating *that they sold their house* as subordinate to only *that he heard that they sold their house*.

GCE uses the term CLAUSE not only for FINITE CLAUSES, clauses with finite verbs, but also for NON-FINITE CLAUSES, those with non-finite verbs, and for VERBLESS CLAUSES, those without a verb (GCE: 11.4). GCE also distinguishes three types of non-finite clauses according to verb types:

INFINITIVE CLAUSES (subdivided into *to*-INFINITIVE CLAUSES and bare INFINITIVE CLAUSES), -*ing* PARTICIPLE CLAUSES, and -*ed* PARTICIPLE CLAUSES (GCE:11.5). Non-finite and verbless structures are termed clauses because we can analyse their internal structure into the same functional elements that we distinguish in finite clauses. For example, the analysis of the infinitive clause in

The best thing would be *for you* (S) *to paint* (V) *the room* (Od)

depends on the analogy with the analysis for the corresponding finite clause:

You (S) *should paint* (V) *the room* (Od)

Similarly, the verbless clause *when ripe* in

When ripe, these apples are delicious

is analysed as consisting of the conjunction *when* and the subject complement *ripe* by analogy with their functions in the corresponding finite clause:

When (conj) *they* (S) *are* (V) *ripe* (Cs), these apples are delicious

The use of the term CLAUSE for non-finite and verbless structures is established in the grammatical tradition; for example, in Poutsma 1928–9: 746–996; Jespersen 1924:122; and Curme 1931:176–80.

Non-finite and verbless clauses can be superordinate to finite clauses as well as to other non-finite or verbless clauses. For example, the -*ing* participle clause *knowing that they would not pay him voluntarily* in

Knowing that they would not pay him voluntarily, he hired a lawyer

has as its direct object the finite clause *that they would not pay him voluntarily*. Similarly, the verbless clause in

Often indecisive when a crisis occurs, he is unlikely to be promoted

has the finite clause *when a crisis occurs* as an adverbial.

GCE recognizes at least three sentence types: SIMPLE SENTENCE, COMPLEX SENTENCE, and COMPOUND SENTENCE. This typology indicates the relationship between the sentence and the clauses that are its immediate constituents. The simple sentence is coextensive with its clause. The complex sentence has one or more of its elements (subject, direct object, etc) realized by a clause. The immediate constituents of the compound sentence are two or more clauses of equivalent status; the clauses are not elements of the sentence. The term COMPOUND SENTENCE is referred to only in a footnote (GCE:9.39), but the existence of this type is implicit (*eg* GCE:11.2).

The SIMPLE SENTENCE is a finite clause that does not have another clause functioning as one of its elements. However, it may contain another clause functioning within a phrase. Thus, the sentence

The girl *who waved to you* is Mary

is considered a simple sentence (GCE : 13.1) because the relative clause is not a sentence element, merely a modifier within a phrase.

Strictly speaking, 'S, V, O, C, and A are elements of clause structure rather than elements of sentence structure' (GCE : 7.1) and therefore we should say that the simple sentence

The girl is Mary Smith

consists of the clause

The girl is Mary Smith

and the subject of that clause is the noun phrase *the girl*. However, it is convenient – and should not lead to misinterpretation – to say also that *the girl* is subject of that sentence. In a compound sentence, on the other hand, we cannot speak of the subject of the sentence. Thus, in

The girl is Mary Smith and the boy is Bob Jones

we can refer only to the separate subject of each clause.

The distinction between simple sentence and complex sentence could be usefully applied to clauses. We could then distinguish between a SIMPLE CLAUSE and a COMPLEX CLAUSE. The complex clause, unlike the simple clause, would have one or more of its elements realized by a subordinate clause, which in turn could be simple or complex. The availability of the term COMPLEX CLAUSE will enable us to refer easily to one set of clauses in a hierarchy of multiple clause structures (GCE : 11.80–4). To turn again to an earlier example, in the complex sentence (also a complex clause)

He said *that he heard that they sold their house*

the direct object *that he heard that they sold their house* is a complex clause, since its direct object *that they sold their house* is a clause.

A finite clause, whether simple or complex, may be an INDEPENDENT CLAUSE. That term suggests a contrast with DEPENDENT CLAUSE. GCE sometimes uses DEPENDENT CLAUSE as a synonym for SUBORDINATE CLAUSE (GCE : 2.3), but a distinction is available where needed (*eg* GCE : 11.3). SUBORDINATE is paired with SUPERORDINATE as relative terms for a syntagmatic relationship between clauses, whereas DEPENDENT is paired with INDEPENDENT as terms for the paradigmatic relationship between clauses. A dependent clause can be at the same time a superordinate clause and a subordinate clause, superordinate to one clause in the syntagmatic chain and subordinate to another.

The independent clause is defined in GCE negatively as a clause that is not subordinate to another clause; that is to say, the independent clause does not function as an element in another clause, nor indeed as an element in any other unit, for example a noun phrase (GCE:11.3). The negative definition of independent clause has the effect of equating INDEPENDENT CLAUSE with MAIN CLAUSE in GCE.[2] A main clause is a simple or complex clause viewed as a constituent of a sentence (GCE:7.1, 11.2). Consistent with its analysis of a subordinate clause as functioning within its superordinate clause, GCE follows the general trend in the scholarly grammatical tradition (cf Jespersen 1924:105f; Poutsma 1928-9:544; Long 1961:Ch 3) in regarding subordinate clauses, including adverbial clauses, as incorporated within their main clause. As Jespersen (1924:105f) rightly argues, there is no value in a term for what is left in the principal clause (his equivalent of main clause) after the subordinate clauses are detached. There is no more reason for suggesting that *I am going home* is a clause in its own right in *I am going home because he insulted me*, when the adverbial is a clause, than in *I am going home because of his insulting remarks*, when the adverbial is a prepositional phrase. The ultimate absurdity would occur in an instance like *What I'd like to know is why he did it* where *is* alone remains after the subordinate clauses are removed.

We need the category of main clause because some rules refer to main clauses. For example, the rules for forming imperatives and direct questions apply to them. (For some recent discussions of the rules for main clauses, see Hooper and Thompson 1973, Green 1976, and Bolinger 1977.)

The independent clause is also defined positively in GCE by its potential function: 'a clause capable of constituting a simple sentence' (GCE:11.3), in that it is not marked by any of the signals of subordination (GCE:11.8-12). The positive definition permits a clause to be identified as independent in isolation. In general, dependent clauses are marked as such. All non-finite and verbless clauses are dependent, and finite dependent clauses usually have a subordination marker. Two exceptions are noted: nominal *that*-clauses from which *that* has been omitted and the type of comment clause exemplified by *you know* (GCE:11.2, 11.65-6). If the tag question is considered a dependent clause, it is a third exception.

The positive definition in GCE:11.3 is not consistent with the use of the term INDEPENDENT CLAUSE elsewhere in GCE. An independent clause can be either simple or complex (GCE:7.1, 11.3) and hence can constitute either a simple sentence or a complex sentence. We can bring the definition in line with the use of the term by omitting *simple*: an independent clause is a clause capable of constituting a sentence. Alternatively, we can restrict the use of INDEPENDENT CLAUSE in GCE to clauses capable of constituting a simple sentence. The present use of the term views the independent clause as a potential sentence, whether simple or complex; since potential sentences

---

2 GCE exceptionally analyses one type of main clause as incorporated within another main clause. The direct speech that is marked by quotation marks is said to retain 'its status as a main clause' (GCE:11.73). In fact, since one or more sentences can occur in reported speech, sentences too can be incorporated within a main clause (cf Longacre 1976:146).

can be main clauses in a complex sentence, the potential sentence is also a potential main clause. It is not clear what function the restricted use would have in the grammar.

The positive definition of an independent clause (capable of constituting a simple sentence) and the negative definition (not functioning as an element in another clause, a definition identifying independent clause with main clause) are not necessarily congruent. The two definitions conflict on the inclusion of main clauses that cannot constitute sentences. One example is the elliptical coordinated clause, as in

John has written a poem and *Bob a short story*
John was the winner in 1970 and *Bob in 1971*

Such sentences are analysed in GCE as consisting of two clauses, the second being elliptical (GCE:9.66). GCE is generous in positing ellipsis in coordination. Most instances could be analysed alternatively as involving phrasal coordination within the one clause, for example of verbs, predicates, or predications. However, we cannot analyse the above two examples as the coordination of two units below the clause level since there is a gap between clause elements. Although there is no explicit mention of their status, those elliptical clauses are presumably to be considered main clauses; since they are not functioning as elements within other clauses, they cannot be treated as dependent clauses. On the other hand, the elliptical main clauses are not independent clauses according to the positive definition: we could not say that *Bob a short story* and *Bob in 1971* are capable of constituting a sentence.

A sentence can contain more than one main clause. If it contains two or more main clauses, they may be coordinated or juxtaposed or there may be a combination of both types of relationship. If they are coordinated, the coordination may be syndetic or asyndetic (GCE:9.24). In syndetic coordination a coordinating conjunction is present; in asyndetic coordination there is no overt coordinating conjunction, but one can be inserted. Thus, both the following sentences contain coordinated main clauses; whether the coordination is syndetic or asyndetic depends on whether the coordinating conjunctions *and* and *but* are inserted or not.

He tried hard, (and) yet he failed
Robert is secretive; (but) David is frank

Juxtaposed clauses, like asyndetically coordinated clauses, are not linked by a coordinating conjunction; they differ from the latter in not admitting a coordinating conjunction:

She understood the rules of the game; I could see that immediately

The punctuation indicates that the juxtaposed clauses are felt to belong to one orthographic sentence (GCE:App III.18*f*). There are no clear criteria

[23]

in the spoken language for distinguishing between juxtaposed clauses and juxtaposed sentences (*cf* also Crystal's paper in this volume).

It would be useful to introduce into GCE the traditional terms PARATAXIS and HYPOTAXIS for types of clause relationship. PARATAXIS, with its corresponding adjective PARATACTIC, would cover both coordination (syndetic or asyndetic) and juxtaposition, while HYPOTAXIS and HYPOTACTIC would refer to superordinate-subordinate relationships. The terms are relative, since a paratactic construction can contain a hypotactic construction in one or more of its constituent clauses and a hypotactic construction can contain one or more paratactic constructions.

The identification of the main clauses in a sentence is often dependent on whether two or more clauses are analysed as coordinated or as related hypotactically. GCE recognizes the possibility of hierarchical relationships within coordination when three or more clauses are coordinated. While all the clauses may be on the same level, it is also possible for one set to be coordinated to another set (GCE:9.36, and *cf* Dik 1968:231–6):

(X) I play the piano and (Y) my sister plays the violin, but (Z) my brother is not interested in music at all.

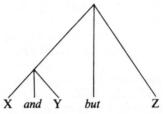

Fig 2 Hierarchical coordination

We could distinguish levels of coordination by introducing the term COMPOUND CLAUSE for clauses that are coordinated at the same level. The above sentence would then be a COMPOUND SENTENCE consisting of two main clauses: a COMPOUND CLAUSE coordinated with a SIMPLE CLAUSE. GCE does not make this distinction; presumably the sentence would be considered to consist of three coordinated main clauses.

Disagreement over whether a clause is coordinate or subordinate arises from disagreement over whether certain items are to be analysed as coordinating conjunctions, subordinating conjunctions, or conjuncts (the last a term used in GCE for certain connective adverbs, *cf* GCE:8.2–5, 89–94). It is generally agreed that *and, or*, and *but* are coordinating conjunctions and therefore the clauses they link are coordinated. Opinion is divided on whether other items are to be considered coordinators; the most common additional candidates are *for* and *nor*. GCE identifies *and, or*, and *but* as coordinators, though it also recognizes that there is a gradience from the clear coordinators to the clear subordinators (GCE:9.28–38, and *cf* Jacobsson 1977). In GCE, therefore, the conjunctions that link main clauses can only be *and, or,* and *but*. GCE categorizes as subordinate such clauses as are introduced by *for* and resultative *so that*, although they resemble coordinated clauses in their fixed position in relation to a preceding clause and in not allowing another conjunction to link them to a preceding clause. Clauses introduced by *nor* or *neither*, by immobile conjuncts such as *so* and *yet*, or by mobile conjuncts such as *therefore* and *however* are considered to be asyndetically coordinated, but become syndetically coordinated if a coordinator is inserted (GCE:9.26).[3]

Coordination and subordination are treated in GCE as syntactic phenomena. The implied semantic relationships between coordinated clauses may be similar to those expressed more explicitly by subordinating conjunctions (GCE:9.26, 11.52, 11.83, 13.15):

He tried hard, *but* he failed
Although he tried hard, he failed

She heard someone trying to force the lock *and* she phoned the police
When she heard someone trying to force the lock she phoned the police

The similarity is particularly conspicuous in ASYMMETRIC COORD-INATION, the type of coordination where the two clauses cannot be reversed without changing the semantic relationship between them (GCE:9.27, 9.40, and *cf* Lakoff 1971):

He died and he was buried in the cemetery
He was buried in the cemetery and he died

In those two examples, the distinction arises from the perception of a different chronological sequence in the two events and a consequent contrast in the cause-effect relationship. In asymmetric coordination, it is generally the first clause that is presupposed in the interpretation of the second clause (*cf* Lakoff 1971:128). Thus we interpret

He was buried in the cemetery and he died

as

He was buried in the cemetery and he died because he was buried in the cemetery

3 British and American speakers seem to differ on the applicability to *nor* of one of the tests for coordination. British speakers allow *and* and *but* to precede *nor*, while American speakers find the co-occurence of *nor* with another conjunction to be unacceptable (GCE:9.28, 55, and Long 1974:203 and 1975:93–4). The requirement for subject-operator inversion with *nor* indicates a measure of integration within clause structure (GCE:9.55), and that requirement applies to American speakers too.

An adverbial can make the anaphoric link explicit (GCE:9.41–8):

He was buried in the cemetery and *as a result of that* he died

One type of *and*-coordination approaches subordination syntactically in that it is possible to move the *and*-clause from its sequential position and insert it within the other clause, though this is not an institutionalized device (GCE:9.44 Note):

Many students at our university – *and it is difficult to explain this* – reject the proposed reforms in university administration

The motivations for choosing between coordination and subordination when similar semantic relationships are found in both are mentioned only very briefly in GCE. One factor is stylistic: coordination is said to be preferred in spoken English (GCE:11.83); that is probably so for parataxis in general. Another factor is said to be the greater importance given to the information conveyed in coordinated or juxtaposed clauses within the discourse, in that the information within a subordinate clause is more likely to be known or already given (GCE:8.92, 9.26, and *cf* Smaby 1974 and Edgren 1971:239–40). While this generalization has some basis, there are many instances where the more significant information seems to be in the subordinate clause or where there seems little or no difference between the two types of construction in this respect (Curme 1931:175, and *cf* Gleason 1965:334–433). The subordinate clause has more information value than its superordinate clause most obviously in cases where the superordinate clause contains a performative verb or an expression of conviction:

I bet you he won't be at home yet
I'm certain I wrote to you

We have so far assumed the identification of the unit SENTENCE. The sentence is not defined in GCE. Previous attempts at defining it have proved to be fruitless exercises that have failed to achieve a generally acceptable formulation (*cf* Fries 1952:Chs 2–3 and Allerton 1969). It is no wonder, therefore, that Gleason (1965:330) recommends 'It would seem best to abandon the attempt, and to apply the effort to more promising endeavours'. In generative grammar, the assumption is that the sentence is defined by the rules of the grammar (*cf* Morgan 1973:719–20). In GCE the sentence is assumed to be a syntactic prime which the grammar describes but does not define. The orthographic sentence signalled by punctuation is not necessarily identical with the syntactic sentence (GCE:App III.1, 18–19). And in speech we do not have unequivocal devices corresponding to punctuation that will mark the beginning and end of a unit that we can term a spoken sentence.

Essentially, GCE views the word as the minimum syntactic unit and the sentence as the maximum syntactic unit. The word enters into syntactic relationships in two ways: (*a*) directly for most closed-system items, such as pronouns, prepositions, and conjunctions, and (*b*) indirectly for most open-class items, such as nouns and adjectives, because the choice of item as head of a phrase determines the type of phrase (noun phrase with noun as head, adjective phrase with adjective as head) and therefore the syntactic relationships into which the phrase can enter (GCE:2.12–5, 7.8–12). Below the level of the word, inflections are described, but no attempt is made to imitate the rigorous morphemic analyses of (say) irregular verbs that are characteristic of some linguistic descriptions; word-formation is relegated to an appendix. At the highest level, GCE does not recognize a syntactic unit above the sentence, for example 'paragraph'. It recognizes that there are relationships between sentences; indeed, the connections between sentences are treated in far greater detail in GCE, particularly in Chapter 10, than in previous reference grammars. But the syntactic relationships are expressed in terms of syntactic devices that link sentences or sets of sentences, such as logical connecters, substitution, and ellipsis. The sentence is not said to be included in any higher-ranking unit, nor can a sentence contain another sentence.

There are several reasons for the difficulties in arriving at an agreed definition of the sentence. In the first place, with paratactic constructions we can often choose whether to include independent clauses within one sentence or to separate them as different sentences, the choice depending upon the extent to which we want to show the closeness of connection between the clauses (GCE:App III.19). This choice is manifested clearly only in the written language, where it is signalled by the punctuation selections we make.[4] Secondly, linguists have different preconceived notions of what constitutes a sentence. Those differences are compounded by a common tendency to identify sentence with utterance. Bar–Hillel has warned repeatedly against the confusion that results from the failure to distinguish between SENTENCE, the abstract linguistic entity, and UTTERANCE, the physical product of a linguistic act (Bar-Hillel 1970:165–170, 195–7, 279–84, 364–9). One consequence of that confusion is that SENTENCE is commonly defined in terms of what can be isolated in linguistic acts.

The norm for the sentence in GCE is identified by its internal structure: one or more clauses that are not subordinate to other clauses (GCE:7.1, 11.1–3). GCE also recognizes minor sentence types that are defective in clause structure, such as *The more, the merrier*. It is not clear from the description whether GCE recognizes as sentences such constructions as *If only I'd listened to my parents* or *To think I was once a millionaire*, which contain markers of subordination, or formulae such as *Yes* and *Goodbye*, which do not permit analysis into elements of clause structure, or many

---

4 On the other hand, an orthographic sentence need not be a sentence or a clause syntactically (GCE:10.1 Note).

instances of block language, such as *Entrance* or *Danger: Falling Rocks,* which are likewise inaccessible to clause element analysis (GCE:7.86–90). They can all be utterances – spoken or written – but we would be classing together dissimilar units and therefore complicating our description needlessly if we considered them sentences. GCE explicitly classes as sentences the elliptical responses, questions, and comments made by a second speaker, where the ellipsis is dependent on the previous linguistic context, even when the elliptical construction is not capable of being a main clause (GCE:10.74–8):

A: Who told your father?
B: *Mary.*
A: I'm studying grammar.
B: *What?*
A: He is cleverer than you.
B: *Unfortunately.*

In those instances we can apply a clause element analysis if we take account of the ellipted elements; in the first example, *Mary* has the function of subject, as it would have in the non-elliptical *Mary told my father.* In some instances, however, the elliptical utterance would have to be analysed as an utterance of only part of a clause element; for example, *very* in

A: Are you angry?
B: *Very.*

is an adverb which in the reconstructed *I am very angry* is a modifier within an adjective phrase functioning as subject. It seems best to treat all such instances and the previously-mentioned subordinate clauses (*eg If only I'd listened to my parents*) as utterances of grammatical FRAGMENTARY SENTENCES. Acceptable utterances that are not accessible to clause element analysis should be treated as grammatical NON-SENTENCES.[5]

Even if we do not recognize a higher unit than sentence, it would be useful to be able to refer to dependency relations between sentences, though we can only speak of sentences as being relatively independent and relatively dependent. The dependency relations are those discussed in Chapter 10 of GCE and in Halliday and Hasan 1976 (*cf* also Waterhouse 1972 and Pike and Pike 1977:22–3, 262–3). The dependency may be on the situational context or the linguistic context. Dependency on the linguistic context can be defined as in Halliday and Hasan 1976:4: one sentence is dependent on another sentence (whether preceding or following) if the interpretation of some part of that sentence presupposes the interpretation of some part of

5 For some references to the status of what are here termed sentence fragments and non-sentences, see Jespersen 1924:305–8; Long 1961:19–20, 494; Bowman 1966; Allerton 1969; and Morgan 1973.

the other. The common syntactic devices marking dependency are reference, substitution, ellipsis, and explicit logical connecters. The dependency may be bidirectional, as when there is a listing by enumerative conjuncts (GCE: 10.19), and may involve sets of sentences (GCE: 10.1).

The metalanguage for clause and sentence in GCE is largely based on the grammatical tradition, but since that tradition is not completely uniform, choices have been made in terms and in their use. I have suggested some extensions and adjustments of the metalanguage that might be incorporated within the grammatical tradition to meet more fully the descriptive values of economy and consistency.

COUPLE: AN ENGLISH DUAL
DWIGHT BOLINGER

In his 'Grammatical and Pragmatic Aspects of Countability' (Quirk 1978), Randolph Quirk renews his interest in the number system of English with a masterly analysis of the types of nouns that are variously conceived as singular or plural, or that can be viewed either way – adding, to the latter, the previously unrecognized class of 'aggregate', the typical example being the noun *data*. His evidence makes it clear that number in English is far more complex than it is usually thought to be.

What follows is an attempt to single out a further complexity, one echoing a lost category that is still explicit in the morphology of many languages: dual number. Though English has no dual inflection, duality may need to be recognized as one of those categories that Benjamin Lee Whorf called COVERT.

The dual faded out of the English personal pronoun system in the thirteenth century. It has long been considered not to be a part of English grammar. Yet duality is a fact of life, and is apt to persist in out-of-the-way places, even to reestablish itself where it had not existed before. Something of this kind has happened to the English determiner system.

Lexically, of course, the dual is as strong as ever: *two, both, either-or, pair, twosome, duo, duet, brace, dyad, between*. Grammatical manifestations are something else. Supposedly the plural took over the functions of the dual. Are there places where 'more than one' requires specification beyond mere plurality, where the language compels the speaker not to be indifferent to the distinction between two and more than two?

[30]

If someone exclaims *Look at those lights!* we will be surprised if we see only two. There may be any number from three up, but if the number is two, it will almost certainly be specified in a situation like this where 'how many' is strongly in focus. But if the number is known to be two, it need not be specified: *Your parents are here; What have you done with my books?; I'd like you to meet my neighbours here, Jack and Mary Jones; Put out those lights, you're wasting electricity.* Even the exclamation is possible with known pairs: *Look at those hands!; Look at those burners!* (on a stove that has only two); *Look at those duelists!*

There is also a required dual, *pair of*, with plural nouns of the *shears, trousers, pliers, tongs* type in contexts where in the singular the indefinite article would refer to a particular item: *I squeezed it tight with a wrench, I squeezed it tight with a pair of pliers.* The unadorned plural here would acquire a generic, definitional sense: *I squeezed it tight with pliers* means that I did not do it with a vise, or a wrench, or my bare hands. In this case *An awl is a useful tool* = *Tweezers are a useful tool*. A generic in a sentence that is not specifically definitional (*Bees are insects*) probably implies an underlying sentence that is: *I squeezed it tight with pliers* = *I squeezed it tight with X tool + X tool was pliers*.

The generic sense attaches to unmodified plurals, whether of the *pliers* type or not, as well as unmodified mass nouns: *I lifted it with crowbars* and *I paid for it with money* identify the nature of the tool and of the medium of exchange. But what interests us here is that the plural is also non-dual (unless it refers to some crowbar contraption where 'two' is known). If only two crowbars were used, the fact would be specified: *I lifted it with two crowbars, I lifted it with a couple of crowbars*.

Couple is what shows best how systematic the dual still is in English. We need the generic/non-generic distinction (see Burton-Roberts 1976:427–9) to place it properly. *Couple* can be used for either specific or non-specific indefinites, but not for generics:

> I found a couple of handymen to help out; *they* were unskilled, but willing.
> I needed a couple of handymen to help out, but I couldn't find *any*.
> *A couple of handymen have to know their tools.

The singular article is possible in all three cases, but plural *some* is like *couple*:

> I found a handyman to help out; *he* was unskilled, but willing.
> I needed a handyman but I couldn't find *any*.
> A handyman has to know his tools.
> I found some handymen to help out.
> I needed some handymen to help out.
> *Some handymen have to know their tools.

[31]

The non-generic paradigm thus works out as follows, in singular, dual, and plural (I use specific examples, but non-specific would work just as well):

A man is waiting to see you.
A couple of men are waiting to see you.
Some men are waiting to see you.

Though the verb is indifferently plural with both *a couple of* and *some*, the article forces the distinction: *Some men are waiting to see you* is not apt to be used if the speaker knows there are two. (*Men are waiting to see you* is again generic – it would be strange except to suggest something like 'Those who are waiting for you are men and more deserving of attention than women or children'.)

The generic paradigm has only the article and zero:

A man needs appreciation.
Men need appreciation.

This is to be expected, since there is no need, for purposes of inclusion and exclusion, to specify a number other than one or totality. The reference is to a universe of discourse, which can be covered either distributively (one by one) or collectively (all at once): *A screwdriver drives screws, Screwdrivers drive screws; An elephant has a trunk, Elephants have trunks.*

The plural member of the non-generic paradigm, *some*, is restricted in the same way as was noted above for the plural form of nouns. Both may refer to 'two' when the items in question are known to come in twos. This makes *some* the indefinite counterpart of *pair*:

You'll need some glasses to read this print.
Go get me some pliers to open up this can.
I'd better put on some shoes before I go out.

If the number of pans is already known to be two, one may say *You'd better get some lids for those pans* to refer to two lids. One could not say here

*You'll need a couple of glasses to read this print.

There are apparent counter-examples where *some* is excluded:

I need a minute to finish here.
I need a couple of minutes to finish here.
*I need some minutes to finish here.

These contrast with

Give me a friend and I'll be happy.
Give me a couple of friends and I'll be happy.
Give me some friends and I'll be happy.

WHERE the restriction occurs is clear enough – it is with numeral classifiers, such as *spoonful, inch, spool, pound, grain*, etc:

> It would taste better with a little pepper – throw in a dash.
> ... throw in a couple of dashes.
> *... throw in some dashes.

The WHY is more difficult, but I suspect it reflects the relationship between the classifiers and the numeral system. The more like a 'counting' unit the determiner is, the better it accords with the classifier:

> I'm going to need a few hours to finish.
> ?I'm going to need more hours to finish. (OK more time.)
> A sweater that size will require several skeins.
> ?A sweater that size will require lots of skeins. (OK lots of wool.)

If this surmise is correct, the problem with *some* is its vagueness. *A, an* and *couple* are more in the nature of counters.

But not precise counters. As indefinites, they allow a certain latitude in the sense of 'minimal amount'. The 'minimal plurality' of *couple* has often been noted in sentences like *All I had was a couple of beers*, where the speaker evades the exact number. This is typical of duals: 'Commonly duals are extended to become *paucals* – referring to a few, more than one, but not so many as would call for a plural. In a system such as that of Marshallese, the dual may refer to "a few", the trial to more than that, but still a clearly limited number, and the plural to "lots", depending on the sort of object referred to and the discourse circumstances' (Anderson 1978:37). Such relative imprecision applies to the singular as well. In *He gave me a book* the speaker probably refers to just one book, but is not explicit about it; on the other hand, if someone offers a dish of peanuts and says *Have a peanut*, the listener will be imputing a joke if he picks just one. Both the indefinite singular and the indefinite dual can be used in a plural situation where a precise number might seem to be untruthful:

> What have you got in there, a rabbit?—Yes, in fact I have two.
> What have you got in there, one rabbit?—*Yes, in fact I have two. (OK No, I have two.)
> What have you got in there, a couple of rabbits?—Yes, in fact I have four.
> What have you got in there, two rabbits?—*Yes, in fact I have four. (OK No, I have four.)

It would be surprising if *some* did not share in this imprecision. Actually, given its indefinite range upward, it is more imprecise than its partners *a, an,* and *couple.* But it overlaps downward too, as was noted earlier – when the focus is elsewhere, *some* may embrace 'two'. But the distinction between dual and plural is not erased, only suspended. *Some* for 'two' is open to question or denial. This can be shown intonationally in examples like those of the last set:

What have you got in there, some rabbits?—Yes, ten.
What have you got in there, some rabbits?—Yes, two.

Ten would most likely have a terminal fall; that high a number definitely affirms 'some'. But *two* is more apt to have a rise-fall-rise, implying 'if two counts as some' (Ladd 1979:103). The reply *No, I don't have sóme rabbits, I have just twó* would also be normal. In a sentence like

I wonder if some rocks might work to keep the thing from blowing away.

'two' satisfies the possibilities, but the probability is more. In one such as

We're having some people to dinner this evening.[1]

the speaker is noncommittal and 'two' is possible. Similarly in

Who are Lou and Jane Carson?—Just some friends of ours.

but not in

Who are Lou and Jane Carson?—*Just some of our friends.

where the partitive puts more emphasis on plurality. *Couple of* is normal in either context:

Who are Lou and Jane Carson?—Just a couple of friends of ours (just a couple of our friends).

The partitive of course uses the pronoun *some* rather than the article *some*.

Fitting the pronoun into the overall scheme calls for a look at the common etymological source of both pronoun and article. We know that the singular indefinite article comes from a de-accented numeral 'one' in its OE form *ān*, whose consonant is retained in the alternate form *an*. The fading of the accent accompanied the semantic bleaching that reduced 'one' from a number to a signal of unspecified presence or existence. It developed farthest as a pre-adjunct, losing not only its full vowel but also its consonant in some positions. The reduction has not gone so far in pre-pausal environments, where we still have *one* with unreduced vowel in the indefinite pronoun,

I took a break because I badly néeded one.

but with optional reduction when the word is used to turn an adjective into a nominal:

This is the bést one [wṇ].
Give me a néw one.

The pronoun is not accented: *I badly needed óne* refers to number, not

1 Example from Geoffrey Leech, personal communication.

identity. The nominalizer may be accented for climax – the accent belongs to the sentence, not the word:

Thanks, but I'm not going to take your véry lást óne!

The pronominal use, with its accent, concerns us because paralleling the article paradigm we find a pronominal paradigm using the same words (if we count de-accented *one* the same as *a, an*). All three are de-accented, but *some*, like *one*, has its unreduced form [sʌm]:

There aren't any pigeons around here. – You're mistaken. I just sáw one (a couple, some).

The dual is used if the number is two. But if the numeral *two* is used, it attracts the accent – *couple* and *twó* (like *some* and *séveral, tén*, etc) pattern like *one* and *óne*:

There aren't any pigeons around here. – You're mistaken.
I've already seen óne (twó, séveral, tén).[2]

The indefinite pronoun, like the article, is a special form of the quantifier, whose accentual behavior symptomizes its pronounness, that is, its relative redundancy. The responses *one, couple,* and *some* to *There aren't any pigeons* have one thing in common: affirmation. Having one, two, or any number is sufficient to establish this, but the quantifiers actually used are the minimizing indefinites. In the following,

I didn't offer him any apples because he already hád one (a couple, some).

the particular amounts are not important beside the fact that – and the sentence can be so worded – *he was already provided*. As with the article, the focus is on the existence of the entity, not the amount of it. The invitations in

Do you like them? Táke one!
Do you like them? Táke a couple!
Do you like them? Táke some!

are equivalent to *Help yourself* or *Be my guest* – any of the quantities mentioned suffices to affirm the action of taking.

The minimizers reveal what might be called the Redundancy of Modest Amounts. Here we see the cluster of *one-couple-some* at the closed end of an open-ended category of minimizers. *Couple* can be replaced by *one or two* or *two or three*, *some* by *a few, two or three, three or four*, and other expressions

---

2 The intonation may differ, with the smaller numbers, *one* and *two* especially, tending to take the rise-fall-rise ('if one or two counts as "any"') and the large ones a terminal fall. The same intonational behavior is found with *couple* and *some* when used as non-pronominal indefinite quantifiers – they have the terminal rise:
Are there any pigeons around here?—Well, I've seen óne (a cóuple, sóme).

(given appropriate contexts) such as *a little* and *a fair amount* with mass entities and *a fair number*, *a dozen or so*, etc, with countables. Definites, however small, attract the accent, as do non-minimizing indefinites: *several* would be unusual as a replacement of *some*, and *a large number* even more so as a replacement of *a fair number*.

If *one-couple-some* were quantifiers to begin with, and even today are interchangeable to such a degree with other minimizers, what right do we have to regard them as a special set? The semantic justification is that they, more than any of the other minimizers, deflect the focus from amounts and put it on existence. The *Táke one!* of the last set of examples affirms the taking. The *one* is for whatever reason obvious under the circumstances – the objects being offered are of such size or value that taking more than one would be unexpected, or the speaker has in mind that the hearer is hesitating to take even one. And so with the amounts in *couple* and *some*. On the other hand, the examples

Do you like them? – Táke one or two.
Do you like them? – Táke a few.

do not contain an unstinting invitation. Despite the shift of accent to the verb, the amount is still important. *A few* probably comes closest to the article-pronoun paradigm, and outside the paradigm – as accented quantifiers – *some* and *a few* are extremely close:

These are only sóme (a féw) of the reasons he gave.

But *a few* does not quite make the grade. In the following it is unsuitable as an article:

Who are Jack Nelson, Joe Riggs, Clyde Hampstead, and Merve Little?— Just some friends of ours. (?Just a few friends of ours.)

The effect of *some* is to make *friends* identifying rather than defining. (*Just friends of ours* would be defining.) In this context, even the slight emphasis on quantity contained in *a few* is inappropriate.

As for *couple*, there are at least two things that are unique about it and confirm its tie to *one* and *some*. First, it is the only quantifier other than *one* that refers to a particular number and yet is indefinite – to the extent that it would rarely be used with the definite article or other definite determiner. (The sense 'coupling' or 'married couple' of course is irrelevant here.) In this respect it is like *some*, and unlike other quantifiers, even indefinite ones:

?What did you do with the couple that you had?[3]
*What did you do with the some that you had?

3 Leech suggests the following exchange (personal communication):
  I'm just looking for a couple of screws to finish fixing that mirror.—What did you do with the couple that you had?

What did you do with the ten (dozen, score) that you had?
What did you do with the few (little, several, many, more than ten) that
   you had?

The one is not a counter-example, for *one* belongs equally to the definite
quantifiers.

The second quality of *couple* is that it is the only COUNTING unit
incorporating the indefinite article that minimizes without being qualified
in some way. Other counting units to be so used require some means of
suggesting 'loose approximation' (it may be no more than an intonation plus
a shrug of the shoulders). The answers in the following are intended to
signify essentially 'minimal affirmation':

Does he have employees?—A dozen, I guess.
                        A score or two.
                        A hundred or so.[4]

Similarly with the numeral classifiers that accompany mass and mass-like
countable nouns (*eg, soybeans* is similar to *corn*):

Does he have land?—An acre, maybe.
Does he have soybeans?—Oh, a bushel, I guess.
Does he have motor oil?—A quart, perhaps.
Does he have time?—A minute or so.

But the language has gone farther and created rather highly specific minimal
classifiers. In the following, the answers are to be read with an intonation
that de-emphasizes the amount – a low or not very high pitch on the stressed
syllable and a slight terminal rise:

Does he have followers?—A scattering.
Does he have knowledge?—A smattering.
Does he have friends?—A handful.

This I think is by way of a quotation. It is not uncommon for one speaker to parrot another and
violate a rule in the process:

   I intend to have my way.—What do you do when 'my way' collides with other people's way?

If the first speaker does not actually use the word *couple*, I find the response doubtful:

   I'm just looking for one or two screws to finish fixing that mirror.—?What did you do with
   the couple that you had?

There may be some dialectal variation here, especially in the range that *couple* is allowed to
cover. I find the definition 'several' in the *American Heritage Dictionary* incorrect except as a
figure of speech. But the words referring to indefinite amounts are by their nature apt to shift
meaning. The word *several* itself is variously understood. For one person of my acquaintance it
has to be 'at least ten'. Going in the opposite direction, there is a tendency now to turn it into
a minimizer. An episode of the Cousteau Odyssey has *only several miles away*; news accounts
mention *no more than several hundred*. I would require *a few* in these contexts.

4 Large numbers can always be used figuratively as minimizers, of course, with low-pitched
accent and terminal rise:

   Did you lose much?—A million or so.

Does he have hope?—A glimmer.
Did he have food?—A bite.
Did he have fruit juice?—A swallow.
Did he have fresh air?—A sniff.
Did he find historical evidence?—A trace.
Was there snow?—A flurry.
Was there rain?—A sprinkle.
Do you want salt?—A dash.

In this next group, there is no accent at all on the classifiers:

You'd like to see it? Táke a squint.
　　　　　　　　Táke a glance.
　　　　　　　　?Táke a look.
You'd like to enjoy its perfume? Táke a sniff.
　　　　　　　　　　　Táke a whiff.
　　　　　　　　　　　?Táke a smell.

As with other similar categories (of countability or transitivity, for example), there are some items that are shared with the complementary category. This is true of words that in a given context are equivalent to 'one'. In *Do you like these apples? Táke one!* the unit is naturally *one*. (Or conceivably *a box*, in a large display.) But in *Do you like these checkers?* it might well be *a set*, or with cards, *a deck*, or in a display of eggs, *a dozen*. We may then get – as further minimizers – *a couple of decks* (*sets*, etc), but not *some decks* (compare *some dashes*, above). Some items are stereotyped as minimal classifiers, others are not.

Lying outside the category are not only precise amounts above unity, but also imprecise ones that approach them – this includes *approximately* and *about*. The following examples are unusual with the low-pitched accent described above, but would be normal with the 'if that counts' rise-fall-rise:

Does he have time?—A second.
Does he have friends?—Five, anyway.
Does he have motor oil?—About (approximately) a quart.

Also outside the category, as already pointed out, are indefinites that do not minimize. Regardless of intonation, the following could not signify 'minimal affirmation':

Does he have money?—He has scads (heaps, piles, gobs).
Does he have friends?—he has lots (a great many, any number, dozens).

This look at the indefinite minimal classifiers has taken us some distance from the paradigmatic relationships of *couple* but it was necessary to assess the nature of the paradigm itself. *Couple* has been attracted from the broader range of indefinite quantifiers into the orbit of the articles, whose chief

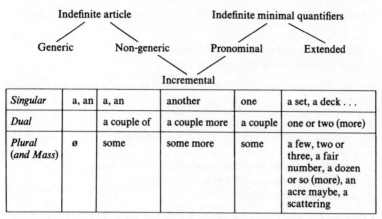

Singular	a, an	a, an	another	one	a set, a deck ...
Dual		a couple of	a couple more	a couple	one or two (more)
Plural (and Mass)	ø	some	some more	some	a few, two or three, a fair number, a dozen or so (more), an acre maybe, a scattering

Table 1 summarizes the articles and the quantifiers.

function is not to quantify but to oppose the generic sense of the unmodified mass and plural noun.

The picture would be clearer if this were the ONLY function of the singular *a*, *an*, but as we have seen the singular article is shared with the generic paradigm. What confuses things is that *a*, *an* has been called upon to fill several roles, including prosodic ones. In the following it separates two accented syllables (*fine lóoking*):

The Major did not smile in the least, though he had every reason to be amused. 'Monstrous handsome young man that – as fine a looking soldier as I ever saw,' he said to Costigan. (Thackeray 1848.)

The intrusion of *such* on the semantic realm of *so* responds to the same problem of rhythm: *so good an investment*, **a so good investment*, *such a good investment* (cf Bolinger 1972a: 137–45). In *It's a sort of a squeegee* the second article was probably a hesitation sound to begin with, coming at a point where the speaker pauses and thinks; but later, *sort of (a)* was specialized as an adverb: *It's a squeegee, sort of*; *It's funny, sort of*; *It's sorta funny*. And so with *kinda*.

The generic use is not inherent in the meaning of the indefinite singular article, but has developed from a series of oppositions in the system. It was still used only about half the time, in Middle English, in constructions like the following singular:

John and James are lawyers.
John is (a) lawyer.

[39]

(Mustanoja 1960:260–2; Visser 1970:230–1.) Relics of this are still found:

I can be more than sister to you.
Teacher I am and teacher I shall remain.
I saw somebody.—Was he man or boy?

But for the most part, absence of the indefinite article in the singular indicates

(1) a proper noun (*Nurse says to behave*),
(2) a unique-referent noun (*I'm lord of the manor here, He's low man on the totem pole*),
(3) a predicative adjectival (*He's Catholic, *He's Methodist*),
(4) an intensified noun (*He's 100 per cent boy*), or
(5) a mass noun (*It's sugar*).

The last example shows the trouble we are in if we try to use an unmodified singular to identify a countable: *They are lambs* is countable, but *It's lamb* can only be mass – it must refer to meat. The article restores the singular: *It's a lamb*. A similar problem occurs with personal nouns, only now it is the possessive that the older form would create an ambiguity with: *John's baker*. This explains why the generic paradigm is incomplete, why *a couple* and *some* are absent – the indefinite article itself, in a sense, does not belong there.

As for *couple*, its place in the paradigm is supported not only by the syntax but by the phonetic reduction that it shares with *a, an, some*. Mencken records *coupla* alongside of *kinda, sorta,* and *woulda* (Mencken 1936:443, 471, 570).[5] *A couple of* has become or is becoming as much a unit article as *kinda* and *nice'n* are unit intensifiers in *kinda cute* and *nice'n hot*.

The indefinite paradigm has a lateral branch in the shape of an incremental paradigm. It might appear that the only thing needed to express that which is additional would be to add the word *more*. With the definite quantifiers that is exactly what is done: *two more, a dozen more, a hundred more*. But with the indefinites, a problem is created by the ambiguity of *one*. *One more* is definite. To replace it on the indefinite side, *another* is used. Also, *of* is dropped from *a couple of* (and *some more* becomes *s'more*):

I want another peanut.
I want a couple more peanuts.
I want some more peanuts.

---

5 Leech points out the parallel reduction in *pint of milk* and *bottle of beer*. So perhaps the appeal here should be not just to the phonetic reduction but to the eye-dialect spelling, which is what Mencken actually reports. *Pint of*, too, is found as *pinta* with the sense 'pint of milk', in British usage (nobody, apparently, writes *bottla*). The spelling *kinda* and *coupla* probably reflects the writer's feeling about the special status of these 'words'.

COMPLEX INTRANSITIVE CONSTRUCTIONS
P. H. MATTHEWS

1 Introduction

In sentences such as [1]:

[1] They made it green

the construction is of a type that GCE:850 *ff* describes as COMPLEX TRANSITIVE. Of the elements in question, *it* and *made* are related as in the simple transitive:

[2] They made it

while *it* and *green* are related as in a simple copular sentence:

[3] It is green

of the type that, following Lyons (1977:469 *ff*), we will call ASCRIPTIVE. But *green* also stands in a direct relationship to *made*, the object and adjective exemplifying a single pattern of VERB COMPLEMENTATION. This pattern can be said to represent a FUSION (GCE:850) of the simpler transitive and ascriptive types.

If the ascriptive can be fused with the transitive can it also be fused with the intransitive? In sentences such as [4]:

[4] It turned green

the construction is usually identified with that of [3]; in both examples the verb is described as copular or, in the terminology of GCE:820 *f*, as taking 'intensive' complementation. But neither description is quite appropriate to both cases. In the ascriptive sentence there is indeed no more than a copula, or grammatical link, between the adjective and its subject. But plainly this is not true of [4], whose verb, TURN, has its own specific meaning. If *turned* is a full verb it must then be the governor of *green*, as *made* is in [1]; in that sense there is complementation. But we express nothing by assigning such a complementation to the copula. A solution is to class [4] as a COMPLEX INTRANSITIVE, its construction being an extension of the simple intransitive:

[5] It turned

precisely as that of [1] is extended from that of [2].

2 Fused constructions

Let us take our cue from GCE's reference to 'fusion'. In the simple or unfused transitive [2], the construction consists of a single predicator (*made*), which in a dependency analysis has both the subject and the object as its dependents or, to adapt GCE's term, has both a subject and an object as its complementation. In that sense [2] has a KERNEL construction (Lyons 1977), which cannot be reduced to more elementary relationships of predication. So too has the simple intransitive [5], with *it* dependent on, or forming the complementation of, *turned*. So too has the simple ascriptive [3]; its predicator, on the analysis of Lyons and others, is the adjective *green*. One reason for relating the subject to the adjective is that the elements are jointly subject to selectional restrictions. A reason for not relating either to the copula is that the latter stands aside from these restrictions, adding none of its own.

In a fused construction the pattern is neither strictly kernel nor straightforwardly non-kernel. In the complex transitive [1], both *it* and *they* are again direct dependents of *made*; these relations are shown below the words in *Fig* I, by directed arcs (labelled *a* and *b*) leading outward from the

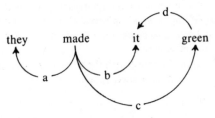

Fig I

predicator. So is *green* (arc *c*), this too being supported by selectional restrictions. We are therefore dealing with a single clause, rooted in *made*, of which each word is a distinct element. But *green* is also a predicator in relation to *it* (arc *d*). In that way we are dealing with two kernel patterns, the four-term clause incorporating both the three-term transitive and the two-term ascriptive.

In *Fig* 1 we have diagrammed what any grammarian will propose, provided that his terminology, or his notational apparatus, allow him to say it. But similar reasoning applies to the construction which we have called the complex intransitive. Of the relationships shown in *Fig* 2, that of *green*

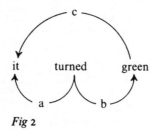

Fig 2

to *it* (arc *c*) is again as in the ascriptive, and needs no further comment. But the final element is clearly subject to additional restrictions. With TURN it must be either an adjective or an undetermined noun (*He turned pink, He turned king's evidence*); a determined phrase is excluded (*He turned a frog*), unless the prepositional form is also considered (*He turned into a frog*). With GO the exclusion is absolute: one cannot even say *He went into a criminal*. The adjective is also limited to specific collocations. For example, one can say *It turned sour* or *It went sour*, but it is harder to accept *It grew sour*. Conversely, one can say *He grew old*, but not *He went old*. On that evidence we may establish a relationship of dependency between *green* and *turned* (arc *b*). The verb too can then be related to the subject (arc *a*).

In both our examples there is one term, *it*, which is a dependent in both the ascriptive and the verbal kernel (*Fig* 1, arcs *b* and *d*; *Fig* 2, arcs *a* and *c*). The fusion is then effected by a further link (*Fig* 1, arc *c*; *Fig* 2, arc *b*) in which the second of the two predicators, *green*, is incorporated as a dependent of the first. It is to this last relation that Quirk and his colleagues, in the case of the complex intransitive, have applied the term 'intensive complementation'; we might accordingly describe the valency of TURN, or of TURN in this use, as that of an 'intensive intransitive'. But the insight may also be extended to the complex transitive. In that spirit MAKE, or MAKE as used in sentences such as [1], might appropriately be described as an 'intensive transitive'.

3 Distinctions between the complex intransitive and other, partly similar, constructions

For a three-term construction, *Fig* 2 shows the maximum number of interconnections, with each term related to each of the others. The minimum is one; thus for the ascriptive [3] we have adopted the structure shown in *Fig* 3, with the second term no more than a marker, or supporting element, for the predicative relation between the first and the third. But this leaves five other possibilities, which in theory might be realized. Just as the second element can be a marker, as in *Fig* 3, so too might the third; in that case only

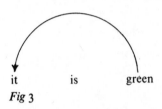

it   is   green

Fig 3

the verb would be a predicator, with only the subject related to it. This structure does not seem to be realized, at least not in a way which is relevant to our analysis. A second possibility is that only the verb and the adjective might be related; in that case both predicators would be impersonal, with the subject a mere place-filler. This structure might conceivably be suggested for examples such as [6]:

[6] It got mistier

with a so-called 'ambient' *it*. But although *it* may indeed be ambient with respect to *mistier*, it need not follow that it is ambient with respect to *got*.

In the remaining cases no element is a marker; but there are only two, instead of three, interconnections. If there were no link between the subject and the verb (*Fig* 2, arc *a*), the verb itself would again be impersonal. In transformational terms, its surface subject would be derived by raising (Postal 1974) from a subordinate adjectival clause. If there were no 'intensive' link between the first and second predicators (*Fig* 2, arc *b*), the verb would be a simple intransitive, taking just the subject as its complementation; the construction of the adjective would then be CIRCUMSTANTIAL. In [7], for example:

[7] He arrived sober

grammars do not establish an intensive, or copular, use of ARRIVE. Finally,

[44]

if the ascriptive link were broken (*Fig 2*, arc *c*), the third element would no longer be a predicator. Its role would instead be ADVERBIAL as in [8]:

[8] He ran fast

There is no doubt that the intensive construction is distinct from the adverbial, and that *sober* in [7] is at least more circumstantial than *green* in *It turned green*. But the subject-verb relation is more problematic, in that a raising transformation has been proposed for one, at least, of the GCE's intensive verbs. Let us therefore take that distinction first.

3.1

Of the twenty or so 'most common' intensive verbs (GCE:821), SEEM and APPEAR particularly lend themselves to transformational analysis. On the evidence of sentences such as [9]:

[9] It seemed that they were green

it is natural to establish an underlying structure:

(*a*) ₛ[they were green]ₛ seemed

in which *seemed* is related not to *they* and *green* individually, but to the whole ascriptive kernel. From the same structure a sentence such as [10]:

[10] They seemed to be green

can then be derived by further transformations of subject raising and infinitive formation. From the structure realized by [10], we are naturally tempted to derive the complex intransitive [11]:

[11] They seemed green

by a further transformation deleting the copula.

For SEEM the rules deriving [10] and [11] would both be optional. But for other verbs, such as TURN or GO, we could make them obligatory: so, *It turned green* could be the only realization of an underlying ₛ[*it was green*]ₛ *turned*, the 'ambient' *It got mistier* – [6] above – a realization of, say, ₛ[*mistier*]ₛ *got*, and so on. If the obligatory rules were then restricted to the copula, we would also ensure that any other form of embedded structure (ₛ[*he left*]ₛ *turned* or ₛ[*he kissed her*]ₛ *grew*) was filtered out. By such means a treatment which is widely accepted for SEEM, and for which the evidence is at first compelling, could be extended, if it were thought appropriate, to the entire intensive intransitive class.

There are good reasons for not thinking it appropriate. In a sentence such as [12]:

[12] Harry got drunk

one is not simply talking of a state that resulted ('It got so that Harry was drunk', or 'Harry's drunkenness happened'). Nor is *Harry* a mere theme or topic ('As to Harry, drunkenness happened to him'). The subject is, potentially at least, an actor: getting drunk was something that Harry did. The verb may accordingly take a 'subject adjunct' (GCE:466*f*): thus *I deliberately got drunk* or *He foolishly turned traitor*. It may also supply the complement of a conative verb (*I did try to get drunk*), may appear in the imperative (*Don't get drunk!*), and so on. For some collocations this potentiality is doubtless harder to realize (compare *He deliberately turned blue* with *He deliberately turned nasty*, or *He tried to grow older* with *He tried to grow fatter*); but that is precisely the case for subjects and predicators generally. It is this semantic role that justifies the first link shown in *Fig 2*, which an impersonal structure, as in (*b*):

(*b*) ₛ[Harry was drunk]ₛ got

would relegate to the surface.

If (*b*) is wrong for *Harry got drunk*, a transformationalist should consider more carefully whether a similar structure is correct for *Harry seemed drunk*. Let us assume that it is correct for the construction with a *that*-clause (*It seemed that Harry was drunk*); for SEEM and APPEAR a clausal complement does form one possibility. Let us also accept that SEEM has a constant sense in all its constructions. But for other 'current' intensives (GCE:820*f*) the evidence is more complex. With SOUND a *that*-clause can be forced: for example, if a dative is inserted (*It sounds to me that they aren't coming*). There is also an impersonal construction with *as if*:

[13] It sounds as if they were green

which might be thought to derive from the same source. The construction of [13] is also acceptable with LOOK (*It looks as if they aren't coming*). But between it and the complex intransitive we can find clear disparities in meaning. In [13] the judgment is based on indirect clues: what 'sounds', or appears from audible information, is indeed the whole proposition 'they were green'. But in the complex intransitive [14]:

[14] They sound drunk

it is based on sounds that *they* are making. For that reason it is harder to make sense of *They sound green*. Likewise *They look drunk* means that they, from their appearance, are so. But in *It looks as if they are drunk* the speaker does not even imply that he has seen them. (Compare *From what you say, it looks as if they are drunk*.) If we wanted a complex source, it would be tempting to relate [14] not to the impersonal [13], with raising, but rather to the personal [15]:

[15] They sound as if they are drunk

with the second *they* deleted.

[46]

Personal and impersonal are often hard to separate, as Palmer (1972) and before him Bolinger (1961*a*) have shown. Of this group of intensives, TASTE and SMELL are the most restricted in meaning, and it is with these that the impersonal construction, as in [9] and [13], is least acceptable. With TASTE neither seems likely: *It tastes to me that the soup is salty, It tastes to me as if they are sweet.* If the second example can be interpreted, it is by virtue of a blending with the personal construction (compare *It tastes as if it* . . .). With SMELL the construction of [13] may be more acceptable (*It smells to me as if dinner is ready*), but the blending remains. With FEEL a non-tactile sense is possible (*It feels likely*), but is less established than the broader senses of LOOK or SOUND (compare *It looks likely, It sounds likely*). It is in this case that my judgment is least secure: would one say, for example, *It feels* (or *It feels to me*) *as if they were green*? With SOUND and LOOK the general sense is well established, as in [13] or *It sounds likely*; but there is still a sensory meaning, as in [14] and [15], which inhibits the pure impersonal with *that*. With SEEM and APPEAR we are at the end of the continuum, both having general senses only. Hence the construction of [9], alongside the impersonal with *as if* (*It seems as if they were green*). Hence, perhaps, the infinitive construction of [10]; with SOUND and the others this too is awkward (*They looked to have arrived*, or *It tastes to me to be sweet*). But it does not follow that the semantically general *They seem drunk* differs in syntax from the specifically sensory *They sound drunk* or *They smell drunk*. We can even force an active interpretation of the subject: thus *They tried to appear drunk*, or *I deliberately seemed irritated.*

3.2

As [11], with SEEM, lies on a gradience between personal and impersonal, so there are others which raise problems in distinguishing intensive from adverbial and circumstantial constructions. For there is no criterion which is both sufficient and necessary.

The obvious step is to test for simpler transforms. Thus for [12], *Harry got drunk*, we can compare the simple ascriptive *Harry was drunk*; this is a TRANSFORM in that, firstly, it is acceptable and, secondly, the predicator DRUNK has not altered its sense. But [12] has no intransitive transform *Harry got*, as this use of GET is not acceptable. Nor has [4], *It turned green*, an intransitive transform *It turned*, since this involves a different sense of TURN. If there is an ascriptive transform but no simple intransitive, the third element must be a complement; so [4] and [12] must be complex intransitive. If there is neither transform it MAY be complement, but the collocation of verb and adjective might reasonably be classed as idiomatic. Thus *The roses have run wild* has no transform *The roses have run*, nor does it strictly match *The roses are wild*. But WILD is at least an adjective, and must stand in some relationship to the verb; therefore RUN WILD is rightly classed as a 'result' intensive (GCE).

If there is a simple intransitive but no ascriptive transform, the construction must be adverbial. Thus, trivially, *He ran quickly* has no ascriptive transform *He was quickly*; less trivially, *He travelled light* does not match *He was light*. But what if we find both? *They stood still* has an ascriptive transform *They were still*; so *still* may be a complement or circumstantial, like *silent* in *They stood silent*. But there is also the simpler intransitive *They stood*; so *still* might be an adverb, like *silently* in *They stood silently*. Since there is no distinct form *stilly*, the latter is hard to rule out. For *It shone white* we can compare the formally adjectival *It shone bright*; again there are both transforms (*It shone, It was white*). But *It shone bright* is close in meaning to the formally adverbial *It shone brightly*; could *white* be an adverb, in default of, or as the commoner alternative to, *whitely*? Blending may also be found in idioms. For example, it is fruitless to ask if *doggo* is an adjective or an adverb in *He is lying doggo*.

For the circumstantial case both transforms are necessary: thus [7], *He arrived sober*, has the transforms *He arrived* and *He was sober*. We would also expect that the verb and adjective should be free of collocational restrictions: so *He arrived sober, He left sober, He left satisfied, He arrived satisfied,* and so on. But it is very hard to say when such a requirement is met. One does not say, for example, *They stood noisy* or *They stood peaceful*; on that evidence *They stood silent* might be classed as complex intransitive. But neither is one likely to say *They arrived noisy*, or *They arrived kind*. Is that too a matter of collocational restrictions, so that [7] is also intensive? Or is it merely that NOISY and KIND are ill suited to this construction? At this point it is tempting to distinguish degrees of circumstantiality. The extreme case would be represented by such sentences as [16]:

[16] They stood there, exhausted

(likewise *They have arrived, quite sober*), where the adjective and verb are marked as separate. Beside [16] the construction in [7] is less clearly circumstantial; in *They stood silent* or *They stood fidgeting* it is perhaps even less so. But this last might still be seen as less intensive than, for example, *They stood amazed*. Likewise *They fell exhausted* is less clearly intensive than *They fell sick*, since it involves no special sense of FALL.

The problem also arises for the complex transitive. In *They found him guilty* there is a special sense of FIND, as of MAKE in *They made it green*. In *They met him sober* there is no special sense of MEET; by that test *sober* is more circumstantial. But one is unlikely to say, for example, *They met him meditative*.

4

Finally, there is an obvious gradience between the complex intransitive and the simple ascriptive. With TURN or GROW there are narrow selectional restrictions, as we have seen. With SEEM or STAY they are far fewer;

nevertheless one cannot say, for example, *He seemed chairman* (compare *He stayed chairman* or *He was chairman*) or *It stays obvious that . . .* (compare *It seems obvious that . . .* or *It remains obvious that . . .*). With REMAIN it is hard to find any; but at least the intransitive exists (*He remained*) and their senses can be related. With BECOME that evidence too is lacking. *He became drunk* can be distinguished from the ascriptive *He was drunk* only by arguing from its resultative meaning.

This merging has led grammarians to treat the constructions together. But we can do this only by assimilating BE to the model of verb complementation (as in GCE), not by assimilating TURN and so on to the model of a copula. Like the complex transitive, the complex intransitive is a poor candidate for what must then be a kernel structure.

SOME ENGLISH VERBS
AND THE CONTRAST
INCOMPLETION/COMPLETION
SVEN JACOBSON

In this paper I will discuss the acceptability of the two-sentence example [1] with its four verb + object alternatives. The purpose is to test to what extent it is possible, simply by using a negated non-progressive past in the second sentence, to assert that the incompletion denoted by the use of the progressive past in the first sentence was not followed by completion. The referent of the subject is the same in both sentences. In case of disturbing ambiguity or no acceptability for any alternative I will discuss possible ways of amendment. In this connection I will also demonstrate differences between some of the alternatives as regards verb-adverb collocation. Various recent approaches to verbal aspects will be used in order to find an adequate system and set of terms to describe certain interesting results of the test.

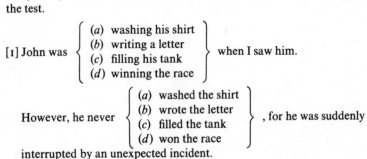

[1] John was
- (a) washing his shirt
- (b) writing a letter
- (c) filling his tank
- (d) winning the race

when I saw him.

However, he never
- (a) washed the shirt
- (b) wrote the letter
- (c) filled the tank
- (d) won the race

, for he was suddenly interrupted by an unexpected incident.

Alternatives (*a*) and (*b*) are not acceptable since their sentences are contradictory; if one says that John was washing his shirt or writing a letter, one cannot state in the next sentence that he never washed the shirt or wrote the letter. What has to be expressed more clearly is the fact that the second sentence is meant to deny the completion of the activity described by the first. This can be done as in [2].

[2] John was $\left\{ \begin{array}{l} (a) \ \text{washing his shirt} \\ (b) \ \text{writing a letter} \end{array} \right\}$ when I saw him.

However, he never $\left\{ \begin{array}{l} (a) \ \text{finished washing it} \\ (b) \ \text{finished it} \end{array} \right\}$, for he was suddenly interrupted by an unexpected incident.

Here it is to be noted that in the situation of (*a*) one thinks of the washing of the shirt, rather than of the shirt itself, as never finished, whereas in that of (*b*) one tends to think more of the letter, and less of the writing of it, as never finished.

The verb *fill* in alternative [1*c*] is ambiguous between the two senses 'pour (*eg* petrol) into' and 'fill up' or 'fill to repletion'. If the first sense is taken to apply to *was filling his tank* and the second to *filled the tank* in [1*c*], the example sounds quite reasonable. In order to make this change of meaning quite obvious to a listener, the speaker must give contrastive stress to the verb the second time it appears. If this is not done, the listener may take *fill* to mean 'pour (*eg* petrol) into' also in the second sentence and is then disconcerted by what he feels to be a contradiction. The possibility of his understanding *fill* to mean 'fill up' in both places seems more remote. *Cf* the discussion about [1*d*] below.

The difference between the ambiguous verb *fill* and the unambiguous *fill up* can be clearly seen in such cases as [3].

[3] I'll look at the oil. Meanwhile you can start $\left\{ \begin{array}{l} (a) \ \text{filling.} \\ (b) \ \text{filling up.} \end{array} \right\}$

By saying (*a*) the speaker can imply that he himself will soon take over the job, whereas this implication is less plausible if he says (*b*), since it stresses that the filling has to go on until the tank is full.

The possibility that the unmodified verb *fill* has of either ranging over the whole scale 'empty–full' or denoting the reaching of the end-point 'full' is not open to the adjective *full*. When it is unmodified, it can only denote the end-point 'full', and only by being modified, as in *partially full, half full,* or *almost full,* can it be used about other points. This difference is shown by [4].

[4] A: When did you last fill the tank?
   B: Oh, I filled it yesterday, but unfortunately I only got it half full, for something went wrong with the pump.

The same distinction applies to the verb *empty* and its corresponding adjective.

In alternative [1*d*] the meaning of *John was winning the race* can be represented as 'Everything pointed in the direction of John's winning the race' or, in more technical terms (*cf* GCE:95), 'John was approaching the transition involved in winning the race'. In other words, the first sentence of [1*d*] contains no assertion that John actually won the race and therefore the second sentence, where it is asserted that he did not win, does not contradict it. [1*d*] is thus acceptable as it is, without any amendment or special stress and intonation.

Other verbal expressions that it seems possible to substitute for *was winning/won the race* in [1*d*] are, for example, *was leaving/left the country* and *was reaching/reached the top*.

After this preliminary discussion of the alternatives of [1], we will look at some recent ways of approaching the field of verbal aspect and verb classification, in the hope that this will give us deeper insight into how and why the four alternatives fail or succeed in expressing the contrast between incompletion and completion.

In GCE:90 it is said that 'English has two sets of aspectual contrasts: PERFECTIVE/NON-PERFECTIVE and PROGRESSIVE/NON-PROGRESSIVE'. Four pages later non-progressive aspect is called 'simple' aspect, a term which is based on form rather than on meaning, as the term 'non-progressive aspect' is. In fact, the distinction made between aspects in GCE is largely formal: for example, the progressive aspect is recognized by the use of the auxiliary *be* + present participle. Another approach to aspect is that of Verkuyl 1972, whose classification is based on the semantic qualities of the verbal expressions, including objects and adverbial modifiers. See *Fig* 1, which sums up *pp* 5–6 and 36 of Verkuyl 1972.

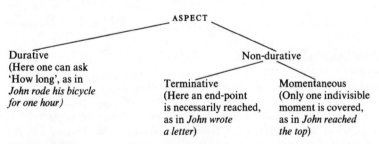

Fig 1 Verkuyl's classification of verbal aspects

This system is matched in GCE:95–6 not by 'aspects' but by a set of verbal subclasses denoting, respectively, activity (*eg* ride), process (*eg* deteriorate), bodily sensation (*eg* feel), transitional event (*eg* leave), momentary action (*eg*

kick), inert perception and cognition (*eg guess*), and relation (*eg include*).
Verbs belonging to the first five subclasses are called dynamic, the others
stative.

In Verkuyl's system *wash the shirt* apparently can have double aspect. It
can be assigned to the durative aspect, since we can very well ask [5]:

[5] For how long was he washing the shirt?

However, it can also be said to have terminative aspect since an end-point
is necessarily reached when the shirt is clean. Similarly, *fill the tank* can be
assigned to more than one aspect. In the sense 'pour (*eg* petrol) into the tank'
it normally (*cf* Vendler below) has terminative aspect, while it has
momentaneous aspect in the sense 'fill the tank to repletion'. *Write a letter*
and *win the race*, on the other hand, can only be assigned to one aspect,
respectively: the former to the terminative aspect and the latter to the
momentaneous aspect. The difference between the progressive and non-
progressive forms in English is of no special concern to Verkuyl, since he
bases his discussion on Dutch examples with English translations.
Nevertheless, his classification of aspects can be used as a basis for a general
statement about the acceptability of the alternatives of [1]: only those
containing verbal expressions that have, or can have, the momentaneous
aspect are acceptable. The subclassification of verbs in GCE:95–6 can be
brought in to make this general statement more specific: both *won the race*
and *filled the tank*, when used in the momentaneous aspect, denote
transitional events.

Like GCE, Vendler 1967:100–3 makes a clear distinction between verbs
admitting continuous, *ie* progressive, tenses and those lacking them. See
Fig 2.

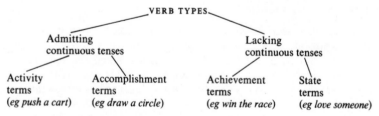

Fig 2 Vendler's classification of verbs

According to Vendler, verbal expressions like *win the race* and *reach the
top* are achievement terms and as such lack continuous tenses. Obviously
the latter is not true, since [1*d*] must be described as acceptable. Vendler,
however, indirectly gives a key to the use of the progressive here. He
discusses a sentence like [6] and says about it that it does not mean that the

'reaching' of the summit went on during three hours, for obviously it is the climbing that preceded it that took that time.

[6] It took him three hours to reach the summit.

This suggests that the notion of progressiveness in *was winning the race* does not apply to the actual 'winning' of the race but to the racing immediately preceding it (in the form of running, riding, driving, etc). We are also given a reason why the second sentence in [1*d*] is not contradictory in relation to the first: what is not completed in *was winning the race* is the racing, and *never won the race* states that the racing did not end in the form of victory for John since he was interrupted in it.

On the whole Verkuyl's durative aspect covers Vendler's activity and state terms, and the former's terminative and momentaneous aspects correspond, respectively, to the latter's accomplishment and achievement terms. One striking difference is that the designations for Verkuyl's aspects are based on the temporal ideas associated with the use of the different verbs, *eg* the notion of duration, whereas Vendler's terminology attempts to catch the ideas embodied in the verbs themselves, *eg* the notion of activity. Vendler, as well as Verkuyl, however, frequently uses temporal expressions as criteria. As regards the distinction between accomplishment terms and activity terms Vendler points out that, for example, drawing a circle has to be finished, while it does not make sense to talk of finishing pushing a cart. In the first case he says we can ask *How long did it take to do it?*, in the second *How long did he do it?* As has already been shown in connection with Verkuyl's aspectual system, *wash the shirt* can be substituted for *do it* in the second of these questions (*cf* [5]) and is then to be regarded as an activity term. It can, however, also be substituted for *do it* in the first question, as in [7], where it thus functions as an accomplishment term.

[7] How long did it take to wash the shirt?

It is the fact that *wash the shirt* can be used as an accomplishment term that makes it possible to add the verb *finish* in [2] in the case of that verbal expression, just as in the case of *write a letter*, which can only be an accomplishment term. While in [2*a*] *wash* can be either an activity term or an accomplishment term in *was washing his shirt*, depending on whether we think of the result of getting the shirt clean or not, it thus must be an accomplishment term in *finished washing it*.

In the sense 'pour (*eg* petrol) into the tank' *fill the tank* is as a rule to be regarded as an accomplishment term, since the question *How long did it take to fill the tank?* sounds appropriate, while the question *How long did he fill the tank?* sounds a bit odd, at least under normal circumstances. (A situation can of course be imagined where the rate of filling is measured by the clock, not by other instruments or by eyesight.) In the sense 'fill the tank to repletion' *fill the tank* is, however, clearly an achievement term. When [1*c*] is accepted, *was filling his tank* must be taken as an accomplishment term, just like the racing involved in *was winning the race*, and *filled the tank* must be interpreted in its achievement sense. While the fact that the progressive-ness of the racing in *was winning the race* is expressed by the verb *win* suggests that the achievement denoted by that verb is close at hand, a similar idea of closeness is far-fetched in *was filling his tank*, since it sounds natural to take *fill* here to mean 'pour (*eg* petrol) into'.

Activity and process verbs are two separate subclasses in the verb taxonomy used by GCE, but to Dahl 1974 activity is a subordinate category in relation to process: on *p* 25 an activity is defined as the intentional bringing-about of a process. A process, in its turn, is described by Dahl roughly as a sequence of events. An event denotes a change from one state to another, *ie* a transition, and the intentional bringing-about of an event is called an act. On the basis of Dahl's discussion we may diagram his model of what verbs or verb phrases describe as in *Fig* 3, where 'a bounded process' means a process that has a definite end-state. Although Dahl speaks of, for example, state-describing and activity-describing *sentences*, his model is actually an analysis of what is described by verbs and verb phrases rather than by sentences (*cf* Jacobson 1978 : § 2.3). A distinction is necessary, since such negated sentences as *John was not ill* and *John was not working* describe circumstances (*cf* Bartsch 1976 : 74), whereas their verb phrases, looked upon independently of the negation, describe, respectively, a state and an activity.

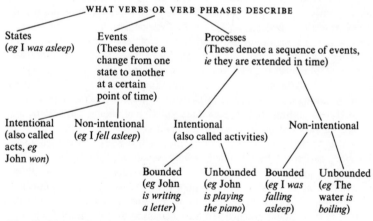

Fig 3 Dahl's model of what verbs or verb phrases describe

Dahl's classification makes it possible to analyse the activity of moving as a series of intentional changes, *ie* acts, which successively result in new states, involving as their main characteristic a sequence of new positions.

An activity like writing includes, amongst other things, moving. However, an act of writing cannot be said to have taken place until at least one of the letters making up a word has been formed or typed out.

The progressive verb form in [1a] can describe both a bounded and an unbounded activity, whereas that in [1b] can only describe a bounded one. That in [1c] also suggests a bounded activity. Finally, in [1d] the bounded activity of racing with the intention to win is described by means of the object *the race* preceded by the progressive form of *win*.

In [1a] and [1b] the non-progressive expressions *never washed the shirt* and *never wrote the letter* fail in denying the completion of what is described by the preceding progressive forms because they express the denial of any act of the washing involved in washing the shirt or of the writing involved in writing the letter. However, the fact that John was interrupted suggests that the negation in *never* covers more than that. Washing a shirt can be, and writing a letter is, a bounded activity whose end-state is 'the shirt is clean' or 'the letter is complete', and the act of reaching this end-state is also denied. (Actually the latter act can be analysed into an act of causing and an event of transition, *ie* beginning to be clean or complete.) If the denial had only applied to the act of reaching the end-state, then alternatives [1a] and [1b] would have been successful in stating that the activity described by the progressive forms was not completed. This is exactly what is achieved by adding the verb *finish*, as in [2]; since this verb expressly refers to the act of reaching the end-state, the negation by *never* in [2] can only apply to that act. *Never filled the tank* in alternative [1c] is ambiguous between, on the one hand, a sense where any act of pouring (*eg* petrol) into the tank and the act of reaching the end-state 'the tank is full' are denied, and, on the other, a sense where the negation affects only the act of reaching that state. In the latter sense *never filled the tank* is successful in denoting that the preceding activity of filling was not followed by completion. *Never won the race* in [1d], finally, can only mean that the act of reaching the end-state intended by John in taking part in the race is denied, and this expression is thus successful in stating that the bounded activity of racing implicit in *was winning the race* was not completed as intended.

Dahl 1974 thus gives us a system by means of which certain phenomena described earlier can be explained, *eg* why the addition of *finish* amends [1a] and [1b]. However, it gives no clue to why in the situation of [2a] one thinks of the washing of the shirt, rather than the shirt itself, as never finished, whereas in that of [2b] one tends to think more of the letter, and less of the writing of it, as never finished. To find a solution to this question we must first complement Dahl 1974 with Dahl 1975, where (on p 453) a distinction is made between cumulative and non-cumulative processes. Writing and reading a letter are of the former type, since word after word is added until the process is finished. When only part of the writing or reading is performed, the rest of the letter remains to be written or read. Washing a shirt and baking a loaf of bread, on the other hand, are non-cumulative processes. If in this case the process is interrupted, we cannot say that the rest of the shirt remains to be washed or the rest of the loaf to be baked. Secondly, we must distinguish between *effected* objects, *ie* those which come into existence as a result of such processes as writing and baking, and *affected* objects, *ie* those which exist from the beginning but are influenced by processes like reading and washing. *Cf* GCE:355. See also Lyons 1968:439, where *a letter* in a context like *write a letter* is called an object of result. The reason why one thinks of the washing of the shirt, rather than the shirt itself, as never finished in the situation of [2a] is thus that the shirt itself had been present from the beginning and that therefore only its cleanness could be brought to completion. It is, on the other hand, natural to say in the situation of [2b] that the letter, whose existence was due to a cumulative process of writing, is what was never finished. What results from a non-cumulative process, however, is not finished. For example, a baker does not 'finish a loaf', since it does not exist until the end of the baking is reached.

A shirt is, at least normally, washed with the intention of getting it clean. The possibility of reaching that result is dependent on the degree of perfection with which the washing is performed. The fact that washing is gradable in this way and that the *whole* shirt is affected all the time gives the expression *wash a shirt* different collocational properties from those of *write a letter* in relation to the adverb *completely*, which denotes the highest degree of perfection. See [8] and [9].

[8] He washed the shirt completely.
[9] *He wrote the letter completely.

The reason why [8] is acceptable, whereas [9] is not, is that the degree of perfection of washing, but not of writing, can be measured along a scale where one pole is denoted by *completely*. For example, a washing-machine can have several programs, which differ as to the degree to which the laundry is washed. Then if someone used a program not thorough enough for a very dirty shirt, one might say [10].

[10] He washed the shirt incompletely.

No typewriter, pen, or pencil has a similar set of programs.

Since *completely* can be added to *washed the shirt*, a suitable way to amend [1a], besides that suggested in [2a], would be to say [11a].

[11] He was $\left\{ \begin{array}{l} (a) \text{ washing his shirt} \\ (b) \text{ filling his tank} \end{array} \right\}$ when I saw him. However, he

never $\left\{ \begin{array}{l} (a) \text{ washed it} \\ (b) \text{ filled it} \end{array} \right\}$ completely, for he was suddenly interrupted by an unexpected incident.

[57]

When *fill the tank* denotes a cumulative activity, *ie* when part after part of the tank is regarded as affected by the filling, modification by *completely* cannot occur, whereas this is quite possible when only the end of that activity in the form of reaching the state 'full' is meant. For this reason [1c] can be fully disambiguated by the addition of *completely*, as in [11b]. In this connection it is worth quoting GCE:450, where it is said that 'a non-gradable verb can become gradable when the focus is on the result of the process rather than on the process itself' and that this can occur in the perfective aspect or when the perfective particle *up* is added, as in *He has completely drunk his beer* and *He completely drank up his beer*. If we take 'cause to become full' to be the unmarked basic sense of *fill*, since it directly reflects its derivation from *full*, this verb represents a case where a gradable verb develops a marked sense where it is non-gradable, when the focus is not on the result of the process but on the process itself, *ie* a change in the opposite direction to that of a verb like *drink*. What has here been said about *fill* also applies to its antonym *empty*, the only difference being that **empty up* does not occur. However, the verbal expression *pour* (*eg petrol*) *into the tank*, which has been used above to paraphrase the process sense of *fill the tank*, cannot be used at all to denote an end-result in the same way as *fill* and *drink*. Thus both [12a], where the perfective aspect is used, and [12b], where the perfective particle *up* is added, are impossible.

[12]a *He has poured petrol into the tank completely.
   b *He poured up petrol into the tank completely.

Writing a letter has been described above as a cumulative process and it has also been said that filling a tank in one of its senses can be looked upon as such a process. However, while in the situation of [2b] one tends to think more of the letter, and less of the writing of it, as never finished, one thinks in a similar situation of pouring petrol into a tank of the filling, rather than of the tank itself, as never finished. The reason why *fill a tank* in this respect resembles the non-cumulative process *wash a shirt* is that the tank exists from the beginning and thus is no object of result like the letter that is produced by writing. However, it differs from *wash a shirt* in that the *whole* tank is not affected until the end-state 'full' is reached.

For further illustration of the contrast incompletion/completion we will now look at [13], which in some respects resembles [1]. However, that which is expressed by the non-progressive form in the second sentence is asserted, not denied.

[13] John was
{
  (a) washing his shirt
  (b) writing a letter
  (c) filling his tank
  (d) winning the race
}
when I saw him.

I therefore know that he
$\left\{\begin{array}{ll} (a) & \text{washed the shirt.} \\ (b) & \text{wrote the letter.} \\ (c) & \text{filled the tank.} \\ (d) & \text{won the race.} \end{array}\right\}$

Alternative (a) must be considered an acceptable English sentence if *washed the shirt* is taken to denote an unbounded activity; in other words if it asserts that John just washed the shirt, not that he also got it clean. However, this verbal expression denotes completion only in the sense that it tells us that at least those acts of washing were completed which took place when the speaker saw John. The speaker is thus non-committal as regards the completion of the whole activity implied by the progressive form of the first sentence. Alternative (b), on the other hand, contains a debatable assertion, for from the acts involved in writing a letter that the speaker saw he cannot really draw the conclusion that they actually resulted in a finished letter. As regards alternative (c) it has been said above that *fill a tank* normally denotes either a bounded activity or the reaching of an end-state. In the former case the intention is to get the tank full, and in the latter case the end-state 'full' is stated to be reached. Only if it is possible for the speaker to make his listener(s) interpret *filled the tank* in the second sentence as a case where only an unbounded activity of pouring (*eg* petrol) into the tank is meant, is alternative (c) acceptable. This verbal expression then denotes completion in the same limited way as *washed the shirt* in (a). Alternative (d), finally, is not acceptable, since the speaker cannot conclude from what he saw that John actually completed the race by winning it.

I will now sum up the discussion in this paper by pointing to some conclusions that can be drawn from it.

(a) In three of the four verbal expressions used in [1] the contrast between incompletion and denied completion is not sufficiently expressed or made clear enough by simply opposing the progressive and non-progressive forms of the same verb. These forms therefore must be supplemented by other expressions, *eg* a verb like *finish* or an adverb like *completely*, or, in the case of the ambiguous verb *fill*, by the use of contrastive stress. When the second sentence of the alternatives of [1] is changed as in [13] to test whether it can express asserted, not denied, completion, acceptable English sentences only occur in those alternatives where the non-progressive form can be interpreted as referring to an unbounded activity, *ie* one where no special end-state is thought of at least for the time being. This is the case with *washed the shirt* and possibly also with *filled the tank*. However, from the point of view of the contrast incompletion/completion these alternatives, too, are to be regarded as failures since they do not expressly say that the whole activity was completed, only those acts of it that the speaker actually saw.

(b) In Thomason and Stalnaker 1973 : 218 there is an enumeration of some inferences that are said to fail. One of these is [14].

[14] He filled the tank halfway.
    Therefore, he filled the tank.

With normal interpretation it is true that [14] has to be described as an unacceptable inference. However, on the basis of the discussion about [13c] it can be claimed that due to the ambiguity of *fill* the inference does not necessarily fail. This can perhaps be shown most clearly by adding a sentence which disambiguates *filled the tank* in the second sentence, so that it can only refer to an unbounded activity of pouring (*eg* petrol) into the tank. See [15]:

[15] He filled the tank halfway.
    Therefore, he filled the tank.
    However, he did not fill it completely.

(c) For the description given in this paper of the extent to which the contrast incompletion/completion can be expressed by simply opposing two forms of the same verb, the distinction made in GCE between progressive and non-progressive aspect and between various verbal subclasses was used as a starting-point, to which it turned out that the descriptions of aspects in Verkuyl 1972 and of verb types in Vendler 1967 could add little new. Dahl 1974 and 1975, on the other hand, proved to be very useful by providing a workable model of what verbs or verb phrases describe and by making some distinctions that helped to explain certain observations made in the preliminary discussion of the four alternative verbal expressions.

ON BEING TEACHING
M. A. K. HALLIDAY

In G CE, in the section concerned with tense and aspect in the English verb, the authors refer to the gap in the non-finite system: there is no non-finite form constructed with what they refer to as 'aspect auxiliary *be*' (*ie* 'present in present' in the interpretation in Halliday, 1976: Ch 10). Thus on *p* 75 Note [*a*] it is stated that '*examining* is used for the unacceptable **being examining* and *being examined* for the unacceptable **being being examined*'.

As this footnote implies, the paradigm is defective at this point. Yet precisely because this is so notable a gap, in a paradigm which is otherwise remarkable for its regularity and consistency, one might expect it to begin to be filled; and there are clear signs that this is happening, at least in the active voice. The following are some examples I have observed over the past twelve years ([1] and [2] were recorded in 1965).

[1] Is the deadline a rigid one? Can you ever get an extension?—You can get an extension, on the grounds of being teaching.

[2] I've missed endless buses through not being standing at the bus stop when they arrived.

[3] We're never going to get this stuff out on time. Everything's late this year.
—That's what comes of Martin being teaching again.

[4] I'm always in favour of being doing something when guests arrive. I don't really like to have everything ready and finished beforehand.

[5] What happened to all those field notes?
—They're still there somewhere. I just never got back to them. It's one of the things I neglected to do as a result of being moving around so much.

[6] The water's gone off again, look. The tap's only just dripping.—It's after being running all that time it starts to do that.

[7] So they'll be able to do something in both departments?
—Yes. But there'll be no question of them being doing Sanskrit here and Sanskrit there. They won't be doing the same course twice.

These were all spoken by different speakers, six British and one Australian. During some four years spent in the United States between 1967 and 1975 I never noticed one of these forms used by an American speaker; nor did I notice any of the more complex tense forms that can be heard from British speakers, such as *they'll have been going to have been doing it*. But this may have been simply because I was not adept at picking up casual speech in what was to me an unfamiliar dialect.

The most closely related finite forms would be something like the following:

[1'] You can get an extension on the grounds that you're teaching.

[2'] I've missed endless buses because I wasn't standing at the bus stop when they arrived.

[3'] That's what happens now that Martin's teaching again.

[4'] I always like to be doing something when guests arrive.

[5'] It's one of the things I neglected to do as a result of the fact that I was moving around so much.

[6'] It's after it's been running all that time that it starts to do that.

[7'] There'll be no question that they'll be doing Sanskrit here and Sanskrit there.

A comparison of these with the non-finites [1–7] suggests at least in some instances why the non-finite form is used. In [1], for example, the meaning can be captured in the finite form only by some such locution as *on the grounds that you're teaching, if you are*. Similarly [3] embraces the meanings of both *now that* and *because*. Here the non-finite forms neutralize the unwanted contrast between types of dependence. In [2] there is some conflict of tense in the finite form: *I've missed* suggests *haven't been standing*, whereas *when they arrived* requires *was standing*. Here again the non-finite neutralizes a contrast that is present in the more specific finite forms, in this case a contrast between tenses. On the other hand neutralization does not seem to figure in the other examples; in [4], [5] and [7] the non-finite is used in colligation with the choice of *in favour of, as a result of, no question of*, and in [6] perhaps to avoid a repetition of *it's* (*it's after it's been running* . . .).

[62]

Given that the non-finite form is selected, what determines the choice of this previously non-existent tense? Here the effect is rather to avoid neutralization. In [1] and [3], the simple present *on the grounds of teaching* and *that's what comes of Martin teaching* would entirely fail to capture the required sense of 'at that/this particular time'. In [2] and [4] the 'present in present' is clearly demanded by the dependent *when* clauses: 'just at the moment of their arrival'. In [5], [6] and [7] the finite tense would have contained some non-present element, past in *was moving around* and *has been running*, future in *will be doing*; this is absent in the non-finites – it could have been selected (*as a result of having been moving around, after having been running, no question of them going to be doing*), but there is no general requirement of tense concord here as there is in the finite – and the 'present in present' form takes its place.

It is interesting to note that compound tense forms with the secondary present (*ie* the same aspectual *be*) in the middle, which have hitherto been even less acceptable, are also now beginning to appear. Here are two examples noted recently, again from British speakers:

[8] It's been being occurring to me for some time.
[9] Our plant's going to be having been without water for three days.

Here [8] is present IN PRESENT in past in present, [9] is past IN PRESENT in future in present. Essentially the same processes are at work as in the present in present non-finites; the speaker forces the system to accept an interpolated 'in present' component because *it's been occurring to me* (present in past in present), *is going to have been without water* (past in future in present), fail to capture the required sense of 'for some time the situation has been that it keeps occurring to me', 'our plant's going to be in a situation of having been without water'.

I have not yet observed any instances of present in present non-finites in the passive. There is a tendency in the English verb for the passive forms to catch up with the active after a lapse of time; the finite tense system seems for the moment to be identical in the two voices, although if the stop rule precluding interpolated presents is disappearing, as [8] and [9] suggest, it will probably disappear in the active first. The resistance to *being being examined* may be purely morphological, like the stop rule precluding double secondary futures of the type *he's going to have been going to do it* (future in past in future in present); the latter can be resolved by the use of *about* to replace one occurrence of *going*, and I have in fact observed one instance in which it was resolved in this way: *he's going to have been about to do it*. But there is no such alternative form available to replace *being being*. To give an idea of how this form would sound in the passive, here is a made-up example:

[10] Don't take that away; I'm using it. It's being used as a support.

—What's the good of it being being used as a support if it won't even stand up by itself? [invented example]

Forms such as those cited above will be found only in informal spontaneous conversation, where the contexts build up rapidly, in a continuous ebb and flow, and speech is produced and decoded at a rapid pace. The more leisurely modes, of writing and formal speech, make it difficult to process the highly complex structures that are the stock-in-trade of casual exchanges. It is in spontaneous conversation that we can explore the frontiers of the system and observe the foreshadowing of some coming linguistic change. In particular, we can observe the tensions that arise between opposing features, and see how new forms are created by the conflicting demands of interacting semantic systems.

CRITERIA FOR AUXILIARIES AND MODALS
RODNEY HUDDLESTON

I shall use 'catenative' as a pre-theoretical term for verbs taking non-finite complements, as for example TRY, DARE, BE in *He tried to leave, I dare not tell you, It is raining*. A number of catenatives are highly grammaticized in the sense that they have various syntactic and morphosyntactic properties that are shared by only small classes of items. These special properties of the catenatives in question have led to the claim that they are not verbs at all or, more commonly, that they are not 'full' verbs, claims that have been the subject of a good deal of controversy over the last few years.[1] The main issue, I believe, is whether the properties which differentiate CAN, HAVE, BE, etc from the less highly grammaticized TRY, KEEP, TEND, etc justify assigning different constituent structures to pairs like *He was watching* versus *He kept watching* such that in the former *watching* is the superordinate (main) verb with *was* subordinate to it whereas in the latter *kept* is the superordinate verb with *watching* its complement. Put in this way, the issue arises in essentially the same terms whatever descriptive framework one is using: transformational grammar in any of its versions, systemic grammar, tagmemics or the more informal frameworks of studies like GCE, Palmer 1974 and so on.[2]

1 See Pullum and Wilson 1977 for references; some more recent additions are Akmajian, Steele and Wasow 1977, Huddleston 1976, Starosta 1977.
2 Proponents of the full-verb analysis have typically assumed that catenatives have full clauses as complements, functioning as underlying subject or object, but this is in no way entailed by that analysis: the question of whether the complements are underlyingly full clauses or not is quite independent of the auxiliary versus full-verb controversy.

My aim in the present paper is not to argue the case for one view as against the other in this controversy, but rather to provide a fuller presentation of relevant data and potential evidence. Some of the arguments in the debate have, in my view, been based on quite insufficient and selective data: it is an area where Bolinger's (1976) warnings on the methodological dangers of assuming too great a homogeneity in the system are highly pertinent. I accordingly believe that it will serve a useful purpose to examine in detail various criteria that have figured in discussions of auxiliary verbs in general or modal auxiliaries in particular with a view to determining the precise membership of the classes they define.

The table following presents a classification of thirty-seven items in respect of thirty criteria. The items are in general lexemes (represented by small capitals) as opposed to particular word-forms (given in italics); thus CAN subsumes the forms *can, can't, could, couldn't*, and so on. I have distinguished various sets of complete or partial homonyms (partial in that the paradigms of inflectional forms are not completely identical), where the distinctions are relevant to the properties under investigation; at the pre-theoretical level at which I am working here it does not matter if two or more 'homonyms' should rather be analysed as different senses of a single lexeme. For BE, I distinguish the progressive and passive catenatives, the BE of the idiom BE *going* (as in *It is going to rain*), the copula, and the 'modal' BE of *She was to die the next year, You are not to touch it*, etc. The last takes a *to*-complement, but so too can the copula (*To say that is to miss the point*); what distinguishes 'modal' BE is that it has only finite forms.[3] The main basis for the distinction between 'modal' and 'lexical' DARE and NEED is the inflectional contrast of modal *dare/need* versus lexical *dares/needs* with a 3rd Person Singular subject and the fact that the modal DARE and NEED are confined to non-assertive contexts; when these properties do not serve to determine whether a given instance of DARE or NEED is modal or lexical, the assignment is made on the basis of whether it is behaving like a paradigm modal such as CAN or a paradigm non-auxiliary catenative such as WANT, as in *I daren't answer* and *I did not dare to answer* respectively – though, as we shall see, not all tokens of DARE fall clearly into one or other of these categories. For DO, I distinguish the imperative DO of *Do hurry, Don't move*, the periphrastic DO of *Does it work?, I don't like it*, and the substitute DO of *Will he win? — He may do*; I do not treat various other DO's, such as those of *He did his best, Who did it?, She did so*. Five HAVE's are distinguished: the perfect aspect catenative, the HAVE of the idiom HAVE *got* in its obligational sense, 'central' HAVE indicating possession and similar relationships, 'necessity' HAVE as in *You have to be joking, I have to go*, and 'special' HAVE used causatively or as a variant of TAKE, and so on, as in *She had them move*

---

3 The first BE of *These insects are to be found in NSW* (for which there is no active counterpart) must likewise be finite.

	MAY	MUST	NEED (modal)	(lexical)	OUGHT	SEEM	SHALL	TEND	TRY	USE (aspectual)	WILL	WOULD[*rather*]
1 Non-catenative use	−	−	−	+	−	+	−	−	+	−	−	+
2 Inversion	+	+	+	−	+/−	−	+	−	−	+/−	+	+
POLARITY												
3 Negative forms	+/R	+	+	−	+/−	−	+	−	−	+/−	+	+
4 Precedes *not*	+	+	+	−	+/−	−	+	−	−	+/−	+	R
5 Emphatic positive	R	+	−	−	+/−	−	+	−	−	−	+	+
STRANDING												
6 *So/neither* tags	+	+	+	−	+/−	−	+	−	−	−	+	+
7 SV order, verb given	+	+	+	−	+/−	−	+	−	+	−	+	+
8 SV order, verb new	+	+	+	−	−	−	+	−	+	−	+	N
9 Complement fronting	+	+	+	−	?+	−	.+	−	−	−	+	−
10 Relativized complement	+	+	+	−	+/−	−	+	−	−	−	+	+
11 Occurrence with DO	−	−	−	+	+/−	+	−	+	+	+/−	−	−
12 Contraction	−	+	−	−	−	−	+	−	−	−	+	+
POSITION OF PREVERBS												
13 Precedes *never*	+	+	+	−	(+)	−	+	−	−	(+)	+	+
14 Precedes epistemic adverb	+	+	N	−	?+	−	+	−	−	−	+	+
15 Precedes subject quantifier	+	+	+	−	+	+	+	+	−	+	+	+
INDEPENDENCE OF CATENATIVE												
16 Temporal discreteness	+	+	+	+	+	+	+	−	−	−	R	+
17 Negative complement	+	+	+	+	+	+	+	+	+	+	+	+
18 Relation with subject	−	−	−	−	−	−	−	−	+/R	−	−	+
TYPE OF COMPLEMENTATION												
19 Base-complement	+	+	+	−	−/R	−	+	−	−	−	+	+
20 *to*-complement	−	−	−	+	+/R	+	−	+	+	+	−	−
21 *-en* complement	−	−	−	−	−	−	−	−	−	−	−	−
22 *-ing* complement	−	−	−	−	−	−	−	−	+	−	−	−
INFLECTIONAL FORMS												
23 3rd Singular	−	−	−	+	−	+	−	+	+	N	−	−
24 *-en* form	−	−	−	+	−/R	+	−	+	+	−	−	−
25 *-ing* form	−	−	−	+	−	+	−	+	+	−	−	−
26 Base-form	−	−	−	+	−/R	+	−	+	+	−/R	−	−
27 Past Tense	−/R	−/R	−	+	+	+	+	+	+	+	R	−
28 Unreal mood: protasis	?−	−	−	+	−	+	−	+	+	−	+	−
29 Unreal mood: apodosis	+	+	+	−	+/−	−	+	−	−	−	+	−
30 Unreal mood: tentative	+	−	−	−	−	−	+	−	−	−	+	−

the sofa, She had her breakfast/baby before daybreak.[4] The *had* of *You had better hurry* I treat as belonging synchronically to a distinct lexeme HAD rather than as being a form of HAVE. Likewise the *would* of the idiom *would rather/sooner,*[5] as in *I would rather you didn't tell her*, is analysed as a distinct lexeme, though that of *He wouldn't help me* is a form of WILL. The idiom BE *going* consists of a sequence of two catenatives; the column headed 'BE [*_going*]' gives the properties of the first, that headed '[BE_] *going*' gives those for the second. Analogously for the idiom HAVE *got*. The idiomatic nature of these expressions (the meanings are not derivable from 'progressive'+GO or 'perfect'+GET) should not be allowed to obscure the fact that they do have internal syntactic structure. The only other GET considered is the one used in the passive construction, as in *It got broken*, and the only other GO is the dialectally-restricted one of *He would usually go have a swim* – this I have labelled 'quasi-modal', following Shopen (1971), who observes that some speakers have other verbs, *eg* COME, HURRY, RUN, behaving in like manner. The LET is the one used in 1st Person imperatives like *Let's go* rather than the less grammaticized catenative of *He let her watch*, etc.

I assume that aside from verbs having negative forms in *n't*, all non-defective verbs have seven inflectional forms in their paradigm – four finite forms: 3rd Sg non-Past Indicative (*takes*), non-3rd Sg non-Past Indicative (*take*), Past Indicative (*took*), Unreal (*took*); and three non-finite: *-ing* form (*taking*), *-en* form (*taken*) and base-form (*take*) (*cf* Huddleston 1975). The imperative I take to be a base-form.

I turn now to a brief explanation and commentary on the thirty parameters. (1–18) bear on the question of defining auxiliaries in general, (19–30) relate more specifically to modals. The entry 'R' in the table means that the verb has the given property but under restricted conditions, as outlined below. 'N' signifies that the question is not applicable. Entries separated by obliques apply to different dialects or varieties of English, but I have certainly not attempted a comprehensive coverage of the variation.

1 Non-catenative use

The first question asks whether the verb can be used without a non-finite complement (other than in the case of ellipsis), *ie* whether it has a non-catenative use. Those that can would not be candidates for auxiliaryhood in the traditional sense (where an auxiliary is a verb used to form a tense, mood, voice, etc of another verb), unless it could be established that the catenative and non-catenative uses involved homonyms, as one might

---

4 Zwicky (1970:329) subsumes 'necessity' HAVE under the 'special' category, but certainly in British English it differs in respect of numerous relevant properties.
5 I have found one example where RATHER is inflected as a verb: *She would have rathered there were no risks involved at all* ('The Australian', 14 May 1977), but for most speakers there is no inflectional or distributional evidence for departing from the traditional analysis of it as an adverb.

distinguish the TRY's of *He tried to see* and *He tried the water*. The non-catenative use of WOULD is exemplified in *I'd rather you didn't tell her*. The positive answer for substitute DO is based on the conservative assumption that *Will you win?—I may do* involves pro-form rather than zero (elliptical) anaphora.

2 Inversion

Can the verb precede the subject in interrogative or similar constructions (*eg Never had I seen such fun*)? The question is not applicable to [BE_] *going*, [HAVE_] *got* and LET, which do not have subjects (in the relevant sense). The entries for necessity and central HAVE, OUGHT and USE reflect the well-known dialect and/or style variation in *Used he to go?* versus *Did he use to go?*, etc.

3–5 POLARITY

There are four parameters relating to positive-negative polarity; I deal first with those that correlate most closely with (2), deferring the fourth till later (17).

3 Negative forms

Does the verb have negative forms in *n't* in its paradigm? Apart from imperative *don't* (whose analysis as a negative base-form is in any case arguable), negatives are confined to the finite section of the paradigm. Answers are the same as for (2), except that the BE's lack negative counterparts of *am* (except for interrogative *aren't*) in most standard dialects, and in many dialects MAY has only the negative form *mightn't*, not *mayn't*.

4 Precedes *not*

Can the verb precede a *not* in whose syntactic scope it lies? The syntactic scope is determined by the Klima (1964) tests for the polarity of a clause. Thus the MUST of *You must not go* is within the syntactic scope of the *not* because the finite clause behaves like a negative with respect to coordinate and reversed-polarity interrogative tags: *You must not go and nor must she, We must not go, must we?* Conversely, the TRY of *He tried not to be seen* is outside the scope of *not*, as is evident from the tags ... *and so did she, ... didn't he?* Note that it is syntactic scope that is at issue: from a semantic point of view, MUST is here just as much outside the scope of the negative as is TRY. The Klima tests apply only to finite verbs – hence the 'N' answers for the four non-finite entries. There are interesting differences between HAD *better* and WOULD *rather*: the normal position for *not* is in both cases after the adverb, but whereas the catenative is inside the scope of the negative in *You had better not tell him* (*had you?*), it is outside in *You'd rather not go* (*wouldn't you?*) – the syntax matches the semantics with WOULD but not HAD. The *not* can come between the *would* and *rather* only when one is denying the corresponding positive (*You would rather stay*

[68]

here—No, I would not rather stay here), and in these restricted conditions the WOULD is inside the negative scope. With HAD the *not* can come before the *better* without changing the syntactic or semantic scope, though in this case the *not* is most likely to be criticized: *You hadn't better go* is equivalent to *You had better not go.* The denial use is also marginally possible (*He'd better be told.—He had 'not better be told*), in which case HAD *better* is brought within the semantic scope too. With *He dared not go* and *He dared not to go,* which are found in some dialects (*cf* Greenbaum 1974), it is difficult to say whether we have the modal or the lexical DARE – usages like these (and see further examples below) show that tokens of DARE do not fall clearly into 'modal' and 'non-modal' categories. It may be appropriate for certain purposes to idealize and exclude the 'blended' constructions, but it should be acknowledged that this would be significant idealization: the primary data cannot be used as evidence for a sharp division between modal and non-modal catenatives.

5 Emphatic positive

Can the verb carry emphatic stress to mark a polarity contrast with the corresponding negative? We are concerned with cases like: *He can't swim.— Oh yes, he 'can swim.* The second *swim* here would of course be frequently omitted, and then we have a special case of the various 'stranding' constructions to be dealt with below. Any verb can carry emphatic stress to contrast with another lexical verb or with absence of the verb: *Did you buy it?—No, but I 'tried to* (*buy it*); we are thus concerned here only with polarity contrast. The answers are not completely the same as for (2). I believe that USE carries emphatic stress only when the contrast concerns the temporal aspect rather than the polarity (but *cf* Palmer 1974 : 162). The non-assertive condition on modal DARE and NEED excludes **He 'dare/need go*; an exception to the condition, however, is that with ellipsis it is possible to have *You/he daren't tell her.—Oh yes I/he 'dare.* I have marked imperative DO with 'N', for the *Do tell him* type hardly involves the kind of polarity contrast at issue here, which applies only to finites. I am hesitant whether modal BE should have a '+': *We aren't to tell her.—Oh yes we 'are* and the like sound highly unlikely (and it is not simply that BE is outside the semantic scope of the negative, for the corresponding example with MUST is much better). MAY has the property only in its root (permission) sense: in epistemic *He 'may have seen her* the contrast applies to the modality not the polarity; it may be that the corresponding restriction holds for MUST.

6–10 STRANDING

I shall say that a verb is 'stranded' when it occurs immediately (or, if subject-verb inversion has applied, with only the subject intervening) before a 'deletion site', a position vacated by elements deleted by ellipsis or moved to another place in the sentence: stranding thus covers Palmer's 'code' plus a little more besides. It is necessary to distinguish various types of stranding, for the ability of a verb to be stranded is not the same in all cases. One type that I have not included in the table (because the answers are in all relevant cases the same as for (2)) is that of the interrogative tag, with reversed or constant polarity, as in *You can't see her, can you?, So you can solve it, can you?, *So you began it, began you?*.

6 So/neither tags
The next type involves anaphoric constructions of the form *so/neither* (or *nor*) + subject + verb, as in *Ed is ill and so is Max; Tom won't go.—Neither will I.* The same verbs can be stranded here as in interrogative tags, except that USE is excluded in all dialects: *She used to be a member and so used Tom.*

7 SV order, verb given
Here the verb follows the subject and is stranded before a deletion site vacated by ellipsis – the most straightforward type of ellipsis, where the ellipted material can be replaced without loss of well-formedness. The verb is 'given', in the sense that it also occurs before the antecedent of the ellipted material – thus *John can swim and Bill can too* illustrates the stranding of CAN in this type of construction. The restrictions noted for BE are that in some dialects the form *being* cannot be stranded in examples like *Sam was being examined by a psychiatrist and Bill was being too* (cf Akmajian and Wasow 1975, Pullum and Wilson 1977), but there are certainly dialects where such sentences are acceptable. I believe that in dialects having the restriction it applies only when the progressive BE that precedes the stranded *being* is also given: when it is new, as in *When is the building going to be demolished?—It already is being*, the stranding of *being* is allowed. With 'special' HAVE, some dialects allow stranding in (7), although none do in (6) – cf Halliday and Hasan's (1976:202) *Has she had her breakfast?—Yes, she has had.* Most dialects exclude the stranding of the form *having* (cf Karlsen 1959:269), but it is allowed by Halliday and Hasan (1976:173). Some dialects extend the restriction to other non-finite forms of HAVE, except for perfect HAVE: thus Akmajian and Wasow asterisk *Johnny can't have an ice-cream but Billy can have.* In my judgment this type is completely acceptable if the verb preceding stranded *have* is 'new', as in *John has a copy and Ed may have as well.* I have marked substitute DO as 'N' because it involves substitution rather than ellipsis: in *John likes her and Max does too* the DO does not precede a deletion site and is not 'given' in the sense defined above. A number of catenatives can be stranded in (7) but not (6) – eg TRY and HELP, but not SEEM or lexical NEED: *Liz tried to open it and then Ed tried* versus *Tom seemed to understand her and Max seemed as well.*[6] The latter can be made acceptable by inserting *to* after *seemed*, but in that case it is *to* rather than the verb that is stranded, and the ability to occur before a

6 BEGIN, HELP, and TRY allow the understood complement to be recovered from context instead of an antecedent (cf Hankamer and Sag 1976:410–15).

stranded *to* does not yield a special subclassification of catenatives. BEGIN can apparently be stranded only when its subject is interpreted as having an agentive role: compare *Tom began to learn the piano and soon afterwards his brother began too* versus **Tom began to feel ill and soon afterwards his brother began too.*

8 SV order, verb new

This is the same type of construction as the last except that the stranded verb is new, not given, *ie* it does not also occur before the antecedent of the ellipted material: *John won't swim, but he can* exemplifies the stranding of CAN in type (8). Comparison of (7) and (8) shows that certain verbs can be stranded only when they are given. This applies to modal BE (*I expect John to do it.—*Well, he was*), and the non-perfect HAVE's (*I don't want to go.— *But you have; I'm looking for a pen.—*Well, I haven't*). There are clear differences in well-formedness between such examples and, say, *Have you a pen?—No, I haven't.* The same difference is found with OUGHT: compare 'given' *Ought I to tell him?—Yes, you ought,* with 'new' **Even when a linguist can analyse, it does not necessarily follow that he ought.* The new type is better, but still appreciably less acceptable than the given, if the antecedent also contains *to*: *?*Even if he is legally entitled to sell it, it doesn't follow that he ought.* Stranding of a new progressive BE seems hardly possible, except perhaps where there is an appropriate time adverbial to help retrieve the progressive meaning: compare *Will they play the match?—*They are/?They already are.* A functional explanation for these conditions on the stranding of a new BE is probably that when it occurs before a deletion site there is not enough information to enable the decoder to determine easily which BE it is. With passive BE stranding is in general not possible unless the antecedent contains a passive too: *Tom said he saw them beaten.—But they weren't* is clearly much better than *Could she see?—*Yes, but she herself couldn't be.* I have marked BE [*_going*], HAD [*_better*], HAVE [*_got*] and WOULD [*_rather*] with 'N' in (8), for if they were new the rest of the idiom would be new too and hence could not be ellipted; the adverbs *better* and *rather*, however, can be stranded when new: *I haven't read it.—Well, you'd better.*

9 Complement fronting

Here we are concerned with what Akmajian and Wasow call VP Fronting, where a verb is stranded through the movement of its complement to initial position: *They said he would be drinking rum and drinking rum he was, *They deny that she is to marry a prince but to marry a prince she is.* This is a stylistically highly 'marked' construction and there are many places where acceptability judgments are uncertain (I think one should accordingly be wary of attaching too much weight to it as a criterion for constituent structure). According to Akmajian and Wasow (1975), passive and copula BE cannot be stranded here if they are within the complement of progressive BE. They thus accept examples like *They said he was being noisy and being* *noisy he was*, but not *They said he was being noisy and noisy he was being*. These seem to be among the cases where acceptability is not clear-cut; I myself find little to choose between the two examples, and in cases where the progressive in the second clause is new rather than given, as in the above, the form with stranded rather than fronted *being* sounds more natural: *She hadn't expected him to be sadistic but sadistic he undoubtedly was being* (rather than . . . *but being sadistic he undoubtedly was*). The questioned '+' answers for BEGIN, special HAVE and OUGHT reflect my judgments of examples like *They wanted her to sing, so to sing she quickly began, They said she'd have a swim and a swim she had, They say she ought to go and go she ought* (this last sounds surprisingly good considering the absence of the second *to*). HAD [*better*] and WOULD [*rather*] both have negative answers since the verbs themselves can't be stranded, but the idioms differ in that the adverb can be stranded much more readily in the former than the latter: *She said you'd better go and go you'd better, ?*They say she'd rather go and go she'd rather*. In examples like *They said he would win and win he did* I have assumed that we have the periphrastic DO, as in the non-fronted . . . *and he did win*, rather than the substitute, which does not elsewhere take a complement, but it is a construction where the distinction between the DO's is somewhat problematic.

10 Relativized complement

The last stranding construction I shall consider is that exemplified in *They say she's going to win, which she is*. The answers here are in general the same as in (7), except that BEGIN, HELP and TRY (which are in any case special in (7): see footnote 5) are excluded. It is in some respects a puzzling construction. It is normally assumed in the transformational literature that *which* arises through relativization of the complement, but this analysis is difficult to reconcile with examples like *If you'd rather stay, which I suspect you would*, . . . , *If you'd rather Bill went instead which I suspect you would*, . . . , for there is no apparent independent evidence for saying that the adverb is part of the complement: the natural bracketing of *would rather Bill went instead* is [*would rather*] [*Bill went instead*], not [*would*] [*rather Bill went instead*]. Thus *which* appears to correspond to a non-constituent in the unreduced form of the sentence. Analytic problems arise also with *They want her to resign, which she may do*: this cannot be the periphrastic DO, but if it is the same DO as in . . . *and she may do*, which we have treated as substitution rather than ellipsis, what is *which* the pronominalization of?

11 Occurrence with DO

Can the verb occur as complement to periphrastic constructions considered in (2–6), etc? Examples like *John used to live there and so did Max* do not involve the occurrence of USE with DO, for although USE is understood in the second clause, it is not overtly expressed. The 'R' answers for BE relate to the *Why don't you be a lawyer?* or *If he doesn't be a good boy* constructions mentioned in Palmer 1974:153-4; the progressive and passive BE's are somewhat unlikely here.

12 Contraction
Can the finite forms of the verb be phonologically reduced to the extent of losing their vowels? (Verbs without finite forms are marked 'N'.) Answers here are based on the comprehensive list of contracted forms in Palmer 1974:241; Zwicky's (1970) rule of Auxiliary Reduction (dependent on prior Glide Deletion) is more restrictive, applying only to *is, has, would, had, have, am, are* and *will*, the only cases yielding non-syllabic forms. BE [_going] and HAD [_better] can be reduced to zero.

13–15 POSITION OF PREVERBS
The next three questions involve the linear position of the verb relative to various 'preverbs' – frequency adverbs like *always, never*, 'epistemic' adverbs like *certainly, probably, possibly*, quantifiers like *all* or *both* associated with the subject, and so on. According to Jacobson (1964:54) auxiliaries 'are usually followed, not preceded, by typical mid-position adverbs, eg *never* and *always*. This is a feature not shared by other similar words, eg *have* (*to*) or *get*.' We shall not of course be interested in cases where the catenative is outside the scope of the following preverb, as in *I hope never to see him again*, where the position of *never* after *hope* needs no special explanation. From a semantic point of view, however, it is not always easy to determine whether the catenative is within the scope of the preverb; in (13), therefore, I have used the negative preverb *never* as model, for here we can establish the syntactic scope using the Klima tests mentioned in (4).

13 Precedes *never*
Can the verb precede a *never* in whose syntactic scope it lies? The question as phrased does not refer to the notion of usual position that figures in Jacobson's account: it assumes that if the verb can occur before *never* then some rule will be needed to handle that position (*cf* Baker's Auxiliary Shift rule, 1971). There are, however, some clear differences in preferred orderings. *He is never angry* and *He had never any money on him* are both acceptable, but while the first is preferred over '... *never is* ...', the second is not preferred over '... *never had* ...'. A '+' answer indicates that the verb + *never* order is preferred, a '(+)' that it is possible but not preferred. We note that there is a sharp difference between modal NEED and DARE: *He need never know* is the normal order, but *?*I dare never go with him* is hardly acceptable. The 'N' entries are for verbs which do not fall within the scope of *never*; with HAD, **He never had better* ... and **He had never better* ... are both deviant, and in *He had better never tell her*, HAD seems to fall outside the scope of the negative. Baker notes that epistemic MAY cannot follow *never*; when it precedes, as in *Ed may never have met her*, it is not clear

whether it falls within its scope (the Klima tags, . . . *and so/neither may Bill*, sound somewhat unnatural, whatever their polarity, though some speakers accept the *neither* tag).

14 Precedes epistemic adverb

Can the verb precede an epistemic adverb like *certainly, probably, possibly* (excluding cases where the adverb is set off intonationally from the rest of the clause)? I have not here recorded information about preferred orderings, but it may be noted that with necessity and central HAVE and with OUGHT the usual position for the adverb is before the verb. I have answered 'N' for modal DARE and NEED because of the interference caused by the negative that must accompany them in relevant examples.

15 Precedes subject quantifier

Can the verb precede an *all* that is semantically associated with its subject? In *The children could all swim*, for example, *all* quantifies the subject, the sentence being equivalent to *All the children could swim*. Noting the grammaticality difference between *They are all leaving early today* and **They leave all early today*, Pullum and Wilson include (15) within their criteria for auxiliaries. Outside the catenative construction, BE, central HAVE and WOULD are, I believe, the only verbs exhibiting this property, but within the catenative construction it does not yield a subclassification that correlates closely with the more usual criteria. The test is, moreover, not at all straightforward to apply. Variation in the position of *all* may change the meaning: this is very clear, for example, in a pair like *They would all rather go* versus *They would rather all go*. In the first, each of them would rather that he went than that he didn't; in the second they would rather that all went than that not all of them went. In the second I regard the *all* as being semantically associated with the complement rather than the subject, and such complement-associated quantifiers have been discounted in answering (15). Yet the distinction between a subject- and a complement-oriented quantifier is often difficult to make – note, for example, that *They had all better go* and *They had better all go* do not differ in the same way as the WOULD *rather* pair, and nor do *They all seemed to like her* and *They seemed all to like her*. The question marks in row (15) reflect my doubts as to whether a following *all* is properly to be regarded as associated with the subject in examples like *I doubt whether they dare all take part*. In general I feel a good deal of uncertainty about the data and its interpretation on this dimension.

16–18 INDEPENDENCE OF THE CATENATIVE

The next three properties concern the degree of independence of the catenative as reflected in its ability to contrast with its complement in temporal specification and polarity, and in its relationship to the subject. One significant facet of the grammaticization process is that the separate identity of the catenative may in some respects be lost or diminished, so that the catenative and its complement verb may seem to merge into a single unit, analogous to the unit formed by a verb and its inflections – it is this analogy between the grammaticized catenatives and inflections that underlies the traditional concept of auxiliary. For this reason I think that this area is important for any investigation of auxiliary verb as a category of universal grammar, but limitations of space preclude more than a cursory treatment here (see also Palmer 1974, on which the criteria are based, and Huddleston 1976). This dimension does not correlate closely with the more commonly invoked ones – for example, passive GET and imperative LET are among the least independent of the catenatives but are rarely classed as auxiliaries in modern studies.

16 Temporal discreteness
Can the complement contain a temporal adjunct indicating that the time associated with the complement is distinct from (either earlier or later than) that associated with the catenative? In *They had to abandon the match when the rain came*, it seems semantically irrelevant to ask whether the *when*-clause relates to the abandoning or to the necessity: they are not distinct, so that it appears to relate to *had-to-abandon* as a unit. Similarly, it will often make no difference whether we say *You have to return next week* or *You will have to return next week*. But there is potentially a contrast, as with *You now have to return next week* versus *If you don't finish the job today you will have to return next week*. Such contrasts show that we must allow for temporal discreteness between the HAVE and its complement, even if the potential often remains unexploited or is lost. Necessity HAVE clearly differs here from the passive catenatives BE and GET, where there is simply no potential for discreteness: in *He was executed at dawn* we cannot make any temporal distinction between BE and EXECUTE. The three 'N' entries are for the verbs that do not take complements. Progressive BE is temporally discrete only in its non-aspectual sense, as in *I am now meeting Tom tomorrow*. The complement of perfect HAVE can have its own specifier when HAVE is Past (*He had left three hours early*), but there are well-known restrictions when it is non-Past (*I have read it before/*yesterday*), and the temporal discreteness is lost in cases like *He must have left yesterday*, which are not semantically perfects. WILL is temporally discrete in *I will now give my paper next week*, though the potential is rarely realized and is lost altogether in such Past tense uses as *In those days she would smoke sixty cigarettes a day* or *When Liz tried the door it wouldn't open*.

17 Negative complement
Can the verb take a negative complement? If it can, this will indicate that it can select independently for polarity instead of fusing with its complement verb to form a unit that is positive or negative as a whole. It will be convenient to relate this question to (4) above. Of the catenatives with a '−' answer to (4), only GET and, probably, GO require a positive

complement: *He tried not to be seen* but **He got not arrested*. With finite catenatives having a ' + ' answer to (4), a post-catenative *not* will belong to the complement only if stressed and separated from the catenative by juncture[7] (*We could 'not answer*), an adverb (*He was always not listening*), *to* (*Beryl had to not sleep with her boyfriend*, 'New Statesman' 29 August 75) or another negative (*I daren't not tell him*). The latter double negative seems to be possible – if sometimes highly marked and contrived, especially perhaps with HAVE [*_got*] – in all cases, and I have accordingly marked all with a plus. But again it must be emphasized that this indicates the potential for independent polarity: for several of them, this potential will be only rarely realized.

18 Relation with subject

Is there a direct semantic relation between the catenative and its grammatical subject, such that semantically the subject NP should be analysed as an argument of the catenative predicate? Three commonly-cited symptoms of such a direct semantic relation are:

(a) selectional restrictions between subject and catenative
   (*The waitress*/**water hoped to remain cool*);
(b) the impossibility of having *there* as subject
   (**There hoped to be a church on the site*);
(c) a difference in the truth conditions of sentences of the form $NP_1 V_1$ (*to*)
   $V_2 NP_2$ and $NP_2 V_1$ (*to*) BE V_2-*en by* NP_1
   (*Robin hoped to escort Kim* $\neq$ *Kim hoped to be escorted by Robin*).

Replacing HOPE by USE removes the deviance of the first two examples and the truth-conditional difference in the last pair – HOPE has its subject as a semantic argument but USE does not. In answering question (18) I have given most weight to (a) and (b), for with (c) there are considerable difficulties in determining whether there is a truth-conditional difference between relevant pairs (*cf* Schmerling 1976, Huddleston 1976, Mittwoch 1977, for recent contributions to this much discussed question). It must be admitted, however, that there is some untidiness in the data: not all verbs behave either wholly like HOPE or wholly like USE. There are, for example, speakers who accept sentences like *Inflation is a problem which dare not be neglected* (*cf* Pullum and Wilson 1977), which suggests that we should group DARE with USE. But we find other data supporting a grouping with HOPE: we cannot acceptably replace MUST by DARE in examples like *The weight must not exceed 50 lbs* or *There must not be any typing errors*, while *The Mail's reporter daren't interview the premier* hardly entails *The premier daren't be interviewed by the Mail's reporter*. Moreover the 'unexpected' *Inflation dare not be neglected* type can be matched with examples containing TRY: *The few voices of dissent against socialism in South Australia are trying to be won over*

7 This prevents cliticization: in *We couldn't answer*, CAN must fall within the scope of the negative.

(attested in a recent Australian radio programme with the intended interpretation 'we are trying to win over...').[8] In the table I have accordingly marked modal DARE (I have no comparable data for lexical DARE) and TRY with a dialect-variable 'R' to reflect this limited use. Non-catenatives and those which do not have a grammatical subject are marked 'N', though we may note that [BE_] *going* and [HAVE_] *got* clearly do not have a direct semantic relation with the subject of BE and HAVE respectively.

19–22 TYPE OF COMPLEMENTATION

Here we are concerned with the kind of non-finite complement that the verb takes: can it have a bare infinitive (base-form) as complement, (19); an infinitive with *to*, (20); an *-en* form, (21); an *-ing* form, (22)? Little commentary is needed. In some dialects OUGHT takes a bare infinitive in non-assertive contexts (*cf* Greenbaum 1974:247; Svartvik and Wright 1977). Lexical DARE certainly allows both bare and *to*-infinitives, as is evident from the classical handbooks (*eg* Visser 1969:1432–40; *cf* also Greenbaum), though there may be some limitations concerning dialects and types of construction; I have shown modal DARE as taking only a bare infinitive, but as noted above the modal-lexical distinction is difficult to draw in cases like *dared not to V*, which are used by some speakers.

23–30 INFLECTIONAL FORMS AND THEIR USE

Here we consider the ability of the verb to carry certain inflections, either in general or in specified uses.

23 3rd Singular

Does the verb have a distinct inflectional form for the 3rd Person Singular non-Past Indicative? Verbs which cannot occur in the non-Past Indicative with a 3rd Person Singular subject are marked 'N'; I have assumed that *had* [_better_] and *would* [_rather_], which exhibit no contrast in Mood, are synchronically indicative.

24 -*En* form

Does the verb occur in the *-en* form? The dialect-limited '–' answers for BE [_going_] are based on the data in Emonds (1976: 106) and Jenkins (1972: 42), the '+' reflecting the complete acceptability in British English of examples like *He had been going to help her*. In certain non-standard dialects, OUGHT has an *-en* form restricted to occurrence after *hadn't*.

---

8 Another way in which passivization may be applied to NP_1 V_1 (*to*) V_2 NP_2 to make NP_2 subject of the main clause is to passivize both verbs, as in such attested examples as *to explain what was attempted to be achieved, a general idea of what is intended to be achieved, grants were threatened to be cut*. Superficially, these look like the quite standard construction *He is known to be feared*, but semantically they are different in that the 'logical subjects' of ATTEMPT and ACHIEVE are the same, while those of KNOW and FEAR are not.

25 -Ing form

Does the verb occur in the -ing form? Perfect having can occur after verbs like REMEMBER, but not after aspectuals like BEGIN or progressive BE; central having does not occur readily after BE: *She is having blue eyes.

26 Base-form

Does the verb occur in the base-form? As in (24), the answer for BE [_going] reflects the difference between the Emonds-Jenkins dialect and, say, British English with respect to the acceptability of He can't be going to resign and the like. OUGHT has in some non-standard dialects a base-form restricted to occurrence after DO (like that of USE) or should.

27 Past Tense

Does the verb have one or more inflectional forms that can be used to express past time? I exclude the special case of indirect speech, as in He said he must leave immediately. With modal DARE the usual form is dare(n't), though some speakers have dared; it may be that others would have a '–' entry here. Might and must appear here only in certain dialects and uses (cf Leech 1971:91, Zandvoort 1969:69–70); would is restricted to certain uses of WILL, eg volition but not futurity.

28 Unreal mood: protasis

Can the verb occur in the protasis, the if-clause, of an unreal condition? The '–' for MAY perhaps needs qualification: We would be very grateful if we might invite Tom may be acceptable for some.

29 Unreal mood: apodosis

Can the verb occur in the apodosis, the main clause, of an unreal condition? The variable answers for OUGHT reflect differing judgments on the acceptability of examples like If he were to need help, he ought to ask me (cf Palmer 1974:144).

30 Unreal mood: tentative use

Can the verb occur in the Unreal Mood form in a main clause where the mood expresses something like tentativeness, rather than being determined by an unreal condition? The only verbs with positive answers are CAN, MAY, SHALL, WILL, as in If John calls, could/would you tell him I'm in the garden; You might be right; I should think so.

SEMANTIC INDETERMINACY AND THE MODALS
GEOFFREY LEECH AND JENNIFER COATES

1 Introduction

The English modals in many ways epitomize the problems which beset modern semantics. Among important questions which are particularly difficult to answer are:

(a) Are linguistic items MONOSEMOUS or POLYSEMOUS?
(b) Are meanings strictly CATEGORICAL ('discrete, invariant, qualitatively distinct, conjunctively defined, and composed of atomic primes' – Labov 1973), or NON-CATEGORICAL?
(c) Can factors of speaker- and hearer-involvement be integrated into the LOGICAL representation of meaning, or should they be given an extrinsic PRAGMATIC explanation?

It would be easy, though time-consuming, to list previous studies of the modals which (implicitly or explicitly) take up different positions on (a) – (c), and thereby offer conflicting models of modal meaning. But it is a measure of the intricacy of our subject that the answers to these questions, with respect to the English modals, seem to be 'sometimes yes, and sometimes no'. This argues for a more multi-faceted approach to natural language semantics than has generally been adopted.

In this paper we investigate some aspects of semantic indeterminacy in the modals, in order to suggest answers to questions (a) and (b). The answers

[79]

are interrelated: those who have looked for a 'basic meaning' common to all uses of a modal (such as Ehrman 1966) have almost inevitably given up the strong assumption of semantic invariance; and those who have taken a polysemous approach (such as Leech 1969) have in general operated with categories they have assumed to be discrete. The latter has been true both of traditional categories such as 'permission', 'possibility', and 'ability', and of logical categories such as 'epistemic', 'deontic', and 'dynamic'.

We shall largely ignore question (c) (and therefore choose our examples so as to minimize interference from the direction of pragmatics). But it is notable that logical formalizations of modality in natural language (and we include here 'deep structure' formalizations) have typically evaded the problem of indeterminacy, which is inimical to the precise operation of logical rules. There is a strong association, in other words, between the orientations which we may label 'polysemous', 'categorical', and 'logical'.

This brings us to a crucial problem in modal semantics, and in semantics in general. On the one hand, logical formalism has provided the basis of explicitness and precision on which most advances in the semantics of modality have been made (for a survey, see Lyons 1977: Ch 17). For example, if one abandoned such formalism, one could no longer state such uncontroversial 'laws' as that of the inverseness of possibility and necessity:

not (POSSIBLE *p*) = NECESSARY (*not p*)
POSSIBLE (*not p*) = *not* (NECESSARY *p*)

On the other hand, if one attempts a semantic classification of modals as they occur in real language data, one is inevitably confronted with unclear cases: tokens which cannot be clearly assigned to one category or another, except arbitrarily. This was the case with our own analysis of modals sampled from two written corpuses of English.[1] As a result of this analysis, we came to the conclusion that a correct description of modal meanings must achieve a reconciliation between categorical and non-categorical approaches. Palmer takes a similar view of the modals:

> It has been increasingly apparent in recent years that there are many areas of syntax and semantics where no clear, discrete categorization is possible. This does not invalidate any attempt to categorize; it simply means that the model must recognize that there are often continua with extremes that are clearly distinct, but with considerable indeterminacy in the middle. (Palmer, 1979: 172–3)

But if linguistic description is to be explicit, it is necessary not only to acknowledge indeterminacy, but to define its nature and extent. A valuable

---

1 The two corpuses were Brown University's computer corpus of printed American English, and a corresponding corpus of British English. The corpus analysis was supported by Social Science Research Council research grant HR/3791. This paper is partly based on our Final Report to the SSRC. For further details, see Coates and Leech (forthcoming).

parallel here is furnished by studies of syntactic indeterminacy, notably the pioneering work of Quirk (see especially Quirk 1965). It is significant that both Quirk (in his general study of gradience) and Palmer (in his more recent and specific study of modality) have based their analyses on corpus data, *viz* that of the Survey of English Usage. Corpus study not only compels one to recognize indeterminacy as a serious factor in modal semantics, but is a prerequisite to its precise analysis.

2 Three types of indeterminacy

We distinguish three types of indeterminacy, two of which are well represented in our data. The most important kind is GRADIENCE (Bolinger 1961*b*), to which Palmer refers above, and which exists between two categories *a* and *b* when there are intermediate cases which cannot be clearly assigned to *a* or *b*. It is normally assumed that the intermediate cases show varying degrees of similarity to *a* and *b*, so that they can be placed on a scale running from 'full membership of *a*' to 'full membership of *b*'. But for semantic indeterminacy, one has to entertain a weaker concept of gradience (perhaps in terms of a partial ordering or preordering of intermediate cases), since even the criteria for determining relative similarity cannot always be strictly applied. We illustrate gradience in 3 below.

In addition to gradience, however, there are two other reasons why a token may not be non-arbitrarily assignable to one semantic category or another. First, a token may be AMBIGUOUS, yielding more than one interpretation. The two (or more) meanings are in an either-or relationship, so that in making sense of the passage, we select one meaning only. Ambiguities are rare in actual texts, because contextual clues generally make clear which meaning is appropriate. But it is not difficult to find instances of ambiguity if we isolate a sentence from its context: in *He must understand that we mean business*, for example, the modal may be given either an epistemic or root (obligational) interpretation.

But a more important source of indeterminacy is what we have called MERGER. This term applies where a token yields two interpretations, and where the meanings are mutually compatible in a reading of the passage; *ie* are in a both-and relationship. Merger may be regarded as a special case of ambiguity, in which the meanings are so closely related that, whichever we choose, the passage makes sense in roughly the same way. One may alternatively regard it as a 'contextual neutralization' of meanings which in other contexts would be clearly distinct. An example outside the sphere of modality is the merger of the collective and distributive interpretations of a clause in which a plural noun phrase and an indefinite singular noun phrase are in a transitive relationship:

[1] *The leaders* decided to hold *a meeting*.

[2] *The children* in the senior classes are allowed to ride *a bicycle* to school.
[3] This autumn *the farmers* are expecting *a bumper harvest*.

In [1] it is clear that the leaders collectively decided to hold a single meeting. In [2], it is equally clear that the children do not ride a collective bicycle: that each child rides a separate one. But in [3], either type of interpretation is possible: in fact, it matters little whether we think of the farmers collectively anticipating a single (nation-wide) harvest, or think of each farmer looking forward to his own individual harvest.

Merger is not easy to detect, since the whole principle of it is that speakers are unlikely to notice a difference between the two meanings. Moreover, it is difficult to find a reliable criterion for distinguishing merger from gradience: in both cases we shall find instances where the context clearly indicates one category or the other, and other instances where it does not. The most reliable criterion we have found depends on paraphrase; *ie* if paraphrase formulae A and B are criterial for clear instances of semantic categories a and b, then either A or B or both will fail to provide satisfactory paraphrases of an intermediate case (gradience); whereas for a case of merger, both A and B will be satisfactory paraphrases (see 5 below).

3 Gradience

To illustrate semantic gradience of modality, we shall confine ourselves to two kinds of indeterminacy in the interpretation of *can*.

3.1 *Can* ('possibility') and *can* ('permission')
These two senses are related through a gradient of RESTRICTION (*cf* Lyons 1977:828–9). At the possibility end, *can* can be glossed 'Nothing at all prevents p from taking place', while at the 'permission' end it means 'Nothing prevents p from taking place in a specific world of man-made freedoms and obligations'. We can think of *can* as presupposing a universe of possible worlds. Such a universe may be an unrestricted universe in which 'everything goes' except what is contrary to so-called natural laws; or it may be to a greater or lesser degree restricted by what a human being, human institution, or human code permits at a given time or place. At the man-made end of the gradient, a paraphrase with *allow* or *permit* is acceptable, while at the other end one with *possible* is more acceptable. Different points on the gradient are illustrated by:

[4] You can't do that – I forbid it. (most restricted)
[5] You can't do that – it's against the rules.
[6] You can't do that – it would be breaking the law.
[7] You can't do that – everyone would think you were mad. (*ie* a breach of conventions of acceptable behaviour)
[8] You can't do that – it wouldn't be reasonable.

[9] You can't do that – it wouldn't be right.

[10] You can't do that – it's contrary to the law of gravity. (least restricted)

In [4] the imposition of human constraint is absolutely clear and direct, but in [5] and [6] it is less direct, in [7–9] it is less direct again, and in [10] it is absent. Only this last example corresponds to possibility in its usual logical sense. In the other cases, it is possible to add *If you do/did* . . ., implying that in some less restricted universe, the action is possible. But paraphrases with *possible* are often accepted for sentences referring both to unrestricted and restricted universes. There is no non-arbitrary way to draw the line between 'possibility' and 'permission'. Further, we cannot insist on a strict ordering of universes (*eg* the ordering of [4–10]) according to degree of restriction: it is not the case, for instance, that the universe of social acceptability presupposed by [7] is a sub-universe of the ethical universe presupposed by [9], for it is quite conceivable that what is forbidden by an ethical code will be permitted by social convention, and vice versa.

The gradient of restriction is selectively illustrated by the following textual examples:[2]

[11] You *can* start the revels now.   [L] (personal authority)

[12] The allowance *can* be paid to a woman widowed over sixty years of age only if her husband was not receiving a retirement pension. [L] (regulation)

[13] We *can't* expect him to leave his customers.   [L] (reasonableness)

[14] How, then, *can* I help other people to impose a ban in which I do not believe?   [L] (ethical/moral)

[15] You *can* look as fit as a fiddle and yet be bloodless.   [L] (natural law)

3.2 *Can* 'possibility' and *can* 'ability'

These two senses are related through the gradient of INHERENCY, at one end of which *can* means 'the circumstances which enable *p* to happen are independent of the participants in *p*', and at the other end 'the circumstances which enable *p* to happen are inherent to the performer of *p*'. This gradient operates at the unrestricted end of the gradient of restriction.

If we first contrast clear cases such as *Oil exploration can be very costly* and *She can dance beautifully*, the 'ability' category is distinguished by the following factors:

(*a*) the subject-referent has an agentive function;

(*b*) the main verb denotes a physical action or activity;

(*c*) the possibility of the action is determined by inherent properties (whether physical or psychological capabilities) of the subject-referent.

---

2 These and subsequent examples are from our corpus sample. Examples marked '[B]' are from the Brown Corpus of American English, and those marked '[L]' are from the Lancaster Corpus of British English.

Thus if the subject is inanimate [16] or the verb is not an activity verb [17], *can* is less securely assignable to the 'ability' category:

[16] It's time this country spent a bit more money on canals . . . they *can* still do a lot for this country.   [L]

[17] She doesn't understand how her husband *can* be so dumb.   [B]

[18] . . . and [crochet] edgings . . . *can* fulfil a variety of functions.   [L]

It will probably be agreed that [18], in which neither subject nor main verb is of a kind typically associated with ability, is less 'ability-like' than [16] and [17]. But the third factor, that of inherency, gives rise to a more serious problem of indeterminacy. In practice, an action may be possible by virtue of a multiplicity of factors, some of which may be inherent to the subject-referent, and some not. A relatively simple case is:

[19] Would the man with an empty lifeboat row away from a shipwreck because his boat *could* not pick up everyone?   [B]

The possibility of saving survivors in [19] is presumably determined by at least two circumstances:

(*a*) the size of the boat (inherent) and
(*b*) the number of survivors (non-inherent). In

[20] You *can* build this vacation cottage yourself.   [B]

the enabling factors are more diverse, and may include

(*a*) the addressee's physical capacities,
(*b*) his technical know-how,
(*c*) his financial resources,
(*d*) the simplicity of the house's design,
(*e*) the availability of land,
(*f*) the availability of building materials, etc.

Only the first two of these are inherent properties of the subject-referent, and only in a wider context could we judge whether the writer intended the inherent factors to be more or less important than the others.

4 Monosemy and polysemy

Because all uses of *can* (except possibly for the use of *can* with verbs of perception – *I can see/hear/etc*) fall within the scope of these two gradients, *can* is essentially a monosemous modal: there are no clear divisions between permission, possibility, and ability. The three senses are in a relationship indicated by this diagram (in which the arrows represent gradients):

[84]

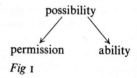

Fig I

The special status of 'possibility' here is that it is the unmarked meaning with respect to both gradients: it is the meaning which applies where there is no positive reason (restriction or inherency) for choosing otherwise.

As both permission and ability are associated with an agentive subject function, it might be argued that the lines of demarcation are clearer than we have indicated. But firstly, agency is not incompatible with possibility, and secondly, the role of agent is a complex of factors (*cf* Cruse 1973) which may or may not be simultaneously present: *ie* agency itself is a 'fuzzy' concept.

Few modals, however, are monosemous like *can*. In particular, *may* is polysemous: it has an epistemic sense ('It is possible that . . .') which is clearly distinct from the root senses of permission and possibility which it shares with *can*. Thus the semantic overlap of *can* and *may* is approximately as follows:

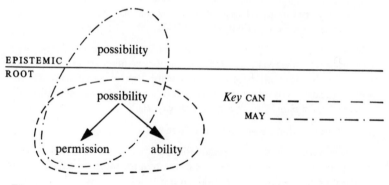

Fig 2

The epistemic-root boundary for *may* (as for other modals like *must*) is clear-cut for the following reasons. (*a*) The distinction is associated with clear syntactic/semantic criteria, such as scope of negation, and the non-occurrence of the perfective aspect with root meaning. (*b*) Epistemic meaning (so far as our corpus analysis shows) has no gradients; *ie* in contrast to root meaning, it is non-fuzzy. (*c*) The two paraphrase formulae (*It is possible that p* and *It is possible for p*) which distinguish epistemic and root possibility are qualitatively distinct, and allow no intermediate gradations. This seems to be because the *p*s in these two formulae belong to different levels of abstraction: *p* in the epistemic formula stands for a proposition, while *p* in the root formula stands for what Palmer calls an 'event' (1979, 24–6). Such a distinction is consonant with the familiar observation that epistemic modality concerns the status of a sentence or proposition with respect to truth value.

5 Merger

This brings us back to merger. For although the epistemic-root contrast is discrete, ambiguous instances of *may* are rare. Instead, we find instances which could be interpreted either as epistemic or as root with little difference of effect. The common semantic element of possibility (as shown in the paraphrase formulae) is indicative of the close connection between the two meanings. Before illustrating this semantic convergence, let us first consider clear cases of the two meanings, noting what semantic tests (apart from the paraphrase formulae above) distinguish them:

[21] I *may* not get back there today – it depends on the work here. [L] (epistemic)

[22] There are many theories about the balance of these forces in a perfect society, and many reasons for believing that X's party, class or nation *may* be trusted with them where Y's cannot. [L] (root)

The epistemic *may* of [21] may be followed by *well* or *possibly*. Two other variations which leave the epistemic sense of *may* intact are (*a*) the addition of *or may not* after *may*, and (*b*) the substitution of a construction with *perhaps (I perhaps won't get back there today)*. Yet again, we can replace the construction 'x *may* Y' by '*it may be that* x *(will)* Y':

[21]*a* It *may* be that I won't get back there today.

All these variations provide reasonable paraphrases of [21], but none of them apply to [22]. On the other hand, the root meaning of [22] allows the substitution of *can* for *may*, a substitution which is not acceptable in [21].

Consider now the following sentence:

[23] With tone, individual differences *may* be greater than the linguistic contrasts which are superimposed on them. [B]

All the semantic tests applicable to [21] apply to [23], and at the same time, [23] also satisfies the test of substituting *can*. This then is a case of merger: in generic statements of this kind, the message conveyed is approximately the same, whether we choose the epistemic or root meaning.

The root-possibility meaning of *may* is often ignored or regarded as a rarity of formal literary style. In fact, our analysis shows that in scientific and other learned texts it occurs more frequently than the equivalent sense of *can*. It is in such texts, also, that merger tends to occur.

Another type of merger is seen in these examples of *should*:

[24] You *should* complain. [B]
[25] It is in some ways distasteful that some people *should* be endowed with greater gifts than others. [L]
[26] Rutherford suggested to Marsden . . . that he *should* follow this up. [L]

Whereas [24] illustrates a straightforward obligational use of *should*, [25] illustrates the quasi-subjunctive or putative *should* (see GCE:874), which is chiefly found in certain kinds of *that*-clause. The two meanings converge in [26], which may be read as purely putative, or as an indirect speech equivalent of [24]. (The obligational meaning can be alternatively expressed by *ought to*, while the putative meaning can (if somewhat archaically) be rendered by the present subjunctive in examples like [25] and [26].) The putative meaning cannot occur in [24], which lacks the right syntactic environment. Conversely the obligational meaning could not occur in a sentence like [26] unless the force of the verb in the main clause were compatible with the attenuated obligation expressed by *should/ought to*. *Demand*, for example, would imply obligatoriness of too absolute a kind:

[27] Observers said the biggest obstacle to agreement was the Soviet 'Troika' proposal, demanding that the International Control Commission *should* be headed by three administrators. [L]

The area of undecidability is therefore chiefly limited to *that*-clauses which complement a main clause expressing a degree of constraint consonant with *should*'s obligational sense.

6 Theoretical and descriptive implications of indeterminacy

6.1 Gradience

With reference to gradience, the question remains: how do we determine the extent and nature of indeterminacy? This question is of some importance, since we have assumed that labels such as 'possibility' and 'permission' are meaningful, and this can scarcely be justified if these are merely arbitrary reference points in a welter of gradience.

One way to determine gradience is to use Quirk's method (1965:210-11) of plotting instances against criteria in a serial-relationship matrix. Quirk has demonstrated this method with reference to syntactic gradience, but it is also applicable to semantic gradience, even though one must reckon with a greater subjective variation in the application of semantic criteria. A simplified example of such a matrix is the following, which displays the gradient of restriction relating possibility to permission:

[87]

Criteria

	1	2	3	4	5	6
A	+	+	?	+	?	−
B	−	+	+	+	−	−
C	−	?	+	+	+	−
D	−	−	?	+	+	−
E	−	−	−	−	+	−
F	−	−	−	−	+	+

Examples

Fig 3

Examples

A: The car? Of course you *can* have it. [B]
B: But this is a public park and it's a city ordinance that the statues *cannot* be crawled on. [B]
C. 'Promise? On the honour of a soldier?' The large eyes lit up. 'I *can* do that?' [L]
D: How, then, *can* I help other people to impose a ban in which I do not believe? [L]
E: The mind is a simple thing . . . You *can* make it swing like a pendulum. [L]
F: A fussy referee *can* ruin a bout. [L]

Criteria

1: x can Y = I'll let x Y; I'll allow x to Y
2: x can Y = x is allowed to Y; it is permitted for x to Y
3: x can Y = it is permissible (for x) to Y
4: x can Y presupposes a restricted universe
5: x can Y = it is/will be possible (for x) to Y
6: x can Y = x sometimes Y(s)

The queries in the matrix are a reminder that the criteria themselves are gradable in their application; a paraphrase formula may be more or less appropriate to a given sentence. In a more sensitive version of this technique, informants would be asked to rank paraphrases in order of appropriateness, so that the $+/-$ rating would be replaced by a numerical ranking.

Another technique that may be used is cluster analysis, the degrees of similarity between classes of tokens being displayed by a dendrogram, or hierarchical tree structure (Everitt 1974).

Although we have only just begun to apply these techniques, our work tentatively indicates that the postulation of gradience is necessary for only a minority of textual instances. In other words, most instances of root modality are assignable to 'core' meanings corresponding to such traditional notional categories as 'possibility' and 'ability'. If it proves true that 'core' examples are in a substantial majority, then one may speculate that the interpretation of root modality proceeds by matching an instance to a particular stereotype which is quantitatively and hence psychologically predominant. The notion of a 'quantitative stereotype' is likely to apply to other linguistic classifications, both syntactic and semantic.[3] For example, despite Ross's 'squish of noun-phrasiness' (Ross 1973), it is probable that in

3 The psychological concept of 'prototype', as investigated by Rosch and others (see for example Rosch and Mervis 1975), has much in common with that of 'quantitative stereotype' proposed here.

a quantitative analysis, the vast majority of NP-like constructions will prove to be what he calls 'copper-clad, brass-bottomed NP's'. Similarly, although Labov (1973) shows that the meaning of the word *cup* is to some extent a more-or-less rather than all-or-nothing matter, it would not be surprising to find that in real life, English-speakers are normally exposed to vessels which they can clearly identify as cups or non-cups.

This conjecture implies that in language acquisition, core meanings are established before, and as a point of reference for, the accommodation of less determinate cases. (Anderson 1975 provides some support for this, in showing that a child's understanding of the word *cup* and related items becomes more, rather than less, fuzzy as he gets older.) On the theoretical level, our conjecture suggests that the statistical study of corpus data, far from being peripheral or irrelevant, has a fundamental role in the definition of linguistic categories.[4] However, there is much work to be done before these speculations can be substantiated.

6.2 Merger

The importance of merger, from the theoretical point of view, is that it bridges the gap between monosemy and polysemy. We can acknowledge the existence of categorical distinctions of meaning within the semantic range of a single modal, and yet show (as in the epistemic and root possibility senses of *may*) that there is a common element of meaning that connects them. The fact that such distinctions can be contextually neutralized may well be a significant factor in semantic change. It cannot be accidental that related root and epistemic meanings have come to be expressed by the same modal.

7 Conclusion

We have argued, with reference to the questions with which this paper started, that modal meaning is characterized by a mixture of monosemy and polysemy, and a mixture of categorical and non-categorical contrasts. Where the 'strict categorical view' (as defined by Labov 1973) cannot be sustained for modal semantics, we suggest that a weaker definition of 'category' (as a 'quantitative stereotype') may be justifiable, so that the

---

4 To establish a quantitative basis for category recognition, it would therefore be more relevant to analyse a corpus of parents' and children's language, than an adult corpus. It is evident from a comparison of our findings with those of Wells forthcoming that the frequencies of semantic types in an adult written corpus are vastly different from those in a developmental corpus. In Wells's material (up to $3\frac{1}{2}$ years) the 'ability' and 'permission' senses of *can* are in the overwhelming majority, whereas in ours the 'possibility' sense predominates, and the 'permission' sense is rare. Wells reports (personal communication) that he found no significant problems of indeterminacy in his children's corpus.

existence of semantic indeterminancy can be reconciled with approaches to meaning (including logical formalizations) which rely on discrete categories. What is needed is a more subtle model of natural language semantics which will enable us to describe the combination of discreteness and non-discreteness, variance and invariance, homogeneity and heterogeneity, which is manifested in the field of modality.

CAN, WILL, AND ACTUALITY
F. R. PALMER

In a previous paper (Palmer 1977:5–6) I offered an explanation for the fact that we cannot normally say *I ran fast and could catch the bus.* What I suggested was that CAN is not used if there is an implication (in a non-logical sense) of actuality (*ie* that the event took place) in the past, because the factual status of the event is known and a modal verb is inappropriate in such circumstances. In contrast, it is perfectly possible to say *I ran fast and was able to catch the bus*, because in spite of the close similarity of meaning, BE ABLE TO is not, like CAN, a modal verb. A rather different issue is raised by the perfectly possible *I ran fast, but I couldn't catch the bus.* Negative modality implies (in a more logical sense) negative actuality; if I couldn't, it follows that I didn't.

While I still believe this is basically correct, a close examination of the data in the Survey of English Usage at University College has convinced me that the picture is much more complicated than I had realized. I intend in this paper to illustrate the problems with respect to both CAN and WILL, as far as is possible, with examples taken from the Survey, and to suggest an explanation. (Survey examples are identified by their bracketed references; other examples are invented.)

1 CAN and BE ABLE TO

We shall be mostly concerned with CAN and the apparently suppletive BE

ABLE TO, because with these the situation is more complex, and yet, in a way, clearer than with WILL (and the less clearly suppletive BE WILLING TO).

1.1

In the simplest form the rules for past tense are:

(a) Positive *could* is not used to refer to a single action;
(b) there is no similar restriction on negative *couldn't*;
(c) *could* may be used if there is reference to habitual or repeated actions;
(d) there is no restriction similar to (a) on the forms of BE ABLE TO.

Paradigm examples are:

(a) *I ran fast and could catch the bus.
(b) I ran fast, but couldn't catch the bus.
(c) I used to run fast and could always catch the bus.
(d) I ran fast and was able to catch the bus.

Examples of *couldn't* from the Survey are:

I didn't go in a mask. I couldn't with a child that small. (S.1.8.98)
Your mother was out and couldn't leave the key. (S.2.13.29)

But it is not simply the form *couldn't* that may occur, but also *could not*, and *could* with any negative form:

Why was Chetwyn Road so cheap?—Ah that! There's an answer to that.
Nobody could get a mortgage on it.
(S.4.2.21)

Equally, though this is not a matter that will continue to concern us, *could* may occur in interrogation, where the actuality is questioned as much as the modality:

Could you reach it?
How could you do such a thing?

Interrogation and negation function generally in very similar ways, and, indeed, are conveniently handled together as 'non-assertion' (GCE:54).
   There is a potential ambiguity with *could* and *couldn't* in that they may also be conditional, expressing what would or would not be possible, rather than what was or was not possible. In all the examples I have quoted either the immediate context or a wider context indicates that the interpretation is one of past. It should be noted, in support of (a), that *could* without a negative form would be possible in similar sentences only with a conditional interpretation, and not to refer to past time.

Examples of (*c*) (habitual or repeated actions) are:

> I could get up and go to the kitchen whenever I wanted to. (S.2.7.57)
> Yet my father could usually lay hands on what he wanted. It all seems to have a purpose. (W.1.3b.20)

As further evidence it can be seen that *could* would be perfectly possible in place of *couldn't* in:

> She couldn't be left alone. She couldn't do anything. She couldn't sleep, eat, anything. (S.6.2.84)

There are plenty of examples of *was/were able to* being used to refer to a single event in the past:

> I was able to finish reading R. S. Bentley's play 'The Burning Bush'. (W.8.3a.1)
> I was able to lead this chap into directions that I knew about, you know. (S.2.9.12)
> He and Professor Huxley working together were able to establish the actual nature of the excitation process which occurs at each point of a nerve. (W.4.2a.18)

Notice once again, in support of (*a*), that *could* would not be possible here.

It is possible, however, to use positive *could* if the context clearly suggests that there is no implication of actuality. This I take to be the explanation of Ehrman's (1966:50):

> I was plenty scared. In the state she was in she could actually kill.

This means, I think, that although she was able to kill, she did not. But, although this is an unusual use of *could*, it actually supports the general thesis that positive *could* will not be used where there is an implication of actuality.

It should be added here that the rules we have been discussing do not apply to the 'private verbs' (Hill 1958:207) and, in particular, not to the verbs of sensation. *Could* may occur, for instance, in:

> I could see the moon.
> As he leaned on the ropes, I could hear the ropes and ring creak. (S.10.3.23)

With such verbs CAN occurs with little or no suggestion of ability or possibility. I shall, therefore, treat them as a special, idiomatic case and ignore them for the rest of the discussion, though Johannesson (1976:46–8) attempts to provide an explanation.

1.2

The restrictions on positive *could* are not as simple as the previous section suggests.[1]

Could occurs with *hardly* and *scarcely* in such sentences as:

> He was laughing so much he could hardly get a word out.   (S.11.3c.5)
> He could scarcely get a word out.
> Fulham's extreme expedience of first flooring Banks could hardly escape
>   Mr Walters.   (W.12.5g.3)

Hardly and *scarcely* are 'semi-negatives' (Palmer 1974:28–9); they function formally as negatives in some syntactic circumstances, *eg* in tag questions and with *some/any*:

> It's hardly good enough, is it?
> He's hardly done anything.

If *hardly* were not negative we should expect:

> *It's hardly good enough, isn't it?
> *He's hardly done something.

If, then, we consider the issue in syntactic terms we should not be surprised to find that *could* occurs with *hardly* and *scarcely*.

Yet this does not conform with the semantic explanation suggested at the beginning of this paper. For *hardly* and *scarcely* do not suggest that the event did not take place, but only that it almost did not, or that it did so only with difficulty. The argument, then, that the negation of the modality implies the negation of the actuality does not apply here and cannot, strictly, be used to account for the occurrence of *could*.

This might seem to suggest, then, that the occurrence of *could* is a purely syntactic matter, *ie* in that it may occur with forms that are syntactically negative and that the semantics is not at issue. This is sufficient to explain the occurrence of *could* with *only* in the following example, since *only* also has negative characteristics syntactically.

> Well she was the only one of the family there who could do it.   (S.1.13.103)

We may compare with (unstressed) *any*

> Well she was the only one of the family there who did anything.

Yet semantics must, surely, be a crucial factor, as shown by:

> One moment I seem to be everything to him, and then all he could think
>   of was this child.   (W5.2.61)

The occurrence of *could* here seems to be explained by the semantics as

---

1 I am grateful to Mr P. S. Falla for some very helpful observations.

shown by the paraphrase 'He could not think of anything but this child'. It is the meaning here, not the syntactic form, that is relevant.

Consider too:

I could just reach the branch.
I could almost reach the branch.

Neither *just* nor *almost* are formally negative in the sense that *hardly* and *scarcely* are. Unlike *hardly* and *scarcely* they take negative tags in tag questions and occur with *some*, not *any*:

It's just good enough, isn't it?
It's almost good enough, isn't it?
He's just bought some.   (*any)

The syntactic explanation is not, then, available for these (unless we make a purely ad hoc rule that they are negative for the purposes of accounting for *could*). *Almost*, however, implies that the event did not take place; it is, thus, semantically negative and could account, in semantic terms, for the occurrence of *could*, for actuality is not implied. But this will not work with *just*, for *just* suggests that the event did (just) take place; *just* is neither syntactically nor, in a strict sense, semantically negative.

It is fairly clear, then, that it is semantic negation that is at issue, but in a wide sense, to include not only non-occurrence of the event but also its occurrence under difficult circumstances, or its 'almost-non-occurrence'.

This may, perhaps, account for the possibility of:

I could get in, because the door was open.
The door was open, so I could get in.

There is no doubt that these sentences can be used with the implication of actuality but there is a negative implication of the 'almost didn't' kind; it was only because the door was open that I succeeded.

1.3

We saw in 1.1 that BE ABLE TO may be used where CAN is not permissible, to refer to a single action in the past with the implication of actuality (subject to the remarks in 1.2). There are, however, circumstances in which, although CAN is possible, BE ABLE TO is preferred.

First, in the past, even if there is reference to repeated actions, BE ABLE TO is preferred if there is a very strong implication of actuality:

Most people worked harder than me during the University, of course, and when it came to the exams, they were able to draw not just upon two weeks of knowledge. They were able to draw upon three years of knowledge.   (S.2.9.52)

Secondly, BE ABLE TO is preferred in the present, if actuality is implied:

> . . . and yet you are able to look at the future of it in this very objective way. (S.6.4a.73)
> By bulk buying in specific items, Lasky's are able to cut prices on packages by as much as 30 per cent or so. (W.15.4c.13)

The implications are that we did draw on the three years of knowledge, that you do look at the future in this way, that Lasky's do cut prices. Here the implication of actuality does not require BE ABLE TO, but it makes it much more likely.

In conclusion, then, it can be seen that the occurrence of CAN and BE ABLE TO is conditioned by questions of actuality, tense and negation. In particular the following points may be made:

(a) The strongest restriction on CAN in terms of actuality is in the past where a single action is involved.

(b) Even in other circumstances BE ABLE TO may be preferred if the implication of actuality is strong.

(c) 'Negation' permits the occurrence of CAN in the past, provided this term is taken to include the semantics of *hardly*, *just*, etc, the almost-non-occurrence of the event or its occurrence only with difficulty.

2 WILL

We will first discuss the use of volitional WILL and then two interesting, but debatable examples.

2.1

In basic terms volitional WILL functions like CAN, but there are differences.

The rules for past tense are similar, except that there is no verb to parallel BE ABLE TO (BE WILLING TO is the obvious candidate, but by comparison with BE ABLE TO it is very rare). I will not set out the rules again, but merely give a paradigm of examples:

(a) *I asked him and he would come.
(b) I asked him, but he wouldn't come.
(c) I used to ask him, and he would (always) come.
(d) (I asked him and he was willing to come.)

Examples from the Survey are:

(a) Melissa was very noisy at night and wouldn't sleep. (W.8.2.27)
(b) Married to a woman who wouldn't sleep with him after the birth of her second son. (W.7.5c.6)
(c) . . . and whenever she gardened, she would eat with dirt on her calves.

(*d*) So it appears that the skipper was willing to sacrifice a win over a team we had never beaten before for a 'moral' victory. (W.7.3–46)

The third example, which is taken from Ehrman (1966:46), may be thought to be rather different in that *would* is used in the very specific context of 'habitual activity' with no clear sense of willingness or volition. But it is still interesting that it is habitual.

Would is also possible in some of the circumstances similar to those discussed in 1.2. Certainly it would be possible in the semantically negative environments, *eg*:

Well she was the only one of the family there who would do it.
All he would think of was this child.

It does not, however, seem to occur with *hardly, scarcely, just* or *almost*, except in a conditional or habitual sense. With WILL, therefore, negation can be defined in its stricter, more usual, sense.

2.2

The following passage occurs in the Survey:

There are certain arguments which will work and they work in times of prosperity; in, of course, the times we're in now they don't work at all. (S.11.2.55)

Here we have the sequence *will work, work* and *don't work* and the choice of these different forms is easily explained. *Will work* indicates what 'will' conditionally work; or, possibly, it is to be interpreted in terms of 'power' (Jespersen 1909–49:VI 239), which is essentially volition ascribed to inanimate objects. *Work*, in the simple form, is used in a habitual sense. *Don't work* indicates the present non-occurrence of the event. Here the three forms are clearly in contrast semantically. Yet earlier there was the following sentence:

They know that there are certain arguments which work and certain arguments which won't work. (S.11.2.54)

Here there is no contrast in meaning, except wholly in terms of negation. Why, then, is *work* used in the positive, but *won't work* in the negative? It is not merely accidental, for, if we reverse the forms with *will work* and *don't work*, the resulting sentence is much less natural:

They know that there are certain arguments which will work and certain arguments which don't work.

The choice of *work* and *won't work* is, then, deliberate. It is, of course, easily explained in terms of modality, negation and actuality. The modal WILL is appropriate in the negative because negative modality implies negative

[97]

actuality, but is less appropriate in the positive because positive modality does not, or does not so clearly, imply positive actuality; the non-modal simple form, which asserts actuality, is, therefore, preferred.

2.3
Even more surprising, perhaps, is the alternation of forms in:

> You don't seriously suppose that children are going to start saying 'trash can' and, indeed, of course, they won't. (S.1.10.50)

Here both BE GOING TO and WILL are used to refer to the future. Again the question is why BE GOING TO is used in the positive and WILL in the negative, and again it is clear that this is not accidental, since, if we change over the forms, the result is much less natural:

> You don't seriously suppose that the children will start saying 'trash can' and, indeed, of course, they're not going to.

It is, in fact, clear from the Survey that, in general, where the negative is required, there is a greater tendency to use WILL than BE GOING TO; indeed, examples of negative BE GOING TO are, comparatively, quite rare.

Once again the actuality explanation is available. If WILL is a modal, even when it refers to the future, while BE GOING TO is not, it is to be expected that where there are implications of actuality WILL may be used in its negative, but not in its positive, forms. But this suggests that even 'futurity' WILL is essentially modal. This is, perhaps, not surprising in view of the close semantic relationship between modality and futurity (cf Lyons 1968:310; 1977:816).

3 Other verbs

Finally, it is worth noting that it is not only CAN and WILL that raise issues of actuality. Consider:

> It's a slow walk down, he's got to fight his way through the crowds. (S.10.3.3)
> It's a slow walk down, he must fight his way through the crowds.

With the first sentence it may well be that the person referred to (a boxer coming to the ring) is actually engaged in fighting his way through the crowd; with the second using *must*, this interpretation would be impossible. Although the distinction can be seen in terms of time, *ie* that *must* must refer to the future here, it can obviously also be seen in terms of actuality.

It would be nice if we could show that similar considerations hold for past tense: that with HAVE TO and HAVE GOT TO actuality is implied, while with MUST it is not. This is not so, because MUST has no past tense form. It is true, however, that the past tense forms of HAVE TO and HAVE GOT TO imply actuality as in:

We had to make a special trip down to Epsom to collect the bloody thing. (S.2.13.28)

It might be argued that it follows that past necessity must imply actuality, because, if the event did not take place, the necessity is, thereby, disproved. But this is valid only if the event is in the past. There is no reason why we should not refer to the necessity in the past of an event that is still future. It is possible to say *Yesterday he had to come tomorrow* (*but today he doesn't have to*). Yet we almost never need to express this; for usually, if the event has not yet taken place, the necessity is still with us and can be expressed in the present. But it may be that part of the reason why MUST has no past tense forms is that there is little or no need for a past tense form of a necessity modal that, by virtue of being a modal, does not imply actuality. The contrast supplied by CAN and BE ABLE TO in the past is simply not needed for MUST and HAVE TO/HAVE GOT TO.

WILL IN *IF*-CLAUSES
R. A. CLOSE

For such an occasion as this, it would be fitting to refer to no less a grammarian than Otto Jespersen and try to deal with a point in English grammatical usage concerning which that great scholar, firmly grounded on 'historical principles', found himself faced with the inexorable nature of contemporary fact.

Jespersen 1909–49: Part IV, 2.5 (4) states: 'the present tense . . . is used in *if*-clauses with the main verb in the future . . . But *if* + *will* implies volition.' The author's line of thought is sometimes difficult to follow in this work, compiled over a period of four decades and running into over 3,000 pages.[1] In Part V, 21.64, he was more categorical on the question of *if* + *will*, establishing the rule that 'a future time is regularly denoted by the present tense' in the conditional clause of a sentence on the model of

[1] If he comes tomorrow he will tell him everything,

and that *will* after *if* always denotes volition, as in the quotation from the 1611 translation of the Bible:

[2] If any man will come after me, let him denie himselfe[2]

---

1 I know that Professor Quirk holds the view that the present usefulness of Jespersen's *Modern English Grammar* would be enhanced by a radical revision. That would, of course, require immense labour, preferably by a team, as well as a very expensive publishing operation.
2 The obsolescence of this example is relevant to the theme of my paper.

In Part IV, 15.9 (1), Jespersen tells us that a modern translation of *if any man will*, as in example [2], is 'if any man wishes to', but paradoxically he also says '*will turn* means the future, and not volition' in the quotation he cites from Hughes T 1.69:[3]

[3] If he'll only turn out a brave, truth-telling Englishman, . . . that's all I want.

It is later in Part IV (in 16.5) that he produces the much discussed example

[4] I will come if it will be any use to you,

defending his rule by maintaining that *if it's any use to you* would be 'decidedly more natural'. To that same section he adds the fragmentary

[5] If that'll do.

The undeniable acceptability of [4] and [5] must have troubled him, for under CORRECTIONS at the end of Part IV, he concedes that '*Will* is quite natural (with non-personal subject) in *I will come if it will be (of) any use to you*'; and he goes on to quote the following from J. B. Priestley's *The Good Companions*:

[6] Now if all the dresses will be finished by about next Monday, why don't you bring them yourself?

In attempting to account for those exceptions to his rule, Jespersen is unconvincing. Of [3], he suggests: 'probably . . . *if* does not imply a condition' in that instance; of [4], '*if it will be* perhaps is a shade politer than *if it is*'; of [5], '*If that'll do* is, of course, all right, as *if* here has no reference to the future'; while on [6] he makes no gloss. His explanations of [3] and [4] are weakened by tentative disjuncts: in any case, I consider that [3] states a condition as definitely as other examples of *if*+ non-volitional *will* given in this paper do. On [4], I agree that *if it will be* may be politer than *if it is* and shall explain why this should be so; but any shade of politeness cannot hide the fact that a non-volitional *will* is here 'quite naturally' preceded by *if*. As for Jespersen's comment on *if that'll do*, that certainly will *not* do: there is undoubted reference to the future in

[7] I've got a luggage rack you can borrow, if that'll do (*ie* if that will prove useful on your forthcoming journey).

Subsequently, most grammarians have adopted without question the same rule as Jespersen. Kruisinga 1931–2 and Zandvoort 1975 repeat it in traditional terms. McCawley 1971 conforms in more modern metalanguage, thus: 'The future marker is replaced by a present tense in conditional clauses'. Leech (1971:60) closes the door firmly against any exception to the

---

3 From the popular Victorian novel *Tom Brown's Schooldays*.

'rule', saying 'When *will* appears in a dependent conditional or temporal clause, it requires a volitional interpretation, because ... the sense of prediction is not available in that position'. F. R. Palmer has been particularly insistent on this point. In Palmer 1965, his summary of the various uses of *will* included:

(a) Futurity – Not after *if*
(b) Volition – Occurs after *if*.

In Palmer 1974 (5.5.6), he wrote: 'It was clearly shown in 5.2.1 (and again in 5.5.2) that WILL and SHALL do not occur in an *if*-clause merely to indicate futurity'. In Palmer 1977, he distinguished between the grammatical use of *will* and its modal use, asserting that the former refers to time and does not occur in an *if*-clause. Yet he had previously (Palmer 1974: 149) published this enigmatic sentence:

[8] If he'll be left destitute, I'll change my will.

He saw two interpretations of that: (a) If it is likely that, with my will in its present form, he'll be left destitute, I'll change it in his favour; and (b) If, by changing my will, I can leave him penniless, then I will cut him out of it.

It is significant that in both Palmer's paraphrases of [8] *if he'll be left destitute* refers to a possible event in future time. A third interpretation, which would accord with Jespersen's decisive '*will* after *if* always denotes volition', namely (c) 'If he is willing to live in absolute poverty after I die, I will leave my money to someone else', did not, apparently, occur to Palmer. Nor would it, I believe, be the first interpretation to spring to the mind of other native speakers of English in this period.

I shall attempt to show that *if* + non-volitional *will* can occur naturally, with both personal and non-personal subjects, though instances of it may be comparatively rare;[4] I shall consider explanations of that phenomenon, apart from Jespersen's, which I regard as quite inadequate; and I shall suggest an explanation which would account for all the examples I have on file, only a selection of which are cited in this paper. Other examples are given in Close 1977: 142–4.

Two of the examples quoted in Close 1977 were taken from the corpus of the Survey of English Usage at University College. Another from the same corpus is

[9] I know that if medicine will save him, he will be safe.

Note, with reference to F. R. Palmer's paper in the present volume, that *will* in [9] is replaceable by *can*.

Mine of information though a large corpus may be, striking examples are often met with outside it. In April 1977, a blow-out from the Ecofisk oil-rig

---

4 Wekker (1976) found no examples of it in his corpus of 600,000 words.

poured 20,000 tons of potential pollution into the middle of the North Sea. While one group of experts laboured to stop the gush, another sought to predict towards which coastline the vast oil-slick would be carried by wind and tide. The BBC invited members of the second group to debate their forecasts on television (25 April 1977), when the Norwegian Minister concerned was heard to say:

[10] If the slick will come as far as Stavanger, then of course I must take precautions on a massive scale.

In that context, the Minister's *will come* was, in my view, both logical and grammatically acceptable. The group was discussing predictions, in the narrow sense of 'forecasts', and the Minister was, in his statement, assuming predictability: he was not making a prediction, in the broad sense of that word, and therefore not relating a prediction to assumed future actuality (see Leech 1971:60). If he had used *comes* instead of *will come*, he would have been saying, in effect: 'If one can consider the arrival of the slick at Stavanger as actually occurring (rather than as likely to occur), then I must take precautions to prevent a disaster which I envisage as having already taken place'. That would of course have been absurd and totally irresponsible.

A similar example had been noted in January 1973, when a BBC reporter, shouting above the roar of an erupting volcano off the coast of Iceland, and pointing to a cluster of modern villas, informed the world:

[11] How far the flood of molten rock behind me will spread is anybody's guess. If it will come down to where I am standing now, all these lovely villas are doomed.

His reference to 'anybody's guess' suggests that the reporter, like the Minister, was thinking about likelihoods. I interpreted his message as follows: If a certain event is likely to happen, then the writing is on the wall, as far as these houses are concerned. That is not the same as saying: If that event actually takes place, these houses will be swallowed up. The distinction would have been very clear if an Icelandic official had made one or other of these declarations (as well he might have done):

[11]*a* If the lava will come down as far as this, all these houses must be evacuated at once.
[11]*b* If it *does* come thus far, anyone still here will stand no chance of survival.

GCE:11.68 Note gives these examples of *if*+non-volitional *will*:

[12] If it will make any difference, I'll gladly lend you some money,

which bears resemblance to Jespersen's [4]; and

[103]

[13] If he *won't* arrive before nine, there's no point in ordering dinner for him.

In [13], the *if*-clause, which isolated would be ambiguous, is obviously meant to be non-volitional. Note the difference between [13] and 'If he *won't* get here before nine, we shall have to terminate his employment', where the stressed *won't* expresses strong volition without any doubt.

If another example will help (and that was supplied unintentionally), here is one seen on a poster displayed two weeks before Christmas on the door of a social welfare centre in London:

[14] If you will be alone on Christmas Day, let us know now.

Are could replace *will be* in that sentence, but only if it meant 'are scheduled to be', which would be more likely to apply to a busy executive than to anyone in need of charity. It could not possibly mean: 'If, when Christmas Day comes, you find yourself alone, let us know two weeks before.'

We have so far had eight sentences – [4], [6], [7], [9], [10], [11], [11*a*] and [12] – in which a non-personal subject, presumably incapable of having volition, is followed in an *if*-clause by *will*; and four sentences – [3], [8], [13] and [14] – where the personal subject of an *if*-clause is associated with *will*, without volitional colouring. It might be argued that beneath the surface of the passive verb phrase in [6] lies the notion of somebody's determination to finish the dresses; and anthropomorphists might imagine Vulcan deliberately exploding with wrath off the coast of Iceland, or Poseidon vomiting up oleic bile in revenge for the desecration of his bed. Even then we are left with enough evidence to cast doubt on Jespersen's contention that '*will* after *if* always denotes volition'.

The difference between the grammatical and the modal uses of *will* was neatly drawn by the unknown writer of:

[15] Where is the man who has the power and skill
To stem the torrent of a woman's will?
For if she will, she will, you may depend on't;
And if she won't, she won't, so there is an end on't.[5]

Despite the date of that doggerel (pre-1829), *will* in the sense of *be determined to* and *won't* signifying a stubborn refusal are still familiar features of the idiomatic English of today. Yet, as Jespersen himself pointed out, much of the volitional force of *will* has been lost. The use of the word in Matthew Arnold's

[16] We cannot kindle when we will
The fire that in the heart resides,[6]

5 Inscribed, according to the *Oxford Book of Quotations*, 'on the Pillar Erected on the Mount in Dane Field, Canterbury' and reported in *The Examiner*, 31 May 1829.
6 Opening lines of *Morality* (1852).

would now be regarded as obsolete and unacceptable; for, if we agree with
F. R. Palmer (1974:163) that there is 'no demonstrable difference between
WILL/SHALL and *be going to*', and if we agree that *I will but I'm not going to*
is nonsense, we must reject *We cannot kindle something when we're going to do
it*.

The full extent to which *will* has lost volitional force does not seem to have
been taken into account even by the most eminent of present-day
grammarians. It is remarkable that Palmer and Blandford 1969:180 should
contain

[17] /hi l'du it/ – He's willing to do it

as if the two sentences were synonymous. We can say *Jack will do it*, though
he might be most *un*willing. Certainly, *I'm willing to go* is not synonymous
with *I'll go*. I happen to have been invited to visit Japan next April. I am
perfectly *willing* to go, but that does not mean I *will* go: health or family
considerations may prevent me. Even Leech (1969:225) gives the following
equation:

[18] 'My chauffeur will help you' = 'My chauffeur is willing to help you';

and he repeats *My chauffeur will help you* as an example of willingness
(1971:78). I have more than once enjoyed the privilege of being told *My
chauffeur will drive you back to your hotel*, when all the speaker meant was
'that is what will happen, what I have arranged for you'. I am sure no
thought of willingness on the part of the chauffeur had entered the speaker's
mind.

This is not to deny that innumerable sentences containing *will* and
carrying a volitional tone have been attested, but in many of them the
volitional tone might have been provided partly, or wholly, by elements in
the sentence other than *will* itself, *eg* an agentive subject, a subject
complement, the lexical verb in the infinitive following *will* (especially if
that verb is dynamic), or an adverb of manner.[7] If example [18] had been

[18]*a* My chauffeur will help you gladly,

I would have read volition into it, the colouring being supplied more by
gladly than by *will*, and the latter serving mainly as a marker of future time.
After ten years of research into the English future, I have come to the
conclusion that present-day *will* is mainly a marker of future time, and is the
commonest and most convenient of the verbal expressions acting in that
capacity.

Moreover, since 'modal and tense values are inextricably mixed', as
Poutsma put it, it is difficult to decide in a given example of the use of *will*
whether volition was intended by the originator of that example, and

7 Further details, and examples, are given in Close 1977.

impossible to measure exactly how much volition, if any, it conveys. Palmer and Blandford (1969:183) admitted that 'Some speakers of English feel modal force much more strongly than others, and in particular the modal force of *will*'. A ruthless fund-raiser, being told

[19] I will subscribe ten pounds, provided that twenty others will do the same.[8]

would not, I think, base his estimates on assumed willingness so much as on cast-iron predictability of what cash would come in. Not surprisingly, therefore, Wekker (1976:3–14) found that of the 1,498 examples of *I/We + will* in his corpus of 600,000 words, 'approximately 78 per cent were ambiguous between a volitional and a simple future interpretation'. Checking through the first 250 of the 1,800 WILL cards in the corpus of the Survey of English Usage, I found the following:

Plain future reference	195 examples
Ambiguous between a simple future and a volitional interpretion	26 ,,
Modal, clearly volitional	27 ,,
Modal, of the type *That will be the postman, I expect*	2 ,,

As the cards examined included a batch recording British Parliamentary Question Time, over half of the 27 clearly volitional examples were of the type *Will the Secretary of State assure the House . . .?*

It is symptomatic of the difficulty of identifying and assessing volition in modern English that grammarians' examples of *if* + volitional *will* tend to be:

(*a*) obsolete, as Jespersen's [2] plainly is;
(*b*) formulaic, as in

Charles: Can I help you, Aunt Mary?
Aunt Mary: Yes, Charles, if you will.

Another formulaic example, taken from the Survey's corpus, is *If the Honourable Gentleman will allow me . . .*;

(*c*) fragmentary, as in Palmer 1974:108: *If he'll come tomorrow*. In that example, the possibility of volition is due largely to the lexical verb *come*: with say, *be (here)*, the fragment might refer to volition or not;
(*d*) apparently made up for the occasion, as in Leech (1971:60), *If you will love me, we shall be happy*.

GCE:11.68 Note gives a more authentic-sounding example in

[20] If you *won't* help us, all our plans will be ruined,

8 Quoted by Kruisinga and Erades from Wyld's *Universal English Dictionary*.

playing for safety by giving an example of 'strong' volitional *won't*.

It is probable that the conviction that '*will* after *if* always denotes volition' has led scholars in a variety of directions to get round the fact that Jespersen's pronouncement is not invariably true. Of the various explanations offered, the least satisfactory is that there has been ellipsis of 'something like' *you think* before *if* + non-volitional *will*. I reject this on the grounds that 'words are ellipted only if they are uniquely recoverable' (GCE:9.2), and I have been unable to find 'something like *you think*' in the co-text of any of the examples given above.

Another explanation is that *if* + non-volitional *will* may be found in a second-instance sentence, *ie* one that re-echoes a construction previously used in the conversation or text, with an effect that would normally be ungrammatical. An example of such an echo occurs at the end of my previous paragraph where *something* is used instead of *anything*. There may well have been such an echo in

[21] If Claude will be here tomorrow, there's no need to call him now.[9]

But the possible existence of an echo in [21] does not make the sentence anything but perfectly grammatical as it stands; whereas 'I have been unable to find something' could not be justified in the above context except as an exact repetition of previous wording.

R. L. Allen (1966:179) presents a stronger case in his argument that the problem we are discussing is a matter of 'free clause' as opposed to 'bound clause', the verb in the 'free' clause not being 'subordinate' to that in the superordinate. There may be a degree of freedom in the *if*-clauses of, say, examples [4] and [7], which could be pronounced after a pause and an intonation break, as if they expressed an afterthought. But that would not apply to other examples I have quoted.

F. R. Palmer (1974:148) explains his own example [8] and Jespersen's [4] in terms of an apparent reversal of the normal time relations in a conditional sentence: in [2] somebody's coming (referred to in the *if*-clause) precedes our telling, whereas in [4] the speaker's usefulness (referred to in the *if*-clause) is imagined as becoming manifest after his arrival. But that 'reversal of time relations' would not apply to examples [6] and [9]; and Palmer admits that his explanation makes the logic of example [4] 'quite complex'.

GCE:11.68 Note observes that 'the future contingency expressed in the *if*-clause determines a present decision'. That happens to be true of their own examples [12] and [13] as well as of [10] and [11*a*], but it is not of, say, [9] and [11].

My own answer to the problem posed in this paper is related to Leech's explanation of *if* + present tense with future reference, and to F. R. Palmer's notion of actuality (1977). Leech (1971:60) argues cogently that a conditional

9 This example, quoted as a 'second-instance sentence', occurs in a paper by N. L. Fairclough of Lancaster, who courteously allowed me to use it in my article in Bald and Ilson.

sentence of the type of example [1] has the semantic structure 'If X is a fact, then I predict Y'; in other words, if we may assume such-and-such an event or state to be a future actuality, then the following prediction can be made. The use of the present tense to express what is imagined as actual fact is very common in English. It occurs not only in conditional and temporal clauses but also normally after *see (to it) (that)*, and *take care (that)* as in *I'll see that no harm comes to him* and *Take care that you don't spill any on your clothes*; optionally after *hope, bet, Let us assume, assuming etc*; and can occur in relative and manner clauses (*eg We must fill up at the next pump we come to. Then we must act as we think best at the time.*). It can account for one of the so-called 'future tenses', as in *We cross the Rubicon tomorrow*; though here we need to remember that one meaning is expressed by the present tense referring to a definitely scheduled future and another meaning by the same tense referring to assumed future actuality, as in

[22] If you leave (*ie* are definitely scheduled to leave) at 6 o'clock tomorrow morning, you'd better get to bed now.

[22]*a* If you leave (assumed future actuality) at 6 . . ., you will be in London in good time for lunch.

This distinction is reflected in my comment on [14].

The context of example [10], which occurred in a discussion of possible forecasts, helps to make it clear that in *if*-clauses containing *will* we are concerned not with assumed future actuality but with assumed predictability. Leech's formula (1971:60) would then change from 'If X is a fact, then I predict Y', to 'If X is predictable, then the consequence is so-and-so'. The consequence may be a present decision, as in examples [11*a*], [12] and [13]. It may be to leave the speaker content, as in [3]; or it may be a suggestion that certain action be taken, as in [6] and [14]; or that a future prediction can be made, as in [9]. The possibilities are unlimited.

In some cases, whether the *if*-clause assumes predictability or future actuality makes no substantial difference in the meaning of the sentence. For example, in [4], we can assume future actuality (*if it is any use to you*) or only predictability (*if it will be . . .*): the former, in which the speaker is assuming that his presence will be useful, may sound rather presumptuous, and that is why I agree with Jespersen that *if it will be* is perhaps 'a shade politer'. In other cases, the replacement of *will* + infinitive by the present tense would necessitate a different completion of the sentences, as in the following:

[3]*a* If he turns out a brave, truth-telling Englishman, . . . I will make him my heir.

[8]*a* If he's left destitute, he can always apply for social assistance.

[9]*a* If medicine saves him, it will be a miracle.

[10]*a* If the slick comes as far as Stavanger, hundreds of miles of our coastline will be spoilt.

[13]*a* If he isn't here before nine, we'll start without him.

[14]*a* If you're alone on Christmas Day, come round here any time you like (on that day).

The notion of assumed predictability seems to provide for a reasonable explanation of all the examples I have of *if*+non-volitional *will*; and it has the advantage of breaking down the barrier between that particular construction and the more familiar *if*+the *will* of volition, since both constructions are basically realizations of assumed predictability. We can therefore classify conditional clauses with future reference according to the following scheme:

Assumed predictability   *Assumed future actuality*
(*a*) with volition
(*b*) without it
(both realized by, *eg if he/it will*)   (realized, *eg* by *if he/it is*)

DISCOURSE IN RELATION TO LANGUAGE STRUCTURE AND SEMIOTICS
J. McH. SINCLAIR

1 Introduction

Explanations that achieve respectability in linguistics are seen as being in an orderly relationship to some model or metaphor. The popular phrase 'account for' conjures up the notion of language phenomena being fixable within a precise apparatus, and the apparatus in truth is essentially a device for restatement, for representing the phenomena in such a way as, without gross distortion, is compatible with the basic metaphor or set of metaphors.

The familiar organizing metaphors of recent linguistics come from disciplines outside linguistics itself – taxonomies, networks, systems, transformations, binary codes – and are tailored to fit as closely as possible to the language events as observed (with an inevitable interaction between the model and the observations). When successful, these processes of adaptation, restatement and fitting stimulate insights into language, and focus a great deal of enthusiastic activity, and arouse the interest of scholars in associated disciplines.

Each set of metaphors can be used not only to select and evaluate language-events but also to contribute to the delineation of the domain of the discipline of linguistics. Further, a particularly successful movement can reach a peak of explicitness and generality which offers attractions to related areas of study – a sort of export trade in models. One approach to the study of general semiotics is by extension of linguistic models of proven value into the description of non-verbal sign-systems.

This paper begins by considering one organizing metaphor that has played a fundamental role in linguistic theory and description – linearity. The reason for exploring the effects of linearity is that it constitutes a good example of a constraint upon language which is characteristic of language but not of every semiotic area. From this notion is developed in outline a way of describing spoken verbal interaction, and this in turn leads to a general statement of interpretation which explicitly links structural aspects of English clause syntax with discourse functions, in terms of the way in which utterances anticipate each other. These detailed observations are then placed in a larger setting of, possibly distinct, semiotic areas.[1]

2 Linearity

The notion of linearity in language is that only one element of a structure is in process of production at any point in the representation of utterances, spoken or written, and that succession is the only ultimate relationship of elements. Since there must be more than one element of structure distinguished, a binary code is the simplest semiotic organization that meets these conditions.

The interpretation of linear succession normally involves postulation of many more complex orderings, but all eventually realized by simple succession of elements. Even in interactive discourse, where it would not be unreasonable to expect structures involving simultaneity ('they were all talking at once') a recent authoritative statement insists that turn-taking (*ie* speakers in succession) is a basic organizing principle of conversation:

> It has become obvious that, overwhelmingly, one party talks at a time, though speakers change and though the size of turns and ordering of turns vary. (Sacks, Schegloff and Jefferson 1974:699)

At the other end of the spectrum of language, the experiments reported in Ladefoged 1967 suggest, if I interpret page 156 correctly, that human aural perception tends to interpret simultaneity in terms of successivity, and thus subjects report inaccurately on the position of a meaningless noise in relation to a meaningful one.

So language structure can be represented by a linear string of symbols, each symbol standing for one element. One important principle of language

---

1 A first version of this paper was tried out in the Centre for Contemporary Cultural Studies of Birmingham University in February 1975, and I am grateful to Stuart Hall, Michael Green and their students for their helpful criticism. The formulation of the general statement of interpretation owes much to continuing discussions with Malcolm Coulthard. David Brazil checked the plausibility of the examples, reserving his own position; Jack Allanson explained the principle of *Table* 1 to me, several times.

A revised version became a working paper at Burg Wartenstein symposium number 66 in August 1975, and as a result of discussions there it has been completely rewritten. Peter Roe, Deirdre Burton and Mike Stubbs have all helped to clarify this final version.

structure, expressed in this way, is that not all the possible strings occur: in fact only a very small proportion occurs. *Table* 1 shows the number of possible structures varying with (*a*) the maximum length in elements, of any one string, and (*b*) the maximum number of different elements that are available.

Table 1

		Maximum length of string in elements				
Maximum no of different elements		1	2	3	4	5
	1	1	2	3	4	5
	2	2	6	14	30	62
	3	3	12	39	120	363
	4	4	20	84	340	1364
	5	5	30	155	780	3905

On the basis of *Table* 1, English clause structure, with primary elements S, P, C, O, and A, has a potential of 3905 different configurations. The number used by the language with any regularity is under 50.

One way of presenting this major restriction upon language structure is in terms of predictability. If there were an area of natural language patterning that utilized all the possibilities of *Table* 1, it would not be possible to predict an element on the basis of what had already been chosen, because any element could occur at any position. (The notation of integers is a ready example.) But in the restricted set of possibilities that are conventionally available to a language user, the predictive power of an unfinished structure must be high.

Statistical studies of the sound and writing systems of English show the large redundancy of those, in terms of the mathematically possible combinations (a useful annotated bibliography is to be found in Zettersten 1969). I should like to emphasize that redundancy is a feature of language structure in general; a major feature that is found in every instance, not only in the surface codes but in any symbolic representation of any part of the structure.

Unfortunately this feature is at best only implicit in grammars – they are preoccupied with occurrence and non-occurrence, and they do not state what the possible occurrence is, given the distinctions that are required to formulate the grammars. Syntax is rarely presented as a set of limitations upon the free combination of those elements that require to be distinguished.

Language structure is far more complex than a linear string might suggest; in fact our familiar descriptive systems are devices for illustrating how non-linear relationships can be represented in linear strings. In order to model the occurrence of the sound or graphic substance, a procession of symbols indicating segments will not suffice, and a many-layered apparatus is required, each layer of which makes a distinctive contribution to the ordering and is in a precise relationship to adjacent layers.

3 Structure and meaning

Of the various types of organization of layers in a description, one is exemplified in *Fig* 1. This is a simplified version of a syntactic system, showing how the choice of MOOD, which contributes to the function of a sentence in discourse, can be related to the elements of the structure of free clauses.

Further instances of particular moods, and further conditions upon the occurrence of structures, can be added by specifying greater detail in the subclassification of elements of clause structure.

The point to be made in this instance is the nature of the relationship between the stages of the hierarchy. The elements S (Subject) and P (Predicator), and their linear placement, are fairly arbitrary signals which in certain configurations realize mood choices. The mood choice itself is no guarantee of the ultimate function of a sentence in discourse, because other factors irrelevant in the consideration of clause structure affect the organization at other places.

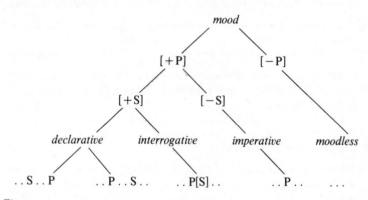

Fig 1

Perhaps 'arbitrary' is a slightly misleading characterization of the relationship between stages in a description. It is no accident that the person to whom a command is addressed does not need to be named, hence the explicable feature [−S] in the imperative mood. But

(*a*) the feature [−S] states that there is no S in the clause, not that it is optional.

(b) commands may be uttered in any of the four moods, and a simple imperative is only used in certain situations where the relationship of participants is clear, and the speaker thinks he has the right of command. Imperatives uttered in other circumstances may be interpreted as suggestions, invitations and the like.

(c) it is possible to command a person to have something done, with or without the agent nominated, so the recipient of a command may not be the same individual as the performer of the action designated.

Because of factors such as these, the occurrence of an English free clause with a certain form of P and the exclusion of an S signifies a choice entirely within grammar, implying no general informal association between meaning and structure. This is the sense of 'arbitrary' used here. Mnemonics such as 'declarative', 'imperative', suggest that some unit of general meaning is delivered by a choice of that branch from the node above, or in the characterization of an . . S . . . P . . clause structure with that label.

Some of the labels may indicate a tendency for the eventual discourse function to be linked to a particular syntactic choice, and it may even be possible, within limited circumstances, to provide statistical evidence to support such a claim. But it is important to note that the type of association between a choice and the syntactic label for it is not itself valid within syntax.

In general, then, an element of structure in a linguistic description may

(a) realize or partly realize another element of structure at a more abstract level

(b) be realized by one or more elements of structure at a less abstract level

– without any systematic selection or ordering of structural elements except the record of choices that have been made, informally represented by the conventional labels of syntax.

4 Conforming and evolving

I wish to develop the point about predictiveness a little further. Those who study the structure of paragraphs, and patterns of contributions to interactive spoken discourse, have long claimed for them a predictive quality, without easily capturing the structural rules. Question-answer pairs are simple instances from conversation very much used in examples, but not very typical, since a question, and particularly a *wh*-question, is highly limiting in its prediction of the set of fitting answers.

It is illuminating to regard each TURN in a discourse as a predictive classification of all possible next turns – and even though literally anything CAN happen it is not difficult to supply a comprehensive guide to the next utterance. The next turn then is classified by its predecessor and

[114]

simultaneously sets up a new prediction, and so on. But each turn, although it must fit into the classification which has been devised for it, can choose which class it will realize – and the classification includes such options as challenging the predictions of the previous turn, and reopening after a conclusion.

Subsentence grammar is not normally represented in this way because it is seen as conforming rather than evolving, but the analysis of discourse advanced here assumes that the same linguistic principles apply both above and below the watershed of the sentence (and its counterpart in speech). The contrast between conforming and evolving is not always obvious in written language because of the further option in writing of tidying up the spontaneous structures that are more typical of speech. It is not yet clear whether the exercise of this option results in fundamentally different structures, or major or minor shifts of emphasis. The rest of this paper therefore concentrates on conversation.

An approach to conversation that expects it to conform to predetermined rules will assume, for example, that when a question of a certain kind occurs the discourse is incomplete unless and until an appropriate answer occurs, even after intervening material such as (Schegloff 1972) 'insertion sequences'. However, a question may just as well be immediately superseded and never returned to; furthermore, an 'answer' to it that does not immediately succeed the question must be prefaced by a phrase such as *well then*, which is otherwise a marker of a considerable structural boundary. Clearly, in terms of some kind of RETROSPECTIVE structuring the answer recalls the question, and this contrasts with the predictive or PROSPECTIVE structuring which signals a break in the evolving pattern of conversation.

5 Structure and function

There is emerging from current research a way of relating structure to function that may provide a framework for the delineation of rules of interpretation and presupposition. It may help to break a vicious circle that has restrained work in socially-sensitive language description for some years – the lack of a classification of situations which can be used to focus language descriptions but which is independent of language. The interpretation potential set out below offers a basis for empirical comparison of verbal encounters where matters of status, role and occasion can be evaluated against structure.

The key unit in discourse structure is the EXCHANGE, which is the minimal unit of interaction (Sinclair and Coulthard 1975). We have postulated several types, but no acceptable generalized structure as yet. See, however, Coulthard and Brazil 1978 and Burton 1977. One guiding criterion for exchange termination is the extent of relevance of those units of meaning which have a prospective function. The exchange can be seen as an accumulation of shared meaning (hence the tendency to elliptical structures in a non-initial position), and some of that meaning is a set of prescriptions for the immediately ensuing utterances. Consider the following sequels to the command 'Sit down!'

(*a*) No I won't.
(*b*) No, I'll stand for a while, if I may.
(*c*) Say that again, will you.
(*d*) Sit where?
(*e*) Come off it, Bill.
(*f*) Don't you boss me around.

The first two examples are refusals to comply, which therefore question whether the assumption of the initiator – that he was in a position to command – was correct. Locally, he has certainly miscalculated either in controlling his addressee (*a*) or in a slightly overbearing politeness (*b*). (*c*) and (*d*) suggest that the command has not been clearly delivered but by not accepting the command without question they establish a basis for sabotaging the prospections, and can carry varying shades of irony and aggression. (*e*) and (*f*) challenge the appropriacy of the command directly. All six examples indicate an exchange boundary immediately before them on the grounds that the basic projection of the initiator is not acceptable. The minimal case, (*a*), will require further elucidation in another paper.

Verbal sequels to a command, then, must all take for granted the right of the initiator to command and the obligation of the addressee(s) to comply: so relevant action will follow, with a murmured apology or an expression of acquiescence. Anything else will terminate the exchange and simultaneously initiate a new one.

Although there are some problems of identification, this criterion for exchange boundary is applicable in general. It thus becomes possible to consider which sequences of move can occur within the same exchange, and which demand a boundary between them.

Those that are identified as potential elements of the same exchange can then be examined to clarify the structure of exchanges, and to add further detail to the criteria for co-presence in an exchange. Simple sequences of question followed by answer, statement or command and acknowledgment, seem capable of systematic description. But many other reasonable possibilities cause descriptive trouble. Examples [1–14] show a variety of possible pairs of utterances, some illustrating points which have already attracted scholarly attention. (Note that only the first word or phrase of the *b* member is given: in most conversation we are not so cryptic, and many of those without asterisks may seem more natural when extended.)

Those that seem to indicate mismatches or breakdown in communication are asterisked. Highly specialized encounters, *eg* quiz games, are not taken into account.

[1]a My name is Smith	*[1]b Yes (low pitch)
[2]a Today is Saturday	[2]b Ah (medium pitch)
[3]a I call my cat Herbert	*[3]b No (low pitch)
[4]a Have you ever had measles?	[4]b No (any pitch)
[5]a Is that a Rembrandt?	*[5]b No (low pitch)
[6]a You'll have coffee, won't you?	[6]b Please
[7]a Do you have a light?	[7]b Here [+activity]
[8]a Where have I told you not to go?	[8]b Here
[9]a Which would you like?	[9]b The tartan one
[10]a When will you be ready?	[10]b Oh sorry [+activity]
[11]a It's stuffy in here	*[11]b I suppose so
[12]a I need a volunteer	[12]b Sir! [+activity]
[13]a There must be an ashtray somewhere	[13]b Just in front of you
[14]a It's nine o'clock, isn't it?	[14]b Oh gosh [+activity]

[1a] proffers information but if interpreted as an introduction, the 'channel-open' response of [1b] is inappropriate. [3a] can be acknowledged, queried or evaluated (*How interesting!*) but not denied on a low pitch. [5a] is apparently an example of a *yes/no* question, but it could only be denied by [5b] if gross contempt was within the conventions of the situation. [8a] is a question for which [8b] is an apparently appropriate answer, since the *b* speaker would normally be in the prohibited place, but woe betide the child who uses [8b]! [11a] has implications of disapproval that [11b] ignores. Among the examples that seem fitting, [6b] is not among the predicted syntactic responses to a tag question, nor [10b] to an information question, while [12b] is hardly a typical way of acknowledging a piece of information.

It seems that some quite elaborate rules of interpretation will be needed to cope with this variety (see Labov 1970) but the first step is simple enough. Grammars would probably set out options for an initiating utterance that relate to the mood system sketched in *Fig* 1 above.

Statement (requires acknowledgment)
Question (requires verbal response)
Command (requires non-verbal or verbal activity)

– with maybe Exclamation as a fourth possibility. However, the evidence suggests that the link between structure and function, while still precise, is not as direct as the above might suggest.

We shall now give a functional categorization of main clause types, choosing a criterion which is very important in the description of oral interaction. A description of conversation has to include how speakers negotiate turn-taking, and how a coherent discourse emerges from utterances which arise from different sources. One aspect of organization that one might expect to find, then, would be PROSPECTIVE patterns: utterances which anticipate or invite verbal or non-verbal contributions from other participants.

It is often held that people use language to transmit information from one to another. Prospectively, a participant receiving information would be expected simply to acknowledge it, with a muttered indication of 'message received' on a low-key intonation, or just a nod of the head. The classic structure which can be used for just this is that where the subject precedes the predicator. So we can produce *Table* 2.

Table 2

FORM	FUNCTION	ANTICIPATION
SP	transmit information	acknowledgment

Another common structure is said to be the *yes/no* question, where a proposition is offered to another person for a simple decision process. The prospection in the question form is that a fitting answer is either *yes* or *no*, delivered in an intonation that implies nothing beyond that decision. The characteristic clause structure is positive (rather than negative) and the subject is inside the predicator, *Table* 3:

Table 3

FORM	FUNCTION	ANTICIPATION
P [S] (positive)	offer proposition for decision	*yes/no*

At this point we must pause and review the functions that we have put forward. Do people say things purely or even mainly for the purpose of transmitting information? Do they go around fishing for simple decisions? A few moments' reflection or observation suggests that no substantial portion of human verbal behaviour is covered by *Tables* 2 and 3. They seem to suggest speech that has content but no purpose which is distinct from the content. Information is offered gratuitously – not in execution of any particular plan. Individuals offer each other decisions in an entirely detached fashion, unconcerned as to what the answer will be so long as it is either *yes* or *no*. The model of semiotic areas which follows in this paper (Section 7) suggests that all communication is the execution of a purpose which originates from a source different from the content.

There are clause structures in English which lie rather ambiguously between statement and question, and which clearly anticipate the listener's acceptance of a proposition.

This is your coat, isn't it? (tag-question)
Isn't this your coat? (negative P[S])

[118]

Various factors, particularly intonation, vary the exact signalling of these utterances, but they all signal that they have a proposition to offer, and invite acceptance of it, *Table* 4:

Table 4

FORM	FUNCTION	ANTICIPATION	EXAMPLE	
SP P[S] (positive)	transmit information offer proposition for decision	acknowledgment *yes/no*	London is the capital of Britain Is this High Street?	A
P[S] (negative) } Tag question }	offer proposition for acceptance	acceptance	Isn't this High Street? This is High Street, isn't it?	B

It is contended that the vast majority of so-called statements and *yes/no* questions are in fact interpreted as being of type B in *Table* 4.

There are other questions in English, often called 'information questions' or '*wh*-questions', which have the following formal features in most instances:

(*a*) the initial word is *who/whose/which/what/why/how/when*
(*b*) the sequence of elements of clause structure is basically interrogative.

The role of these questions is to invite much more particular behaviour of the addressee; they impose a greater control over what follows. To fit their anticipation fully, the response must be propositional, and must retain the framework of presuppositions set up by the original question. Everyone can remember times in crowded pubs or parties where they had to play the role of listener without being able to hear. So long as the discourse is of types A and B there is little danger of a major breakdown; but if the speaker turns to information questions it is suddenly necessary to hear the question precisely.

Syntactically, one can say that the anticipations of structures in *Tables* 2, 3, and 4 are all adequately realized by selections from small closed lists of conventional words and phrases. The *wh*-question demands a response that, however elliptical, is a selection from a theoretically limitless set of alternatives.

Table 5

FORM	FUNCTION	ANTICIPATION	EXAMPLE	
wh+P[S]	offer guidelines to response	relevant proposition	Where is your office?	C

It should be noted here that these questions are peculiarly open to being challenged, *eg* 'I don't have an office', but that such challenges break the continuation of presupposition from initiation to response and therefore introduce an exchange boundary. The same with 'How should I know?' 'Where do you think?' 'Good question' etc.

Many instances of structure-types A and B can be found with a similar function and anticipation to *wh*-questions. Compare the following, finding an appropriate intonation:

[15]*a* Is this a Rembrandt?
   b Is this an ashtray?

(*b*) will normally be interpreted as 'Where can I find an ashtray?', whereas (*a*) merely seeks acceptance.

   c I suppose she's ill again.
     (Why is she not here?)
   d Isn't this the way?
     (How do you do this job?)

The direct question is avoided by substituting a suggestion, perhaps using a reporting structure, like (*c*) or (*e*).

   e I don't know what to wear.

The structural table is completed by the imperative form, which demands activity, with or without acknowledgment. It is readily seen that other clause structures can have the same function. For example, there is a range of *wh*-questions of the type shown in example [8*a*] above, where control over another's activity is intended. A little reflection confirms that any clause structure at all can function in the same way as we associate with the imperative. The full picture is shown in *Table* 6.

Table 6

FORM	FUNCTION	ANTICIPATION	EXAMPLE	
S P P[S] (positive)	transmit content offer proposition for decision	acknowledgment *yes/no*	London is the capital of Britain Is this High Street?	A
P[S] (negative) Tag question	offer proposition for acceptance	acceptance	Isn't this High Street? This is High Street, isn't it?	B
wh + P[S]	offer guidelines to response	relevant proposition	Where is your office?	C
P (no S)	suggest activity	activity ± acknowledgment	Get me a pencil and paper	D

The relation now proposed between form and function is quite different from that suggested in *Fig* 1. One further general statement is required to explain all the mismatches that have been noted:

WHERE CLAUSE STRUCTURES REALIZE INITIATING MOVES IN EXCHANGES, THEY CAN BE INTERPRETED AND RESPONDED TO ACCORDING TO TABLE 6, EITHER HORIZONTALLY OR LOWER DOWN THE TABLE.

Note that this statement concerns the interpretation of forms, which is a mutual activity, and not the province of any one participant. The initiator may choose an SP structure which carries a strong suggestion that it should be interpreted as type B (*That's a lovely dress*), type C (*I must sit down*), or D (*I need a drink*). The details of the encounter, personal and status relationships among participants, personalities, climate, time of day and many other factors may provoke the responder to another interpretation, or several responders to different interpretations. Any participant may re-interpret or discuss the interpretation overtly. *Table* 6 and the statement of interpretation can be used to suggest a reason why the matching of form and function is not one-to-one. The higher the form is in the figure, the less it demands of the other participants, as can be seen

(*a*) by inspecting the ANTICIPATION column, and
(*b*) by noting that level A allows 4 interpretations, B allows 3, C allows 2.

Imperatives are only used in English where their interpretation is guaranteed, because they can only be interpreted as suggesting activity. Keeping to type A forms reduces social risk, but of course also relinquishes clear control.

Halliday (1975 and spoken conference contribution) notes that children's acquisition of communicative competence proceeds in stages up the levels of the FUNCTION column, *Table* 6, starting long before they can control the clause structures. Attempts at the direct control of others precede getting adults to say certain things, which precedes securing acceptance of the child's propositions, and type A behaviour comes late, if ever.

We can now return to examples [1] to [14] and explain the oddities. In [1] the SP structure is interpreted as type A, where it would normally be seen as doing more than transmitting content. In [3] the SP structure is taken as offering a decision, and this is particularly implausible since a type A form exists for this, and conversion to it (*Do I call my cat Herbert?*) indicates how unlikely that interpretation would be. In [5] a P[S] structure is taken as type A where it would normally be read as type B; in [8] a *wh*+P[S] structure is read horizontally instead of as type D, in [11] an SP structure which might be B, C or D is read as A.

6 Intention and effect

The foregoing discussion has tried to suggest that there is a middle ground of mutual interpretation of utterances which is not necessarily dominated by the intentions of any participant and which is independent of what actually happens. A study of what actually happens, related to this account of interpretation, offers new prospects for sociolinguistics. For example, encounters can in principle be classified according to the way in which invitations are characteristically interpreted. An encounter in which one participant's *wh*-questions were nearly always taken as type D (*Where is my pipe?—Oh – sorry, I'll get it right away*) denotes a different relationship from one where they are taken as type C (*Down the side of the chair again, I should imagine*). More detailed classification of type D could add further sensitivity, and lead to a typology of situations based upon the way in which the participants agree on the meaning of what they say. This should be superior to register classifications, based upon the forms only, informal labels for the encounters based on participants and occasions, which are nearly circular, and notional analyses, based largely on informal guesses at the functions.

Formal grammars stop at the sentence for various reasons, some of them good. There may well be an absolute restraint on the range of effect of linguistic choices. Language works by the ordering of very small components, in relation to the broader dimensions of some semiotic systems. A few microseconds of continuously variable sound or a minute squiggle can realize a linguistic unit. It would be reasonable to suppose that as the size of units in verbal communication rises, the chances of linguistics offering a relevant mode of description must diminish. I am not here going to discuss the value of linguistics as a useful general model for all communication, but restrict myself to the detection of large-scale linguistic structures which can be systematically related to the smallest units of language.

There is little doubt that the EXCHANGE is a defensible linguistic unit, the minimum unit of interaction, relatable to a primary structure of Initiation, Response and Feedback. Much of the content of an exchange may be chosen according to the priorities and structure of, or actually realized by, non-linguistic systems, but the rules of exchange structure provide the essential organization of the utterances.

But in discourse extending over a considerably greater extent, it is unlikely that the planning will have much to do with the nature of language. A doctor meeting a new patient will no doubt say things that set up short-term prospective expectations, but a doctor sorting out his appointments and other duties for the day will be unlikely to see the language he will use as a relevant factor in his calculations.

7 Areas of semiotics

SEMIOTICS is not defined in this paper, but certain assumptions need to be made about it. It is thought to require division into several distinct areas which, because of the raw materials each organizes, suggest different categories of description. Three semiotic areas are noted below by way of example, but no claim is made to be comprehensive, exhaustive or even accurate in suggesting divisions.

The area of REALIZATION includes language. The emphasis of organization is on the actual process of signalling among human beings, where the nature of codes, the structure and formation of messages, and the variation between individuals are the primary focus. Language so dominates this area that it may be difficult for us to think separately about other independent systems of realization. However, the case currently being made for the existence of kinesic realization systems, and the international sign-codes (toilet-door languages), and the sophistication of diagrammatic representations in, for example, operating instructions for international products – all these suggest that language has potential rivals, which like the deaf sign languages will start by showing a genetic affinity to natural language, and then may exploit some unique features of their own condition.

The area of CONTENT records, stores, classifies and organizes what is known; Popper's (1972) concept of objective knowledge is a sufficient metaphor for the purposes of this paper while Roe (1977) is much concerned with contrasts between content and realization. It would be imprudent to assume that the categories and relations in the content area are at all similar to those of realization; the constraints of interaction need not be relevant at all. One need only look at the extensive apparatus of diagrams, artificial codes, illustrations, multidimensional models, etc that have been required so far in order to aid the realization of content, to reject the likelihood of systematic similarity of structure between content and realization.

The implications for linguistics (for example the status and design of a semantics) will not be pursued here. Language may very likely reflect, in a partial and ad hoc fashion, some of the major categories of content, and it is difficult to guess in the present state of our knowledge how far the study of this reflection is a wild-goose chase. Certainly much of the staple diet of traditional semantics (kinship terms, colours, seasons, numerals, etc) concerns content which is particularly simple and close to linguistic organization, and therefore most likely to delude the investigator. Testimony from the Arts and Sciences insists that some, if not many, if not all, items of content are genuinely inexpressible despite great skill in the manipulation of realization systems.

The area of PURPOSE concerns plans, goals, intentions, motivations, aims, strategies, tactics, implications, presuppositions. Whatever causes an individual to engage in communications, respond to them, or disengage arises in this area, as does the mass of decisions leading to the particular forms of the utterances produced. It is tempting to consider this area as primary, or dominating, but not necessary, since all three areas contribute to the design of communications. The only point being stressed here is the difference between the three areas. The formulation of purposes and the methods used to further them does not need to have any relationship at all with either the rules for making up messages or the underlying patterns of content that are referred to. Each may well cast a shadow on the other two, and the areas of content and purpose are not yet accessible to direct observation, so their nature must be inferred from various realization systems.

If areas such as those of content, purpose and realization are unlikely to be structured in identical ways, we can postulate certain buffer areas that mitigate the effects of the mismatching. They may be hybrid concoctions, like charts, diagrams, maps and figures, or they may be elastic categories, not rigidly constrained by any one semiotic system. An example of these may be the patterns of style, which are acknowledged to be indefinite, not entirely predictable and capable of producing powerful ancillary meaning (Sinclair 1975). For language, there are such patterns latent in the typography, layout, sounds and shapes of words, patterns of similarity, contrast, oddity and licence.

The argument of this paper is that language description can no longer ignore the distinctive considerations of interactive discourse; that connections between patterns of language and meanings are indeed capable of precise explication, but require new descriptive apparatus; and that semiotics generally will advance at present more surely by assuming that different areas demand bespoke theories, rather than searching for some very general and abstract set of categories and relationships.

POST-INTONATION-CENTRE
PROSODIC SHADE
IN THE MODERN ENGLISH CLAUSE
JAN FIRBAS

It has been rightly pointed out (Crystal 1975:3) that GCE is the first comprehensive grammar for English to give a section to intonation. It is also the first English grammar to devote a special section to problems of 'focus, theme and emphasis', in other words to those of functional sentence perspective. It will therefore perhaps not be inappropriate to honour Randolph Quirk by presenting him with a contribution concerning the relations between grammatical (syntactic) structure, FSP and intonation.

In his well-known article 'Linear Modification', D. L. Bolinger comes to the conclusion that within a sentence, or subordinate clause for that matter, 'gradation of position creates gradation of meaning when there are no interfering factors' (1965:288). In terms of communicative dynamism ($=$CD) this means that in the direction from beginning to end a clause[1] will show a gradual rise in CD provided there are no interfering factors. By a degree of CD carried by a linguistic element at the moment of utterance I mean the relative extent to which at that moment the element contributes towards the amplification (development) of the discourse (*cf*, for example, Firbas 1971).

A clause provides a distributional field of CD (Firbas 1968:41 and 1975:320 *ff*; Svoboda 1968). Within this field, the clause constituents – Subject, Verb, Complement, Object, Adverbial (GCE:35; Quirk and

---

1 In the present paper, 'clause' covers both a superordinate clause (a sentence) and a subordinate clause. It will not be used in reference to a structure lacking a finite verb.

Greenbaum 1973:12) – function as communicative units (Svoboda 1968).[2]
The distribution of degrees of CD over the clause constituents makes the
clause function in a definite kind of perspective (hence the term 'functional
sentence/clause perspective', or for short FSP).[3] Simultaneously, the clause
functions as a distributional field of prosodic weight, the gamut of prosodic
weight being constituted by absence of stress, partial stress, non-kinetic
(non-nuclear) stress and kinetic (nuclear) stress (cf Gimson 1970:267).[4]
Following Leech and Svartvik 1975, one could describe the nucleus 'as a
strongly stressed syllable which marks a major change of pitch direction, ie
where the pitch goes up or down' (1975:36). With, for the time being, one
proviso, I regard the last nucleus within a distributional field as the most
prominent prosodic feature and, following F. Daneš, refer to it as the
intonation centre (= IC; cf Daneš 1957:27, 153). As to the proviso, I do not
regard as an IC a low rise after a fall (cf, for example, Halliday 1970b:38,
O'Connor 1973:82 ff).

It is assumed that there is, if not perfect, then at least very high,
congruence between the gamut of CD and the gamut of prosodic weight. In
keeping with linear modification, the last element within a clause should
then carry the highest degree of CD and bear the IC. This indeed holds
good for the end of an unmarked clause in Present-day Standard Czech. To
a lesser extent, on the other hand, it applies to the end of an unmarked
English, German, Dutch, or even Russian clause.

In the present notes I will deal with such ends of Modern Educated
Southern British spoken clauses as deviate from linear modification. I will
concentrate on the final sections that come after the IC within such clauses
and are, in consequence, prosodically overshadowed by it. Elements
constituting such a final section will be described as occurring in the 'post-
IC prosodic shade', or 'shade' for short.[5]

Examples are mainly taken from three phonetic readers prepared by
prominent British phoneticians: Arnold and Tooley 1972 (A–T), Lewis
1977 (L), MacCarthy 1956 (McC). With a few exceptions, the examples
present the IC bearers in boldface. Examples with no IC bearers in boldface
will be commented on specially. Where necessary, at least the minimum
context will be adduced in round brackets. Within them, the IC bearers will
not be set in boldface. For typographic reasons (and in order to conform to

2 An attribute, in clausal or non-clausal form, constitutes only part of a clause constituent
(Svoboda 1968). The distributional field of CD which an attribute, together with its headword,
provides will not be analysed in this paper. On the possibility, or even necessity, of splitting up
the finite verb into two communicative units – constituted by the temporal and modal exponents
and the notional component of the finite verb – see, for example, Firbas 1975:321.

3 The basic concepts of FSP have been discussed by me in various other places; see Firbas and
Golková 1975.

4 The prosodic weight of a clause constituent (communicative unit) is determined by the
weightiest prosodic feature the constituent (communicative unit) bears.

5 I am intentionally introducing the designation 'shade', for the phenomenon denoted by it does
not always coincide with what has come to be termed 'tail'.

the practice adopted by other contributions to the present homage volume) the different types of tonetic notation used by the readers have not been retained and Crystal's notation (*cf* Crystal and Davy 1969:24–40) has been employed instead.

There are three major causes that make the final elements of a clause appear in the shade.

It is not necessary to dwell too long on the FIRST cause – the context dependence of an element. An element is context dependent if it conveys information derivable from the preceding verbal context and/or if it refers to a perfectly obvious item belonging to the situational context of immediate experience shared by the speaker and listener, context dependence or independence ultimately depending on the communicative purpose entertained by the speaker at the point that, at the moment of utterance, has been reached in the development of the discourse. It should be evident that in regard to context dependence, context is here understood in the narrowest possible way.

Context dependence accounts for the frequent occurrence in the shade of anaphorically used pronouns and anaphorically used pro-words in general. But any element may be rendered context dependent. Context dependent elements will carry the lowest degree of CD and their occurrence in the shade is quite in keeping with this low communicative value. [1] and [2] will illustrate.

[1] (|NÔ| · |THĔY gave me this WRÌST watch| ·) I've |ÀLways| |WÀNTed one| McC 67.24

[2] (|WĔ've all been 'down with FLÙ| – |one after the ÒTHer| . . .) – . . . I'm |SÔRRy to 'hear you've been 'having ↓FLÚ in the 'family| McC 71.16

The SECOND of the causes relegating elements to the shade is to be sought in the character of the semantic content of the relegated element and the semantic relations into which the element has entered. The semantic character and relations either permit or necessitate the relegation of an element to the shade.

In [3–8] the adverbials of time and place, occurring in the shade, provide a temporal and/or spatial environment of an action or event in general, and not belonging to the core of the message merely function as temporal or spatial settings.

[3] (|ₗNÒ| ·) but I |read a re↓vÌEW of it the 'other ↑DÁY| McC 58.04

[4] (and |these ↓LÁdies| · are the famous |FÀLLS| – –) if you can |stop ↓TÀLKing for a ↑MÓment| – (you'll be able to |HĔAR| their |MÌGHTy| |RÒAR|) L 36:2:3.01

[5] you |keep such a 'lot of ↑RÙBBish in your 'bag| A–T 31.02

[6] |WÀITer| · there's a |FLŸ in my soup| L 36:2:4.01

[7] the |tide was ↓ÌN when I 'first 'walked along the ↑FRÓNT| McC 60.18

[8] if you |want to be ↑WÌTTY in 'what you 'say| McC 65.09

The environment of an action or event in general, however, is not constituted by temporal and spatial components only. Other concomitant circumstances are expressed by other types of adverbial, *eg* adverbials of condition [9], viewpoint [10], attendant circumstance [11].

[9] |they can go for ↑WÀLKS if the 'weather's ↑FÍNE| L 44:24.07

[10] (|MÒRNing| · a|NÒTHer cold DÁY|−− |YÈS| · |îsn't it|−) sur|PRÌSingly 'cold for the 'time of ↑YÉAR| McC 71.04

[11] (in the |ŎLD days of 'course| · it was a case of sending |many more ↑TÈLegrams around| · |WÀsn't it|−) or getting a |MÈSSenger| to de|liver a note by HÀND in 'cases of 'real ↑ÚRGency| McC 75.22

Some adverbial elements − if context independent − are conspicuous by their virtual absence from the shade.[6] This applies to adverbials of purpose and cause. (If context independent and occurring in end-position, they carry the highest degree of CD; *cf* Golková 1968.) Let me add that temporal adverbials are far more frequent in the shade than adverbials of place (*cf* Horová 1976).

Concomitant information is also given by various types of sentence adverb expressing the speaker's opinion on the message conveyed [12–15].

[12] |what was it LÌKE on the 'whole| McC 60.15

[13] the |BĚST places| were |more than we could af↑FÒRD of course| McC 60.10

[14] I |wonder whether it's 'best for the 'ordinary PÈRson though| McC 76.24

[15] (|ₗYÈS| · I |ₗHÀVE|−) but I |don't know 'what it MĚANS really| McC 65.05

Phatic elements, *ie* such as convey general sociability rather than specific meaning, naturally function in the shade as well. They would come under the heading of what Kingdon (1958:100) refers to as adjections. Question tags, vocatives and structures of the *I'm afraid/you know* type, and to a certain extent even sentence adverbs, belong here [16–18]. Grammatically speaking, some of these elements − *eg*, the question tags and the *you know* type of adjection − are clausal structures. The very fact that they appear in the shade and in this way function within the prosodic distributional field of the sentence to which they are adjected only testifies to their concomitant character [16], [17].

[16] |MĬNE's from the LÌbrary| · so I |can't ↑"LĚND it you I'm a'fraid| McC 58.21

[17] |I 'never SMÒKE you know| McC 63.01

[18] can you |think of any ↓MÓRE Father| McC 65.15

6 The conclusions to be offered here are partly based on excerpts collected by Miss I. Fialová and Mrs V. Hranáčová, students of the Brno Department of English. Their co-operation is gratefully acknowledged.

Another type of shaded element is constituted by a subject and a verb occurring after a piece of direct speech they introduce into discourse [19]. The degrees of CD carried by direct speech are undoubtedly higher than those of the shaded subject and verb.

[19] a |real BÀRgain the 'man said| A–T 25.30

A case of particular interest is the context independent shaded finite verb. I have attempted to show elsewhere (Firbas 1968, 1969) that in regard to a context independent object, subject complement, object complement, and adverbial functioning as a specification, not as a setting, the verb will as a rule not exceed any of these elements in CD. In the absence of these elements, it will not even exceed a context independent subject in CD. This is because in the development of discourse the primary function of the verb is an introductory one. It consists in introducing into the discourse notions conveyed by context independent elements. This explains why the verb comparatively rarely comes to carry the highest degree of CD and to function as IC bearer. It also explains why in [20–26] the verb is prosodically overshadowed by the subject.

[20] |miss JÒNES is coming to lunch to↓MÓRRow| L 37:5.01
[21] . . . if |all 'that ↑BÒOZing goes on ↓THÉRE| L 44:24.17
[22] there are |ₗLÒTS| of vÒLuntary| ac|ₕTÌVities laid ↓ÓN| L 44:24.06
[23] |too much like the 'pictures your MÔTHer 'paints| A–T 27.16
[24] |PĂRTly I 'think| · be|cause my ↑PÀRents 'wanted it| A–T 63.30
[25] the |ₗLÉvel of TÈACHing 'drops| A–T 65.29
[26] I |sÀY FÁTHer| · |what does ab'breviÀTION mean| McC 64.06

It is worth noticing that in [27] and [28] the introductory function is taken over by the entire copula-plus-subject-complement combination. Like the verbs of the preceding examples, the combination is overshadowed by the context independent subject.

[27] her |PÀRents were 'keen| A–T 65–11
[28] |I ↑CÀN't| · my |HÀNDS are wet| L 41:16.05

At this point I should like to insert a note on the distinction between setting and specification, at the same time touching on two questions: on that of an unequivocal indication (signalling) of this distinction in written and in spoken language and on that of an unequivocal indication (signalling) of the communicative purpose of the speaker. First some comment on [29–33].

[29] |YÈS · but it's |no 'fun if you 'live well out ↑TŎWN| L 44:23.04
[30] it was a |pity we couldn't 'buy him a 'beer mug in the ↑'Portobello RÒAD| A–T 25.22
[31] (I'm |still 'looking for my ↑NÒTEcase| –) I |know I 'put it in my 'bag

this ↑MǑRNing|–(with my |PÙRSE|–) I |had them ↑BÒTH| · I'm |SÙRE|
· when I |paid the ↑FÀRES| A–T 29.31

[32] (|YÈS|–) and you |had it in the · Portobello RÒAD|–(|don't you
re↓MÉMber|–) I |gave you what was 'left of my MÒNEY| · |after I'd
'bought the CÀNDLE 'sticks| A–T 29.35

[33] it's sup|posed to be 'in by to↑MÒRRow|

In the above examples, the final adverbials are all I C-bearers and cannot
therefore function as settings. Belonging to the core of the message, they are
to be interpreted as specifications. Now written language is not totally
devoid of clues signalling the distinction between settings and specifications,
but the shade and the I C are extra devices employed by spoken language in
lowering the frequency of equivocal (multifunctional) cases, *ie* such as at the
moment of utterance permit of more than one interpretation of their
functional perspective. Let us compare [34] and [35].

[34] (I |haven't · finished my ↑ÈSSAY 'yet|–) It's sup|posed to be ↑ÌN by
toMÓRROW| A–T 61.01

[35] it's sup|posed to be 'in by to↑MÒRRow|

Providing the final adverbial with the IC in [35] and placing it in the
shade in [34], spoken language respectively makes it function as a setting
and as a specification. In the absence of tonetic marks, even a wider printed
context of [34] may fail to offer a definite clue to the interpretation of the
adverbial.

But even the system of spoken language may show places where
unequivocal interpretation cannot be ensured. A case in point is, for
instance, parallel nuclei, *ie* successive nuclei having the same tonetic
realization; *cf* [36] first version, [37], [38], [39].

[36] you can be |ₗLÓOKing 'over that 'last ↑CHÀPTer| · while the |KÈTTle
boils| McC 70.31
you can be |ₗLÓOKing 'over that 'last ↑CHÀPter| while the |ₗKÉTTle
boils|
you can be |looking 'over that 'last 'chapter while the ↑KÈTTle boils|
|while the ↑KÉTTle boils| · you can be |looking 'over that 'last
↑CHÀPTer|

[37] we |DÌD try a ↓PÉRcolator| · |ₗÓNCE| McC 79.02

[38] at |HǑME| |we don't DRÌNK much ↓CÓFFee| · |ₗÁCtually| McC 79.32

[39] oh I ex|pect we shall go to the ↑SÈA| · as |Ùsual| McC 67.08

It can be expected that a nucleus occurring later will signal a higher degree
of CD than one occurring earlier. This would show perfect congruence
between the gamut of prosodic weight and the gamut of CD. Yet, an
examination of the mentioned examples raises the question whether the
final nucleus bearers should not be interpreted as prosodically intensified

carriers of concomitant information (*cf* Hartvigson 1969:53). This seems to apply also to [41] and [42] which do not display parallel nuclei. It does not seem to apply to [40] where the two nucleus bearers function as specifications anyhow, the second giving a more detailed piece of information than the first. No uncertainty arises as to the interpretation of the three other versions of [36]. The prosodic means unequivocally signal the temporal adverbial as a setting.

[40] I'll show you them to|MÒRRow| · when you come to |TÈA|
    McC 67.18
[41] though it's |ÒBviously 'indicated| at |TĔA-time| · of |CÒURSE|
    McC 78.29
[42] but I believe they |DÒ come| from a|BRŎAD| |ÀNYhow| McC 79.29

The question of an unequivocal signalling of the distinction between setting and specification also involves the question of an unequivocal indication of the communicative purpose of the speaker. The communicative purpose cannot be disregarded by a functional approach to language, although – especially in written language – it can sometimes be determined only by an analysis of the following context. In spoken language, it is additionally indicated by prosodic features. Signalling context dependence/independence, they prove to be valuable indicators of the communicative purpose.[7] They cannot, however, operate regardless of objective context. A pair of examples must suffice.

[43] |YÈS| · |let's ask the MĀNager| if |anyone's FÒUND a 'notecase|
    A–T 33.37
[44] (it's a |good job you 'didn't spend ↑ĂLL your money on them| –) you'd have |nothing left for 'Robert's BÌRTHday present| A–T 27.01

In [43], if actually putting the question to an uninformed manager, the speaker could hardly have the IC on *found*. Yet in the actual context of [43], the occurrence of the IC on *found* is perfectly acceptable, for the loss of a notecase is the general theme of the conversation.

This interpretation is not contradicted by [44], which occurs in a conversation in which Robert's birthday present is the central theme. The phrase *Robert's birthday present* does not occur in the shade and the sentence produces a kind of summarizing effect, offering a recapitulatory appraisal of the situation. To achieve this purpose, the phrase is presented as context independent, the development of the discourse consisting in an act of recapitulation.

The speaker can subjectively control the operation of context, but only within certain limits. There are certain rules of the game, which have not yet been satisfactorily explored. I assume that there is a cline, the one end of

7 *Cf* Bolinger's conclusion that accent (= the IC) directly reflects the speaker's intent (1972*b*:633 and *passim*).

which is constituted by evident context dependence and the other by evident context independence. Somewhere between is a sphere of potential context dependence/independence. In the absence of unequivocal clues, the sentence becomes equivocal (multifunctional).[8]

Let me turn to the THIRD cause leading to the shading of elements. The shaded elements concerned are, objectively speaking, context independent, but have been relegated to the shade in spite of the fact that their semantic character would enable them to exceed in CD the element that has come to bear the IC and in consequence prosodically overshadows them. Examples [45–51] will illustrate.

[45] (|GÒODness|–) |HÈ's looking 'pleased with himself| A–T 29.26
[46] |THÀT sounds ↓FÚN| A–T 61.11
[47] |THĂT's not 'much of a 'reason| A–T 65.08
[48] I |ₜSÀY|– |ₜ"DÒ shut the ↓DÓOR|– (there's |ₜSÙCH a ↓DRÁUGHT|–)   McC 70.04
[49] he |WÌLL have a 'shock| A–T 27.24
[50] I |ₜDÒN't think you'd ↓BÉTTER| McC 67.31
[51] |NÒW we're in a ↓FÍX|–– (|what's the MÀTTer|––) (we've |missed the 'last TRÀIN|– the porter says it left |five MÌNutes ago|––) (|"my GÒODness|–) |that "ÌS awkward|– |NÒW what do we 'do| McC 81.05

That discrepancy is functional: it renders the sentence marked, emotionally colouring the message. In achieving this effect, it operates either on its own or in co-operation with other devices, such as word order or semantics. As a rule the elements that have in this way been relegated to the shade create the impression of being context dependent. In fact, they are presented as such by the speaker and can therefore be looked upon as pseudo context dependent.

The revaluation becomes especially evident when the primary, unmarked CD load of the element bearing the IC is very low; *cf* the pronouns *you* and *he* in [52] and [53] and the two *that*'s in [54] and [55].

[52] (|HÀLLO MÁRjorie|–) you're looking very |ₜPLÉASed with your'self| A–T 49.06
[53] (|GÒODness|–) |HÈ's looking 'pleased with himself| A–T 29.26
[54] |THĂT's not 'much of a 'reason| A–T 65.08
[55] |ₜTHÁT's the TRÒUBLE|– (I |ₜDÓN't really KNÒW|)   A–T 63.36

Of particular interest are cases in which the IC appears on an element that even after the revaluation can hardly be looked upon as carrier of the highest degree of CD. Such an element serves as a purely emotional signal

8 The present state of knowledge may cause the interpreter to find equivocalness where further research will discover unequivocal clues or even signals. Yet language does not represent a closed and fully balanced system (*cf* Quirk 1965 and also Halliday 1970*a* and Vachek 1958) and equivocalness can by no means be excluded from language.

(see the *or* in [56]; to a certain extent even the *now*'s of [57] and [58] belong here).

[56] (. . . we |shan't 'actually STĂRVE| ·) |ŎR 'die of 'thirst| A–T 47.37
[57] |NÒW we're in a ↓FÍX| McC 81.05
[58] |NÒW what do we 'do| McC 81.09

These cases are peripheral; nevertheless they testify to the operation of the interplay of means signalling degrees of CD. Under special conditions the IC can appear on another element than the carrier of the highest degree of CD provided the signalling of degrees of CD is carried out with sufficient adequacy by other – prosodic and/or non-prosodic – means. The IC is after all only one of the devices signalling the outcome of the interplay of linear modification, semantic structure and context. The interplay of these three factors, the most powerful of which is that of context, makes the sentence function in a definite kind of perspective. Ultimately controlling the placement of the IC, this interplay (producing the functional perspective of a sentence) must be taken into account in determining the relation between grammar and intonation – a relation an inquiry into which has been most aptly and competently reopened by Quirk *et al* (1964).

MARKED FOCUS:
FUNCTIONS AND CONSTRAINTS
NILS ERIK ENKVIST

1.1

In this paper I shall first briefly discuss the information-structuring roles of marked focus in English.[1] I shall then make use of this discussion to comment on constraints on the placing of focus. By marked focus I shall mean that special prominence which is given to elements in a tone group by means of a high-falling or fall-rising tone or an exaggerated movement on the nucleus, often together with increased stress and paralinguistic signals.

1.2

I am thus assuming a contrast between marked and unmarked focus. Such an assumption can, I think, be defended, though we well know that the many gradations of spoken language often make it difficult to assign a pattern unambiguously to the marked or the unmarked category. But I cannot here try to sketch actual physical manifestations of this contrast in acoustic, physiological, phonetic, phonological, and paralinguistic terms (cf Halliday 1967, Crystal 1969 and 1975, Lehiste 1970). Exploring the relations between focus and paralinguistic marking devices would be a particularly challenging task.

---

1 A discussion of focus is wholly appropriate in a book honouring Randolph Quirk. One of the remarkable features of the *Grammar of Contemporary English* is that it is the first compendious description of English to take up focus, theme and emphasis at par with more traditional aspects of syntactic function.

2.1

One classic difficulty in the study of marked focus, or 'emphasis', is that it enters into more functions than one.[2] In this paper my argument will bear mainly on marked information focus, in other words on those functions that are related to thematization and topicalization because they signal distinctions between shared and new information. I shall be less interested in those instances of marked focus that could be labelled as 'corrective' and as 'emphatic'.

2.2

The job of corrective focus is to set right a poorly transmitted or wrongly received part of a message. Therefore corrective focus can fall on any item, such as a form-word (preposition, article, conjunction) or even an individual syllable of a word: *I said DEfensive, not OFfensive.* As corrective focus is to make up for flaws in transmission, it is constrained by success in transmission. And as flaws in transmission are caused by extralinguistic, situational, often haphazard forces such as noise or external interference or the recipient's linguistic or physical handicaps, the motives for the use of corrective focus elude analysis in terms of linguistic and semantic structures.

2.3

Emphatic focus exists to signal, not the difference between shared and new information but rather the relative weight that a speaker wants to attach to a particular element in the speech stream. Emphatic focus might thus be glossed as 'subjective speaker-oriented emphasis'. Like corrective focus, emphatic focus is not primarily conditioned by information structures in the text or by other overtly definable factors in the textual and situational envelopes of the utterance. But unlike corrective focus it is dependent on syntactic and semantic constraints which are similar to those of information focus. Emphasis does not suffice to justify the use of structures such as those cited below in Section 5, which might still be accepted when motivated by corrective principles.

2.4

In the following I shall use the term 'non-corrective focus' to imply 'information focus', but shall leave open the question to what extent the rules governing the placement of information focus might also apply to

---

2 *Cf* for instance Stockwell, Schachter and Partee (1973:34): 'It is not unlikely that [Case Placement Rules] are somehow akin to rules that provide for such notions as Topicalization and Focus Marking, but those notions in turn are related to emphasis and stress marking in complex ways that have not been adequately studied.' It is my belief that such a study must, first, distinguish those instances of emphasis and stress marking that serve to mark informational structures from those instances that mark correction or subjective emphasis, and then, secondly, relate marked information focus to thematization, topicalization, and clefting, including cleft-like hyperonymic structures such as *the girl who came was Liz, the town I live in is Lafayette.*

emphatic focus. Indeed the distinction between information focus and emphatic focus can be blurred, particularly when reasons of information and of emphasis conspire to trigger off one and the same focus placement.

3.1
In the following summary listing of the major informational functions of marked focus, focally marked items will be written in capitals.

3.2
A focally marked item serves to evoke a set of items which has been called its 'presuppositional set' (Jackendoff 1974:245 ff).[3] Thus a person who says

[1] JOHN ate the sandwich.

would normally have presupposed that his interlocutor already knows that somebody ate the sandwich. The presuppositional set of the focally marked item *John* comprises all those values that can be inserted for the corresponding variable 'somebody' in the presupposition. What these values are depends on the situation: we must, in accord with Jackendoff, assume that the presuppositional set is a coherent or well-defined set in the discourse or that it is amenable to, or under, discussion (Jackendoff 1974:246). The set membership is thus defined by the discoursal and situational contexts and by the amounts of information shared by the interlocutors. That *John* was selected by the speaker out of its set in [1] depends on the speaker's intentions and strategy: either the choice of *John* makes the sentence true, or it misleads the recipient of the message in a fashion desired by the speaker. In

[2] John ATE the sandwich.

the presuppositional set consists of all those verbs that express things John could, in the given discoursal context, plausibly have done to the sandwich (*looked at, sniffed at, contemplated*, etc), and from among which *ate* was selected. Note that sentence [1] could have been turned into a passive to place the new information, *John*, into the sentence-final position that we more commonly associate with new information. But the speaker preferred an active, which compelled him to mark the focus. Perhaps he did so for stylistic reasons, perhaps because he expressly wanted to evoke a presuppositional set.

---

3 Those who dislike the term 'presupposition' are free to use some other term, for instance 'lambda-set' from the lambda-operator used in the related logical or quasi-logical formula. I use 'presuppositional set' because 'lambda-set' is opaque. In speaking about markedness one must also be careful to note which type of markedness one has in mind. Thus [1] is focally marked because the nucleus falls on a non-final item. But it is not 'marked' textually if it answers the question, 'Who ate the sandwich?', which requires an answer such as [1], or an answer in which *John* occurs in the rheme (*The sandwich was eaten by John*).

3.3

Selecting one member out of a presuppositional set amounts to contrasting this set member with the other members of the same presuppositional set. This is why so many grammarians have called marked focus 'contrastive stress', though the item or items with which the focused item is contrasted need not be present in the text.

3.4

The result of the selection of one member out of the presuppositional set is new information: the receiver of the message did not know which member was to be chosen. Therefore, in those instances where the focally marked item occurs in a position usually reserved for old (shared or textually given) rather than new information, marked focus also comes to signal the occurrence of new information in an unusual place (in the theme rather than in the rheme, to use one of the possible terminologies). This would have been the case in [1] and [2]. But in

[3] John ate a SANDWICH.

the focally marked item, *sandwich*, has the indefinite article and occurs in a position where we expect the information to be new even without marked focus. In [3], therefore, the evocation of a presuppositional set and a contrast must be primarily responsible for the focus marking. There are informants to whom [3] sounds distinctly odd, at least when uncontextualized. This supports the view that its justification must be sought in the presuppositional set, which in turn is related to and affected by the context.

3.5

As the focally marked item carries new information, it also shows, conversely, that the focally unmarked items carry old (shared or given) information, information that the speaker believes that the recipients of the message already have because of a shared cultural or situational background or because it has been given in the text. Thus marked focus comes to restrict and to pinpoint new information, which conversely increases the range of old information in the tone group. Compare

[4]*a* The tall girl in blue shorts carried the red ball.
   b The TALL girl in blue shorts carried the red ball.
   c The tall girl in BLUE shorts carried the red ball.

In the focally unmarked sentence [4*a*] the theme, which presumably consists of shared information, comprises the entire subject noun phrase. In [4*b*], on the contrary, only *tall* is new information, whereas the existence of more than one girl in blue shorts is presupposed. And in [4*c*], only *blue* is marked as new information, and the existence of more than one tall girl in shorts would be presupposed. Also in [4*b*] and [4*c*] it is possible to regard the rhematic part of the sentence, *carried the red ball*, as old information; this could hardly be so in [4*a*]. Similarly in

[4]*d* The tall girl in blue shorts carried the RED ball.

the fact that the ball was red is marked for its newness, the rest of the sentence being presupposed as shared information.[4]

3.6
In instances where the focally marked item is a speaker-oriented, epistemic or attitudinal adverbial, an intensifier or a downtoner, marked focus tends to be more unambiguously emphatic in function, as in

[5]*a* OBVIOUSLY John is a fool.
   b Her performance was ABSOLUTELY AWFUL.
   c She was INCREDIBLY beautiful.

Here the intensification follows from the fact that the contrasted set members consist of other intensifiers or downtoners, or of zero. And as such items serve the very purpose of emphasizing the speaker's own subjective attitudes, they are usually pronounced with emphatic focus. Indeed sentences such as [5*b*] or [5*c*] sound unusual when produced without marked focus. Such semantic and pragmatic considerations, then, sometimes help us to draw the line between information focus and emphatic focus.

3.7
If the marked focus falls on a temporal auxiliary, the sentence becomes assertive by denying a negative presupposition (*cf* Carter 1972). For instance the sentences

[6]*a* John HAS been to Paris.
   b John WILL go to Paris.

deny the presuppositions 'John has not been to Paris' and 'John will not go to Paris', respectively. There must thus have been a negator in the presuppositional set. If there is no temporal auxiliary to carry the assertive focus, *do* – the *factotum* of English verbs – is inserted as a focus carrier:

[6]*c* John $\left\{ \begin{matrix} \text{DOES} \\ \text{DID} \end{matrix} \right\}$ eat the sandwich.

Here, English makes a distinction neutralized in, for instance, Swedish (where *Johan ÅT smörgåsen* renders both 'John ATE the sandwich' and 'John DID eat the sandwich'). Focal marking of modal auxiliaries evokes

---

4 The reason why sentences such as those under [4] seem artificial is presumably that in natural communication people tend to avoid repeating so much old information: instead of *the tall girl in BLUE shorts* one would prefer to say something like *the one in BLUE shorts*.

presuppositional sets whose members are other modals or zero. Thus in

[6]*d* John SHOULD be able to come.

the focally marked modal contrasts with *will, would, shall, must,* and *ought to.* But there is also a potential contrast between *SHOULD be able* and *IS able,* where, more precisely, *should be* occupies the same slot as *is,* though only *should* is focally marked. Thus here we have an instance where the focally marked member of the presuppositional set fails to fit into a slot precisely identical with that of all the other set members. In this respect the verb phrase works like an idiom: see below, Section 5.4.3.

3.8

Marked focus can signal the scope or range of certain operators: the question operator, the negator, *also, even, only, just, merely, simply, truly, hardly.* Thus a *yes/no* question is ambiguous in as many ways as it can be negated, but focus marking disambiguates the question by widening the presupposed, shared information. Compare

[7]*a* 'Did John fly to Chicago?' 'No, Susie did.' 'No, he drove.' 'No, he flew from Chicago.' 'No, to New York.'
 b 'Did John FLY to Chicago?' 'No, he drove.' *but* *'No, Susie did.' *'No, from Chicago.' *'No, to New York.'

In *wh*-questions, the question word suffices to disambiguate the question, and the focus is free to reflect other presuppositional sets and new information:

[7]*c* 'My book is in my pocket. WHOSE book is on the TABLE?'

Similarly, a negative sentence can be disambiguated by pinpointing the new and widening the presupposed information. Thus a negative sentence such as

[8]*a* John did not fly to Chicago on Tuesday.

is true under any of the following conditions or combinations of such conditions: John did not but *Susie* did, John *drove,* John flew *from* Chicago, John flew to *New York,* John flew *before* or *after* Tuesday, John flew on *Wednesday.* But negator scope can be disambiguated through focus marking, as in

[8]*b* John did not fly to CHICAGO on Tuesday. (He flew to New York)
 c John did not FLY to Chicago on Tuesday. (He drove)
 d John did not fly to Chicago on TUESDAY. (But on Wednesday)

The adverbs listed at the beginning of this section resemble the question operator and the negator in also having ranges specifying what is to be regarded as overt and what as presupposed or implied information (*cf*

Anderson 1972, Frazer 1971, Horn 1969). Thus for instance *John ate also x* signals that 'John ate something else than x', *John ate even x* that 'John ate something else than x, and that he ate x is remarkable' (remarkable, that is, at least in the speaker's opinion), and *John ate only x* that 'John did not eat anything else but x'. Such ranges of *also, even, only*, etc, can be indicated in two ways: either by moving the adverb, or by keeping it in position (and, presumably, in its least marked position) and by pinpointing its range by focus marking:

[9]*a* John only bought beer in the supermarket.
   b John bought only beer in the supermarket.
   c John bought beer only in the supermarket.
   d John only BOUGHT beer in the supermarket.
   e John only bought BEER in the supermarket.
   f John only bought beer in the SUPERMARKET.
   g John only bought beer in the BEST supermarket.

These functions of marked focus and their constraints have been discussed in greater detail for instance by Jackendoff (1972:247–58). A full analysis would have to build on more stringent definitions of old and new information in relation to presuppositions and implicatures of various kinds. A discussion of these controversial concepts would explode the bounds of the present paper and must therefore be omitted.

3.9
There has been a great deal of recent debate about the functions of marked focus in bifocal tone groups (that is, in tone groups with two marked foci). The discussion has, however, centred upon the respective functions of the falling and rising tones of the marked items. It therefore touches upon the general, systemic distinctions between falling and rising tones in English and not on the functions of marked, as contrasted with unmarked, focus as such. For this reason it will not be taken up here. (*Cf*, however, Halliday 1967, Jackendoff 1972, Nyqvist Goës 1974, Brazil 1975, Schmerling 1976, and Ladd 1977.)

3.10
Of greater immediate interest for this paper are bifocal structures of the type discussed *eg* by George Lakoff (Lakoff 1971):

[10]*a* Algernon hit Bert and then $\left\{ \begin{array}{l} \text{HE} \\ \text{CHARLIE} \end{array} \right\}$ hit HIM.

   b Algernon hit Bert and then HE was hit by $\left\{ \begin{array}{l} \text{HIM.} \\ \text{CHARLIE.} \end{array} \right\}$

In the focally unmarked structure

[10]c Algernon hit Bert and then Charlie hit him.

the *him* is in the first place interpreted as referring to Bert; in [10a] and [10b], the focally marked *him* is, on the contrary, coreferential with Algernon (unless it is used to point at somebody present in the setting, as a mechanism of exophoric deixis). Consequently, in [10c] the *and* is additive, in [10a] and [10b] adversative or contrastive. In the active structure in [10a], the antecedent of the pronoun is also shifted further back by the focal marking. This function of marked focus with stress on the pronouns, not on the verbs, is only operative when the verbs of the clauses or sentences are semantically related. Compare

[11]a First Algernon LAUGHED at Bert and then he RIDICULED him.

with

[11]b First Algernon laughed at Bert, and then HE ridiculed HIM.
   c First Algernon laughed at Bert, and then HE paid his respects to HIM.
   d ?First Algernon laughed at Bert, and then HE paid HIS debts.
   e *First Algernon laughed at Bert, and then HE had breakfast with HIM.

[11c] becomes acceptable if *paid his respects* is read as irony; [11d] invites metaphorical interpretation; but [11e] is hard to contextualize without very elaborate assumptions and presuppositions, and therefore also hard to accept. In such instances, then, marked focus serves to indicate chiastic coreference, thus:

[12]a Algernon hit Bert, and then

HE slugged HIM.

The chiastic relation can be maintained even across sentence borders, as in

[12]b Algernon hit Bert. Then HE slugged HIM.

These structures too, which are by the way not peculiar to English alone, can be ultimately derived from the general principle that focally marked items convey new, unmarked ones old or shared, information. Here the new information signalled by the focus marking is a shift in semantic roles. What was the actor becomes the patient and what was the patient becomes the actor, both in the active [10a] and in the passive [10b]. Even though the referents forming the presuppositional set remain the same, they do not maintain their old semantic roles. In terms of linear reference, the focus marking shifts the reference to an antecedent which, in the active, is more distant. And the condition of verb synonymy is an extension of the principle

[141]

that in a structure some of whose items carry marked focus, the focally marked items are the ones entrusted with the new information, whereas the focally unmarked items must convey old information. Thus here 'old' means 'synonymous, or roughly synonymous, with that of the preceding verb'. If the second of the verbs actually carries new information, it contrasts with the first verb and the verbs must be given marked focus, as in [11a]. The acceptability of [11a] depends on whether *laugh at* and *ridicule* can be interpreted as being semantically different enough to justify focally marked contrasting. In [11b], *laugh at* and *ridicule* seem semantically close enough to warrant focally marked chiastic coreference.

4

Under 3.2–10 I have now listed a number of instances in which marked focus occurs in English. The common denominator and thus the basic function of focus marking seems to be TO EVOKE A PRESUPPOSITIONAL SET AND TO PRESENT ONE OF THE SET MEMBERS AS NEW INFORMATION. The other functions, for instance the widening of the range of old, shared, presupposed information, can be more or less directly derived from this basic function. Which of the two subfunctions, evocation of the presuppositional set or the presentation of a set member as new information, is primary and which is secondary depends on the structure and on the context. Thus in [5], set evocation is presumably the primary reason for focus marking. In fact the two subfunctions merge harmoniously and often conspire to bring about focus marking; in this sense they can be said to form one single semantic complex.

5.1

It has been necessary to dwell so long on summarizing the rationale of non-corrective focus marking because, if successfully described, this rationale should at the same time explain the constraints that limit the placement of non-corrective marked focus. Thus if it is true that the function of marked focus is to evoke a presuppositional set and to present one of the set members as new information, contrasting it with the other members, the use of marked focus will be prevented whenever it would be incapable of serving this function.

5.2

First, however, we should not forget that there is a class of constraints on focus placement that arise from an avoidance of ambiguity or change of meaning. David Crystal (1969:264–5) has offered a selection of distinctions in which tonicity (that is, the placing of focal stress and intonation) has a grammatical function and in which a change in focus placement can therefore change the meaning of the structure:

(a) The distinction between restrictive and non-restrictive relative clauses: my |brother who's aBRÓAD|, where the presence of a nuclear tone on 'brother' (usually with a following pause) suffices to make the distinction.

(b) The distinction between end-placed vocative and apposition: it's the |BÀker 'Mr Jones|, compared with: it's the |BÀker| |Mr JÒNES|.

(c) The distinction between apposition and list: |John my SÓN| and his |WÍFE|, compared with |JÓHN| my |SÓN| and his |WÍFE|.

(d) The distinction between parenthetic and main clause; you |know it ↑ìs im'portant . . ., compared with: you |KNÒW it is im'portant. . . .†

(e) The distinction between certain types of idiom and a literal interpretation: |has your 'attitude be'come 'more or less deVÉloped since . . . (answered by 'yes' or 'no'), compared with: |has your 'attitude be'come MÓRE| or |LÈSS de'veloped since . . . (answered by 'more' or 'less'); I can't |stand any MÒRE| compared with: I can't |STÀND any 'more| (which is ambiguous); would you |like 'one or two 'lumps of sÙgar|, compared with: would you |like ÓNE| or |TWÒ 'lumps of 'sugar|; |ÀNY old 'thing will 'do|, compared with: any |ÒLD 'thing will 'do|; that's |not BÀD| compared with: that's |NÒT 'bad|; he |isn't half ↑MÃD| compared with: he |isn't ↑HÀLF MÁD|.

(f) The distinction between different uses of an adverb: it's a |good 'job TÒO| and it's a |good JÒB| |TÒO|; we |went 'home HÀPPily| and we |went HÒME HÁPPily|; he |didn't RÈAD the book 'stupidly| (or . . . STÚpidly|) and he |didn't RÈAD the book| |STÚpidly|.

(g) The distinction between positive and negative implication in some structures: I |thought it would RÀIN| (and it hasn't), and: I |THÒUGHT it would 'rain| (and it has); |John sug'gested a 'means whereby it 'might not be obTÀINed| and: |John sug'gested a 'means whereby it might NÒT be ob'tained|.

(h) Occasionally, a distinction as to whether a structure is a dependent clause or not: |even if he ↑TÒLD me| I'd | GÒ|, compared with: |even if he ↑TÒLD me I'd go| (I wouldn't think of accepting).

(i) Occasionally, a distinction as to whether an item should be treated as an adjective or an adverbial intensifier: I want |more exPÈrienced 'people|, compared with: I want |MÓRE| ex|PÉrienced| |PÈople| (which may be ambiguous if the context is one of irritation).

(j) Certain distinctions between adverbial particle, operating as part of a phrasal verb, and end-placed preposition: I |came across that RÓAD| (when I was |looking for your HÒUSE|), which is ambiguous, compared with: I |came aCRÒSS that RÓAD| (when I was |looking for your HÓUSE|), which is not.

† But not in American English, where 'you know' as parenthesis is regularly nuclear.

It will be seen, however, that several of Crystal's instances involve not only tonicity in the sense of 'placement of focal stress and intonation', but also tonality in the sense of 'the division of the utterance into tone groups'; indeed Crystal is here concerned with pauses, potential or actual. All the same such instances must be borne in mind. If a shift of marked focus changes not only the patterns of old and new information and presuppositional sets, but also the basic meaning of the sentence, the shift is not a shift in the focus system only, but rather in the signals that expose basic grammatical functions.

5.3

There are, however, instances where the placement of marked focus is constrained by tonicity alone rather than by the tonality-tonicity complex. To repeat: as we could expect, focus placement is constrained when the focus cannot evoke a presuppositional set, and when the focus cannot settle on items expressing new information. As implied above in Section 4, both reasons often conspire to prevent a certain pattern of focus placement.

5.4.1

One type of constraint occurs when a sentence contains one overt presuppositional set – overt in that its members are expressly mentioned on the textual surface. In such instances, the focus can only go on the contrasted members of the set, not on any other item:

[13]*a* Joan was wearing the RED dress, not the GREEN $\left\{ \begin{array}{l} \text{dress.} \\ \text{one.} \end{array} \right\}$

   b Joan was wearing her red DRESS, not her red SLACKS.

   c *Joan was wearing her red DRESS, not the green $\left\{ \begin{array}{l} \text{DRESS.} \\ \text{ONE.} \end{array} \right\}$

The overt presuppositional set whose members are contrasted can also occur in two or more sentences and not necessarily within one single sentence, as in these examples cited by Bresnan (1972:340):

[14]*a* I've read some interesting books recently.—What books have you READ? (Not *What BOOKS have you read?)

   b John has many friends.—How many friends does John HAVE? (Not *How many FRIENDS does John have?)

Books and *books, friends* and *friends* cannot form a presuppositional set because they fail to contrast; their repetition also signals old information. Therefore if there is marked focus, it must go on the maximally rhematic element, here the final verb. We should note in passing that the difficulty of contrasting synonymous or hyponymous items and their refusal to enter into the same presuppositional sets can be tested by placing them in frames such as

[15]*a* John did not TRAVEL to Paris, he WENT there.

   b Peter did not drive an AUTOMOBILE, he drove a CAR.

   c Susan did not eat FISH but SALMON.

What justification such sentences may have comes from the lack of complete synonymy of the contrasted items: *automobile* for instance may be given a different stylistic flavour from that of *car*, and [15*b*] may be read to indicate that Peter was a person who liked to call a car a car. Also sentences such as

[15]*d* He didn't eat just (any old kind of) FISH, he ate SALMON.
    e He didn't just TAKE it, he GRABBED it.

are all right as long as it is the superordinate, hyperonymic term that is negated. A more severe test would be that in

[16]*a* *Peter drove an AUTOMOBILE and a CAR.
    b *Susan ate FISH and SALMON.

Synonymy and hyponymy imply old information and preclude contrastive membership in a presuppositional set. Hence the awkwardness of [16*a–b*].

5.4.2
Items that do not contrast with any other items do not enter into presuppositional sets. In English, the only preposition used with *interested* is *in* (there is no *interested of*, *interested about*, etc). Therefore

[17]*a* Elizabeth had always been interested IN playing the violin.

can only be an instance of corrective focus. It is, on the contrary, possible to have non-corrective focus in

[17]*b* Did Susan turn the tap ON before she left the house?

because *turn on* contrasts with *turn off*. That

[17]*c* Did Susan see OFF her children before she left for the cruise?

is a good sentence follows from the fact that in verb-adverb combinations such as *see off*, the adverb can carry the main stress even without a contrast. Another category of items that do not contrast and therefore have no presuppositional sets are form-words such as *there* and *it* in existential and cleft constructions:

[17]*d* *THERE were three books on the table.
    e *IT was John who ate the sandwich.

A deictic *there*, however, enters into presuppositional sets, contrasting for instance with *here*, and can therefore be focally marked:

[17]*f* THERE is a girl dancing on the table.

5.4.3
Within idioms, individual lexical items cannot contrast, and therefore they cannot enter into presuppositional sets. We can thus only focus-mark entire

idioms such as *kick the bucket* (by focusing both KICK and BUCKET), but not place the focus marking on *kick* alone or *bucket* alone without losing the idiomatic sense. Compare

[18]*a* Did Charlie KICK the BUCKET?
 b Did Charlie KICK the bucket?
 c Did Charlie kick the BUCKET?

[18*a*] can be ambiguous, whereas [18*b*] and [18*c*] only allow the literal interpretations.

5.4.4

In phrases, items can form semantic hierarchies, whose most important and high-ranking members are most apt to carry marked focus. Thus in the focal permutations

[19]*a* Does Chris write home because he LOVES you or because he NEEDS you?
 b Does Chris write home because he LOVES you or because he needs MONEY?
 c *Does Chris write home because he LOVES you or because he NEEDS money?
 d Does Chris write home because he loves YOU or because he needs MONEY?
 e *Does Chris write home because he loves YOU or because he NEEDS money?

loves and *you* readily accept the focus, depending on context. But in *needs money*, the focus goes on *money* rather than on *needs*, irrespective of a possible iconic parallel between the focus on the two verbs (*loves, needs*) as in [19*c*]. To focus *needs* in the phrase *needs money* we need structures such as

[19]*f* Does Chris write because he WANTS money or because he really NEEDS money?

Examples such as [19*a–e*] thus suggest that in certain phrases and collocations it is semantic weight, rather than final or non-final position or word-class membership, that decides with what ease the respective items can receive and carry marked focus. We cannot say that it is the last item that always carries marked focus. In *to need money*, *money* is thus informationally more important than *need* (or *money* is 'higher in the rhematic hierarchy', to speak with Contreras 1976:96), and if *to need money* carries focus as a whole phrase, the focus goes on *money* rather than on *need*. But *need* is perfectly capable of taking the focus in structures such as [19*f*], where *money* is old information and *need* contrasts with another verb. As suggested by Bolinger (1972*b*), this may also be connected with predictability. Thus in frequent, predictable collocations such as '*clothes to wear*, the verb tends to be unaccented; in less predictable collocations such as *clothes to 'launder*, the verb is normally accented. To accept this explanation we have to assume that it is somehow more basic or natural to wear clothes than to launder them: clothes exist to be worn rather than to be laundered.

5.4.5

General, superordinate terms such as SUBJECT, TOPIC, MATTERS, PROBLEM, CASE, and the like do not very readily enter into presuppositional sets. Indeed it is not always easy to discover set members they might contrast with. Such superordinate terms can be compared to superordinate verbs or 'pro-verbs' such as *do*, and to pronouns: they are 'pro-nouns' in the etymological sense of the term. They also often enter into fixed constructions classifiable as idioms – *as matters stand, as the case may be* – in which they cannot contrast with other individual words, as noted above under 5.4.3. These reasons explain why focally marked structures such as

[20]a *The $\left\{ \begin{array}{l} \text{TOPIC} \\ \text{SUBJECT} \end{array} \right\}$ he was writing about was marked focus.

   b *As MATTERS stand, I think Algernon ought to move out.

   c *You should say 'good morning, Sir' or 'good morning, Madam', as the CASE may be.

would be hard to accept as instances of non-corrective focus. It is another matter that these words also have specific, non-superordinate uses in which they can contrast with other members of a presuppositional set:

[20]*d* At the meeting we had a great deal of trouble trying to formulate a statute and to decide on a case. The CASE that worried us had to do with affirmative action.

A similar contrast between general, superordinate meaning and a specific sense explains why the sentences

[20]*e* I gave my horse a bit to CHEW.

   f I gave my horse a BIT to chew.

have different preferential interpretations. If *bit* is given marked focus, its presuppositional set consists of all the things a horse might be given to chew and is interpreted as 'part of the harness'; if not, it is ambiguous, unless *chew* is focally marked, when *bit* retains only its superordinate sense, 'a small quantity of something'. Compare also

[20]*g* John has PLANS to leave.

   h John has plans to LEAVE.

   i Susie has plans for DINNER.

   j ?Susie has PLANS for dinner.

   k Susie has CLAMS for dinner.

Sentence [20*j*] would, however, be all right in a context such as

[20]*j* Susie always has PLANS for dinner. But she can never carry them
out.

These and other related examples have been disccussed by Bresnan (1971,
1972) and by Berman and Szamosi (1972). In the contrast between

[20]*l* ANY old thing will do.
   m Any OLD thing will do.

[20*l*] involves an idiom (*cf* 5.4.3) whereas [20*m*] evokes a presuppositional
set (*any OLD thing* versus *any NEW thing*). But *thing* cannot here be focally
marked, except correctively.

5.4.6
The presuppositional sets of grammatical form-words are the closed sets to
which these form-words belong: a focally marked preposition will evoke
other, substitutable, prepositions, and so forth. (Focally marked pronouns,
however, evoke contextually definable noun phrases as well: a sentence
such as *YOU did it* contrasts not only with *I did it* but also with *JOHN did it*.)
The definite and indefinite articles can contrast with one another and with
zero, and have special focally marked pronunciations whose presuppositional sets appear in dialogues such as

[21] Are you THE Professor Smith?—No, I am just A Professor Smith.

A listing of constraints on focus marking should also mention the restrictions
on presuppositional set membership which are caused by membership in
grammatical categories such as word-class. This is related to the principle
mentioned above in Section 3.6: usually, the members of a presuppositional
set should be capable of occupying the same slot in the sentence frame.

5.4.7
As focus marking indicates new information, all those operations –
passivization, topicalization, cleft, *there*-insertion, dislocation, extraposi-
tion, and so forth – that affect the linear order, and therefore the thematic
information structure, of a sentence are also relevant to a study of constraints
on the choice of focally marked elements. Here I shall only exemplify the
connection between information strategies in the text and focus marking
with a few instances of connections between thematization and topicalization, and focus marking. Thus patterns such as

[22]*a* *This book JOHN has read.
   b *Shakespeare SUSIE studied in London.
   c *Move away HE must.
   d *Off IT went.
   e *To London JOHN flew yesterday.

would have very low acceptabilities (except as instances of corrective focus). This is because in a topicalized structure, the least dynamic elements tend to be in the middle of the sentence string. Anaphoric pronouns expressing old information are thus particularly reluctant to accept marked focus when in the middle of the sentence, as in [22c–d]. Note that acceptabilities improve if the marked focus is placed on the initial or final elements or bifocally on both, as in

[22]*f* THIS book John has READ.

The thematic arrangement of the sentence is regulated by three mechanisms. First there are lexical thematizations carried out with the aid of lexical converses (*John sold the car to Peter/Peter bought the car from John*). Secondly, there are syntactic thematizations that bring with them changes in the syntactic pattern (*John ate the sandwich/The sandwich was eaten by John*). And thirdly there are topicalizations or commentizations, which merely front or postpone an element without concomitant changes in syntactic structure (*John has read this book/This book John has read*). Generally speaking, topicalizations are the most strongly marked of the three types of thematic arrangement, and therefore they can also be expected to be most sensitive to conflicts between their own information dynamics and the placement of marked focus. In a topicalized structure, the fronted element often evokes a presuppositional set recoverable from an earlier portion of the text (such linking is indeed a prime motive for topicalization). And the final element is strongly rhematic, carrying new information and often linking up with something coming later in the text. Therefore marked focus goes on the topicalized or commentized elements or on both, rather than on the informationally more neutral elements in the middle of the sentence.

5.4.8
The rhematic hierarchy, or the degrees of communicative dynamism to use the well-known term of Jan Firbas (*eg* Firbas 1974), can also be reflected in the relative degrees of ease and difficulty by which items in specific thematically definable positions receive marked focus. To give just one example of such a hierarchy in a topicalized phrase, let us look at the sentences

[23] She took the basket.
   a Three foreign newspapers had been packed tightly at the bottom.
   b Packed TIGHTLY at the BOTTOM had been three foreign newspapers.
   c Packed tightly at the BOTTOM had been three foreign newspapers.
   d ?Packed TIGHTLY at the bottom had been three foreign newspapers.
   e *PACKED tightly at the bottom had been three foreign newspapers.

The untopicalized sentence is [23*a*]. The topicalization in [23*b–e*] is motivated by the linking of the topicalized phrase to *basket* in the previous sentence; the implication is of course *the bottom of the basket*, also signalled by *the* in *the bottom*. At the same time the topicalization makes it possible to place *three foreign newspapers*, as new information, into the maximally rhematic, sentence-final position. Even after topicalization, however, *at the bottom* (which originally, before topicalization, was the final and most rhematic element as in [23*a*]) is more hospitable to marked focus than *tightly* alone, or *packed*, as we see from the relatively lower acceptabilities of [23*d–e*]. This suggests that the thematic status of elements is another exponent of the semantic hierarchy in phrases, which was also mentioned above in section 5.4.4. And it shows the relevance of the general principle formulated by Heles Contreras for Spanish: 'The acceptability of a sentence decreases in inverse proportion to the number of violations of the rhematic hierarchy' (Contreras 1976:96).

5.4.9

Some of the most precise rules constraining focus placement have so far been given for operators such as *even, only,* and *just*. The reasons why the sentence

[24]*a* John even gave his daughter a new bicycle.

can take marked focus on any one of its lexical items, whereas in

[24]*b* John gave even his daughter a new bicycle.

only *his* and *daughter* can be thus marked, and in

[24]*c* John gave his daughter even a new bicycle.

only *new* and *bicycle* can receive marked focus, have been explained as follows. 'If *even*,' says Jackendoff,

> is directly dominated by a node X, X and all nodes dominated by X are in the range of *even*. Association with focus will be able to take place only if the focus is within the range of *even* . . . if *only* or *just* is dominated by a node X, X and all nodes dominated by X and to the right of *only* or *just* are in the range of *only* and *just*. (Jackendoff 1972:250)

The reason why *even, only,* and *just* allow such stringent rules is that these operators themselves assume the shape of syntactic formatives which can be placed into structures and subjected to formal treatment. Presumably one could also model the ranges of the question operator and negator on the textual surface, which in turn reflect presuppositional sets, by signalling operator scope in an underlying structure. Thus sentences such as

[25]*a* Did Joy go to Paris YESTERDAY?
  b Joy did not go to Paris YESTERDAY.

could be derived from

[25]c Joy went to Paris (Q yesterday)
    d Joy went to Paris (neg yesterday)

where the scopes of the Q and the Neg indicated by the brackets are manifested on the textual surface as focally marked ranges of their respective operators. Such a model can be interpreted also in terms of presuppositional sets: (Q yesterday) would evoke the set of *yesterday* and lead to focal marking, whereas (Q time), (Q place) and (Q manner) would yield a simple *when, where,* and *how,* respectively.

5.4.10
Though clefts will not be dealt with in this paper, it is proper to note in passing that clefted elements – like focally marked ones – express new information and evoke presuppositional sets. Therefore if a clefted structure is to be focally marked, non-corrective monofocal structures should have their focus within and not outside the cleft. Compare

[26]a It was YESTERDAY that I met Susan.
    b ?It was yesterday that I met SUSAN.
    c It was YESTERDAY that I met SUSAN.

[26b] has a strongly corrective flavour, whereas [26c], being bifocal, is all right as a non-corrective sentence. If the clefted phrase consists of several elements, some of them may be given further prominence by marked focus:

[26]d It was the big RED ball that was carried by the girl in blue shorts.

6
To sum up. Apart from instances where changes in the placement of marked focus change the meaning of sentences or disambiguate them (as shown in the quotation from Crystal in Section 5.2), the constraints on non-corrective focus marking are derivable from the two major functions governing the use of marked focus. Thus focus marking cannot be placed on old information, nor can it go on items incapable of evoking contextually relevant presuppositional sets. There are instances where both blocking forces are operative at the same time.

    To analyse such constraints in concrete instances we must venture beyond sentence grammar. Whether an item in a sentence expresses old or new information is a textual and pragmatic question. It is textual insofar as some old information is recoverable from the text itself, and pragmatic insofar as the extent of shared information depends on the interlocutors' extent of shared background and common experience, acquired before as well as during the speech act. Whether a given element has a contextually and situationally relevant presuppositional set is similarly a matter of pragmatics rather than of strict syntax. That some syntactically and semantically definable elements are less apt to carry marked focus than others does thus not follow directly from their syntactic or lexical properties. Rather it follows from the fact that these elements are used in ways which affect their entering into presuppositional sets and the likelihood of their carrying old or new information. Anaphoric pronouns for instance typically refer to old or known discourse referents, and their focusing must therefore be motivated by the need for defining a presuppositional set rather than by their expressing new information. General, superordinate, hyperonymic nouns such as *matter, affairs,* or *things* are often used as thematic fillers and therefore they are rarely apt to form presuppositional sets with other items. All the same there are some connections between syntactically statable classifications and the aptness of an element to assume marked focus. In English, the most rhematic, informationally most strongly focused elements tend to be the last open-class items or proper nouns of the sentence. In active sentences, this position can be taken by adverbials (of which those that are most tightly bound to their verbs need the strongest motives for, or are most resistant against, topicalization). If there are no adverbials, objects and other verb complements readily occupy final position; and if there are no objects or complements, verbs can go last. In passive sentences, the most rhematic positions are those of adverbials and of the agent.[5] In *yes/no* questions, the most strongly focused element tends to go last; and so forth. When the information focus thus coincides with final position, focus placement is clear even without further marking by intonation and stress. But if the information focus goes elsewhere, it must be marked. Sometimes a constituent which goes into the beginning part of the sentence, for instance a subject, conveys new information because the speaker is reluctant to arrange his sentence so as to make it come later. Sometimes new information is contained in a topicalized phrase; if so, marked focus tends to fall on those elements which were maximally focal in their original, sentence-final habitat.

5 This explains why *by*-agents in passives so rarely topicalize. Among the important motives for passivization is the fronting of the object of the underlying active sentence and the concomitant postponement of the agent, and re-fronting the agent would work counter to this purpose. Fronting of a *by*-agent must thus be motivated by other reasons such as iconic cohesion, metre, rhyme, etc.

NEGLECTED GRAMMATICAL FACTORS IN CONVERSATIONAL ENGLISH
DAVID CRYSTAL

The judicious blend of meticulous observation, experimental enquiry and theoretical insight concerning the English language, which characterizes the writing of Randolph Quirk, has regularly provided linguistic theory with both an example and a challenge. The example lies especially in the complementary roles given to corpus, acceptability test, and intuition in the elucidation of problems. The challenge is to construct a model which will satisfactorily account for the diverse data which these different methodologies uncover. Nowhere is this challenge more disconcerting than in the need to provide an account of that English variety assumed to be the basis of our routine behaviour – informal domestic conversation – for it is here that the discrepancy between standard descriptive statement and observed reality is most noticeable. The aim of the present paper, accordingly, is to identify some of the neglected linguistic features of this variety, which will have to be incorporated into standard descriptions if this discrepancy is to be removed.

The reasons for the comparative neglect of domestic conversational analysis are well-recognized. It is difficult – if not impossible – to capture the informal spontaneity of this variety using a process of controlled intuitive reflection. And corpus-based techniques are problematic, because of the difficulty of obtaining uncontaminated samples of data – uncontaminated either by observer presence, informant self-consciousness, or poor recording quality. The data on which the present paper is based avoided these problems, using a technique which retained the strengths and eliminated the weakness of the hidden microphone method. Without extremely expensive equipment, this method is of limited value, as the speed and low volume level of much conversation makes for obscure reproduction of one and often all participants. But by using the following strategy, unselfconscious and high-quality recordings were obtained. Friends of the author were invited to his house for a social occasion, but with a specific request to help participate in an 'experiment' on accents. The room was prepared with centrally placed, visible microphones apparently attached to a visible tape recorder; in reality, the microphones were linked to a mixer and recorder in an adjacent room. When the informants arrived, they were given an experimental task to do (such as reciting the alphabet). Once this was completed, the visible tape recorder was ostentatiously switched off, and the microphones pushed back somewhat, but left directly in front of the participants. The hidden recorder was of course permanently on, and thus a good quality record of the relaxed spontaneous speech which subsequently emerged was obtained. Permission to use the material was of course always sought before the tape was replayed, and was always given.

The original aim of the enterprise was to provide advanced learners of English as a foreign language with more realistic samples of conversation than are routinely available in language-teaching courses, and it is in that form that extracts of the material have been published (Crystal and Davy 1975), including the whole of the data used in the present paper.[1] It was in fact the accumulation of unexpected analytic difficulties in processing this material which motivated the present argument. To illustrate the nature of this data, an extract is printed in full below: | marks tone-unit boundary; ' ' etc mark direction of nuclear tone; | marks the first pitch-prominent syllable of the tone-unit; ↑ marks a step-up in pitch; ' indicates other stressed syllables (" extra strong stress); · – etc mark degrees of pause length; the word containing the tonic is printed in capitals.

A well |what's the · |what's the 'failure with the ↑FÒOTBALL| I
   mean |this · |this I don't 'really ↑SÈE| I mean it · |cos the
   ↑MÒNEY| · |how 'much does it 'cost to get ÌN| |down the ↑RÒAD|
   |NÒW|
B   I |think it ↑probably – it| 5
   |probably 'is the ↑MÒNEY| for |what you ↑GÈT| you |KNÓW| – erm
   I was |reading in the ↑paper this ↑MÒRNING| a a | CHÀP| he's a
   DI|RÈCTOR| of a |big ↑CÒMPANY| in |BÌRMINGHAM| – who was th
   the |world's ↑number 'one ↑FÒOTBALL 'fan| he |used to ↑SPÈND|
   a|bout a 'thousand a ↑YÈAR| |watching FÒOTBALL| you |KNÓW| 10

1 The tape-collection as a whole is lodged in the files of the Survey of English Usage, University College London. Extracts 1, 3 and 8, the three longest extracts in Crystal and Davy 1975, are used in the present paper (13 minutes of conversation). Reference numbers cite the extract number and line(s) involved.

David Crystal

(C: |còo|) – he's he's |watched 'football in ↑every n · on
↑every 'league · 'ground in ÉNGLAND| |all 'ninety TWÓ|
(A *laughs*) – and he's |been to A↑MĒRICA| to |watch ↑West
BRŌMWICH 'playing in A'merica| he's · he's |been to the la
· to |ÒH| · the |LÀST| f f |two or 'three 'world CÙP| · |world   15
CÙP| · mat |THÍNGS| you |KNÓW| · |TÓURNAMENTS| – – and he |goes
to ↑all the 'matches AWÁY| you |KNÓW| |European ↑CÙP 'matches
and 'everything| that |ÈNGLISH teams are PLÁYING in| he's all
'over the ↑WÒRLD 'watching it you SÉE| – |THÌS YÉAR| he's
|watched ↑twenty 'two GÀMES| – |SÒ 'far| |this YÈAR| which is   20
a|bout · FÌFTY per 'cent| of his |NŎRMAL| (C: |good LÒRD|) · and
|even ↑HÈ's getting 'browned ↑ÓFF| and |HÈ was SÁYING| that
erm – you can |go to a NĬGHTCLUB| in |BĬRMINGHAM| – – and
|watch ↑Tony BÉNNET| · for a|bout ↑thirty ↑BŌB| – |something
like THÍS| a |night with ↑Tony ↑BÉNNET| – |have a 'nice ↑MĒAL| 25
· in · |very · ↑plushy SURRŌUNDINGS| very |WĀRM|
|NÍCE| |PLÈASANT| – says it |CÒSTS him| a|bout the ↑SÀME
a'mount of MÓNEY| to |go and ↑sit in a ↑breezy 'windy STÁND| –
(A & C *laugh*) on a · on a |WÒODEN BÉNCH| – to |WĂTCH| a |rather
BÓRING 'game of ↑FÒOTBALL| with |no ↑PERSONÁLITY| and |all   30
DEFÉNSIVE| and |ÈVERYTHING| he |says it's just ↑KÌLLING itself|
you |KNÓW|

Sentences

Any attempt to analyse this data in terms of sentence structure and function
is beset with difficulties from the outset. Sentence identification and
classification is a much greater problem here than in any other variety of
English. Three factors seem to account for the majority of cases:

(*a*) indeterminate connectivity;
(*b*) indeterminate ellipsis;
(*c*) intercalation of structures.

1 Connectivity

The analytic problem is how far a distinction between simple (mono-clausal)
and complex (multi-clausal) sentences can be maintained. In subordinate
clauses, the semantic dependency involved is usually sufficient to guarantee
the obligatoriness of the connective (*eg He came after the man left*), and often
there is a grammatical criterion, regardless of semantics and intonation (*eg
He told us what the answer was*, where the omission of *what* produces an
utterance whose acceptability cannot be salvaged). But regularly in
coordinate clauses, and also in some cases of subordination, there is no clear
semantic distinction between the presence or absence of a connective, and

formal criteria can be found to support the analysis of an utterance as EITHER a single complex sentence OR as a set of simple sentences. The problem is best illustrated by the use of *and*, which introduces nearly one-quarter of all the clauses in the data (see *Table* 1 on *p* 160).[2]

3.115–20

[1] ... he |gets 'on the 'wrong TRÀIN|
[2] and |ends 'up in the 'wrong PLÀCE| – –
[3] and |finds that he's ↑in a PLÁCE|
[4] that's |perfectly QUĬET|
[5] and |perfectly ÍNNOCENT|
[6] and there's |no ↑STÒRY| –
[7] and |so he 'just ↑WRÌTES 'one| –
[8] and with|in a ↑WĔEK| he's |managed to cre'ate ↑RÌOTS| you |KNÓW|

On syntactic grounds, only the connective in [4] is obligatory. In this variety of English, it is quite normal to have the first part of a clause omitted (*eg looks like another nice day*; *cf* GCE : 545), and this would permit the omission of the *and* in [2], [3] and [5] (*cf* also below). Omitting *and* in [7] and [8] also seems to make no semantic difference, and the grammar and prosody can be used as they are. [6] is somewhat debatable: it might be argued that the *and* here is less likely to be omitted on the grounds that it marks the end of this first sequence of events (= 'and as a result'); but the intonation, and accompanying linguistic and extralinguistic context, could be used for this purpose instead, and the *and* is certainly not obligatory. Presumably, then, an analysis would pay attention to the optionality of these connectives, and count the above as seven sentences (or eight, if [5] is viewed as clausal, instead of phrasal). The alternative, to call the whole of the above utterance a single complex sentence, is possible, but vacuous (on this basis, some extracts, such as Extract 5 in Crystal and Davy 1975, would have to be considered as containing but one or two sentences, each consisting of several dozen clauses).

If all the cases were as clear as the above, there would be no problem. 3.93–7 illustrates a more difficult case:

[9] they |go to the · 'Ledra 'Palace HOTÈL for EXÁMPLE|
[10] and they |sit at the BĂR| –
[11] and they ab|sorb you know 'one or two FÀCTS| from a |few PÈOPLE|
[12] but |they 'don't 'know the ↑LĀNGUAGE|
[13] and they |don't 'know the ↑PĒOPLE|
[14] and they |don't · ↑really 'know the 'SITU↑ÀTION| –

2 The sample contained 420 clauses, this excluding a further 120 minor sentences and comment clauses (*cf* GCE : 778) and incomplete sentences. All examples are given with clauses on separate lines, each clause being numbered separately.

Here, to make the contrast between [9–11] and [12–14], *but* (or some such phrase) seems essential: omitting *but*, and changing the intonation of [12–14], does not avoid the ambiguity of these lines appearing to be part of the same list as [9–11]. Given the above reasoning, we should therefore conclude that there are five sentences here: [9], [10], [11–12], [13] and [14]. But as [12] is in no way in semantic contrast with [11] alone, but with all of [9–11], this solution is hardly satisfactory.

2 Ellipsis

Unless one wishes to include a general and uncontrollable notion of 'being understood' into one's analysis, it is essential to introduce specific constraints onto the notion of ellipsis. On this basis, it is possible to separate cases such as *Lunch?*, where there is no unique elliptical derivation, and *The man went out and bought a paper*, where there is (*cf* GCE:568, 707 *ff*). In conversational data, however, one frequently encounters cases of an isolated clause or phrase, where it is wholly unclear whether the utterance is colloquially reduced, independent of the linguistic context, or is an utterance in a relationship of ellipsis to some nearby clause. If the latter, it is often unclear which of two competing relationships is correct. An example of all these problems is 1.22–7.

[15] and |HÈ was SÁYING|
[16] that erm – you can |go to a NĬGHTCLUB| in |BĬRMINGHAM| – –
[17] and |watch ↑Tony BÉNNET| · for a|bout ↑thirty ↑BŌB| –
[18] |something like THÍS|
[19] a |night with ↑Tony ↑BÉNNET| –
[20] |have a 'nice ↑MĒAL| · in · |very · ↑plushy SURRŌUNDINGS|
[21] very |WĀRM| |NÍCE| | PLÈASANT| –

In this sequence, several problems arise. Is [21] related to [20] by ellipsis (*which are*), or to [19] (*which is*), or is it a new sentence with colloquial omission of SV (*it is*), or is it an example of 'postponement' (*cf* GCE:963) (*and this is*)? From the point of view of sentence identification and classification, is [21] a separate, coordinate, or subordinate clause? Similarly, is [20] an ellipsis of *you can* (from [16]), *that you can* [16], or even *and you can*? [18–19] are more obviously appositional, to [17]. [15] and [17] have optional *and*, already discussed under 1 above; *that* in [16] is also optional, with the clause following subordinate to [15]. However, the question here is how much subsequent structure is to be analysed as also subordinate to [15]. Are [20–21], with all their problems, also subordinate to [15]? It does not seem possible to choose between these various analyses on empirical grounds. As with 1, the question of how many and what kind of sentences we are dealing with seems incapable of receiving a definite answer.

3 Intercalation

Frequently in this data, an utterance is produced which seems to contain two interlaced sentences, as in 3.54–60.

[22] I'm |very sus'picious of the PRÉSS| |GÈNERALLY|
[23] and I can |TÈLL you|
[24] be|cause · |not 'only I |mean 'that's ÒNE 'case|
[25] that you've |GÌVEN|
[26] but |ÀLSO| |in in their RE↑PÒRTING| of erm af|fairs ↑foreign
    AF↑FÀIRS| –
[27] be|cause · ↑LÌVING in 'Cyprus|
[28] I've |seen · ↑quite a 'number of HISTÓRICAL E↑VÈNTS| you |KNÓW|

From the context, it is plain that the reason for [22] is given in [24–26]. The reason for [23], *ie* why the speaker is an authority, is given in [27–28]. What we have, therefore, is a structure of the following type:

Main Clause A + Main Clause B + Subordinate Clause A + Subordinate Clause B

and it is this kind of pattern which is here referred to as 'intercalated'. The situation is however more complex than this. [26], from a semantic viewpoint, relates to both sentences: it is half of the reason for [22], along with [24–25], but it also provides the new theme which is the link with [27–28]. Syntactically, [26] has no main verb, and there is thus some motivation for seeing this as a complex adverbial, linked (via the *because* of [27]) to [28]. Because of such complications, we are once again faced with an unclear analysis in terms of sentence structure.

A similar sort of disassociation of structure which raises problems of sentence analysis is 8.48–52:

[29] |I dis'covered that the ↑MŎTHER|
[30] |who had been ↑THÈRE the 'day BEFÓRE|
[31] |wasn't ↑ÌN it|
[32] and |who was ↑now ↑so BĪG|
[33] having |had ↑two LĬTTERS|
[34] that she |couldn't · ↑easily ↑GÈT through the BÁRS| ·
[35] just |wasn't ↑THÈRE|
[36] which was |very ÓDD|

The second relative clause [32] might again be taken as an example of postponement, in view of the main clause conclusion in [31]; but the main clause is repeated in [35], presumably for a mixture of emphasis and clarity of exposition, following the sequence of subordinate clauses [32–34]. We are thus faced with a problem: do we take [35] as a separate sentence, with elided subject, or do we take [31] as an anticipatory performance 'error', or do we recognize a new type of sentence with a 'double' VP?

The problem caused by a lack of correspondence between syntactic and semantic structure is seen again in 3.75–80; the context is an event in Cyprus:

[37] I mean [w] |that's how 'most [pe] 'people ↑TÒOK it|
[38] and erm |so many ↑ÒTHER 'cases| as |WÈLL|
[39] |where there've 'been · erm ↑inter'national 'SITUǍTIONS|
[40] that erm – |people [re] · have ↑really just ↑taken as 'part of their 'normal LǏFE|
[41] and it |"hasn't AF↑"FÈCTED| the |everyday ↑LÌFE of CÝPRUS| at |ÀLL| ·

Here, the sequence sounds like a single sentence; but the initially plausible analysis of [38] as coordinated object of *took* is put in question by the semantic generality (and switch in tense) of [39–40]. Because 'most people' refers to Cypriots, the implication in [38] is that the 'other cases' are also going to be Cyprus-based; but this is unlikely, given the mention of 'international situations' in [39]. It is [41] which takes up the specificity of the Cyprus example (note the use of *it*); though it also shows, inappropriately, the influence of the perfect tense from [39–40]. If this is so, then [38] must be analysed as a new sentence, with elliptical S V, and presumably [41], also, with optional *and*. The overall structure, then, seems to be

Main Clause A + Main Clause B + Subordinate Clause B + Coordinate Clause A

which allows us several options for sentence classification.

These problems are not isolated cases. A more detailed analysis of connectivity items, for instance, shows that of the 420 clauses in the sample, 267 contain at least one connective (64 per cent); there are 322 connectives, and nearly a third of the cases involve 'optional' *and* (see *Table* 1). Moreover, when a distributional analysis is made of the connectives, in terms of whether they occur initially, medially or finally in clause structure, the bias towards initial position is evident: 281 out of 322 connectives are clause initial (87 per cent) (see *Table* 2). If we then exclude the 72 obligatory conjunctions and the 11 cases of optional *that* (which are of a rather different type), we are left with 198 'optional' connectivity features in the sample: in other words, 47 per cent of clauses pose problems of the type discussed above.

It is arguable that all of the above problems arise solely because of the attempt to impose a descriptive model on the data which uses *sentence* as a primitive term. This variety of English, however, does not seem to be readily analysable in terms of sentences. Rather, the *clause* is the unit in terms of which the material is most conveniently organized (as illustrated in the examples above). A model of Clause + connective + Clause ... makes far fewer assumptions about the organization of the data, and avoids the arbitrariness involved in the discussion of **1–3** above. To work in terms of

Table 1 Frequency of connectives in the sample

OBLIGATORY

Subordinate conjunction	60
Coordinate conjunction	12

OPTIONAL

and	99
but	13
well	18
because	8
Exclamatory (*eg oh*)	12
Comment clauses	
you know	32
I mean	17
Other	11
that, etc (in Object and Relative clauses)	11
Other	29

TOTAL CONNECTIVES	322 in 267 clauses
ZERO CONNECTIVITY	153
TOTAL CLAUSES IN SAMPLE	420

Table 2 Distribution of connectives in clause structure

	Initial	Medial	Final	Zero
Simple sentence	81	9	15	46
Clause in complex sentence	200	9	8	107
Total	281	18	23	153

clauses, moreover, correlates much better with a prosodic analysis of such data, and thus with a possible model of speech production, where the role of intonation (especially the tone-unit) is central (*cf* Laver 1970: 69 *ff*). *Table* 3 shows the correlation between tone-units and clauses in the sample: 54 per cent of clauses are exactly one tone-unit in length (228 out of 420), which is more than twice the frequency of any other correlation.

Adverbials

The lack of clear sentential organization is thus one of the main factors accounting for the discrepancy between conversational data and standard descriptive statement, referred to at the beginning of the paper: almost all such statements insist on the theoretical priority of the sentence. But this is not the only area where the discrepancy is marked. If we look now at the

Table 3 Correlation between clauses and number of tone-units

Number of tone-units	Simple sentence[a]	Clause in complex sentence
less than 1	1[b]	92[c]
1	129	99
1 plus	2	14
2	23	35
3 or more	14	11

[a] Ignoring connectives
[b] This solitary example can be found in Crystal and Davy 1975:1.127.
[c] Largely indirect speech clause sequences

elements of clause structure, a further problem is posed by the category of adverbial, which emerges as a rather more central notion than is to be found in either traditional or most linguistic accounts (an important exception is Jackendoff 1972:47 *ff*; see also Crystal 1966). From a syntactic point of view, adverbials are always considered to be optional elements of clause structure (apart from the few exceptions, such as with *put*, *be*, etc), and unless a special point is being made, they are not usually to be seen in the sentences which constitute the evidence in linguistic papers. The first point to be noted about the present data, then, is the frequency of adverbials: 246 of the 420 clauses contain an adverbial (59 per cent). But the distribution is more interesting (see *Table* 4). Of those clauses NOT containing adverbials, 38 are the introductory clauses of indirect speech (*eg He said X, I think X*, where *X* is usually a clause), and 12 are items of an idiomatic or phatic kind (*eg they're tremendous, that's right, and that was that*). If these are excluded, on the grounds that they do not display the syntactic variation typical of other clause types, the proportion of clauses containing adverbials increases to 66 per cent.

Table 4 Distribution of adverbials in the sample

ADVERBIAL PRESENT		ADVERBIAL ABSENT	
Syntactically obligatory	51		
Semantically obligatory		Indirect speech	38
Main clause	88	Main clause	56
Subordinate clause	31	Subordinate clause	68
Optional modification	71	Phatic	12
Ellipsis	5		
TOTALS	246		174

Table 4 summarizes the main types encountered. Only 51 adverbials are syntactically obligatory, the majority of these co-occurring with the verbs *be*, *go* and *get*, eg

[42] and he's |been to A↑MĒRICA| (1.13)
[43] and he |goes to ↑all the 'matches AWÀY| (1.16)
[44] |was it in MADRÌD| (1.54)
[45] |PÀKI-bashing| was – |at its ↑HÈIGHT| |THÉN| I SUP|PÓSE| (3.17)
[46] but he |gets 'on the 'wrong TRÀIN| (3.116)
[47] and |ends 'up in the 'wrong PLÀCE| (3.116)

and an interesting relative clause example

[48] |worst 'game they ↑ever PLÀYED| (1.117)

On the other hand, only 71 of the adverbials are clearly optional, in the sense that their omission would make no difference to the syntactic or semantic acceptability of the clause sequence in which they occur. These can be broadly classified into two types. Firstly, there are adverbials expressing personal emphasis or attitude, *eg*

[49] |this I don't 'really ↑SÈE| (1.2)
[50] |CÓVENTRY 'maybe| (1.67)
[51] |they 'rather 'liked the ↑WÒRD| (3.21)
[52] you |probably DÌD| (3.31)
[53] I'm |very sus'picious of the PRÉSS| |GÈNERALLY| (3.54)
[54] I mean |FÓRTUNATELY| he |WÀSN'T SHÓT| (3.74)

Secondly, there are adverbials which provide detail that is redundant, either because the information is already present elsewhere in the clause, or a previous clause, or it leads nowhere in the subsequent discourse, *eg*

[55] I mean they're pro|gressively ↑getting ↑WÒRSE| (1.39)
[56] I was |reading in the ↑paper this ↑MÒRNING| (1.7)
[57] we'd |taken a 'school 'trip to ÌTALY| (3.14)
[58] and ex|aggerated them ↑out of ↑all PRO↑PÒRTION| (3.49)
[59] I've for|gotten the 'details NÓW| (3.115)
[60] and · |blocked 'up 'one sÍDE| · with |TĬSSUES| (8.67)

It can be reasonably argued, in all such cases, that if the adverbials were not there, no one would have noticed. In isolation, of course, this cannot be justified, but if we restore the context to each of the above sentences, their optionality becomes clear, *eg* in [57] no subsequent reference is made to Italy – it is the school trip which is taken up as the relevant theme.

The remaining adverbial examples in *Table* 4 are all the reverse of this second type. In isolation, they might all be taken as optional, syntactically and semantically, but in context their presence is crucial. Three main types can be recognized:

(*a*) the clause would be ambiguous or false without the adverbial, *eg*

[61] I mean they |never DÒ these 'grounds ÚP| |DÒ they| (1.38)

[62] but there |WÀS an 'interesting 'programme on these 'grounds| (1.52)
[63] |we 'had – to↑matoes in there RÍPENING| (8.104)

(*b*) the meaningfulness of a later clause is dependent solely upon the presence of the adverbial, *eg*

[64] he's a DI|RÈCTOR| of a |big CÒMPANY| in |BÌRMINGHAM| (1.7)
      (*cf* 1.13, 'and he's been to America to watch West Bromwich playing')
[65] |I went to 'Stamford ↑BRÌDGE last year ÓNCE| (1.107)
      (*cf* 1.111 *ff*, where the situation at Stamford Bridge is taken up)

(*c*) the meaningfulness of the clause is dependent on the adverbial recapitulating or contrasting with information from a previous clause, *eg*

[66] did you |GÉT that in 'Cyprus| (3.2)
      (the Cyprus theme had been discussed earlier)
[67] but |people 'went 'on 'living 'quite ↑NŎRMALLY| (3.72)
      (*cf* 3.71, where the point is made about tension in the area)

Sometimes two of these functions can be found in a single adverbial, *eg*

[68] [he said] there was ↑only "one 'modern GRÓUND in ↑ÈNGLAND| (1.65)

where without *in England* the statement would be unclear, and a subsequent contrast with grounds on the continent would be unmotivated.

Quite often, the item which the first adverbial relates to is itself an adverbial, and an interesting situation of 'mutual dependence' develops, *eg*

[69] [there was] the |sea of – ↑bodies in ↑front of you ↑MÒVING| and |people 'started to PÙSH| BE|HÌND you| (1.125)
[70] |one 'minute there was · 'seventy THÒUSAND in the GRÓUND| and about · |thirty 'seconds LÁTER| or a |minute 'later they were ↑CLÈAR| (1.93)
[71] it was just |boys who went 'round with short ↑HÀIR| |rather 'like · you KNÓW| · |teddy 'boys in the 'mid ↑FÌFTIES| |went 'round with ↑LÒNG 'hair| (3.45)

Semantically obligatory adverbials occurred altogether in 119 clauses (28 per cent), and were particularly common in main clauses (3:1, according to *Table* 4). We may thus conclude that for the data as a whole, 41 per cent of all clauses (170/420) contain an adverbial that is in some sense obligatory. A further 20 per cent of clauses have an adverbial which is optional. The prominence of the adverbial is also underlined by prosody: 78 per cent of all adverbials carry a nuclear tone, and though there are only 241 adverbials in the data, they account for nearly one-third of all the nuclear tones used (of 654 tone-units, 187 have the adverbial carrying the nucleus).

In short, the traditional view of adverbial use, reflected in the standard descriptions of English, seems better reversed: instead of needing a special reason to put an adverbial into a clause, one might say there needs to be a special reason for leaving one out. The clause structure in the present data would be far more satisfactorily accounted for if more attention were paid to the adverbial at an early analytic stage. One might even introduce it obligatorily at such a stage (*eg* Clause $\longrightarrow$ V+NP+AP), specifying its deletion only in contexts where its use would be incompatible with other features of clause structure, or redundant, in view of the presence of an adverbial in a previous clause. Such an approach might ultimately produce a far more economical syntactic analysis, and a more intuitively acceptable semantic analysis, than one based on repeated application of an optional rule.

Moreover, when one looks in detail at the nature of the NPs in the data, a further contrast with expected descriptive statement emerges: in the sense of 'Premodification + Head + Postmodification', there are only 233 such structures, *ie* at least 44 per cent of all clauses have no such NP. *Table 5* gives the exponence of the pre-verb and post-verb elements of clause structure. The most striking characteristic is the pronoun category: 325 of the clauses have a pronoun or 'empty' word (*it, there*) as Subject, *viz* 77 per cent. In post-verbal position, the situation is almost exactly reversed, with 80 per cent of the exponence going to the combination of NP, Adverbial, and Clause (Object/Complement). The end-weight of clauses in English is something which has often been pointed out (*eg* GCE:943). What has been less remarked for conversational data is

(*a*) the fact that NPs account for so little clause element exponence (28 per cent), and

(*b*) the powerful role played by pronouns and adverbials, which together account for 57 per cent of all exponence.

The limited power of statistical reasoning is acknowledged. On the other hand, tendencies such as the above are sufficiently dominant to suggest that

Table 5 Exponence of pre- and post-verbal elements of clause structure

	Pre-verbal	Post-verbal
Pronoun[a]	325	42
NP	43	190
Zero	52	33
Adverbial		113
Clause		32[b]

[a] Including *it, there*
[b] All the clauses as object of indirect speech verbs

they cannot be dismissed as 'mere performance'. It is quite possible that an interesting grammar might emerge if a formalization were attempted using the following two rules:

$$\text{Utterance} \longrightarrow \text{Clause} \,(+\,\text{Connectivity} + \text{Clause})$$

$$\text{Clause} \longrightarrow \text{Pronoun} + V + \begin{Bmatrix} NP+A \\ A \end{Bmatrix}$$

Apart from any interest such a proposal may have at descriptive and explanatory levels, one of its merits is that it provides a better fit with the analytic frameworks used in some other areas of language study. There is a parallel with some work in sociolinguistics. For example: Labov (1972) has analysed narratives of personal experience in black vernacular style as a clause sequence, and has also emphasized the role of conjunctions, simple subjects and adverbials. He views his narrative clause patterns as contrasting with ordinary conversation, however (1972:378), whereas the present data – white, middle-class vernacular – hardly justifies the need for such a contrast. As a further example, we may take child language acquisition, where most analyses of the young child credit him with cognitive or semantic discriminations involving location, time, frequency, and a whole range of deictic expression (*eg* Clark 1973). The importance of pronouns in relation to NPs is recognized (*eg* Limber 1976), as is connectivity, especially with *and* (*eg* Lust 1977, Crystal, Fletcher and Garman 1976:76). Adverbials are the main means of expressing spatio-temperal notions, and items such as *there, again,* etc are common in early samples. Later, adverbials are often used in the process of acquiring modal and other such structures (*eg maybe him go* for *he might go*). Given the recognition of these matters in this literature, which usually takes as its data-base domestic conversation, the contrast with standard adult grammars, which do not give them such emphasis, would be somewhat puzzling, without the hypothesis of the present paper. There is no evidence to support the view that the child in some way uses adverbials, pronouns or connectivity features less as he grows older. On the contrary, domestic performance, according to the present paper, stays very much the same, and a significant continuity can thereby be pointed out.

Looking at the data used to illustrate theoretical accounts of language, it has often been remarked that the examples cited are frequently somewhat contrived. This of course is inevitable if the aim of the exercise is to demonstrate the potential of language, for example defining the boundaries of grammaticality by repeated application of a set of rules until structures are generated which are wholly unacceptable. Lists of sentences of varying form, complexity and acceptability are the normal paradigms of illustration in linguistic writing. The value of this way of proceeding is undeniable, but it is a discovery procedure which, because of the way it is structured (involving an initial delimitation of a topic, and a systematic working through of as exhaustive a range of formal permutations as one's ingenuity permits) is unlikely to encounter the data of spontaneous interaction. Because all such sentences – or at least most of them – are speakable, it is easy to imagine that there is no problem – that the grammar of informal domestic conversation is basically a reflection of that of the written language, with a few additional conventions such as ellipsis, intonation, and emphatic word order, and a few omissions, such as the structures characteristic of the more formal and literary modes of expression. The argument of the present paper, on the contrary, is that the linguistic organization of this variety of English has been fundamentally misconceived, due partly to the absence of data, partly to the uncritical application of traditional paradigms of enquiry. Considerable detailed descriptive work is now needed to take this claim further. Whatever the outcome, progress will be largely dependent on the use of the rigorous techniques of corpus-based analysis pioneered by Randolph Quirk. And with such precedent, an interesting outcome seems assured.

WELL IN CONVERSATION
JAN SVARTVIK

In 1953, in a lecture on 'Careless Talk – Some Features of Everyday Speech', Randolph Quirk drew attention to the 'recurrent modifiers' *you know, you see* and *well*:

> It is easily demonstrable that these play, from the point of view of grammatical structure, no part in the transmission of information, yet not only is our present-day colloquy constantly embellished with them, but popular talk stretching back to Shakespeare and beyond has been similarly peppered with these apparently useless and meaningless items. . . . since the desire to feel that the hearer is *sharing* something with one seems to be fundamental in the urge to speak, these sharing devices, these intimacy signals in our everyday talk, are of considerable importance.
>
> (Quirk 1955:178–9).

Since then we have witnessed impressive activity in the study of English linguistics. Yet in spite of the fact that print represents a fraction of total language use, only comparatively modest progress has taken place in the study of everyday speech. The lexicographer still has a tendency to consider the occurrence of a word in print the chief or sole criterion for its inclusion in the dictionary; the grammarian rarely ventures beyond the safe confines of the sentence, a unit that is of doubtful value in the description of casual speech.[1] In recent years, however, the study of talk has gained momentum

---

1 See Crystal's contribution, *p* 153. I want to thank D. Bolinger, S. Greenbaum, G. Leech and J. McH. Sinclair for comments on a draft version of this article.

with the advent of new approaches, such as discourse analysis and sociologically oriented research into the structure of conversation (*eg* Sacks, Schegloff and Jefferson 1974), and many odd grammatical or lexical items are, hopefully, being released from the 'lunacy ward ... where mindless morphs stare vacantly with no purpose other than to be where they are' (Bolinger 1977*b*:ix).

This study will be devoted to *well* in its function of sharing device on the basis of data in a selection of texts from the London-Lund Corpus of Spoken English (for a description of the corpus and the notation, see Quirk and Svartvik 1979). Some of the uses of *well* we will be concerned with here can be illustrated by this extract from a surreptitiously recorded conversation:[2]

|and they said ↑ÒH yes| |David ↑PRÈNDERGAST| the |man from
OVER↑SÈAS| [prə] |PRÈNDERGAST| he's |been in ↑Southern
RHO↑DÈSIA| · [ə] |this is FÍNE| what's |HÈ [wi] |which |where'll HÈ be
[1] working| · |ÔH| [ə] |WĒLL| of |course he'll be working with overseas
[2] ↑STÙDENTS| · |well [ə] ↑YÈS| |but ↑he's WÓRKING with ↑DÌBBLE|
[3] |well NÔ| he's in the |Yiddish [dipaː|] de|part((ment of)) Yiddish
:LÌTERATURE| – and it |FÌNALLY turns ÓUT| ((that)) |this is · |this is
the |chap to double Mark ↑PÒOLEY| |you SÉE| – and |he is · |he is |he's
a · {LÍTERATURE} MÁN| and he's |going to work in Mallet's
DEPÀRTMENT| – and [ə] at ↑THĬS stage| |they |they threw up their
[4] ↑HÀNDS| and |said well ↑LÒOK| · |these are |these are "[ðəː] two ·
↑{PÈRMANENT} AP{PÒINTMENTS} that have been :MÀDE| (1.2.44–6)

There are certain facts about *well* that can be stated at the outset. First, there is little agreement as to the function or word-class status of *well*. It has, for example, been labelled 'adverb', 'interjection', 'filler', and 'particle'; those grammars that mention it at all assign various names to it in specific uses, such as 'hesitator' (Francis 1958:428), 'utterance-initiator' (Strang 1968:96), 'initiator' (GCE:274). We will here settle for the suitably vague and neutral term 'particle' in contrast to the *well* used as a manner adverb (*He speaks well*) or as a degree word (*You know that perfectly well*; see Bolinger 1972*a*:28–43).[3]

Second, it is obvious that lexicographers find it peculiarly awkward to define the particle *well*. The great OED disposes of this item in six lines (*v* adv, VI. 23):

Employed without construction to introduce a remark or statement, sometimes implying that the speaker or writer accepts a situation, etc,

2 | marks tone-unit boundary; the word containing the tonic is printed in capitals and the direction of nuclear tone is marked ˇˇ etc, for example ÔH, NÒ;| marks the first pitch-prominent syllable of the tone-unit; :, ↑ mark a step-up in pitch; ·, –, etc, mark degrees of pause length; { } denotes subordination.

3 Hines (1977) presents evidence to suggest that there is in fact a relationship between *well* used as an introductory word and *well* as an adverb.

already expressed or indicated, or desires to qualify this in some way, but frequently used merely as a preliminary or resumptive word.

Contrary to its usual practice, Webster's *Third New International Dictionary* gives no exemplification (*v* ⁵*well*):

> **1** – used to express satisfaction with what has been said or done **2a** – used to express assent or resignation **b** – used to express surprise and expostulation and often reduplicated **3** – used to indicate resumption of a thread of discourse or to introduce a remark

Third, particles like *well* are notoriously difficult to translate idiomatically into another language. For example, among the Swedish equivalents provided by standard dictionaries are the following: 'nå!', 'nåväl!', 'se så!', 'nå ja!', 'välan!', 'ja visst!', 'jo!', 'jaa!', some of which seem awkward or even outright impossible to use in casual conversation.

Fourth, the particle *well* is virtually restricted to spoken language, where it is one of the most frequent words. For example, in Jones and Sinclair (1974, Appendix A), *well* has rank 13, and is found in the same frequency range as *is*, *was*, and *that*. Lacking a frequency list with grammatical tags, we can only assume that the vast majority of these instances represent the particle rather than the adverb or degree word. This assumption is endorsed by the fact that, in the Brown Corpus (of written English), *well* has only rank 99. In the material from the London-Lund Corpus (of spoken English) which has been used as a basis for this study, there were, on average, one particle *well* for every 150 words. (The figure would be even higher if all auditorily unclear instances had not been excluded.)

The data of this study consisted of nine surreptitiously recorded Survey texts of casual conversation, each of about 5,000 words, totalling some 45,000 words. Excluding non-particle uses and incomprehensible stretches marked (( )), 303 occurrences of *well* were analysed, ranging from 21 to 51 instances in the texts. The instances of *well* were analysed in terms of seven parameters: position in discourse, collocation, prosody, pauses, incomplete surrounding structure, functions and Swedish equivalents.

Well occurred with equal frequency at the beginning of a new turn, *ie* after speaker switch, and embedded in a single speaker's utterance. One third of the instances in the first category introduced a response to a question or other response-initiation. Among the responses prefixed by *well*, there were more responses to *wh*-questions than to *yes/no* and tag questions, for example:

C: |what's your plan if · this doesn't come ÔFF|
[5] A: *well* I've |been accepted at Pemberton HÀLL| |you *sÉE|*
C: *[m]*
A: – – – which is |obviously going to be much :LĬVELIER| (1.3.60)

Well introduces an indirect answer to C's question 'What's your plan . . .?'.
Speaker A seems to imply 'It's not exactly a plan, but . . .'. *Well* embedded
in discourse has been illustrated above in examples [1–4]. *Well* is typically
prefixed to a following structure. However, it is occasionally used in isolation
and repetition (example quoted by Persson 1974:154):

Developing your muscles, eh? And character. (Pause)
Well, well, well.

It seems possible to analyse such exceptions in the same way as regular uses
of *well*. In this example, the speaker might continue: 'That's what you think
is important but . . .', *ie* challenging the presuppositions of his conversation
partner.

Well frequently occurred with other items: *oh well, well then*, etc. The
following are the most common collocations with *well* in the material: a
form of *say* or *think, you know, you see, I mean, look, really, then, so, no, yes.*
The most frequent type was *say* or *think* + *well* + direct speech:

[6] – – and I |SĀID| *well* I |don't RÈALLY think | I could |WRÌTE| – – and
     this was a sort of |ninety-six page ↑BÒOKLET| |you KNÓW| about |that
     BÌG| (1.3.9)

Of all the instances of *well*, 44 per cent were unstressed, mostly occurring in
pre-onset position (example [5]), but also within the tone unit (example [4]);
56 per cent were stressed, half of them bearing the nucleus. The different
tones on *well* were distributed as follows:

		(per cent)
Fall	53	(62)
Level	14	(16)
Rise	10	(12)
Rise-fall	5	(6)
Fall-rise	3	(4)
Total	85	(100)

If simple and complex tones are conflated, in the case of the latter according
to the final pitch-movement, we get the following distribution:

		(per cent)
Fall or rise-fall	58	(68)
Rise or fall-rise	13	(16)
Level	14	(16)

If these figures are compared with those reported in studies of overall tone
types, for example Crystal (1969:225), we find that the proportion of level
tone is considerably higher (16 per cent here compared with 4.9 per cent in

Crystal's study), and that of falling tone somewhat higher (62 per cent compared with 51.2 per cent), whereas that of rising tone is lower (12 per cent compared with 20.8 per cent). Unfilled pauses before and after *well* occurred as follows:

	Before *well*	After *well*	Total
Brief pause (·)	19	24	43
Unit pause (−, − ·)	22	7	29
Long pause (−−, −−−)	14	2	16
Total	55	33	88

The pauses before *well* occur mostly embedded in discourse, which means that it is typical for *well* in this position to be preceded by silence, in particular a unit or long pause. In addition, there occurred different forms of filled pauses, *ie* voiced hesitation, for example [m, əm, ə, əː, mhm], particularly before *well*.

Well frequently occurred in a context of incomplete structures. Anacolutha were noted in 23 cases before and 44 cases after *well*. In some cases *well* was followed by repetition, such as [ði ði], *I'm I'm*. Here are two examples of incomplete structures with *well*:

B: |on the FLÒOR|·
[7] A: |on [ð?] |on [ðiː] *well* |on [ðiː sʔ] you |know on [ði] "↑HÀTCHWAY
THÉRE| (1.7.123)

Here the use of *well* is that of a temporizing or delaying tactic.

and Aus|tralia's a ↑special ↑CÀSE of CÓURSE| be|cause · it 'has a ↑lot of
[8] · *well* it |has a "↑FÈW| · A|merican ŌVER'TONES| |not "MÀNY| be|cause
it's ↑{MÀINLY} ↑BRÌTISH| (1.10.37)

Well here modifies a claim the speaker decides is excessive.

The difficulties that we experience in stating the functions of *well* can be explained in various ways. For one thing, spoken language has been comparatively little studied and the use of items which are typical of or practically restricted to conversation is therefore bound to be little known. Furthermore, its function is largely pragmatic and not describable in ordinary grammatical terms. The use of such words whose functions are related to phatic communion rather than intellectual reflection (*cf* Malinowski 1969:315) is parallel to the role of intonation. A native speaker, naive or otherwise, may be aware of violations of such a rule, yet will be incapable of providing a rational explanation of it. To take an example: if a foreign learner says *five sheeps* or *he goed*, he can be corrected by practically every native speaker. If, on the other hand, he omits a *well*, the likely reaction will be that he is dogmatic, impolite, boring, awkward to talk to etc, but a native speaker cannot pinpoint an 'error'. Yet inappropriate use of particles like *well* may have more unfortunate consequences for communication success than elementary grammatical errors.

One of the few contributions to the description of *well* is by Robin Lakoff (1972, 1973), who noted that 'there are two major circumstances under which an answer prefaced by *well* is not possible' in answers: 'when a direct answer is given' ('What time is it?'—'*Well, three o'clock') and when 'the response does not constitute a reply to the question in the sense of providing the information sought' ('What time is it?'—'*Well, none of your business'; 1973:458). The conditions under which *well* can be used are '(1) when the answer sought can only be obtained by the questioner by deduction from the response given, and (2) when the reply is directed toward a question other than the overt one: that is, when a different *question* can be deduced by the respondent because of the conversational situation' (460). *Well* is used 'in case the speaker senses some sort of insufficiency in his answer, whether because he is leaving it to the questioner to fill in information on his own or because he is about to give additional information himself' (463). While Robin Lakoff's paper is full of interesting observations, it is limited to the use of *well* in answers.

Crystal and Davy (1975:101-2), who provide a more comprehensive account, including non-answers and prosodic features, state that *well* has three distinct pronunciations and meanings. Initially in utterances

(a) It may be said slowly, drawled, usually with a falling-rising or rising tone, to imply such attitudes as reservation or doubt. The use means 'I'm sorry I have to say this, but . . .'

(b) It may be said in a rapid, clipped manner, in which case the attitude involved would be more business-like, implying that the speaker wishes to get on with his narrative. This may at times lead to an impression of abruptness, impatience, or something similar.

(c) Drawled with a level tone, it is simply an exponent of hesitation, indicating indecision, or, quite commonly, a casual or leisurely attitude on the part of the speaker, which he might be deliberately introducing in order to maintain the informality of a situation.

In the present study, no such distinct correlations were however found between prosody and meaning. It seems that Crystal and Davy interpret not differences in the meaning of *well* but differences in the intonational meaning, which they then attribute to *well* itself.

In order to establish the functions of *well*, paraphrases were used. However, paraphrasing different instances in context as a means of establishing its meanings, let alone defining them, did not turn out to be easy. Yet certain functional categories will be suggested here with English paraphrases and Swedish equivalents, all of which will of course not be possible in every instance but still have enough in common to justify their being grouped together. Since Swedish has no direct counterpart to *well*, the

Swedish rendering can be seen as serving a dual purpose: to provide contrastive statements as well as to further highlight the meanings of *well*. The differences should be linguistic since the social rules of conversation are very similar in the two societies.

There appear to be two major uses of *well*: as a qualifier and as a frame (*cf* Hines 1977). As a qualifier, *well* is closely connected with previous and/or following discoursal context, serving as a link between the two. We can distinguish certain subcategories in terms of paraphrases.

Agreement, positive reaction or attitude: 'yes', 'indeed'; Sw 'ja (visst)', 'jo (visst)'. (Subject: film-making):

> A: *and |can* you ASSÈSS |can you · [kəv'æʔ] |what's the WÒRD| ·
>   con|nect them in 'such a 'way that they ↑just go ÒN| **so |nobody
>   can DE↑TÈCT ((it))|**
> [9] B: **|*well* there's [əːm] |there's a ↑MÀRK** on the on [ðiː əːm] – –
>   (1.7.141)

Even when the answer prefixed by *well* is positive, as here, it is not straight, but saying 'this information is the best I can do in answering your question'.

Well can also indicate reinforcement: 'as a matter of fact', 'actually', 'certainly', 'really'; Sw 'ja (då)', '(ju) faktiskt', 'nog', 'då', 'ju förstås', 'verkligen'.

> B: I |think they've got quite a good O↑PÌNION of him| –
> [10] A: |*well* [ə] ↑I ↑I have TÒO| (1.1.38)

A here adds information but also suggests that B has overlooked a point.

> C: **yes he's** |very busy at the MÒMENT|
> [11] A: |YÈS| · *well* he's |{ÀLWAYS} frantically BÙSY| (1.3.62)

A does not disagree with C but points out that what he has just said is not exactly new information.

Well is also used in collocations like *Well I'm damned!* to express exclamatory surprise, etc. However, this function of *well* represents the smallest category in the data, which suggests that the place given to exclamations in dictionary definitions of *well* is out of proportion to its actual use, at least in spontaneous conversation.

In view of its frequency as an answer prefix, *well* in this use may be considered to have a separate function:

> B: |if it could be DÓNE| |WITHÓUT| · [ə] · |ÈITHER| – |TRÉADING| |or ·
>   ↑even AP↑PÈARING to TRÉAD| · |on the TÓES| of ex|isting
>   AR↑RÀNGEMENTS| ·
> A: |what ex:isting arrangements *:ÀRE they|*
> [12] B: *|*well* you* see they're ((the)) ar↑rangements for EXÁMPLE with
>   ↑MÀCE| · (1.2.37)

Here *well*, together with *you see*, softens the non-straight and incomplete answer to the *wh*-question: 'they are the arrangements for example with Mace' would be an unnaturally brusque answer in a casual conversation. *Well* is particularly common in responses to *wh*-questions but also occurs after *yes/no* questions which are not answered by a simple *yes* or *no* (it is in fact rare for a speaker to utter simply *yes* or *no* in response to a *yes/no* question; *cf* Brown 1977: 112), as in:

A: |are these *CÓPIES|*
[13] B: *well* |THÀT'S a CÓPY| [ə] |that's 'only a ↑Stoke 'student has ↑made a 'copy of the ↑PÀINTING which| the |painting's in MA↑DRÌD| – |I ↑THĬNK| it's |not in LÒNDON| (1.4.29)

Well here (corresponding to Swedish 'nja') introduces a non-direct or qualified answer (*cf* Lakoff); it suggests that the answer is not complete, *ie* 'as far as this painting is concerned, the answer to your question is yes but as for the others . . .' The suggestion of incompletion produced by *well* is enhanced by the following fall-plus-rise intonation. Thus, there seems to be no reason to treat *well* prefixed to answers as a special category, since the same basic qualifying function obtains in answers and non-answers alike. B's '*well* that's a copy' in [13] could equally well occur if A had said, for example, 'I believe these are copies'.

The second major use of *well* is as a 'frame' between two discourse units (for this term, see Sinclair and Coulthard 1975). Unlike the qualifier, which is typically initial and linked to turn-taking, *well* in its framing function normally occurs non-initially, embedded in discourse. Some subcategories can be distinguished.

Closing previous discourse and focusing on following discourse: 'all right then', 'so', 'OK', 'consequently'; Sw 'alltså', 'nå (då så)', 'hur som helst'.

A: but if |they wanted people A↑RÒUND| · |to TĂLK to| – |then I would be very happy to ↑STÀY| – ((and)) |got a letter back SÀYING| we
[14] have AR|RÀNGED| for |you to STÀY| – – "|WÈLL| · |let's take the interview FÌRST| (1.3.14)

In this example, *well*, typically pronounced with a falling tone and preceded by a long pause, shifts the topic focus to one of the topics which have already been under discussion: zooming in on the interview, the setting of which has been given previously.

Another very similar type of frame introduces explanations, clarifications, etc. However similar, the paraphrases seem different enough to call for a separate category.[4] Also, in this use collocations are different: *well you see*,

---

4 One problem with paraphrases is that, as here, the paraphrases themselves can sometimes be preceded by *well*: 'well it's like this', etc. It might therefore be better to talk of 'expansions' rather than 'paraphrases'.

well I mean, etc. Paraphrases: 'it's like this', 'the thing is', 'now listen to me', etc; Sw 'jo (det var så att)', 'ja (du förstår)', etc.

> A: |I acquired an ↑absolutely mag↑nificent ↑sɛ̀wɪɴɢ machine| by
> |foul mɛ̀ᴀɴs| |did I tɛ̀ʟʟ you about ᴛʜᴀ́ᴛ|
> B: |ɴɔ̀|
> [15] A: *well* |when I was · doing freelance ↑ᴀ̀ᴅᴠᴇʀᴛɪsɪɴɢ| – [ðiː]
> ↑ᴀ̄ᴅᴠᴇʀᴛɪsɪɴɢ agency| that I · |sometimes did some wɔ̀ʀᴋ for| ·
> *|ʀᴀ̀ɴɢ*me| and said [əm] –   (1.3.6)

This is a partial shift of topic in that the preceding question has cleared the way for the story to be told but does not directly indicate that the speaker intends to tell the story.

In their analysis of classroom discourse Sinclair and Coulthard (1975) found that a small set of words – *right, well, good, OK, now* – 'functioned to indicate boundaries in the lesson, the end of one stage and the beginning of the next', for example '*Well*, today, erm, I thought we'd do three quizzes' (22).

The use of frames is obviously particularly important in classroom discourse where the teacher's task is to monitor the discourse pedagogically. In casual conversation with speakers on equal and intimate terms such structuring by one of the participants is less likely to occur. Schegloff and Sacks (1973:303) use the term 'possible preclosing'. Yet this is only one of the uses of frames, which may open as well as shut down a topic.

Another use of *well*, which is very similar to its frame function in the classroom, is the common collocation of verbs like *say* or *think* and *well* introducing direct speech, as in [4]:

and |said well ↑ʟɔ̀ᴏᴋ|

In such cases *well* is usually prosodically unmarked and can often be dropped without notable change of meaning. Its function can then be taken merely as a signal indicating the beginning of direct speech, parallel to that of quotation marks in writing. However, in such collocations, *well* can also have the same functions as a turn opener in regular conversation between two or more participants.

Another use of *well* in its framing function is as editing marker for self-correction: 'what I mean is', 'I mean'; Sw '(ja, jo) alltså', 'jo, jag menar'. Du Bois (1974) discusses four types of editing markers: *that is* for 'reference editing', *rather* for 'nuance editing', *I mean* for 'mistake editing' and *well* for 'claim editing', in which case 'the speaker modifies a claim he decides is excessive, or a description he decides is too extravagant' (4), for example:

[16] I drove 90 miles an hour –
$\begin{Bmatrix} \text{well} \\ \text{?rather} \\ \text{*I mean} \\ \text{*that is} \end{Bmatrix}$
85 – all the way to Santa Fe.

[175]

Well as an editing marker, indicating a new start, frequently occurs in a context of hesitation phenomena, for example '. . . it has a lot of · well it has a few . . .' (see examples [7] and [8]).

The basic use of *well* should be seen as a sharing device, highlighting what is perhaps the primary distinguishing feature of informal conversation: 'since its *function* is to maintain (or establish) social relationships, the information content is of secondary importance' (Brown 1977:117). Apart from this basic social function we may detect a variety of specific, additional and optional, uses related to discourse techniques: as floorholder, hesitator, or initiator.

The attempts at paraphrasing *well* turned out to be no more than moderately successful, which is only to be expected since its basic function is pragmatic rather than semantic. We may contrast conjuncts like *in addition* or *by the way*, which retain at least in part some semantic content. The varying applicability of the Swedish equivalents indicates that there is no directly corresponding Swedish item, and furthermore, that *well* in fact displays a much wider range of functions than those discussed here. However, the translations also provide some evidence for the distinction between *well* as a qualifier and *well* as a frame. In particular, items like 'visst', 'ju', and 'förstås' demonstrate the qualifying function in that they express the speaker's attitude to the discoursal context, their pragmatic function being to signal that it is already familiar or obvious to him (*cf* Aijmer 1978).

From the very limited material of this study, there appears to be no clear evidence that there is a close correlation between prosody and the two major uses of *well* as a qualifier and a frame. The most probable explanation for the failure to find a correlation is that the analysis of prosody was too superficial in concentrating on *well* and paying too little regard to the surrounding context. Hence, conclusions drawn from this study can only be tentative.

In spite of lacking support for viewing binary intonation choice as primary, it is tempting to mention certain similarities between our categories of *well* and the referring/proclaiming distinction made by Brazil (1975). He argues that, by choosing the fall-rise tone (the 'you know' type), a speaker can indicate that the content of those tone groups is regarded as part of the shared, already negotiated, common ground; by choosing the falling tone (the 'I mean to say' type) he can indicate that new experience is being introduced. We may compare the 'you know' type, which is said to have a referring function, to our qualifying function, for example [11] above: 'well he's always frantically busy' where 'you know' could be added. The 'I mean to say' type, which is said to have a proclaiming function, can be compared to our framing function, for example [15] above: 'well when I was doing freelance advertising' where expressions with a proclaiming function like 'you see' might be added. In [11] a fall-rise intonation would seem possible but hardly in [15]. Certain collocations also tend to support the distinction.

Again, the distinction parallels that between backgrounding and foregrounding. In its qualifying, referring function, *well* may be seen as a device for backgrounding old information which is common ground (when the utterance prefaced by *well* agrees with, reinforces, challenges the views, etc, of the previous speaker) as well as a device for foregrounding the pragmatic function of the following contribution (such as indicating insufficiency). In its framing, proclaiming function *well* may be seen as a device for foregrounding new information, such as announcing a new topic, a new start, etc.

The two major functions should however be seen as places in a spectrum, ranging from the qualifying functions of polite disagreement [2, 3], qualified refusal [6], reinforcement [11], modification [8,16] and indirect, partial answers [1, 5, 9, 10, 12, 13] to delaying tactics [7] and the framing functions [4, 14, 15]. The common denominator of the uses of *well* in the corpus seems to be that of shifting topic focus in discourse. It signals that the speaker is going to shift ground, *ie* that he is going to modify one or more assumptions or expectations which have formed the basis of discourse so far. *Well* signals a modification or partial change in the discourse, *ie* it introduces a part of the discourse that has something in common with what went before but also differs from it to some degree.

SOME FUNCTIONS OF
YES AND *NO* IN CONVERSATION
WOLF-DIETRICH BALD

1 Introduction

Sir Thomas More observed a functional distribution of *yes/no* and *yea/nay*, perhaps already expressing a conservative usage, which was later recorded in the Oxford English Dictionary (*sv* 'nay', 'yes' *etc*, with a reference to More):

[1] As for ensample, if a manne should aske Tindall hymselfe: ys an heretike mete to translate holy scripture into englishe. Lo to thys question if he will aunswere trew englishe, he muste aunswere nay and not no. But and if the question be asked hym thus lo: Is not an heretyque mete to translate holy scripture into english. To this . . . he must aūswere no, & not nay. And a lyke difference is there betwene these two aduerbes ye, and yes. . . . If an heretique falsely translate the newe testament into englishe . . . be hys bookes worthy to be burned. To this question . . . he must aunswere ye, and not yes. . . . If an heretike falsely translate . . . be not his bokes well worthy to be burned. To thys question . . . he maye not aunswere ye, but he must aunswere yes, and say mary be they, bothe the translation and the translatour, and al that wyll holde wyth them. (More 1557:448, I/II)

In present-day educated British English usage only *yes* and *no* prevail, with *yeah*, [m] or [mhm] bordering on intimate or colloquial styles, and apparently these two words have to serve for all the distinctions once covered by four terms. The aim of our analysis is to investigate which functions *yes* and *no* may have as responses in English conversations, what they 'mean', and which correlations exist with intonational features. Our study is based entirely on corpus material,[1] since it would be futile to speculate about the possible turns of a conversation with the two words as responses. The advantages and disadvantages of corpus analysis need not be discussed here (*cf* Bald and Ilson 1977:3 *ff*), but it will be obvious that this investigation would be virtually impossible without a corpus of data.

2 The data

The analysis of the data was greatly simplified by the almost completed computerization of the spoken material from the Survey of Spoken English at Lund University. The computer provided an output with all the occurrences of *yes* and *no* on slips of paper which also contained a few lines of context. For the investigation we selected five texts which consisted of approximately 5,000 words each of surreptitiously recorded unscripted conversation between disparates, interviews of senior university staff with student or staff applicants. Occasionally, examples contain, for context, sentences spoken by participants for whom the recording was not surreptitious, but any responses of such speakers (symbolized by a small letter 'a' prescript in the examples) were discarded. In a number of instances the context was, however, insufficient so that the original transcriptions in the Survey of English Usage had to be consulted. This was also necessary with regard to various paralinguistic and also linguistic features (tonal range, etc) which are not stored in the computer (*cf* Quirk and Svartvik 1979).

Reasons of space compel us to limit our attention to occurrences of *yes* and *no* only, thus rejecting items like *yeah* and [m] or [mhm] for this investigation. It seems, however, that the picture would not substantially change if such items were included, apart from the fact that the number of elements expressing agreement would increase.

The total number of *yes* and *no* responses in the texts selected, including repetitions, was 372, *ie* 309 for *yes* and 63 for *no*.

The notation used with the examples is that of Crystal (1969), Crystal and Davy (1975:17), simplified by leaving out most of the paralinguistic features

1 I would like to express my deep gratitude to Professor Randolph Quirk for giving me access again to the files of the Survey of English Usage, and also for letting me use the research facilities at University College London. I should also like to thank Professor Jan Svartvik and his team for providing neatly ordered computer-printouts of the occurrences of *yes* and *no* from the Survey of Spoken English at Lund University. The editors of this volume, Miss J. Carter, Dr K. Sprengel, Mrs A.-B. Stenström and Dr H. W. Viethen improved my English and pointed out various errors, while Mrs H. Höhlein typed several versions of this paper; I am very grateful to all of them. The work reported in this article was carried out during my sabbatical year, which was financed through a grant from the *Stiftung Volkswagenwerk*, Hanover.

(*cf* Quirk and Svartvik 1979 and Svartvik's contribution, fn 2, *p* 168). The classification number at the end of each quotation is the slip number of the Survey under which the original text can be found.

3 Analysis

Quotation [1] and the OED entries for *yes* and *no* already illustrate that a classification of the functions of the two words depends at least partially on their contexts. The data in our corpus suggested several subdivisions which will be explored below, namely contexts in which *yes* and *no* retain their polarity of agreement and disagreement, and others in which this polarity is neutralized; thirdly there are instances in which *yes* or *no* select different sections of the context to which they refer as responses, and finally reduplications of the responses will be examined.

One typical feature of spoken language has to be mentioned, namely the interruption of one speaker by another. For instance:

[2] A: ... the |life of an :urban UNI:VÈRSITY| |like this ìs| · "|must be
    {|DÌFFERENT|}·
    C: *|m̀|*
    (A: from |Green 'Field :CÀMPUS| |where ·
    C: |oh YÊS|
    (A: [i] in the ↑ĔND| ...   (3.3.124)

Such cases did not present a special subclass as regards the functions of *yes* and *no* and were hence included in the other sections, according to their contexts.

3.1 Agreement/disagreement polarity

In our material several types of context may be distinguished in which *yes* and *no* retain their basic polarity. The most neutral context calling for a response seems to be a *yes/no* question; for example:

[3] A: in |due CŌURSE| |would you ↑stick that in his ↑PÌGEONHÓLE| ·
    B: |YÈS| (3.2c.34)
[4] A: [ə:m] |ís this a'vailable| – [ə:m]
    C: |NÒ|· ((there |aren't)) ...   (3.3.30)

Tag questions[2] also ask for a response, but here the speaker may influence the answer by choosing a certain tone and a negative or positive correlation with the main clause (*cf* GCE:390 *ff*). The small number of tags in the

---

2 Tags on statements and tags on imperatives seem to have different functions; with statements they appear to draw the listener's attention to the 'truth value' of the statement, whereas the imperative is modified along a scale of politeness from order to request, but remains at least a request; the truth value cannot come into the picture at all.

sample did not reveal any pattern as regards these factors.[3] Questions with a negative may contain 'an element of surprise or disbelief which adds implications of positive meaning' (GCE:389); the four examples in our data were all followed by the response *yes*. We found only one imperative with *let's* whose expected response would be, and actual response was, *yes*.

Positive statements very often do not exhibit any overt triggers for a response, but in a conversation it seems to be a general rule that the partners comment on one another's utterances, if only to show interest or that they understood a certain point. There are, however, two kinds of statement which contain an address-like phrase [5a, b][4] or the subject *you* [6a, b] which sometimes makes these almost functionally equivalent to a *yes/no* question.[5] Compare the following examples:

[5]*a* B: it's |{RÈALLY sort of} : what the ↑MÒNEY 'is| I |mean ↑not |YŎU
     know|
   A: *|YÈS|*
   B: |not – [ə:m] – :wanting to be . . .   (3.2a.25)
   b B: be|cause · ↑after I'd :done the M:À| |straight after DÒING a
     DEGRÉE| I |just felt ↑YÒU know|
   A: *|YÈS| |yes ↑QUÌTE| – |YÈS|*
   B: *I |didn't want · ((to be))* ↑pressurized . . .   (3.2a.41)
[6]*a* B: you |read 'Troilus and 'Cressida be:fore you ↑SÀW it|
   A: |YÈS [əm]|| · I |read it TWÌCE| be|fore I · WÈNT| (3.5a.25)
   b a: you've read a good deal of Chaucer to be able *to make this
     statement*
   A: *|no ↑not – *[ə:]· this is |only – :going :from [ə:] · The
     ↑PÀRDONER'S 'Tale|·   (3.5b.18)

A separate examination of these various contexts did not show any characteristics specific to a certain subclass. *Table* I displays the distribution of *yes* and *no* with relation to their position in the tone unit (TU) and to the nuclear tones with which they occur.

3 The types of tag were distributed as follows:

statement	tag	total
pòs	nég	1
pòs	pós	4
pòs	nèg	10

4 *Cf* Svartvik's contribution, *p* 174. A few borderline cases of the inclusive *we* and the indefinite *you* 'one, people' are included in the figures because they function similarly.

5 Since the statement is structurally and hence functionally the most neutral form, it can be used as imperative, question, or request with the help of intonation, context or situation, whereas question or imperative structures do not exhibit the same range of possibilities. When *you* is the subject of a statement it is often indistinguishable functionally from a question.

Table 1

YES	total	pre-onset	onset bearer	nucleus bearer	＼	／	∨	∧	–	＼+／	／+＼
TU alone	165	–	165	165	134	9	3	4	15	–	–
part of TU	18	I	II	12	10	–	–	I	I	–	–

NO	total	pre-onset	onser bearer	nucleus bearer	＼	／	∨	∧	–	＼+／	／+＼
TU alone	15	–	15	15	10	I	2	I	I	–	–
part of TU	14	I	13	6	3	–	I	–	–	2	–

Several tendencies become very clear. *Yes* occurs far more frequently than *no*. One reason is that there is a preponderance of positive statements in the data and, as *Table* 2 shows, *yes* tends to occur mainly after positive statements:

Table 2

	Responses		Total
	YES	NO	
yes/no question	34	25	59
tag question	14	I	15
question with negative	4	–	4
imperative	I	–	I
positive statement	130	3	133
Total	183	29	212

But another factor is represented by the type of text, *ie* the interview situation prompts the interviewee to agree rather than disagree with the interviewer.

Most *yes* responses are in a tone unit of their own, whereas about half of the occurrences of *no* are part of a tone unit. In 96 of the 165 occurrences of *yes* as a separate tone unit, it is also the complete utterance of the speaker (disregarding repetitions or additions of [m]), while it is the complete utterance in only two instances of 15 occurrences of *no* as a separate tone unit. These figures illustrate the conversational convention, or even necessity, that disagreement has to be explained. The following passages provide typical examples:

[7] B: and |then you · might 'go back to the 'play and 'look at it and 'say
       does it WÒRK| · |is that ↑RÌGHT| –
    A: |YÈS| – –
    B: you've |never THÒUGHT of it like 'that | – – –   (3.5b.50)
[8] B: *|what do you* 'find UN:PLÈASANT a'bout · {|studying FRÈNCH|}|
       TRANS|LÁTING|
    A: |NÒ| I |don't find :French UN:PLÈASANT| at |ÀLL| I |just . . .   (3.5b.6)

The fall is the most frequently occurring and the most neutral tone. As has been stated in many studies of intonation, rising tones and (often) level tones signal continuation and sometimes hesitation ('the speaker is thinking'); on the other hand, the fall-rise adds considerable emphasis. Compare the illustrations below:

 [9] a: [ə:] is that because you dislike French literature
     A: [ə] |NǑ| · |NÓ| I |I [ə] · :thought I would – :learn
        FRÉNCH| · . . .   (3.5b.5)
[10] A: *((|Jake if))* you 'want to say something IMMÉDIATELY|
     B: [ə:] |YĒS| · [ə:] |I can [s] · fore'see a :PRÒBLEM 'here| (3.4.64)
[11] A: |NŌW| · |have you COM↑PLÀINED about 'this| –
     C: ((|NŌ| I |HÀVEN'T|))
     E: |YÊS| · |YÈS|[6]   (3.3.34)

The next two quotations deserve to be especially noted, since the rising tone leads the response beyond the agreement/disagreement polarity. It indicates that the speaker does not concentrate on the utterance immediately preceding but refers to a more general line of thought or argument. This function is typical for contexts as discussed under 3.3.1:

[12] B: . . . "|WÈLL| the |usual 'mixture of · ↑FÒRMS of
        'teaching| · |LÈCTURES| – |SĒMINARS| · [ə] · |SUPERVÍSIONS| or
        TU|TÒRIALS| – – |do you want 'something more PRE:CÌSE than
        'that| –
     A: [ə] |YÉS| well |that's FÎNE| [əm] . . .   (3.6.26)
[13] A: it |seems to 'be a · :fairly :solid ad'miration of · the ":CŎURT
        in| · the |SQUĬRE'S 'Tale| – . . .
     B: the |CHÚRCH| – – –
     A: |YÉS| I |don't think he – :criticizes the :{CHŬRCH}
        PAR↑TĬCULARLY| –   (3.5b.24)

6 This example is particularly interesting since the speaker E answers *yes* to A, but his rise-fall intonation takes C's statement into account.

On the whole the number of non-falling tones was too scarce to permit generalizations as to their effect in our data. The same holds for other prosodic or paralinguistic features, which occurred fairly rarely in the material and did not form any generalizable pattern.

3.2 Neutralization of *yes/no* polarity

Both *yes* and *no* can express agreement with a negative statement:

[14] B: I |didn't want · ((to be)) ↑pressurized like *'that any MǑRE|*
    A: *|YÈS| · |YÈAH|*
    B: |but [əː] · well . . . (3.2a.42)
[15] B: . . . be|cause · pre'sumably one wouldn't be 'teaching it 'single-
      ↑HÀNDED|
    E: |NÒ| (3.6.24)

The neutralization of *yes* and *no* in such instances is demonstrated through the interchangeability of the words; agreement remains irrespective of which item is present. There are examples, however, whose contexts seem to exert a certain pressure towards one response:

[16] A: they |DǑN'T use the 'library| because they |take 'books ÒUT|
    C: |YÈS| (3.3.27)
[17] A: the |ǑNLY thing you ↑want to do is to get A"↑WĂY from the 'people|
    and you *"|CÀN'T|*
  VAR: *|m̃|* |m̀| |YÈS| (3.3.124)

The contexts contain both negative and positive clauses. Perhaps this is the reason for the occurrence of *yes* to signal agreement, because in [16] a *no*

Table 3

YES	total	pre-onset	onset bearer	nucleus bearer	ˋ	ˊ	ˇ	ˆ	−	ˋ+ˊ	ˊ+ˋ
TU alone	9	−	9	9	8	−	1	−	−	−	−
part of TU	−	−	−	−	−	−	−	−	−	−	−

NO	total	pre-onset	onset bearer	nucleus bearer	ˋ	ˊ	ˇ	ˆ	−	ˋ+ˊ	ˊ+ˋ
TU alone	8	−	8	8	5	1	1	1	−	−	−
part of TU	7	−	7	2	2	−	−	−	−	−	−

might be misunderstood as disagreement with the final clause. Yet it is uncertain whether *no* would in fact be an impossible substitute in the two quotations.

If a speaker wants to disagree with a negative statement, *ie* retain the agreement/disagreement polarity, he has to respond with *yes* plus an expansion which makes the contradiction explicit (*cf* Pope 1973:483):

[18] a: but you wouldn't have put that [= *Romeo and Juliet*] in the
　　　 tragedies – –
　　 A: *((ə:m)) – –* ''|YÈS| · |yes I · I |WŎULD| – –　(3.5b.33)

Yes or *no* alone would signify agreement.

The analysis of tones and tone unit structure of the responses in this section is summarised in *Table* 3.

Although the total number of negative statement contexts is rather small, it is remarkable that the *no* responses outnumber the *yes* reactions. Yet the other tendencies are manifest again: the most frequent nuclear tone is the fall; *yes* forms a tone unit of its own, whereas half of the *no* responses are part of a tone unit. Despite the small data basis it should be noted that the number of examples in which *yes* or *no* represent the whole utterance is slightly more balanced: four cases with either word; this may also be interpreted as supporting the substitutability of *yes* and *no*, both signalling agreement.

3.3 Changing referent of the response

3.3.1

A very small number of context sentences other than those discussed above occurred in the data. There was one alternative question and one *wh*-question:

[19] B: [ə:] |can we [ʔ] · 'work out :SCHÈMES| · and |send them to YÓU| or
　　　 |send them to the ap|propriate AUTHÓRITIES| for |DÒING 'that sort
　　　 of 'thing| it *|does mean 'knocking out a WÀLL|*
　　 A: *|YÈS| · don't |send them to ''MÉ|* but |send them to the
　　　 BÙRSAR|[7]　(3.4.81)
[20] B: |what's |what's '[ði:] · |what 'are the :main 'points that the 'ghost
　　　 :MÀKES in 'that 'speech ((now))| – –
　　 A: [ə:m] – – |yes (· coughs)
　　 B: ((come |on)) you've :LÉARNT the PÀRT|　(3.5a.49)

The response does not refer to the immediately preceding structure but signals that the speaker has understood the preceding utterance(s) or the argument in general and is thinking about an appropriate answer. *No* did not appear after one of these contexts in the data, although it could replace

7 The overlapping passages marked by the asterisks and the statement following A's *yes* show that A refers to the alternative question and not to the remark about the wall.

yes after the alternative question, responding, however, to only one part of the question. The distribution of prosodic features can be seen in the quotations.

3.3.2

Disregarding items like [ə:], [ə:m], [m], [mhm], *oh*, and occasionally *well*, then *yes* and *no* were always the initial elements of the responses dealt with in the previous sections. Our present concern is with those instances of *yes* and *no* which occur later in a speaker's utterance. Compare the following examples:

[21] A: oh |THĂT 'side| is |noisier than "↑↑THÌS|
      B: oh |CÈRTAINLY| |YÈS| (3.4.43)
[22] B: |can you re'member 'what the 'officer SÁYS| · the |GÍST of the 'thing| ·
      A: . . . and |he's pur↑sued by [ði] · the 'RÈST of [ði:] BÓYS| – |he 'comes :ÙP to him| – but I |can't re'member the :actual wŏRDS| |NÔ| – · (3.5a.17)
[23] B: . . . but the |KÈTTLE is [əm]
      A: {DIS|ÌNTEGRATED|}| *((is it))*
      B: *|well it's* an ↑ÌNVALID| |YÈS| (3.3.104)
[24] B: . . . I am |very re:sentful about ↑((LÈAVING)) in a wÁY| |YŎU *know|
      A: *|ÁRE you|*
      B: I* |WÀNT ((to go back))| |YÈS| it's it's |very 'very NÌCE| (3.2a.8)
[25] A: does |that in a ↑WŎRKING 'way| |consti'tute a PRÓBLEM| or |is it 'just [ə:] 'something you 'needn't :BÒTHER 'with| . . .
      B: I |think [i?] for the |kind of 'book I'm :WRĬTING| it |is 'something I 'have to 'BÒTHER with *:{|YÈS|}|*
      A: *|YÈS|* (3.6.71)

In the first three examples we have clear cases of agreement or contradiction as they were already listed in previous sections. Yet the postposed *yes* or *no* is preceded by lexical elements so that the speaker has an opportunity to modify the utterance of his partner more substantially. In example [21] B expresses only a certain amount of emphasis; in [22] and [23] *no* and *yes* are preceded by a reformulation of the content of the preceding utterance, thus still indicating disagreement and agreement. But in [24] it is no longer obvious whether *yes* refers to the other speaker's utterance or whether it is a one-word summary of the speaker's own statement. This latter function dominates clearly in example [25] in which one part of an alternative question is reformulated, followed by *yes*.

The function of *yes* which appears in quotations [24] and [25] shades into another one of *yes* or *no* when the speaker interrupts himself. Compare the following instances:

[26] C: ... and this {|WÀS} AR:RĂNGED *for us|
      ?: *|m̄| |m̄| ((|after 2 to 3 sylls))*
      (C: ((I mean in)) a *|very 'short :TĬME| I |mean · |WÈLL| · "|Y`ES| · but
      we |didn't 'start :ÀSKING| un|til a'bout · :five or six :WÈEKS
      a'go| · (3.3.79)
[27] B: |well · ↑last |last YĔAR we had a · we |had a DÌNNER| |no it was a
      :finalists' RE↑CÈPTION| |WÀSN'T it| · in which ... (3.3.114)

The *yes* in example [26] would seem to be a summarizing word of agreement,
whereas the *no* in [27] shows that the speaker has clarified his thoughts (or
words). Generally, this summarizing function of *yes* and *no* appears to be
linked with its non-initial position in the utterance. But we did find two
examples of cataphoric *yes* and *no* in the data, summarizing the utterances
that followed:

[28] A: ... I mean |English ìs {as I |SÀY this 'this|}| – [ʔə] |subject which
      is · is an "↑{ÈNDLESS} DIS:CÙSSION| * · * |it |isn't a 'business of of
      ?: *|m̄|*
      (A: ":LĔARNING| · [əm] – – well |{YÈS} there ÀRE tech'niques to
      LÉARN| · but ... (3.3.127)
[29] D: but |I would 'like to 'say CON↑{SÌDERING the CON}:DÌTIONS| · I
      |think – it's · very GÒOD| –
      C: |m̀| * – |YÈS|*
      A: *|YÈAH| – * ((|MÀRVELLOUS|)) ↑[əm]↑
      D: ↑|no ↑ [ə] |not RĔALLY| |anything to COM:PLĂIN of ((in
      'fact))| (3.3.68)

No pattern seems to evolve in our data with regard to functions and positions
or tones of non-initial *yes* and *no*. The summarizing or clarifying use of the
words can be detected when they are the final elements of an utterance or
when they appear in the middle after a well-formed clause or when they are
obviously interruptions. There is also no clear pattern as regards reference
of *yes* or *no* to the previous speaker's utterance or to the speaker's own; both
types occur in the data whichever position *yes* or *no* occupies.

   An analysis of the distribution of tones and position in the tone unit of all
the instances of postposed *yes* and *no* yields the picture in *Table* 4.

   The co-occurrence of tones with *yes* and *no* is similar to that in the
previous sections, with falls outnumbering by far any other tone; as usual
nearly all *yes* responses constitute a tone unit of their own. A different
tendency can be seen, however, in the set of *no* utterances, despite the rather
small number of examples: *no* as a separate tone unit is considerably more
frequent than *no* as part of a tone unit, whereas in all the previous categories
the figures were fairly evenly distributed. The reason for this tendency
seems to be connected with the postposing of *no*, but the examples do not
furnish any evidence for a more exact examination of it.

Table 4

YES	total	pre-onset	onset bearer	nucleus bearer	ˋ	ˊ	ˇ	ˆ	–	ˎ+ˊ	ˊ+ˎ
TU alone	59	–	59	59	54	I	–	I	3	–	–
part of TU	2	I	I	–	–	–	–	–	–	–	–

NO	number	pre-onset	onset bearer	nucleus bearer	ˋ	ˊ	ˇ	ˆ	–	ˎ+ˊ	ˊ+ˎ
TU alone	I I	–	I I	I I	9	–	–	I	I	–	–
part of TU	3	–	3	–	–	–	–	–	–	–	–

3.4 Repetitions of *yes* and *no*

There are a number of passages in the data in which *yes* or *no* is repeated. One may distinguish between repetitions by the same speaker or repetitions of one speaker by another. Compare the following illustrations:

[30] B: |ÈDWARD|
        D: |oh YÈS| |YÈS| (3.3.105)
[31] a: [əː] is that because you dislike French literature·
        A: [ə] |NǑ| · |NÓ| I |I [ə] · :thought ... (3.5b.5)
[32] B: oh |CÈRTAINLY|* |YÈS|*
        D: *|YÈS|*
        C: |YÈS|
        ?: |YÈS| – (3.4.43)
[33] A: [əːm] |ís this aˈvailable| – [əːm]
        C: |NÒ| · *((there |aren't))*
        A: *|how many* 'copies of the 'Great +TRAD+:ÌTION 'are there|
        B: +|NÒ|+
        C: |NÒ| · I |think ... (3.3.30)

The examples demonstrate that both *yes* and *no* may occur in the two types of repetition, although there are far more instances with *yes* in both of the subdivisions. Example [31] demonstrates also that the speaker can vary the nuclear tone. *Table* 5 summarizes the analysis of the repetitions in our material.

The same speaker repeats *yes* or *no* in most cases only once, without changing the nuclear tone, the most frequent of which is again the fall. There are only five examples of a tone change. In nine instances the

Table 5[8]

	Repetitions of the same speaker		Repetitions of one speaker by another	
	YES	*NO*	*YES*	*NO*
I OCCURRENCE	–	–	9	I
2 OCCURRENCES	23	2	–	–
3 OCCURRENCES	8	I	I	–
4 OCCURRENCES	–	–	–	–
5 OCCURRENCES	I	–	–	–
` `	16	I	9	I
` ` `	4	–	I	–
´ ´	2	–	–	–
^ `	I	I	–	–
^ ^	I	–	–	–
` – –	I	–	–	–
– ` `	I	–	–	–
– –	I	–	–	–
– – –	I	–	–	–
` ´	I	–	–	–
ˇ ´	I	I	–	–

sequence of repetitions is interrupted by phrases like *it is*, and in six cases a repetition coincides with *yes* changing the position in the tone unit, as is illustrated in the following quotation; *yes* carries the onset once, and the onset plus the nucleus twice:

[34] A: |YÈS| |yes ↑QUÌTE| – |YÈS| (3.2a.41)

For *no* we found one insertion of |not at ÀLL| and one shifting of *no* before the onset. Repetitions by the second speaker consist in the majority of cases of one *yes* or *no*; only falling tones appeared in the material, and there were no intervening phrases. As regards the constitution of single tone units, the

8 The numbers in the two parts of the table differ since not all repetitions bear a nuclear tone.

small numbers do not permit an inference for *no*, but *yes* forms a tone unit of its own in the great majority of cases, as in the other sections.

4 Summary

The investigation of *yes* and *no* as responses in spoken English, based on texts from the Survey of English Usage, established two kinds of correlation: one between the preceding context and the response – some of these facts were, of course, already known[9] – and another between the responses and parameters selected from intonation.

With the exception of one type of context, and provided that the choice of tone does not counteract it, *yes* and *no* retain their fundamental polarity, signalling agreement and disagreement, respectively, in all the instances we examined. The exception consists of negative context statements after which *yes* and *no* lose their polarity and may be substituted for one another. If a negative statement is contradicted, *yes* has to be expanded by an utterance making the contradiction explicit. Another phenomenon was noted in the analysis: apart from two examples in which *yes* and *no* cataphorically summarize the speaker's own utterance that followed, the initial responses react to the previous speaker. But with non-initial ones a certain vagueness appears as to which utterance the response refers to; there are also several clear cases where *yes* sums up the speaker's own opinion and does not refer to what his partner said. Two other kinds of context also affect the referent of the response, namely *wh*-questions and alternative questions: in these cases the response is not aimed at the immediately preceding utterances but signals that the speaker has understood the line of argument, the given problem generally, and is thinking of some reply.

The various context-response classes examined do not show a correlation with tone unit structure, selection of tone, or paralinguistic phenomena. These features remain fairly constant in all cases. It is notable that *yes* in most examples from the different sections constitutes a separate tone unit, whereas approximately half of the *no* responses form part of a tone unit. Only non-initial *no* shows the same tendency as *yes*. This observation is linked with the fact that in a great many of the occurrences, *yes* not only constitutes a separate tone unit, but also forms the whole utterance of the respective speaker, whereas *no* is more frequently followed or preceded by more speech of the same speaker. While this seems to be a conversational requirement, to make one's reasons for objection explicit, it would appear that the overall majority of *yes* responses could be a reflection of the type of text in which the inferior speaker in an interview situation is perhaps

9 *Cf eg* the OED *sv* 'yes' and 'no', or Zimmer (1957), who comments very briefly on the two words. Kruisinga (1908) contrasts the meanings of *no* with Dutch *ja*, and Pope (1973) compares several languages with English.

generally inclined to agree with the interviewer rather than disagree. As regards the choice of tones, it appears that the fall is the most frequent and most neutral one. Any other tone has an additional signification, which can counteract the signification of *yes* and *no* such that responses turn into borderline cases between different functions.

Our analysis had to be restricted to one type of text. Only a brief look at surreptitiously recorded unscripted conversation between intimates (Survey texts 2.1–2.5) reveals, however, that several observations recur. See *Table* 6.

Table 6

YES	total	pre-onset	onset bearer	nucleus bearer	＼	／	∨	∧	–	＼+／	／+＼
TU alone	139	–	139	139	105	16	1	7	10	–	–
part of TU	39	1	23	17	10	2	–	3	2	–	–

NO	total	pre-onset	onset bearer	nucleus bearer	＼	／	∨	∧	–	＼+／	／+＼
TU alone	49	–	49	49	37	6	1	3	2	–	–
part of TU	32	4	17	11	9	–	–	2	–	–	–

The most frequent response is again *yes* (178 versus 81 *no*), forming separate tone units in the majority of cases, while for *no* the figures are again more balanced. The number of instances in which *yes* constitutes also the whole utterance is larger than for *no*, although the gap between the two responses is not as wide as in the texts 3.1–3.5: of 139 separate tone units with *yes*, 54 were also the whole utterance of the speaker but 14 for 49 occurrences of *no*. The fall is the most frequent tone in all subdivisions. One phenomenon is not represented in the table which was in the data of texts 2.1–2.5, namely the post-nuclear appearance of *yes* (2) and *no* (5).

It will have become apparent that we have concentrated our attention on fairly clear functions of *yes* and *no*. An analysis of real data shows that there are almost no limits to the delicacy of analysis, especially as regards the significance of elements in context. Our aim was to illustrate some generalizable observations, but their generalizability has to pass the test of further corpus studies.

A TAGGED CORPUS –
PROBLEMS AND PROSPECTS
W. NELSON FRANCIS

The linguist approaching a language from the point of view of
PERFORMANCE – an old-fashioned approach, never wholly abandoned and
now returning to favor – is obliged to use a CORPUS, which can be defined
as a collection of actual examples of language in use, considered to be
representative of the aspect or aspects of the language the linguist is
interested in. This has been the method of lexicographers since the
eighteenth century and of the writers of compendious grammars such as
Jespersen (1909–49), Visser (1963–), and GCE. The last of these is based on
the Survey of English Usage, a large corpus which has been one of the major
concerns of the recipient of this volume for nearly twenty years (Quirk 1968,
1974; Quirk and Svartvik 1979). It has provided material not only for the
Grammar of Contemporary English but for many individual studies as well.
It will continue to be exploited, especially now that at least the oral part of
it is being prepared for computer analysis by the Lund Survey of Spoken
English, under the direction of Professor Jan Svartvik.

Another sizeable corpus of present-day English has been available for
computational analysis for fifteen years: the Brown University Standard
Corpus of Present-Day American English, commonly known as the Brown
Corpus (Francis 1964). This was the brain-child of Professor Freeman
Twaddell, and was compiled by the present writer in 1963–64, under a grant
from the US Office of Education. Copies of this Corpus and of a complete
index to it have been made available to researchers at cost, and it is in use

at over 160 centers all around the world. A microfiche version, complete with a K W I C concordance of the whole, is now available from the University of Bergen.[1] A volume containing frequency tables, both alphabetical and rank-ordered, as well as a number of special studies of sentence length and word distribution, has been published (Kučera and Francis 1967). Many other studies – lexical, syntactic, morphological, and graphemic – have been based upon it, and it has been used not only by linguists but by psychologists, philosophers, stylisticians, and various kinds of technologists for their special requirements.[2] For some purposes, at least, its frequency tables have superseded older ones such as Thorndike–Lorge. The hope of its compilers that it would become a standard research tool has been largely realized. But it has serious limitations, especially for syntactic and semantic purposes, which we are currently working to remedy. The purpose of this paper is to describe this work and the future research possibilities which it will open up.

For those not familiar with the Brown Corpus, a few facts about its size, sources, format, and limitations are in order. Some of these are the result of conscious decisions, made by a preliminary conference of consultants,[3] by the compiler himself, or by various assistants who worked on the project.[4] Others arise out of the nature of the material itself and the state of linguistic data-processing at the time. All of them affect the usefulness of the Corpus, usually by imposing various restrictions on what can be done with it.

First, as to size. The convenient figure of one million words was decided on as being large enough to be useful for many purposes, yet not too large for the capacity of computers then in use. This turned out to be just the amount of text that could be key-punched, proof-read, and corrected in one year by a single conscientious key-punch operator[5] and fully processed within the modest funds allowed. It was further decided that the million words would be divided among 500 samples of approximately 2,000 words each. Since samples were not to be broken off exactly at the 2,000-word point but allowed to run on to the end of a sentence, the average length of the samples turned out to be 2028 + words, so that the entire Corpus is something over 1,014,000 words. Due to mistakes in counting, a few samples fall a bit short of 2000 words.

The most important decisions, almost all of them made at the preliminary conference, concerned the sources from which the samples were to be drawn. It was felt on the one hand that a corpus even as large as a million

1 This was prepared at NAVF's EDB-Senter for Humanistisk Forskning under the direction of Dr Jostein Hauge.
2 See 'Brown Corpus Bibliography' in Johansson 1979, *pp* 9–12.
3 This conference was held at Brown University in February 1963. The participants were John B. Carroll, W. N. Francis, Philip B. Gove, Henry Kučera, Patricia O'Connor, and Randolph Quirk.
4 Especially Anne Robb Taylor, Henry Hall Peyton, and Mary Lois Marckworth.
5 This work was done by Miss Loretta Felice, whose contribution went far beyond mere mechanical key-punching.

words would be inadequate to represent all the different modes of use and varieties of present-day English. To include samples of a wide range of regional and social dialects, for example, would introduce such variety and so reduce the sample size of any single type that meaningful generalizations would be impossible. To attempt to cover a wide range of literary styles would have the same effect. On the other hand, it was considered desirable that the Corpus should have enough range so that it could be considered representative of a large segment of the actual performance of contemporary writers of English. Accordingly, it was decided to impose certain restrictions, in the hope that others might attempt parallel corpora of other sorts, both contemporary and from older periods. The three major limitations were the following:

1 The type of English to be sampled was EDITED PROSE – by which is meant prose prepared for print and actually printed. Thus not only are all varieties of spoken English excluded, but many varieties of written as well. Printed language normally has been subjected to examination and correction by at least three persons: the author, an editor, whether of a periodical or a publishing house, and a printer. The amount of interference with the author's text exercised by editor and printer varies a great deal, of course, but at the least it tends to eliminate idiosyncratic spelling and punctuation, and may go much farther in the direction of a 'house style'. 'Standard' in the title of the Corpus does not mean to imply that it is a corpus of Standard English (whatever that is), but 'edited' certainly means that unorthodox spelling, for example, will have been eliminated everywhere except within special quoted material. There is some of this in the Corpus: one sample, for instance, contains extensive quotations from letters of semi-literate soldiers in the American Civil War, and another from narratives of sixteenth-century explorers. A problem is presented by dialogue in fiction, which may be full of pseudo-phonetic spelling, eye dialect, and other devices intended to suggest natural speech. It did not seem possible, however, to exclude dialogue without excluding fiction altogether, since a 2000-word sample of fiction without any dialogue at all would be quite untypical. So an arbitrary decision was made to include fiction only if it consisted of less than 50 per cent dialogue. Drama was excluded entirely, on the ground that it consists of pseudo-spoken, rather than edited written language. Poetry also was excluded, because it was felt that both its syntax and its lexicon are so different from those of prose that they would present special problems.

2 The samples were to be, so far as it was possible to determine, AMERICAN English. All samples were first printed in the United States, and all authors who could be identified were native speakers of American English. There are, however, especially in the Press samples, anonymous sections, whose authors may not be American. But it is safe to say that the non-American contribution, if any, is very small. The motivation of this restriction was to

eliminate relatively trivial regional varieties in spelling and lexicon, which might unduly complicate many kinds of study. The hope was that parallel corpora of other national varieties would be prepared which would allow point for point contrasts. This hope has been realized in the case of British English by the Lancaster Corpus, undertaken and nearly completed by Professor Geoffrey Leech at the University of Lancaster, and now located at Oslo.[6]

3 It was felt desirable for the language sampled to be as far as possible CONTEMPORARY. Accordingly it was limited to material first printed in the calendar year 1961. There was no way to be sure, of course, when each sample was actually written, but if there was positive evidence that it was written more than a year or two before it was printed, it was excluded. Second editions, translations, first editions of newly discovered writings –all such material was passed by in favor of samples as authentically contemporary American as could be found. Once again, there are quotations from older English which introduce small bits of older syntax, lexicon, and graphics, but their size in relation to the whole is insignificant. It is safe to say that the Corpus is truly representative of middle twentieth-century American English.

In order to ensure as wide a spread as possible within the restrictions mentioned above, the potential universe from which the samples were to be drawn was divided into fifteen genres, most of them with subdivisions. Six of these were classed as 'imaginative' prose and nine as 'informative', a division suggested by Randolph Quirk. The informative prose comprises 374 samples, or 3/4 of the whole, and the imaginative the remaining 126, or 1/4. The list of genres with their subdivisions and the number of samples allotted to each is given in *Table* 1.

Although the universe to be sampled was theoretically everything printed within the United States in 1961 that was original to that year (with the exclusions listed above), the universe was arbitrarily restricted somewhat in order to facilitate location of the samples to be used. Actually the universe consisted of four large compendia:

(*a*) for newspapers, the microfilm files of the New York Public Library;
(*b*) for detective and romantic fiction, the holdings of the Providence Athenaeum, a private library;
(*c*) for various ephemeral and popular periodical material, the stock of a large secondhand magazine store in New York City;
(*d*) for everything else, the holdings of the Brown University Library.

Selections from these to fill the allotted number of samples from each genre were made by various random procedures which assured freedom from bias.

6 Where it has been completed by Dr Stig Johansson, of the English Department, University of Oslo. A corpus of nearly a thousand sentences of Australian English, taken from newspaper editorials, student essays, and diagnostic reading tests, has been compiled by Dr R. D. Beebe. See Beebe 1976.

Table 1

I INFORMATIVE PROSE 374 *samples*

A PRESS: REPORTAGE

	daily	weekly	total
Political	10	4	14
Sports	5	2	7
Society	3	0	3
Spot news	7	2	9
Financial	3	1	4
Cultural	5	2	7
Total			**44**

B PRESS: EDITORIAL

Institutional	7	3	10
Personal	7	3	10
Letters to the Editor	5	2	7
Total			**27**

C PRESS: REVIEWS

(theatre, books, music dance)	14	3
Total		**17**

D RELIGION

Books	7
Periodicals	6
Tracts	4
Total	**17**

E SKILLS AND HOBBIES

Books	2
Periodicals	34
Total	**36**

F POPULAR LORE

Books	23
Periodicals	25
Total	**48**

G BELLES LETTRES, BIOGRAPHY, MEMOIRS, etc

Books	38
Periodicals	37
Total	**75**

H MISCELLANEOUS

Government documents	24
Foundation reports	2
Industry reports	2
College catalog	1
Industry house organ	1
Total	**30**

J LEARNED

Natural Sciences	12
Medicine	5
Mathematics	4
Social and behavioral sciences	14
Political science, law, education	15
Humanities	18
Technology and engineering	12
Total	**80**

II IMAGINATIVE PROSE 126 *samples*

K GENERAL FICTION

Novels	20
Short stories	9
Total	**29**

L MYSTERY and DETECTIVE FICTION

Novels	20
Short stories	4
Total	**24**

M SCIENCE FICTION

Novels	3
Short stories	3
Total	**6**

N ADVENTURE and WESTERN FICTION

Novels	15
Short stories	14
Total	**29**

P ROMANCE and LOVE STORY

Novels	14
Short stories	15
Total	**29**

R HUMOR

Novels	3
Essays, etc	6
Total	**9**

GRAND TOTAL	**500**

Another major decision, one which has had profound effects on the usefulness of the Corpus, related to the form in which the material was to be coded for the computer. It was decided that, since the sources were printed language, they should be presented as such. Thus the spelling, punctuation, hyphenation, capitalization, word division – even the use of italic and boldface type – were coded exactly as found. Even obvious typographical errors were not corrected, since it was felt that once editorial alteration of the text began, it would be difficult to define the point at which it should stop. Instead, these obvious mistakes of the printer were recorded in the Manual which is issued with copies of the Corpus. Some which were missed are being entered in later editions of the Manual, and the rare errors of the key-puncher which escaped three proof-readings are being corrected on the master tape as they are discovered. But errors and inconsistencies stemming from the original sources are allowed to stand.

Strict adherence to the material as printed meant that there was only one possible way to define a *word*: as a string of one or more alphanumeric characters set off by space or certain marks of punctuation on either side. Hyphens and apostrophes were considered as internal marks, hence no different from the alphanumeric letters and numbers. This has led to some rather curious 'words' in the running text and hence in the frequency tables of Kučera and Francis 1967. Since English has many compounds written as separate words but also permits nonce-compounds to be hyphenated,[7] a sequence like THE *NEW *YORK-*PENNYSYLVANIA *LEAGUE appears as four 'words', one of which is *YORK-*PENNYSYLVANIA. The somewhat redundant phrase THE $100 MILLION DOLLAR BOND ISSUE treats $100 and MILLION as separate words, though the identical expression could have been written either as $100-MILLION or $100,000,000, both of which would be treated as single words. Other inconsistencies of graphic English have created similar anomalies.

A further consequence of accepting the graphic word as the lexical unit is the fact that there is no separation of homographs, which are quite frequent in English. These are of two main kinds: purely accidental ones like *bear* and *sow*, and ones resulting from 'functional shift' or zero-marked derivation, as in *love, hope, ride, swallow, implement, separate*, and hundreds more. In the frequency lists of Kučera–Francis these are entered and counted only once. On the other hand, inflectional variants like *loves, loved, loving* are treated separately; that is, the lists are not lemmatized. These facts have detracted, sometimes seriously, from the value of the frequency tables. It has been our intent from the beginning to correct them by producing lists in which homographs are disambiguated and inflectional variants are brought together.

7 For a discussion of the handling of this problem by dictionaries, see Gates 1977. In the remainder of this paper, actual quotations from the Corpus will be presented as they appear there – in full capitals, with capitalization indicated by a preceding asterisk.

Disambiguation and lemmatization could have been accomplished at least semi-automatically without too great difficulty.[8] But since one of our major aims was to make the Corpus adaptable to syntactic analysis, we decided to combine these differing goals into a single operation, if possible. The means decided on was *tagging*; that is, supplying each word in the Corpus with a symbol indicating its place in a taxonomy based on surface syntactic function. It was felt that such a taxonomy, if sufficiently refined, would automatically separate most homographs (though not those of the identical word-class, like the two nouns *swallow*), and would supply strings of abstract symbols that would be the point of entry for an analysis leading to a performance grammar, which, in a corpus of edited text like ours, would in effect be a grammar of well-formed surface structure. Since the task of manually tagging more than a million words would not only be overwhelming in its magnitude but open to considerable inconsistency, especially if done – as it would have to be – by several individuals, it was decided to do as much of it as possible automatically, hoping to leave a manageable residue for completion by hand.

The development of computer routines for tagging was the work of two graduate students at Brown, and has been described in detail in their joint Master of Arts thesis (Greene and Rubin 1971). Their procedure included three operations, two of them automatic and the third manual:

(*a*) assigning to each word in the text one or more symbols (tags) from a list of 81, each representing a word-class taxonomically identifiable either by morphology or syntactic use;

(*b*) in the case of words with more than one tag, eliminating, so far as possible by computer examination of context, the irrelevant ones;

(*c*) continuing process (*b*) by manual intervention.

The result of these three processes is that in the tagged Corpus each individual word has one and only one tag, appropriate to its grammatical classification in the given context.

Although the full description of the first two of these processes is available in the Greene–Rubin thesis, a briefer account is appropriate here.

1 *Initial tagging*
The full list of tags is given in *Table* 2.

Table 2
LIST OF TAGS FOR THE BROWN CORPUS

Tag	Description	Examples	Tag	Description	Examples
.	period, semicolon, question mark, exclamation mark		)	right paren	
			-	dash	
			,	comma	
(	left paren		:	colon	
*	NOT, N'T		ABL	pre-qualifier	QUITE, RATHER

8 For a method of disambiguating and lemmatizing a limited corpus, see Kelly and Stone 1975.

Table 2 *(continued)*

Tag	Description	Examples	Tag	Description	Examples
ABN	pre-quantifier	HALF, ALL	NNS	plural noun	
ABX	pre-quantifier/double conjunction	BOTH (. . . AND)	NNS$	possessive plural noun	
AP	post-determiner	MANY, SEVERAL, NEXT	NP	proper noun or part of name phrase	
AT	article	A, THE, NO	NP$	possessive proper noun	
BE	BE				
BED	WERE		NPS$	possessive plural proper noun	
BEDZ	WAS				
BEG	BEING		NR	adverbial noun	HOME, TODAY, WEST
BEM	AM, 'M				
BEN	BEEN		OD	ordinal numeral	FIRST, SECOND
BER	ARE, ART, 'RE		PN	nominal pronoun	EVERYBODY, NOTHING
BEZ	IS, 'S				
CC	coordinating conjunction	AND, OR	PN$	possessive nominal pronoun	
CD	cardinal numeral	ONE, TWO, 2, etc	PP$	possessive personal pronoun	MY, OUR
CI	conjunction/preposition (portmanteau)	AFTER, SINCE	PP$$	second possessive personal pronoun	MINE, OURS
CS	subordinating conjunction	IF, ALTHOUGH	PPL	singular reflexive (intensive) personal pronoun	MYSELF
DO	DO				
DOD	DID		PPLS	plural reflexive (intensive) personal pronoun	OURSELVES
DOZ	DOES				
DT	singular determiner	THIS, THAT			
DTI	singular or plural determiner	SOME, ANY	PPO	objective personal pronoun	ME, HIM, IT, THEM
DTS	plural determiner	THESE, THOSE	PPS	3rd singular nominative personal pronoun	HE, SHE, IT, ONE
DTX	determiner/double conjunction	EITHER (. . . OR)			
EX	existential THERE		PPSS	other nominative personal pronoun	I, WE, THEY, YOU
FW	foreign word (hyphenated ahead of regular tag)		QL	qualifier	VERY, LOTS, FAIRLY
HV	HAVE		QLP	post-qualifier	ENOUGH, INDEED
HVD	HAD (past tense), 'D				
HVG	HAVING		RB	adverb	
HVN	HAD (past participle)		RBR	comparative adverb	
			RBT	superlative adverb	
IN	preposition	AMONG, BETWEEN	RI	adverb/preposition (portmanteau)	ABOVE, ALONG
JJ	adjective		RIP	adverb/preposition/particle (portmanteau)	DOWN, IN
JJR	comparative adjective				
JJS	semantically superlative adjective	CHIEF, TOP	RN	nominal adverb	HERE, THEN, INDOORS
JJT	morphologically superlative adjective	BIGGEST	RP	adverb/particle (portmanteau)	AWAY, OFF, UP
MD	modal auxiliary		TO	infinitive marker TO	
NC	cited word (hyphenated to regular tag)		UH	interjection, exclamation	
			VB	verb, base form	
NN	singular or mass noun		VBD	verb, past tense	
NN$	possessive singular noun		VBG	verb, present participle, gerund	

Table 2 (continued)

Tag	Description	Examples	Tag	Description	Examples
VBN	verb, past participle		WPO	objective *wh*-pronoun	WHOM, WHICH, THAT
VBZ	verb, 3rd singular present		WPS	nominative *wh*-pronoun	WHO, WHICH, THAT
WDT	*wh*-determiner	WHAT, WHICH	WQL	*wh*-qualifier	HOW
WP$	possessive *wh*-pronoun	WHOSE	WRB	*wh*-adverb	HOW, WHERE, WHEN

NOTES

a The tags CI, RI, RIP are portmanteau tags which are automatically expanded in the tagging process as follows:

CI = CS – IN   RIP = RP – IN

RI = RB – IN

b Merged constructions are marked by the appropriate tags joined by +, except for *, which is affixed directly. For example:

ISN'T	BEZ*
CAN'T	MD*
I'M	PPSS + BEM
HE'D	PPS + HVD – PPS + MD
THERE'S	EX + BEZ – EX + HVZ – RN + BEZ

c The tags FW, NC, NP are given to single words, phrases, or sentences contained respectively in foreign phrases, cited passages, and compound or complex names. The first two are hyphenated to the regular tag. For example:

MENS	FW-NN	IN	IN
SANA	FW-JJ	DRUG	NN-NC
IN	FW-IN	STORE	NN-NC
CORPORE	FW-NN	THE	AT
SANO	FW-JJ	PRIMARY	JJ
		STRESS	NN
		IS	BEZ
		ON	IN
		DRUG	NN-NC

It will be observed that they are of five kinds:

(*a*) major form-classes ('parts of speech'): noun, common and proper; verb; adjective; adverb; in short, the open lexical classes;

(*b*) function words: determiners, prepositions, conjunctions, pronouns, etc; the closed lexical and grammatical classes;

(*c*) certain important individual words: *not*, existential *there*, infinitival *to*, the forms of the verbs *do*, *be*, and *have*, whether auxiliaries or full verbs;

(*d*) punctuation marks of syntactic significance;

(*e*) inflectional morphemes, notably noun plural and possessive; verb past, present and past participle, and 3rd singular concord marker; comparative and superlative adjective and adverb suffixes.

Thus when the following symbols appear elsewhere than in the first two letters of a tag, they normally have the following equivalences:

S = plural	D = past tense
$ = possessive	Z = 3rd singular
R = comparative	N = past participle

T = superlative   G = present participle
O = objective case of pronoun

As will be seen, the attempt was to give the tags a certain mnemonic value, which it was thought would make it easier for those using the tagged Corpus. There are, as a result, some exceptions to the above equivalences: JJS for semantically superlative adjective and PPS for 3rd singular subject form of pronoun, for instance. It might have been wiser to give each of the inflectional markers a unique symbol, reserving S, for example, for noun plural only and finding other unused characters for the other meanings. It is possible that this would facilitate some operations which scholars will wish to make on the strings of tags. This could be done, of course, quite easily by means of a simple computer program.

The selection of the tag or tags to be applied to each word makes use of two separate look-up procedures, following some pre-editing such as removing final *s* or other suffixes to reveal base forms. The word is first looked up in a dictionary of 2,860 words (the 'word-list'), and if it is found there, it is given the tag or tags listed. About 61 per cent of the words on the list have a unique tag; the rest have from two to four, or in a few cases five by the kind of expansion of portmanteau tags described at the bottom of *Table* 2. If the word is not found on the word-list, its ending is checked against a 'suffix list' of 446 strings of one to five letters found at the end of English words, with appropriate tags, and if its ending matches one of the entries, it is given the tag or tags of that ending. Only 51 per cent of the entries on the suffix list have unique tags. Finally, if the word passes through both of these procedures without being tagged, it is arbitrarily given the tags NN – VB – JJ. The final result of the look-up routines is that every word now has at least one tag, and some as many as five. All those with more than one must now be disambiguated, by machine if possible, or ultimately by hand. In a few cases, owing to limitation of working space, words were not given all possible tags. Thus ROUND is given the tags VB – JJ – RB – IN, but not NN, though, it can, of course, be a noun. The actual frequencies for this word in the Corpus are VB 6; JJ 29; RB 14; IN 4; NN 18. This means that 18 NN tags (and 13 NNS tags for ROUNDS as well) had to be inserted in the manual phase.

2 *Computer disambiguation*

In the case of words with two or more tags, disambiguation is effected as far as possible by 'context frame rules'. In effect, these look at the words immediately preceding and following the word in question, or rather at their tags, to see if there are sequences which automatically either select the correct tag or eliminate one or more of the irrelevant ones. To take a simple example, the sentence THE SHIPS ARE SAILING would emerge from the look-up procedure with the tags AT NNS – VBZ BER VBG. The article tag AT signals the beginning of a noun phrase and cannot be followed directly by a finite 3rd person verb. Hence the machine cancels the VBZ tag on SHIPS and the sentence is now correctly and unambiguously tagged. Many cases, of course, are more complicated than this and involve looking before and after the key word to a depth of two words one way or the other.[9] Particularly difficult are strings of words with multiple tags, where the ambiguities are multiplied. Here the routine begins with the last ambiguously tagged item and disambiguates it, if possible, on the basis of what follows. If successful, it works back through the string. If the last word in the series does not yield, the routine moves to the beginning of the series. With luck, each disambiguation will set up an unambiguous frame for the next word, until the whole is unraveled. For example, the string IN MY FATHER'S VOICE would emerge from the look-up routine as follows:

IN	IN		
MY	PP$		
FATHER'S	NN$	NN+BEZ	NN+HVZ
VOICE	NN	VB	

Since the subject of IS or HAS cannot follow a preposition directly, at least if the verb is contracted, the tags NN+BEZ and NN+HVZ are eliminated, leaving only NN$ for FATHER'S. Since this cannot be followed by a verb in base form,[10] the tag VB is removed from VOICE and the string is now correctly tagged IN PP$ NN$ NN.

But it does not always work that way. Sometimes the context frame rules, for all their ingenuity, are unable to completely disambiguate one or more words in a sentence, and they are left with multiple tags. These constitute the residue – about 23 per cent[11] – which must be disambiguated manually.

3 Manual disambiguation

At this point the computer has done all it can, and a human grammarian must go through the text word by word, reducing all multiple tags to one and replacing erroneous single tags by the correct ones. Even though this involves only about one-fourth of the words, it is a long and tedious process, and is open to human failings of inconsistency, misreading, and all kinds of error stemming from fatigue and boredom. In the case of the Brown Corpus it went on over several years and was carried out by a series of readers, hence inevitably increasing inconsistency. When it was completed, we felt that it was necessary to run a series of checks to correct these errors and inconsistencies as far as we possibly could.

9 It would, of course, have been possible to extend the context further – to three or more words either way. But this would have added tremendous numbers of rules, some of which would apply to very few strings. It is hard to tell where diminishing returns set in.

10 Except in very rare constructions involving 'gapping', as 'I saw my mother's car arrive and my father's leave'.

11 This figure does not represent the whole corpus, which was not counted, but three separate

First, the whole vocabulary of the Corpus was sorted alphabetically and then by tags and the frequencies counted. When this list was surveyed, it immediately revealed several hundred readily correctible errors. For example, the word THINK is shown to be tagged VB 414 times and NN once. Checking the passage in question showed it to be a reference to *think factories*. It was decided to change the tag to VB and consider this a rare instance of a base-form verb as prenominal adjunct. Again, the most common word in the Corpus, THE, occurred 69,182 times with the tag AT and once each with RB, RBR, and VBD. Upon checking, these turned out to be slips of the disambiguator's pen or attention and were changed to AT.

Errors of this sort were easy to detect and remedy. But other errors – or at least inconsistencies – resulting from varying judgments by the disambiguators or from parsing problems in the language itself created problems. The -*ing* words, for instance: when are they participles (VBG), when adjectives (JJ), and when nouns (NN)? The word list gave the two tags VBG and NN to eighteen common words (*eg* FEELING, MEANING, PAINTING) and JJ alone to six (*eg* EVERLASTING, INTERESTING). All the rest were tagged simply VBG by the suffix list. This frequently left it to the disambiguator to insert a tag in a sentence like THE PLAY WAS VERY ENTERTAINING, where the presence of the qualifier VERY marks ENTERTAINING as an adjective, though it would have been marked only VBG by the computer. Similarly, in A SWELLING DEVELOPED IN THE KNEE, the disambiguator had to cancel the unique VBG tag and insert NN, since SWELLING was not included in the word list with both tags. Cases of this sort, where it was not simply a matter of cancelling extraneous tags but where the disambiguator had to recognize that a single tag was incorrect, were particularly prone to error and inconsistency, and we cannot claim to have corrected them all. It is, of course, easy for others

---

samples from different genres: news (sports reporting), A10; learned – natural science, J10; and mystery fiction, L22. In spite of the diversity of subject matter and hence of vocabulary, the figures were very similar:

	A10	J10	L22	Total
⌐*otal words*	2224	2236	2215	6675
single tag	1740	1727	1685	5152
per cent single tag	78.24	77.24	76.07	77.18
2 tags	338	331	325	994
3 tags	128	160	154	442
4 tags	18	16	51	69
5 tags	0	2	0	2

The number of words in each of these samples is considerably over the 2000 word mark because punctuation marks are considered 'words' in the tagged corpus but not in the original running text.

using the Greene–Rubin routines to add to and alter the word and suffix lists as they see fit, as well as to include more and/or different context frame rules.

The most vexing problem faced by the disambiguators – the one most open to indecision and inconsistency – involves prenominal modifiers which occur between various pre-determiners, determiners, numerals and post-determiners and the noun head. The tagging system makes allowances for three kinds: adjectives, participles, and nominals. The problem lies in the fact that by compounding (open, hyphened, or closed), suffixation, or simple adjunction, English permits a wide variety of words – many of them nonce-constructions – to fill this position. Especially troublesome are hyphenated compounds like EARTH-SHAKING, HARD-BOILED, MANY-COL-ORED, LONG-RANGE, FULL-BODIED, etc, and words with certain prefixes, especially UN-. The general policy followed is

a to tag NN those which can be a noun-phrase without the hyphen (*eg* LONG-RANGE, HIGH-ENERGY);
b to tag VBN or VBG those which are bona fide verbs when the -ED or -ING ending is removed (*eg* UNTIED, DOWNGRADED, OUTDIST-ANCING, DOUBLE-CROSSING);
c to tag the remainder JJ. This means that the class of adjectives is a large and anomalous one. Among the curiosities it includes are:

Words ending in -TYPE: SANDWICH-TYPE
Noun-Adj combinations: FANCY-FREE, SCREW-LOOSE, SHOUL-DER-HIGH
Noun-pres part constructions: RUN-SCORING, SALES-BUILDING, LAW-ABIDING
Noun-past part constructions: HOME-MADE, ROCK-STREWN (both of these also occur solid)
Noun-Noun+-ED combinations: SHIRT-SLEEVED
Adj-Noun+-ED combinations: SHORT-SKIRTED, SLIM-WAISTED
Miscellaneous combinations: SHOW-OFFY, SIGNAL-TO-NOISE, SMASH-'EM-DOWN (modifying ADVENTURES), SNOB-CLAN-NISH, TOPSY-TURVY, TO-THE-DEATH, TONGUE-IN-CHEEK, TOO-SIMPLE-TO-BE-TRUE, UNIQUE-INGROWN-SCREWEDUP, ROUND-THE-CLOCK, DAY-AFTER-DAY, etc

Both HIGH-POWER and HIGH-POWERED occur in the Corpus; the procedures outlined above tag the first of these NN and the second JJ.

It remains to be seen whether the inclusion as adjectives of such a large and heterogeneous class of lexemes – one can scarcely call them 'words' – will be the best treatment for syntactic purposes. It is, perhaps, especially questionable in the light of the often erratic and inconsistent use of hyphens.

Study of collocations will no doubt reveal that many hyphen-linked words also appear as open compounds, in which case each word would have its own tag. It might turn out to be the best policy to assign hyphenated tags to hyphenated words. Under such a procedure, the following, now all tagged either NN or JJ, would have the tags indicated:

SANDWICH-TYPE	NN-NN
FANCY-FREE	NN-JJ
HOME-MADE	NR-VBN
SHIRT-SLEEVED	NN-JJ
SHORT-SKIRTED	JJ-JJ
TONGUE-IN-CHEEK	NN-IN-NN
TOO-SIMPLE-TO-BE-TRUE	QL-JJ TO BE JJ

Since this procedure would considerably complicate the tagging system, the decision to adopt it has been reserved until we have the benefit of working with the tagged Corpus in its present form for a trial period.

Tagging problems were presented by three kinds of unusual discourse: proper names, foreign words and phrases, and samples of language – words, phrases, and sentences – cited as such. In the case of proper names containing more than one word – *eg* NEW YORK, PRESIDENT JOHN F. KENNEDY, FULTON COUNTY GRAND JURY – all constituents were given the tag NP, regardless of their normal grammatical categories. Thus when examination of a string of tags reveals a block of consecutive N Ps without intervening punctuation, this substring can be construed as a single name.

In the case of foreign words and phrases and metalinguistic citations, hyphenated tags have been used. Foreign words and phrases were identified as such in the first instance by the fact that they were marked in the original texts by some typographic distinction, usually italics. Other apparently foreign words not so identified were treated as foreign if not listed in the main vocabulary of a recent standard dictionary. Words so listed were considered to be loan-words already denizened, however precariously, in the lexicon of English. It was felt to be desirable to identify foreign words and phrases for two reasons:

a they often are incorporated into the syntax of the English sentences where they occur, and hence must be parsed; for example: 'I was, it seemed, *persona non grata* in every quarter.'
b foreign words which are homographs of English words are thus distinguished: thus IN as an English preposition is tagged simply IN, but as a Latin preposition it is tagged FW-IN.

A similar approach has been used with metalinguistically cited words, phrases, and sentences, as in 'In "All systems are go" the verb *go* functions

[205]

as a predicate complement'. The first part of this will be tagged:

*IN	IN
*ALL	ABN-NC
SYSTEMS	NNS-NC
ARE	BER-NC
GO	VB-NC
THE	AT
VERB	NN
GO	VB-NC
FUNCTIONS	VBZ
etc	

In such cases the continuous string of post-hyphen NC tags signals a structure functioning as a syntactic unit, usually a nominal.

One 'portmanteau tag' has been retained. This is RP, used with adverbial elements closely associated with verbs. At first we attempted to distinguish, in the case of phrasal verbs, between adverbs and particles, as is done in various studies (*eg* Bolinger 1971, Fraser 1974). But, after considerable study, we decided to leave this distinction to future syntactic analysis. There is actually a gradient from pure adverbs (usually locative) retaining their basic meaning, to pure particles, forming idiomatic lexemes when collocated with verbs. An example is THROW OUT. This can have the literal meaning, as in 'The President *threw out* the first ball to open the baseball season.' Here OUT is clearly a locative (directional) adverb, but the combination has various idiomatic meanings, such as 'disengage' (the clutch), 'reject' (a proposal), 'discard', 'utter' (a comment or remark), etc. Webster's *Third New International Dictionary* lists fourteen of these. Just where in this scale OUT loses its locative force and becomes a particle is a matter of the *Sprachgefühl* (FW-NN!) of the individual speaker or grammarian. For this reason, the following ten words have been given the portmanteau tag RP (adverb or particle) in all cases except when they are prepositions (or, rarely, other parts of speech): ABOUT, ACROSS, DOWN, IN, OFF, ON, OUT, OVER, THROUGH, and UP. The individual analyst can decide in each case whether he wishes to call the word so tagged an adverb or a particle.

A final checking procedure is based on a KWIC concordance of the entire tagged Corpus, sorted first by words and then by tags. This has not been printed out in its entirety, but a very flexible access program has made it possible to excerpt any desired subset. Relatively quick scanning of crucial parts of this massive document has revealed other corrections that needed to be made. When these corrections are completed, the tagged Corpus will be ready for use.

Prospects

Once the tagged Corpus has been completed and perfected, what use can be made of it? I can only speak here of our immediate plans at Brown, since it is not too easy to imagine what other uses the ingenuity of others will find. I can only say that, to judge by the inquiries we have received since it became known that the tagging was being done, these other uses will be many and varied, once the Corpus is made available. Our own plans at present involve two major projects: lemmatized frequency lists and distribution studies, and automatic syntactic research including parsing, rule-writing, and transformational analysis.

1 *Lemmatized lists*

I have discussed above the limitations placed on the usefulness of the frequency lists and distribution studies in Kučera and Francis 1967 by the fact that they made no distinctions between homographs and did not group inflectional variants under a single lemma. The tagged Corpus will permit new lists to be made in which these shortcomings are to a large degree corrected.

For the purposes of this work, we will define homographs as graphic words which have the same spelling but different tags. This will distinguish the majority of forms which would be listed in a dictionary as separate words, especially the 'functional shift' items discussed above. It will separate adjectives in -ED and -ING from their homographic participial counterparts (*eg* A HEATED ARGUMENT, AN ENTERTAINING PLAY). And it will distinguish most of the accidental pairs like ENTRÁNCE (VB) and ÉNTRANCE (NN). But it will leave some cases still ambiguous. Some examples:

STALL (NN) 'compartment' ≠ 'loss of lift' ≠ 'ruse to delay'
STALL (VB) 'put into a stall' ≠ 'lose lift' ≠ 'delay by deception'
ROW (NN) 'objects arranged in a straight line' ≠ 'noisy disturbance' ≠
    'act of rowing'
ROW (VB) 'arrange in a row' ≠ 'have a quarrel' ≠ 'propel a boat by oars'
ROE (NN) 'female deer' ≠ 'fish eggs'

Anyone interested in further disambiguating words like these will have to resort to the original text by means of an index or concordance.

The problem of homographs merges into the problem of polysemy. Principally for etymological reasons, dictionaries list the two virtually opposed meanings of FAST (JJ) under the same entry. Yet it is safe to say that most speakers of English consider them separate words, since the semantic connection is remote, to say the least. It is perhaps easier to draw such a connection between STAKE 'a post driven into the ground' ≠ 'sum or object put up in a wager', both of which are listed under a single entry.

Problems of this sort will be avoided by adopting the definition of homograph given above, which may leave some pairs unseparated but will not force us into the kind of close semantic analysis which lexicographers must make.

The other side of the lemmatization process – grouping together of inflectional variants of 'the same word' – will also present some problems. Regular patterns, such as regular nouns and most weak verbs, will easily enough be handled by the computer with simple algorithms. But a sizeable residue will have to be done manually: irregular weak verbs (CREEP – CREPT); strong verbs (RIDE – RODE – RIDDEN); irregular noun plurals (CHILD – CHILDREN, FOOT – FEET); suppletive verbs and adjectives (GO – WENT, GOOD – BETTER – BEST), and other irregularities, including variant and erroneous spellings. The lists will give the frequencies of each form (over all and by numbers of genres and samples, as in Kučera and Francis 1967) and also the total for each lemma. Presumably the rank list will be by lemmata, though it might be desirable to present a second rank list by individual forms.

Although the published volume will consist principally of the alphabetical and rank-frequency lists, we may also replicate some of the distributional studies included in the 1967 volume, especially the detailed distribution by genres of the 100 most frequent words. Some tables of frequency by part of speech will also be included, since these relative distibutions of nouns, verbs, and adjectives might establish some norms which would be useful for stylistic studies. Once this volume has been published, the tagged Corpus will be made available on the same basis as the present text.

2 *Syntactic studies*

Recent stylistic work has been shifting from primarily lexical studies to syntax. The types, variety, frequency, and distribution of syntactic constructions vary extensively from genre to genre, period to period, and author to author. At Brown we hope to be able to establish automatic parsing and rule-writing routines which will be applied first to various parts of the Corpus to establish norms, and can be subsequently applied to other bodies of similarly tagged text for comparative purposes. The value of such comparative studies, not only for primarily literary styles, but also in such fields as child language, regional and social dialect, language pathology, and language teaching should be obvious.

The first task will be to develop a surface-structure performance grammar which the computer can use to analyze sentences consisting of strings of tags. Since, as pointed out above, the Corpus, being 'edited' language, consists primarily of well-formed sentences free of such performance problems as anacolutha, interruption, back-tracking, hesitation, and repetition which characterize impromptu spoken language, such a grammar will be feasible. It will probably first take the form of a context-free phrase structure grammar, developing rules on the basis of bracketed strings and substrings.[12] The identification of at least major transformations (passive, relativization, complementation, etc) will follow. It is to be hoped that eventually the computer will be able to take any well-formed tagged sentence as input and put out a surface-structure bracketing (or tree), a hypothetical deep structure, and a list of the rules involved. This would produce a body of sentence models which would be subject to statistical and comparative manipulation. It is in this direction that we expect our future work with the Corpus to go.

12 Work along this line with a fragment of tagged corpus was begun by Henry Kučera and his students in 1969–70, as reported in Kučera *et al* 1970.

EPISODIC JUXTAPOSITION
OR THE SYNTAX OF EPISODES
IN NARRATION
MORTON W. BLOOMFIELD

'Qu'on ne dise pas que je n'ai rien dit de nouveau;
la disposition des matières est nouvelle.'

Pascal, *Pensées* 22 ed Brunschvicg

Randolph Quirk in his splendid and seminal essay (1963) has shown us how effective stylistically and semantically juxtaposition and repetition of formulas, nouns and epithets work in Old English poetry. Although in many ways basic to the meaning and esthetic effect of narration, episodic juxtaposition as a stylistic principle has as far as I am aware been much neglected in the study of the theory of narration. My purpose in this paper is to call attention to its importance and to make some suggestions toward how it works in narration and how to study the phenomenon.[1]

In the Anglo-Saxon world, the tendency in the study of narration has been to put the matter of episodic juxtaposition at the periphery of an analysis focused on a related topic. Sometimes it is subordinate to time or temporal analysis (for example, in Murillo 1975). Sometimes it appears as a side-issue in the discussion of narrative structure (for example, in Steinberg 1974). Sometimes the notion is related to the general topic of connectedness or linkage, especially spatial relations (for example, in Lipski 1976). A good many comments can be collected on the subject of episodic placing, but

---

1 I have dealt with this subject before although from a slightly different angle (Bloomfield, 1970*a*); see, for example, Greimas and Courtes 1975–6, and Genette 1972.

usually they are not, as far as I can gather, the central theme of the analysis. Here a short introduction to the subject as such will be attempted.

Eugene Dorfman (1969) proposed some years ago the analysis of narrative into narremes, which are to narration what phonemes are to phonology. The narreme is determined by theme and role and hence is based in large measure on subject-matter criteria. A phoneme is determined by its role in the bearing of meaning by sound. It makes a difference in meaning and this difference can be determined objectively. The narreme, however, cannot be determined by tests of difference and opposition. Dorfman also wishes to emphasize surface and deep structure (or substructure) on the linguistic analogy but fails to provide objective criteria for the distinction. In many analyses of narrative, thematic (subject-matter) and deep structural criteria are used. Claude Bremond (1973) weakens in my opinion a brilliant analysis of the French fairy tale by such a method. These criteria are too subjective, and too simplistic and all-embracing. The level of abstraction is too high to indicate the real effect of the episode and forces disparate units into one category. The same criticism can be made of Prince (1973).

In the system here proposed, as we shall see, an episode is totally a surface phenomenon and can normally be distinguished by shifts in location, time or interruptions in the narrative line. I do not claim absolute validity for my divisions, but I think in most cases readers would agree as to when an episode ends or begins.

Narration at its most characteristic is a type of description. It is the recording in word (or visual media) of a real or imagined event or events and their translation into what can be called an episode or episodes. The episode is basically a description unit of action. A description of an action or related action falls normally, if it is of any length, into units. An episode may also include elements other than action such as the description of a character (or characters) or scene (or part of a scene), or comments by the persona or author, or dialogue, or lyric or speculative interludes. A good example of the interruption of an episode may be found in Chaucer's *Troilus and Criseyde*, III, 1373–93 when their union is interrupted by the persona's attack on those 'wreches that dispise/Servise of love.' The essence of the episode is the verbal[2] description of the natural units of motion or action, for it is closely connected with motion and duration in almost every sense of these words.

Description itself, however, is neither durative (except in the sense that it takes time to be read) nor static. Whether it be one or the other depends exclusively on what is being described and how it is described. Narration, the process of describing action and movement, appears in various narrative forms: short and long stories, anecdotes, jokes, novels, novellas, case studies, historical narrative, legal reports, special dramatic forms and so forth. It has analogues in other media, often though not always supplemented with

---

2 For the sake of simplicity here, I am assuming all episodic description to be verbal. I am aware of visual description or imitation but here I am ignoring them.

words: films, radio and TV (especially though not exclusively in drama), comics, certain narrative types of painting such as Chinese or Japanese scrolls or narrative painting and so forth.

When the verbal description presents words by really or fictitiously reporting them (since the exterior world being here described is itself verbal and in the form of a real or assumed speech or comment), we have dialogue or interior monologue. In drama,[3] such verbal description becomes of overwhelming importance and is of its essence. Drama is usually based on a story which is presented through dialogue and/or soliloquy, gesture in the broadest sense of the word, and stage directions, by imitating directly, allegorically or symbolically (not mutually exclusive) life. Presenting ('showing') rather than telling or describing in the usual sense of the word is basic. Imitation of speech can be considered a special kind of description. In that case we may say description also plays a central role in most drama. When performed rather than read, drama is fleshed out by real persons who bring to it special personal qualities of presentation which we usually call 'acting'.

Narration often makes use of dialogue but normally does not present its story or plot through real human beings playing parts in the talk. I am of course assuming throughout written communication. In oral cultures, or when in written cultures literature is read, the role of the presenters becomes much more important. Needless to say, the complexities of dialogue and the differences between telling and showing[4] are only barely touched upon here.

Narration is transmitted through episodes, the usual divisions of the description of action.[5] The first episode in narration lacks a preceding episode, at least on the same level of communication. We may, for instance, have a story within a story, where the preceding episode prepares the way by telling of the origin or *raison d'être* of the inner story. The episode at the end of a tale is not normally followed by another – unless it is a tale within a tale and in that case the subsequent episode is on a different level of communication. There are proper and suitable ways for beginning and ending stories which cannot be reduced to scientific exactitude. They occupy an important place in the evaluation of the narration. The study of

3 Or in the rare narratives which are made up exclusively or extensively by the reporting of dialogue, as for example in the novels of Ivy Compton-Burnett. In mime it should be noted, gesture takes over.

4 Normally speech is presented in written narration by the description or reporting of what the characters say (the sounds of their speech as conventionally represented in alphabets). Yet on occasion the sounds uttered by the character are forsaken for description of what he does. A speech may be interrupted by a purely descriptive word as for instance 'sigh' which does not indicate the sounds indicated by the four letters but rather the whole action of sighing. Description is here not phonetic but rather semantic. The showing and telling distinction is discussed in N. Friedman (1955).

5 For most purposes, as indicated above, one can define an episode as the description of the action between chronological and locational gaps which may be juxtaposed with another action unit or with psychological and meditative units. In most cases these divisions are clear enough for our purposes.

beginnings (see for example Said 1975) and endings (see for example Smith 1968) needs further investigation in spite of the important work already done on the subject.

Besides these beginning and ending episodes, other episodes are juxtaposed through a time gap, forward or backward with another episode or interrupted by a soliloquy, a piece of stream of consciousness, by the comments of the persona, a static description or something similar of a non-narrational nature. These possible transitional sections are not mutually exclusive. Furthermore some narrational episodes are transitional and functional as linking episodes. The non-narrational sections can also be looked upon as episodes, although of a different sort. They certainly have positional force.

The existence of episodes and hence their juxtaposition is normally inevitable in narration because of the difference between time represented in the narration and the time taken to read the narrative. It is impossible to represent everything that happens or could happen in a story. Gaps in narrated events are necessary if they are ever to be told. These gaps are not only dependent on the difference in time represented and time read, but also on the unsolvable problem of all description – completeness is never possible. Description may be suggestive or subsumed under some theme, as Dickens often does.[6] When a long time is required by the narration, the length can only be suggested by words which are redolent of long duration and their reading cannot last anywhere near the length of time involved. Often long periods of time are put into the gap between two episodes with a transitional sentence or two in either or both episodes. The interminable tale of the taking away of a grain of corn from a granary is obviously not going to hold any audience. Even Scheherazade would not have been able thus to save her life.

Gaps are by no means limited to the narrative space between two episodes, for in that case a completely mechanical division between episodes would be available. There are also time gaps within episodes. It is impossible to provide a rule or formula for distinguishing intra- from inter-episodic gaps but in practice it is fairly easy to do so. The dramatic role of time must also be taken into consideration. Sometimes the length of time is decisive. Shifts in character emphases also help. At other times, the location of chapter endings can provide clues. These and other devices or modes of narration provide signs of how and where the gap functions.

The relation of episodes to chapters in novels (when they exist) may create interesting complexities.[7] Normally, however, chapters are signifi-cant episodes. Frequently they are used to indicate a longer gap in time than

6 For instance, the opening of *Bleak House*. Dickens often unifies his descriptions by emphasizing the same aspect of the various objects or people being described.
7 See Raymond S. Willis Jr (1953) on the connection of chapters in *Don Quixote* and Philip Stevick (1966). On occasion, chapter or book divisions may seem to be independent of episodic divisions, as for instance in Ovid's *Metamorphoses*.

usual between episodes. Sometimes they (like episodes) can be used to prolong suspense or cut an event in the middle.

The Russian formalists distinguished between fabula (the chronological and causal sequence of the narrative) and *sujet*, the actual arrangement. The term plot has too many meanings to use in this distinction, but it is obviously closely related to both fabula and *sujet*. If we abstract the plot from a narrative or if we create a plot for a narrative, we usually first translate it into the normal flow of events which are being described. But unless he is a remorseless realist, the author frequently rearranges it – so that it can be effective on its own terms – into a *sujet*. The reader or critic must on the other hand start with the *sujet* and then rearrange it to recreate the fabula or something approximating it, so that we can give some sense to the episodes we read about. Sometimes the difference between *sujet* and fabula is small but sometimes it is very great and may in fact be turned almost upside down. The arrangement of fabula and *sujet* often involves different levels of discourse, *eg*, the author's, the persona's, or the story line. These of course must be clearly distinguished in analysis.

Narration then consists of episodes which are usually its natural units conditioned by the factors of transmission which are proper to its medium, purposes, rhetorical and esthetic requirements, under the limitations of time and human ability. These requirements frequently demand the rearranging of episodes from their normal chronological order. What is juxtaposed to what, is determined by the point or points the creator wishes to make, what significance he wishes to give his meaning and the audience he is addressing. The choice of episodes and their syntax or spatial sequential arrangement in narration is determined then by esthetic, mimetic, formal and rhetorical principles. In some cases of obvious propaganda, the rhetorical principles dominate over the others.

Not all episodes are of equal importance to the effect or telling of a tale, nor do their length and complexity always reveal the extent of their significance to the impact of the tale. Furthermore the number of episodes usually does not determine the importance of an event or events, just as the number of words in a speech does not determine its esthetic impact. A one-or-two-sentence episode, for example, 'He walked away with his head bent' can be of greater impact than an episode of ten pages. We do however on occasion find some correlation between location, length, complexity, and number on the one hand and significance on the other. These elements determine and influence the power or charm of a tale by various causal factors which are normally too complex to analyse, psychological and stylistic factors. Where one is to stop in causal analysis depends on the matter being analysed. In some sense all elements leading to and surrounding a scene in real life or in art have causal impact, but it is normally not profitable to pursue the matter too far. If a man falls over a cliff, the presence of the cliff in that place is a causal factor. But normally one would not carry one's investigations to the point of analysing the geological factors which made the cliff to be there. So too in episodic analysis. One must call a halt.

Novelists like Dickens who frequently emphasize action and motion usually have more episodes than novelists less action-oriented, like Jane Austen. The frequent appearance of new episodes tends, as we have already pointed out, to emphasize physical motion. Certain positions like the beginning and end have a special importance in the economy of a tale. Some novelists, particularly in modern times, tend to emphasize interior dialogue or attempt to represent in words the flow of thought. Their books may be called lyrical novels, the emphasis of which is on characterization and on the psychological reaction to events rather than the events themselves. One thinks of some novels of Virginia Woolf, Proust, or James Joyce. In this case, the episode as an important unit of progression becomes too inclusive; it effectively disappears and must be reconstituted from lyrical or dramatic evidence. The episode is not in such cases useful as a unit for analysis. Usually, however, narration involves, in a fundamental way, action through time. Episode analysis then serves as a useful form of literary study and criticism.

In my earlier article (Bloomfield 1970a) I studied one of the major differences between medieval epic and romance in terms of the motivational relation between episodes and found a significant distinction between them in terms of genre. The episodes in medieval epic tended to be properly, if not always realistically, motivated (not caused) by preceding episodes. In epic there was what one may call horizontal motivation. In other words, the relation between the actions and events of episodes or within an episode was usually explicable in terms of the earlier one in time. Reasons, even if unrealistic or irrational, were given why characters acted as they did – either presented in an earlier episode or within the same episode. Horizontal and rational motivation prevailed.

Romances on the other hand, echoing saint's lives, often left gaps in motivation (as well as, of course, in time) between episodes, gaps which could only be explained by some overarching vertical motivation, usually religious. I am of course using the word 'vertical' (as well as 'horizontal' in the preceding paragraph) metaphorically. I am assuming the motivation for the inexplicable episodes in medieval romance comes from God who is normally considered to be located above, in heaven. The motive is a mystery and comes from a divine force which may be considered to be vertical. When episodes motivate each the other, the motivation is on the same level as the narration. It may then be considered loosely as horizontal. The sense of mystery which is strong in medieval romance is partly and perhaps largely due to this frequent vertical and inexplicable kind of motivation for the actions of its characters and for events. The *aventure*, the core of the romance, often befalls the hero or protagonist, as its etymology indicates.

What is not said of the action is both within each episode and, above all, in the gaps between episodes. These gaps, blanks or vacancies stimulate the reader into an awareness of what is not there. The syntax of episodes, their arrangement, is effectuated by gaps and determined by the demands of plot and esthetic goals.[8] The manipulation of gaps is probably a major factor in producing the esthetic effect of the narration. The total esthetic effect of a narration is of course due to more than the gaps and what is placed beside what. Language, characterization, inner organization, truth and suspense are some of the other esthetic determinants, but if we study the narration as such, that is the arrangement of action and event units, the episode, we get a very strong sense of the fascination and power of what is being narrated. Crucial to this sense is what is left out between episodes and what is placed physically beside what. Episodic syntax which depends on blanks is of the essence of artistic effect in narration. Over-explaining or under-explaining, unpleasing or inappropriate juxtaposition – in short, misuse of gapping – destroys the artistic effect of a narration.

It is obvious that these criteria contain a strong subjective element. Esthetic judgments cannot be made mechanically. This truth does not merely apply to the study of episodes, but indeed to any study of the effect of language, the force of characterization, the appropriateness of plot and so on. If esthetic judgments were a matter of counting, there would be few differences of opinion in judging art. Yet the analysis of episodes provides one more and a much neglected criterion of the evaluation of narration.

Let us look at the episode as a formal sequential feature of narration and particularly of narrative and story. It is common in structural stylistic analysis to point to phonological (sounds, length, stress, etc), morphological and even syntactic patterns of various units, but as far as I know little has been done with episodic patterns. Episodes can have special allegorical and symbolic significances as well as contribute to the movement of the action. They can also repeat and contrast with each other or with earlier or later episodes. In fact they can have the kinds of repetition and parallelism that all the elements contribute to the total effect of the work of art or artifact. They may undergo all the variations that any other element in a story or narrative, prose or poetry can submit to. The syntax of episodes needs to be studied as other elements are.

Episodes may appear in various combinations – aba, aabb, abcba and so forth. The internal structure of an episode may also be used to repeat or vary in parallelism that of another episode. The influence of one writer or another does not only include themes, words, characters, but also arrangement both internally or externally of episodes.[9]

---

8 I am indebted for some of the ideas in this paragraph to Wolfgang Iser's talk (1977). See also his book (1976, *pp* 284 *ff*).

9 A classic example of influence through different styles and modes of writing is J. V. Cunningham's article on the influence of the *Romance of the Rose* on the Prologue to the *Canterbury Tales* (1952).

A rather simple but yet puzzling episodic parallelism may be found in the central episode of the Middle English poem *Gawain and the Green Knight*. As has been frequently noted (first perhaps by Savage 1928), the hunting scenes parallel the love attempts of the lady of Bercilak to seduce Gawain. Their full interpretation is still not understood, especially as the exact symbolism of the deer, boar, and fox (like all medieval and Renaissance symbols) in these scenes has not yet been satisfactorily unlocked. Yet even at its most commonplace level, the parallelism between the pursuit of prey and of a beloved is quite clear and contributes strongly to the extraordinary sense of well-formedness which arises from a reading of *Gawain*. The a : b : a, a : b : a, a : b : a pattern simply as pattern functions in a satisfying manner to strengthen the tight structure which dominates *Gawain*. The stability of the lady's prey (Gawain) contrasts and varies with the three preys of the hunter and the failure of the lady to succeed contrasts with the threefold success of the hunter. Furthermore it reflects the macro-episode which dominates the whole story – Arthur's Court, the absence from Arthur's Court (possibly two major episodes of the journey and Bercilak's castle) and again Arthur's Court (aba or abba).

Another example may be found in Chrétien de Troyes's *Knight of the Cart*.[10] After the sword bridge episode (*ll* 3135 *ff*) and just before Lancelot is imprisoned (*ll* 5359 *ff*), the episodes arrange themselves as abcdcba where

a = arrival and departure scene
b = inconclusive combat (between Lancelot and Meleagant)
c = encounter between Guenevere and Lancelot, the one first rejecting and the second rewarding Lancelot's service
d = first search for Gawain.

The location of this final episode (d) moves between Guenevere and Lancelot, interweaving their fates. It provides a good example of an episode which does not remain in one location. Although an episode usually takes place in one place or in transit between places, it sometimes occurs in two localities (or even more) without a transition between them. This particular long episode (*ll* 4083–4458) could be divided into sub- or micro- episodes.

The pattern of reversal as above – abcdcba – is not common but it does occur. Episodes do not usually appear as a pattern in narratives, but they sometimes do. Episodic juxtaposition is an aspect of narrative technique frequently unanalysed and even unrealized. Todorov (1969, *pp* 68 *ff*) speaks of three types of 'sequence-combinations' (and does not deny the existence of others). He entitles them *l'enchaînement*, in which there is a simple linkage of various episodes, *l'enchâssement*, in which one level of an episode is embedded in another, and finally *l'alternance*, which indicates simple repetition (with minor variations). These distinctions are valuable but they

---

10 I am indebted to F. Douglas Kelly (1966) for a number of ideas and especially this example (*pp* 178 *ff*).

fit rather closely Todorov's own theory of 'propositions' which are rather thematic functions than episodes in my sense of the word.

As Kelly (1966) shows, other episodic patterns are discernible in Chrétien's poem. In fact it offers a remarkably complex example of episodic arrangement, especially remarkable because it occurs in a romance normally considered formless. A close examination of other romances along the lines laid out here and in Kelly would show more patterns than has been previously noticed. Yet it must be pointed out that not all episodes fall into a repeatable or similar structural organization. Some episodes are also gratuitously introduced and seem to have no obvious rationale or fit into no pattern. Sometimes the gratuitousness gives a sense of lightness and indifference, sometimes it gives a sense of mystery and surprise. An episode is gratuitous if it is not a logical consequence of the plot line and if it has no apparent motivation or preparation for itself.

Episodes may be simply repeated with slight variations. They may be balanced and unbalanced against each other. They may be gratuitous, seemingly motiveless, or the result of divine or other worldly intervention. They may even be over-determined. They can be expected or unexpected. Their order can be varied in many ways. The deletion of an episode may at times be of great artistic significance, especially when a pattern has been established and expected. They may be manipulated by the artist as sounds, rhythms, lexical and morphical units and syntax can be manipulated, for the sake of foregrounding.

Motivation can also be backwards when in *Gawain and the Green Knight* we discover towards the end of the romance that Morgan le Fay is responsible for the antics of the Green Knight. We can have episodes which include other episodes – macro-or-micro-episodes or even macro-episodes. Sometimes a whole narration may be considered as a frame for subepisodes. The relation between episodes can be chronological, abrupt, or with a subepisode acting as a transition, a copula so to speak. The relation between episodes can also be analysed as associational, repetitive, contrasting and absent. In fine, the syntax of episodes can be very complex and is indeed a major artistic element in the creation and effect of a tale.

To create a syntax of narrative progression and movement, some unit is needed, and it seems to me that the episode is the most convenient for this purpose. The identification and analysis of episodes can be a most valuable contribution to the understanding of narration. It is of course not the only unit which should be studied, but it is an important part of narrative style analysis. It is a topic as important as the use of the persona, or the method of characterization or thematic analysis and like them contributes to an understanding of the narrational process.

As is clear, episodic analysis has not been totally neglected in the past, but Kelly is not interested in a theory of episodes. Dorfman's scheme (1969) seems to me to have, as indicated above, serious deficiencies. Propp's analysis of the folk-tale is too involved in deep structure. Literature belongs first of all to the surface, and the deep structure of literature is far too complex to analyse at present and possibly ever to analyse.[11]

Here are suggested steps for practical episodic analysis. First, the narrative should be divided into episodes. Normally episodic identification is not too difficult a task except in the case of lyrical novels, which should perhaps be ignored. Episodic analysis is not of great use with this type of novel. A story normally falls into units determined by the normal sequence of its narration and often by gaps in duration. There will be occasional problems of where the division should be, but in my experience, the task almost determines itself if the difficult narratives such as lyrical novels are eliminated. Usually, though not always, a shift in location and/or time indicates a new episode. Chapters often give clues. Non-episodic material, such as musings by the persona, lengthy descriptions, meta-narrative comments, should be ignored if they are extra-episodic. We are in search of narrational units and narration is at present our main concern.

Second, after the episodes themselves have been determined and their status as micro-, macro-, or transitional, they should be counted, their proper chronological order indicated by an ordered system of numbers or letters and their length and duration (insofar as the latter is determinable) should be indicated.

Third, we are now ready to indicate their relation to each other in terms of motivations, gaps, length, repetitions, opposition and syntactic location. The narrational pattern can then be indicated with the sigla offered in my article (Bloomfield 1970*a*: 125–8) together with other signs. A structural pattern in space, time, gaps, and inter-episodic relations, especially in motivation will then emerge.

Motivation and causation are not the same. It is my experience that the proper term and the only usable one in this duo for our purpose is motivation. Few episodes cause later episodes in any normal sense of the word cause. Motivation is determined by the answer to the question of whether an episode provides proper reasons for its sequence or a later episode or episodes. The rarer the motivation, the more mysterious the narration appears. The commoner the motivation, the more rational the narrative appears, even if the rationality is based on folk themes and implausibilities in terms of the modern world view.

The kind of analysis here proposed is quite similar to musical analysis when the various themes in classical music are identified and the pattern of the notes appear. What I am arguing for is a kind of musical or syntactical analysis of our texts similar to what Tovey and many others have done with music.

11 See Bloomfield (1970*b*). I wish to thank the members of the Boston Area Stylistics Club for their helpful criticism when this article was first read before them in November 1977. I am also indebted for several valuable suggestions to my colleague Professor Patricia Eberle.

This study attempts to sketch what the author himself hopes later to develop. Structural analysis (as does all other kinds of analysis) contributes to a deeper understanding of how narration operates and increases an awareness of esthetic effects. It is a type of esthetic analysis which has in the past been much neglected. It should be added to those conceptual tools which are available for the understanding of literary art, especially narration. It is, however, another valuable tool but not the only one. Monistic theories of literary analysis are not enough. No one method is enough.

Looking at the subject of episodic juxtaposition, one can but think that it is a variety of the general notion of place and, in particular, position relative to other positions. The juxtaposition discussed in this article does have the advantage of being especially helpful for narrative analysis. Narration also implies directionality, and in my use of the term juxtaposition I am assuming it implies the direction of the movement of the plot. In general, however, juxtaposition and directionality are of the essence of all genres and kinds of art, not to speak of life in general. Because of its durative nature, narration in particular is especially suitable for this type of analysis, but other non-narrational arts can also be viewed thus. These latter forms may adapt themselves less easily to this method. All structural analysis depends ultimately on position, both literal and figurative, even more than on direction. Such analysis is theoretically available for all kinds of art – lyrical poems, sonnets, paintings, music and so forth. To work out a method for all of them will take time and energy, yet it can and perhaps one day will be done.

NON-RESTRICTIVE MODIFIERS:
POETIC FEATURES OF LANGUAGE
EDMUND L. EPSTEIN

The 'poetic use of language' has usually been described as employing those features of language which are also employed in 'casual' speech, but perhaps more organized, or observed in a different way because of the 'situation' of the text as poetry. However, there are some features of language which seem to be reserved specifically for poetic occasions. Poetic epithets – the 'epitheta ornantia' of classical rhetoric – have been associated mainly or entirely with the creative use of language, as in poetry or 'poetic prose.' Examination of these features can lead to the discovery of important properties of poetry which make it different from other varieties of language.

The classical treatment of epithets can be found in Aristotle, Rhetoric III, ii, 14; III, iii, 3; Cicero, De oratore III, 52–207; pseudo-Cicero, Ad Herenniam IV, 12; and Quintilian, Institutio oratore VIII, 6.40–43. Both Aristotle and Quintilian find in the use of ornamental epithets a specific feature of 'poetic language' as opposed to other uses of the language:

> . . . in poetry it is appropriate to speak of white milk, but in prose it is less so; and if epithets are employed to excess, they reveal the art and make it evident that it is poetry. And yet such may be used to a certain extent, since it removes the style from the ordinary and gives a 'foreign' air. . . . Those who employ poetic language by their lack of taste make the style ridiculous and frigid [by piling up ornament upon ornament], and such

idle chatter produces obscurity; for when words are piled upon one who already knows [*gignóskonti*], it destroys perspicuity by a cloud of verbiage. . . . If the practice [of compound words] is abused, the style becomes entirely poetical. (Rhet III, iii, 3 – Freese trans)

Here Aristotle definitely identifies epithets as 'poetizers', elements whose presence make the text in which they appear seem removed from the ordinary; they make the text appear 'foreign', or poetical – for good or ill.

Quintilian's treatment of epithets is similar.

. . . the *epithet*, of which the correct translation is *appositum*, though some call it *sequens*, is clearly an ornament. Poets employ it with special frequency and freedom, since for them it is sufficient that the epithet should suit the word to which it is applied: consequently we shall not blame them when they speak of 'white teeth' or 'liquid wine'. But in oratory an epithet is redundant unless it has some point [*nisi aliquid efficitur*]. Now it will only have some point when it adds something to the meaning, as for instance in the following: 'O abominable crime, O hideous lust!'. . . Two epithets directly attached to one noun are unbecoming even in verse. (Inst Orat VIII, 6.40–43 – Butler trans)

Despite syntactic ambiguities in the examples chosen, it seems likely that the poetic epithets of Aristotle and Quintilian are the non-restrictive modifiers [N R M s] of modern syntactic studies. For the Greeks, the ornamental epithet first found in the works of Homer – his well-greaved Achaians, black ships, polytropic Odysseus, and Achilles, swift of foot – are not contrasted restrictively in Homer's contexts with badly greaved Achaians (or other sorts of Achaians), ships of other colors than black, badly plotting Odysseuses, or slow-footed Achilleses. (More explicitly, the sentence realizing the proposition that (A) 'Homer describes swift-footed Achilles' always has the same truth-value as a sentence realizing the proposition that (A′) 'Homer describes Achilles, who is/was swift of foot' [A≡A′].[1])

It is not clear from context in Aristotle and Quintilian that their modifiers ARE non-restrictive; each one could bear a restrictive interpretation, although perhaps a bizarre one. However, both Aristotle and Quintilian make it clear that they mean their epithets to be non-restrictive. Aristotle's epithets are 'piled upon one who already knows', and therefore contribute nothing of the type of knowledge that restrictive modifiers [R M s] bear. The same seems to be true of Quintilian; his epithets have no 'point'; that is, they add nothing to the meaning. However, the examples that Quintilian

---

1 This co-implication survives the issue of the possible fictionality of Achilles; that is, whatever the truth-value of A, it necessarily implies the same value for A′, and vice versa. The doubt about tense in A′ could be overcome by declaring that A ≡ A′ [present] V A′ [past]. However, even this is not necessary to assume, I believe, since the proper tense would be indicated by the context (the other sentences in the discourse).

gives of informationally additive modifiers – 'O abominable crime, O hideous lust!' – also seem to me to be irresolvably ambiguous as between NRMs and RMs. He may be really making a distinction between analytic and synthetic modifiers rather than restrictive and non-restrictive ones. An analytic modifier is always non-restrictive, of course, and seems to contribute no new knowledge of any kind, whereas many other sorts of NRM *do* contribute knowledge, though not strictly NECESSARY knowledge in context.

It is certainly easy to find examples of NRMs in recognizable instances of poetry besides Homer's. (In these examples, possible NRMs are italicized; doubtful modifiers are marked by marginal queries; restrictive modifiers are not marked.)

[1] Who will go drive with Fergus now,
And pierce the *deep* wood's *woven* shade,
And dance upon the *level* shore?
Young man, lift up your *russet* brow,
And lift your *tender* eyelids, maid,
And brood upon hopes and fear no more.

And no more turn aside and brood
Upon love's *bitter* mystery;
For Fergus rules the *brazen* cars,   [?]
And rules the shadows of the wood,
And the *white* breast of the *dim* sea
And all *dishevelled wandering* stars.   [?/?]

   (William Butler Yeats, 'Who Goes With Fergus?')

[2] The woods and downs have caught the mid-December,
The *noisy* woods and *high* sea-downs of home;
The wind has found me and I do remember
The *strong* scent of the foam.

                    (Hilaire Belloc, first stanza of
                    'Stanzas Written on Battersea Bridge
                    During a South-Westerly Gale')

[3] Oh! ye that prink it to and fro,
In *pointed* flounce and furbelow,
What have ye known, what can ye know
That have not seen the mustard grow?

To see the *yellow* mustard grow
Beyond the town, above, below;

Beyond the *purple* houses, oh!
To see the *yellow* mustard grow!

> (Hilaire Belloc, first and last
> stanzas of 'The Yellow Mustard')

[4] The Amazons wear balzarine of jonquille
Beside the *blond* lace of a *deep-falling* rill;
Through glades like a nun
They run from and shun
The *enormous* and *gold-rayed rustling* sun;
And the nymphs of the fountains
Descend from the mountains
Like *elegant* willows
On their *deep* barouche pillows,
In cashmere Alvandar, barège Isabelle,
Like bells of *bright* water from *clearest* wood-well.   [?/?]

> (Edith Sitwell, *ll* 35–45 from 'Waltz')

[5] Suddenly I saw the *cold* and *rook-delighting* heaven . . .

> (W. B. Yeats, *l* 1 from 'The Cold Heaven')

[6] At the *round* earth's *imagin'd* corners, blow
Your trumpets, Angels, and arise, arise
From death, you *numberless* infinities   [?]
Of souls, and to your *scatter'd* bodies goe.

> (John Donne, *ll* 1–4, Holy Sonnet IV)

[7] And did those feet in ancient time
Walk upon England's mountains *green*:
And was the *holy* Lamb of God,
On England's *pleasant* pastures seen!

And did the Countenance Divine,
Shine forth upon our *clouded* hills?
And was Jerusalem builded here,
Among these *dark Satanic* Mills?

Bring me my Bow of *burning* gold: [?]
Bring me my Arrows of desire:
Bring me my Spear: O clouds unfold!
Bring me my Chariot of fire!

I will not cease from Mental Fight,
Nor shall my Sword sleep in my hand:
Till we have built Jerusalem,
In England's *green & pleasant* Land.

(William Blake, 'Jerusalem')

This is not to assert that without NRMs a poem cannot be a poem. Indeed, it is easy enough to find distinguished examples to the contrary, Shakespeare's 'Full fathom five', for one, in which all modifiers are restrictive relative clauses. What IS being asserted here is that NRMs, when they are present, act as a 'poetizing' influence on the text, just as Aristotle and Quintilian suggest. Sometimes the 'poetizing' effect of NRMs is unwelcome, as when they appear in high-pressure prose. Here their effect is too strong; consider the following inept bit of journalism:

[8] That *luscious* smoked ham on your dinner table and *sizzling* bacon or
   sausage you enjoy for breakfast are easily come by today . . .

(Port Washington *News*, 5 January 1978, *p* 8)

The two NRMs taint the commonplace prose, giving it an inappropriate and unwelcome 'poetic' tinge.

NRMs therefore play an important if enigmatic role in poetry and 'poetic' prose. Little has been written on the sources of their expressive power, and less on their poetizing effect. Homer's epithets, as identifiable tags to nominals, have only a limited expressive value, in that their use, generally though not always, provides more information to the modern reader about the rhetorical tradition of Greek epic than about Achaians, ships, Odysseus or Achilles, or about Homer's feelings about any of these. However, in poetry later than Homer's and in casual discourse (albeit of an unusual kind) they play an intriguing and sometimes a vital role.

A clue to their nature is provided by Jespersen:

Next we come to *non-restrictive adjuncts* as in *my dear little Ann!* As the
adjuncts here are used not to tell which among several Anns I am speaking
of (or to), but simply to characterize her, they may be termed ornamental
('epitheta ornantia') or from another point of view parenthetical adjuncts.
*Their use is generally of an emotional or even sentimental, though not always
complimentary character*, while restrictive adjuncts are purely intellectual.

(Jespersen 1924:111–12: my italics)

Jespersen comments in another place on the affective charge borne by NRMs; in his description of the style of Carlyle, Jespersen declares that the low percentage of RESTRICTIVE adjuncts in the style of Carlyle shows Carlyle's 'predilection for descriptive and emotional as against purely defining adjectives' (1909–49: III.34).

In the same texts Jespersen also says of NRMs that they 'might be discarded without serious injury to the precise understanding of the sentence as a whole . . . . The sense is complete in itself without the addition of the clause . . .' (30–1). (See also GCE:858–9.)

NRMs, then, display three characteristics, each interesting in itself, and most interesting and paradoxical when viewed together.

(a) They are always 'poetizers', even where this is inappropriate;
(b) They are 'emotional or even sentimental' in character; that is, they strongly bear affect; and
(c) They are in some ways gratuitous for the sense, and may be 'discarded without serious injury'.

Examination of NRMs reveals a fourth characteristic: the affect mentioned in (b) can be subtly weakened by altering the surface structure of the discoursal units which bear the modifier. Consider Jespersen's ambiguous sentence [9] 'The industrious Japanese will conquer in the long run' (1924:112), in non-restrictive contexts:

[9]a There is now an international race for power. The *industrious* Japanese will conquer in the long run.[2]

Note how the affect is weakened in a rewrite of [9a]:

[9]b There is now an international race for power. The Japanese will conquer in the long run. They are *industrious*.

It seems to me as if the writer of [9b] felt less strongly about the admirable qualities of the Japanese than the writer of [9a], who introduces his NRM arhythmically, as a pre-modifier. Therefore, there is a fourth trait of discourses embedding NRMs:

(d) Prenominal NRMs, which could be called 'arhythmic modifiers', bear more affect than modifiers in predicate position in separate sentences, from meaning-equivalent discourses.

Why should the mere fact of non-restriction produce such strong and paradoxical effects? If the answer to this question can be found, an approach to deeply characteristic features of poetry can be discovered.

Three of these characteristics – gratuitousness, affect-bearing nature, and rhythm of presentation – will be examined in turn to discover any possible interrelationships and how they may be related to the poetizing effect of NRMs.

---

2 In spoken discourse there are various intonational features which mark restrictive modifiers from non-restrictive – internal pauses for non-restrictive relative clauses, contrastive stress for prenominal NRMs. These features are redundant, however. As we will see, if it is clear to the intuition of the writer that a modifier is restrictive, the accent need not be marked in written discourse even by such devices as italics or underlining.

Gratuitousness

Jespersen's notion that the sense of the discourse could be 'complete' without the NRM is not in itself complete. Consider the following discourse:

[10] Other virtues than military ones are longlasting. The *industrious* Japanese will conquer in the long run.

If the NRM 'industrious' were omitted, the sense would not be 'complete' in any sense of the word. In fact, if it were omitted, the reader would probably supply some equivalent modifier silently.

It is RESTRICTION which requires explanation, not non-restriction. In some sense, EVERY modifier is 'restrictive', in that it provides some 'necessary' information. H. P. Grice has described a Maxim of Relation – 'Be relevant' – as one of the rules of conversational implicature (Grice 1975). If a listener or reader judges all aspects of a discourse relevant, in the Gricean sense, there is no gratuitous or unnecessary information; everything has a function.

However, except as measured from the heights of Gricean tolerance, all sequence of topics, and all comment on these topics, is unconstrained and unpredictable, in any strict sense of 'prediction'. Surrealist poetry is merely the tip of the iceberg, below which lies all non-phatic utterance. To control this intrinsic and unrestrained freedom of non-phatic utterance, discourses are bound together by restrictive devices and expectations. After the unconstrained establishment of the topic, the other parts of the discourse are 'restricted' increasingly by the primary utterance and then by subsequent utterances, until all the information the speaker wishes to convey, or has at his disposal, is gone through. However, poetic NRMs break into this pattern. NRMs convey the ordinary non-restrictiveness of discourse-beginning modifiers into the increasingly restrictive environs of the discoursal interior; hence both their gratuitousness, and the refreshing affect they bear, as non-restrictive.

This is the pattern of ordinary discourse – an initial and tentative establishment, psychologically non-restrictive, of topic, and an establishment – again psychologically non-restrictive – of one propositional predicate, a comment on the topic. Thence proceeds a growing restriction, as in a chess game, until the comment on the topic is played out, and the speaker comes to the end of his knowledge – a forced mate. 'Poetic' NRMs act as if they were discourse-beginners, but WITHIN the discourse in this schema, and therefore bear a primary affect related to their actual internal position. NRMs acting as true discourse-beginners would lack this primary affect, since their lack of restriction would be inevitable, and it is the displacement of discourse-beginning devices like NRMs to the interior of the discourse

[227]

that accounts for their (primary) affect. Of course, almost all poetry is a fragment of a discourse and does not 'begin', so every poetic N R M would bear primary affect.

The presuppositions that underlie N R Ms should be examined for clues to a way through the tangled bonds of discoursal subordination. The presuppositions that underlie the modifier in Jespersen's ambiguous sentence [9] could be expressed as 'The industrious Japanese will conquer in the long run'.

RESTRICTIVE – Some Japanese are industrious.
NON-RESTRICTIVE – (All) Japanese are industrious.

This assignment of quantifiers seems adequate to express the restrictive and non-restrictive interpretations of the sentence. The formula for presupposition of modified nominals could be expressed as

A: Det Mod N → Some N Copula Mod [= Restrictive]
→ (All) N Copula Mod [= Non-restrictive]

This formulation is not adequate for all contexts, however. Consider the following discourse:

I was walking on the boardwalk the other week, and I saw some girls. The blonde girls waved at me.

By formula A the presuppositions for the subject of the ambiguous second sentence would be

RESTRICTIVE – Some girls are blonde.
NON-RESTRICTIVE – All girls are blonde.

However, the first presupposition, though a necessary condition for the truth of the sentence, is too weak to express the restrictive interpretation of the phrase fully, and the second presupposition is simply incorrect. A contextual limitation must be added to the formula

RESTRICTIVE – Some girls (in this discourse) are blonde.
NON-RESTRICTIVE – All girls (in this discourse) are blonde.

The formula should then read

B: Det Mod N → Some N (disc) Copula Mod [= Res]
→ (All) N (disc) Copula Mod [= N R]

The formula B would work even for unique referents – the *round* earth – since 'all (in this discourse)' may be only one.

Within discourses, however defined, contextual restriction on anaphora operates to produce increasingly confining 'local' restriction. Therefore, the 'gratuitousness' of each NRM represents an unexpected outburst of 'All'-ness in an increasingly 'Some'-ness environment.

Affect-bearing

Examination of the NRMs in [1–8] and in Jespersen's ambiguous sentence shows that there are two possible types of affect associated with NRMs, secondary and primary, or semantic and syntactic. There are NRMs that seem (to me) to be connotationally charged, like 'tender', 'bitter', 'noisy', 'elegant', 'luscious', 'sizzling', 'industrious' – these bear secondary affect. There are also connotationally neutral NRMs like 'deep', 'woven', 'level', 'high', 'yellow' 'purple', 'blonde', 'enormous', 'cold', 'round', 'green', and perhaps 'pleasant' – these bear only primary affect, affect only associated with their syntactic lack of restriction. Neutral, primary NRMs have subtler affect than secondarily charged ones, and the discourse that embodies them is generally of a 'higher' poetic class than one which depends upon 'secondary' overtones. As we have seen, this primary affect derives from emotion associated with small outbursts of freedom within constricted environments.

The primary affect associated with epithets has been held to be valuable since the time of Homer. We must discover why value is imputed to the presence of this syntactic feature, independent of any secondary connotations. What is the value of the 'deep wood' or the 'yellow mustard' or Aristotle's 'white milk'? For this we must consider the third aspect of NRMs, their surface-binding in context.

Value-signs

We have seen how an NRM loses much of its affect if it is placed in a separate sentence, instead of remaining in a prenominal position. This would suggest that the listener (or reader) interprets a premodifying NRM as 'too valuable' for the speaker to postpone to a separate sentence. Prenominal NRMs therefore bear a VALUE, as well as an AFFECT, and act as intrusive evidences of the speaker's value-system. It is as value-system signs that they bear their highest poetic values. The emitter of [8], for example, tells the whole world (and himself) that he values the 'lusciousness' and the 'sizzling' of abstractly presented breakfast meats too highly to postpone his expression of them, and therefore presents himself as mawkishly sentimental to readers whose value-systems differ on these points from his.

A value-system is a system for the weighing of choices. These can be choices what to BE, what to HAVE, what to DO, but also what to NOTICE,

[229]

what to SAY, what to WRITE. Every utterance (except involuntary noises) represents expressive action filtered through the utterer's value-system. Every modifier, restrictive or non-restrictive, is a product of the utterer's value-system, what he has 'chosen to notice' about the referent(s) he is talking about. The value of restrictive modifiers, however, is constrained in discourse by the previous value-choice of noticing multiple referents that need to be distinguished. The distinguishing R M itself does indeed represent a separate value-choice, in that another distinguisher might have been chosen but was not. (It is the rare phenomenon that really differs only in ONE aspect from another.) In the discourse

[11] There were two girls on the deck. The blonde girl waved.

the girls differ in position as well as in hair color, so the R M 'blonde' bears some (limited) value, in that the second sentence could have been 'The girl on the left waved'.

The limited or unlimited constraints associated with restrictive modifiers, the subordinations inevitable with restriction, do not exist for NRMs. From the listener's point of view, NRMs represent unrestricted choices of utterance and can therefore be taken by him as clearly and entirely determined by the free operation of the speaker's value-system.

The value-system of an individual is, to a great extent, what he is. Unless NRMs are Homeric epithets and conventional in origin, speakers presenting prenominal NRMs reveal in flashes to the listener what they are in the depths of their personality. This is most 'poetic' when the NRMs are analytic. When Hilaire Belloc informs his reader presuppositionally that mustard is yellow (example [3] above), he is in effect saying that the perception that mustard is yellow is so valuable to the speaker that he cannot refrain from mentioning it, and mentioning it 'out of rhythm'. 'Yellow' expresses an analytic property of mustard, as 'white' does for milk in Aristotle's 'white milk'. The anticipatory prenominal placement of the modifier suggests the high value placed on it by the speaker, a paradoxical assignment for an analytic property! It seems to me that the gratuitous-yet-valuable affect associated with these analytic NRMs proceeds from the evocation of an unusual, 'poetic' frame of mind, one which is conveyed to the hearer/reader precisely by its heterodoxy.

Other 'frames of mind' are conveyed by non-analytic NRMs. Yeats' 'deep' wood and 'level' shore show a narrator so impressed by attributes of the landscape that he 'interrupts' his own questions and commands with observations. The reader, who may not be so impressed by landscape features as the narrator, may judge these 'interruptions' in questions and imperatives as unjustified; that is, he places lower value on them than the narrator presumably does, and therefore finds the intrusion mawkish, and evidence of sentimentality in the narrator.

There are subtler patterns possible than those Yeats uses in 'Fergus' in the distribution of N R M s. In Donne's lines [6]

At the *round* earth's *imagin'd* corners, blow
   Your trumpets, Angels! . . .

the putative value-system of the speaker reveals a frame of mind far removed from the loose 'wandering eye' of Yeats in 'Fergus'. Where the 'Fergus' speaker values landscape details too highly to keep them out of his commands and questions, and thereby achieves a total effect of wandering attention (see Epstein 1978:12–18), the Donne speaker's mind is engaged on a connected act of geometrizing; the mind revealed is far from mawkish or distracted, and therefore the total effect is unusual and powerful.

This can be made clearer by a method of describing the cognitive system of the total utterance. The normal 'rhythmic' assertion of attribution in a discourse presumably mirrors the pattern of realization in the mind that produces these utterances. So in the tripartite discourse,

Sentences:

[12] 1 A girl was on the deck. 2 The girl smiled. 3 She was *blonde*.

Perceptions:

[12]*a* 1 Notices girl on the deck 2 notices smiling 3 notices blondeness

the value of the blondeness is not great enough to reduce the spoken discourse to a duple one. A discourse like

[13] 1 A girl was on the deck. 2 The *blonde* girl smiled.

seems to be the result of a more syncopated cognitive pattern:

[13]*a* 1 Notices a girl on the deck. 2 notices smiling
                                  2*a* notices blondeness

All discourses can be divided into two classes; those without prenominal N R M s and those with prenominal N R M s. The second class could be analysed as consisting of a MAJOR MODE – the discourse minus the N R M s – and a MINOR MODE – the presuppositions underlying the N R M s, expressed as propositions by Rule B above. Minor-mode 'intrusions' mark value-judgments of the speaker. There is no minor mode in discourse [12]; each of the assertions has a sentence to itself. In discourse [13] the major mode is duple, with a minor-mode insertion in the second sentence, mirroring a syncopated 'arhythmic' cognitive pattern, which is caused by a value-system promotion of what would otherwise have been borne by the third sentence in the discourse, here absent. The characteristic of 'blondeness' is here conveyed as being of great value to the speaker.

[231]

Here, as always, the speaker's value-system is on trial, and if the listener's value-system does not assign as high a value to the notice of 'blondeness' as the speaker seems to hold, the speaker is judged to have been sentimental. In the Yeats lines [1], it seems likely to me that a judgment of sentimentality can be made, all the more so since the minor-mode NRMs are intrusive in syntactic areas that are usually inhospitable to NRMs, namely questions and commands. Consider the following discourses:

[14] There's a girl on the deck. Call to the *blonde* girl!
[14]*a* There's a girl on the deck. Isn't the *blonde* girl pretty?

'Blonde' as an NRM alters the force of the command or the question in subtle and heterodox ways. The directive force of questions and commands requires a high degree of communicative efficiency, which is lowered by NRMs. Perhaps this is so because the field of efficacy of directives either lies in the present – questioners attempt to complete belief-statements – or in the future – commanders attempt to alter the future. However, NRMs represent past perceptions, immediate (by perhaps a fraction of an instant) or remote, and operate as a drag on the communicative efficacy of directives. The speaker of Yeats' 'Fergus' reveals himself as a producer of mitigated directives.

Most of Yeats' mitigated directives, unlike Othello's

Keep up your *bright* swords, for the dew will rust them   (I.ii.59)

have no ironic effect, because they lack the cognitive denseness of Shakespeare's. The Othello line features a controlled use of complex NRMs in a directive environment. 'Bright' is an NRM, and intrusive in a directive, which it indeed weakens. However, as an attribute it is chosen carefully – 'brightness' is the only non-dangerous aspect of swords – and the minor mode in the command becomes the major mode in the conjunct, thereby justifying the choice of attribute.

Major mode: Keep up your swords [Directive]
Minor mode: Your swords are bright/the dew will rust your swords [Non-directive]

No such pattern is evident in [1] – Yeats' NRMs seem casually chosen. Until the last two lines, the cognitive acts that produced them seem to be isolated acts of observation, casually accomplished as acts of memory during directive activity. The 'counterpoint' in most of 'Fergus' is between vigorous major modes and feeble minor ones. The only exceptions occur in the last two lines: 'And the white breast of the dim sea, And all dishevelled wandering stars'. These achieve a cognitive richness which makes 'Fergus' stand out among Yeats' early poetry. 'White' and 'dim' represent CONNECTED minor-mode cognitions, since they are antonyms, and therefore they must be interpreted by a denser cognitive pattern than has been noted for the rest of the poem:

Major mode: the breast of the sea
Minor modes: the breast is *white*. The sea is *dim*.
Minor deep structure: [*white* is not *dim*]

The interpretation of 'all dishevelled wandering stars' is even more complex, and highly complicated by semantic factors. 'Wandering stars' could bear a restrictive interpretation since planets were originally 'wandering' stars (*planētēs*, Gk) as opposed to 'fixed'. Hence, the modifier would be implicitly anaphoric, causing it to be restrictive. The same, however, is true of 'dishevelled'. Comets were originally called 'hairy' stars (*komētes*, Gk) and 'dishevelled' means 'unkempt', *dechevelé*. Therefore, both of these modifiers could in isolation be restrictive, but not when produced together: the 'stars' must either be planets or comets – they cannot be both. On the other hand, a completely non-restrictive interpretation (Presupposition: all stars (disc) are dishevelled and wandering) ignores the undertones of 'planet' and 'comet' that a cultured reader would pick up. A mixed interpretation could indeed be possible – dishevelled (NRM) wandering (RM) stars = dishevelled planets – except that the lack of a conjunction makes the modifiers independent of each other. 'Wandering comets' [dishevelled (RM) wandering (NRM) stars] is, of course, not possible. Sidney Greenbaum (personal communication) suggests that perhaps a double restrictive interpretation is possible – 'dishevelled wandering stars' being equivalent to 'dishevelled stars [comets] and wandering stars [planets]', on the analogy of 'honest and clever students' as opposed to 'old and young men' (citing GCE: 598 *f*). Greenbaum notes that the coordinating conjunction must always be present in the latter type, but suggests that poetic language can relax this rule. I do not feel that this is possible – at any rate, in this context. The semantic complexity and syntactic ambiguity brings about a rich cognitive tangle in the mind of the reader, which may be functional in the poem – lack of focus is the productive (minor-mode) frame of mind of the speaker in producing most of his previous modifiers. Hence the fin-de-siècle vagueness of the first stanza of the poem acquires a richer tone of unresolvable complexity by the syntactic tangle at the end of the poem, and produces an affective closure. In his later poetry, Yeats employs his minor modes with great effectiveness, revealing a mind of powerful focus and sharply detailed values. See, for example, poetic sample [5] above:

Suddenly I saw the cold and rook-delighting heaven.

Analysis reveals a complex subordinating pattern in the NRMs – 'rook-delighting' perhaps BECAUSE 'cold' – a subordination in the minor-mode deep structure that is complex and exciting.

In the Donne lines, the minor mode is not that of casual observation, as in most of 'Fergus', but a much tougher activity, requiring maximal connectivity in the minor-mode deep structure:

Major mode: Blow your trumpets, Angels, at the earth's corners!

Minor modes: the earth is *round*. Corners have been imagined for the *round* earth

Minor-mode deep structure: [draw the earth as round (disc-shaped or spherical) and then imagine corners on the round earth, *ie* draw four lines/planes tangent to the round earth, and locate where lines/planes intersect]

The mind is here not revealing excessive value attached to isolated landscape attributes; it is engaged in a complex geometrical process the results of which are too valuable to postpone, even if it means producing modifiers in a directive utterance.[3] The directive force of the utterance is indeed mitigated as such, but the weakening of the illocutionary force of the command[4] is more than compensated for by the cognitive force of the minor mode.

We are only at the beginning of the study of poetic epithets. Why people say what they say – or why they say anything at all rather than remain silent – is one of the ultimate questions in linguistics and psychology. It is possible to say, however, that the three qualities of NRMs – gratuitousness, affect, value – make them indispensable but dangerous tools of linguistic creation. Their 'poetizing' nature always puts the speaker on trial, even when he has no intention of revealing himself and when the value-system thus conveyed may be that of a trivial personality. Yet enormous, complex personalities and states of being are clearly revealed also: gratuitousness, affect, and value are the three qualities of poetry that make it poetry. As Ibsen said, 'When a poet writes a poem, he holds doomsday over himself'. A poet also reveals to the eye of the reader something of what the soul reveals to the eye of God.

3 The precise geometry of the minor modes may be that of inscribing a circle in a square, or the reverse, but a more interesting possibility is that Donne was 'squaring the circle' – constructing by Euclidean means a square equivalent in area to a given circle. This perennial problem in geometry was finally put to rest in 1882, when the German geometer Lindemann proved the construction impossible.

4 Of course, the 'command' has previously been weakened by violations of several constitutive conditions for commands – proximity and authority mainly. For a related point, on the exclusion of attitudinal disjuncts from questions and commands, see GCE:517.

PRONOUNS OF ADDRESS IN *ANNA KARENINA*: THE STYLISTICS OF BILINGUALISM AND THE IMPOSSIBILITY OF TRANSLATION

JOHN LYONS

The phenomenon with which I am concerned in this article is familiar enough, in a general sort of way, not only to linguists, but to anyone who has even the slightest acquaintance with French, Russian, German, Italian, Spanish, Dutch or Swedish – not to mention a very large number of other European and non-European languages. It has been studied from the point of view of social psychology in a now famous and influential paper by Brown and Gilman (1960); and from a somewhat different point of view, with particular reference to nineteenth-century Russian usage, by Friedrich (1966). If I single out these two works for mention it is because I shall be drawing explicitly upon them in various places. But I will not refer to any other treatments of the same topic. For my article is amateurish, rather than scholarly. It is based upon nothing more than my own reading of *Anna Karenina*, a practical knowledge of Russian, French and English (sufficient for the double purpose of reading the original text and evaluating its translation into French or English at certain points) and, it must finally be admitted, a smattering of good old-fashioned structural linguistics. The details of second-person pronoun usage in Tolstoy to which I shall refer will not be new to Russian scholars. Nor will the general points that I will be making come as a surprise to those who, though they may not have been concerned with Russian, have devoted their energies as Professor Quirk has done over the years, to the complexities of stylistic variation in both spoken and written languages.

Let me begin by identifying the phenomenon to which we shall be addressing our attention; first of all, at the level of generality at which it is most commonly discussed; and subsequently, in something approximating to its full specificity and complexity.

In most modern European languages, though not in standard English (as used by the vast majority of the population in the various parts of the world in which it is used), there is a distinction between what is referred to, conventionally but loosely, as a polite and a familiar pronoun of address: between French *vous* and *tu*, Russian *vy* and *ty*, German *du* and *Sie*, Italian *tu* and *Lei*, and so on. Following the practice initiated by Brown and Gilman (1960:254), I will use the letters T and V (from the Latin *tu* and *vos*) to refer to the familiar and the polite pronouns of address, respectively, in any language that we happen to be dealing with. For example, if John, when speaking French, Russian, German, Italian, etc, employs *vous, vy, Sie, Lei*, etc (or a grammatically related pronominal or adjectival form) to refer to Mary, his addressee, I will say that John addresses Mary as V, or alternatively that John uses V, or a V-form, to refer to Mary. Similarly, for the so-called familiar pronouns of address: John will be said to address Mary as T (or to use T, or a T-form, to refer to Mary). Once we get properly into the more specific question with which I am concerned in this article, we shall have to allow for different senses in which T or V in one language may be used, more or less satisfactorily, either to represent or to translate T or V in another language.

In several languages there are special delocutive verbs which have the meaning 'to address as V' and 'to address as T': for example, French *vouvoyer* and *tutoyer*, or German *siezen* and *duzen*. And they can be employed, not only to describe particular acts of using V or T, but also to describe the relationship by virtue of which one person would normally use V or T to address another. For example, *Ils se tutoient*, when used in this way, means 'They (normally) use T to address one another'; and it is important to realize that what, following Benveniste (1966:277), I have called delocutive verbs – *tutoyer, duzen*, etc – are not restricted to the use of T or V in this or that language. It is possible, for example, to say of two monolingual Russians, or Germans *Il se tutoient*; and this obviously does not imply that they are in the habit of addressing one another by means of the French form *tu* and its congeners. The delocutive verbs can be used, then, in two distinct, but related, senses:

(a) to describe particular acts of using V or T (whether occasional or habitual);

(b) to describe a relationship between two or more persons, who may or may not be interlocutors at the time to which we are referring.

I will refer to these as the active and the stative sense, respectively. When 'X addresses Y as T (or V)' has the stative sense, I will say X is on T-terms (or *V*-terms) with Y. On several occasions in *Anna Karenina* Tolstoy makes explicit the fact that one person is addressing another as *T* or *V* in one language rather than the other; and what Tolstoy has to say about the use of French rather than Russian, or of Russian rather than French, on these occasions provides us, as we shall see, with some of our most important evidence for the thesis that I am advancing with respect to the stylistics of bilingualism and the impossibility of translation.

But before we come to the use that Tolstoy makes of the difference between the Russian and the French *T*/*V* forms, let me make a few general points. The first is that, in concentrating upon the similarity at the macroscopic, social-psychological level of the *T*/*V* phenomenon in various European languages, we must not lose sight of the fact that there may be important grammatical differences among what we identify as roughly equivalent pronouns. For example, the so-called *V*-forms of Italian and Spanish are third-person singular forms; and this means that they operate quite differently syntactically, from the *V*-forms of French and Russian. In German, the singular *du* has a plural *ihr* in correspondence with it, but the *V*-form, *Sie*, which from a grammatical point of view is third-person plural, is employed with both singular and plural reference. In Castilian Spanish, on the other hand, it is the singular *V*-form *usted* that has its corresponding plural form *ustedes*; and this plural *V*-form is now widely used in the colloquial language where the literary language has *vosotros* as the plural *T*-form (*cf* Marcos Marin 1974:150). There are many such differences; and to talk globally of *T*-forms and *V*-forms, or pronouns of address, without first of all describing the grammatical system within which each such form operates can be somewhat misleading.

The second point is that, as Jakobson (1960:278) pointed out in his comments appended to the Brown and Gilman (1960) paper, 'the use of different pronouns designating the addressee is but a part of a more complex code of verbal attitudes toward the addressee and must be analysed in connection with this total code, in particular with the question whether we do or do not name the addressee and how we title him'. Consider, for example, the unacceptability of the French utterance *Et comment vas-tu, Madame?* (This example is not Jakobson's, but mine; and I blush to admit that it was produced by me, on a memorable occasion, when my performance, if not my competence, let me down rather badly.) Jakobson rightly emphasizes the 'danger of reinterpreting the data of one language from the point of view of another pattern'. We shall keep this danger very much in mind. But we shall see that there is a sense in which in reading *Anna Karenina* we are required by Tolstoy himself to interpret one language as if it were another, as far as the *T*/*V* distinction and one or two associated matters are concerned.

Finally, it must be noted that the generalizations that can be made about the reciprocal or non-reciprocal use of *T* and *V* in particular languages, in terms of the social-psychological notions of power and solidarity (*cf* Brown and Gilman 1960), tend to be statistical in nature. Even when quite fine distinctions are made for correlated differences of social class and other relevant variables what are, without doubt, statistically valid generalizations are seldom of such power and precision that we can predict with certainty, in cases where the overall system permits choice, what usage an individual, previously unknown to us as an individual, will adopt in a given situation. As Trudgill says, in his conveniently accessible summary of the Brown and Gilman work: 'in most European languages, the solidarity factor has now won over the power factor, so that pronoun usage is nearly always reciprocal'. (Trudgill 1974:107). This is certainly the case for French: nearly always, but not always. There is one young French woman, of aristocratic parentage, known to me who uses *V* to her father and is addressed by him as *T*. And I understand that, although it is now rare, there are some Parisian bourgeois families in which the husband and wife are on *V* terms, at least in the presence of others. This was the norm in France, for both the aristocracy and the bourgeoisie, in the period with which we are concerned in this article.[1] And it was also the norm for members of the high Russian aristocracy to which Tolstoy belonged when they were speaking French; and not only when they were abroad or conversing with non-Russians, but also when they were speaking French among themselves, as was customary in the salons of Petersburg and Moscow. Their use of the *T*/*V* distinction in Russian, however, was strikingly different; and this fact, as we shall see, is central to the present article. The main point to be made here is that Russian allowed scope, as French did not, for the exercise of one's individual preferences and the expression of one's change of mood or emotion. Since the first law of semantics, in the structuralist's canon at least, is that meaningfulness implies choice, the *T*/*V* distinction was potentially meaningful in Russian, but not in French, for Tolstoy and the readers to whom he was addressing himself when he wrote *War and Peace* and *Anna Karenina* and his other works of the 1860s and 1870s. To quote Jakobson (1960) again: 'In the choice of conventional means to designate the addressee, the addresser exhibits his individuality only by an optional preference for one of the eligible etiquettes extant in the over-all code of the given language'.

Most readers with a knowledge of one or more of the modern European languages in which the use of *T* or *V* currently allows scope for the expression of one's individual preferences will appreciate the force of the general points that have just been made – especially if they have experienced, in their own lives, as lovers, friends, or comrades, the thrill and satisfaction of achieving the transition from *V*-terms to *T*-terms in one or another of these languages. And, as for the failure to make this transition and the offence or

1 Labiche, for example, makes great play with the difference between the usage of the higher bourgeoisie and that of the lower bourgeoisie, in this respect, in his farce *La Poudre aux yeux*, first performed in 1861.

suffering that it can cause, let me give just one example. It comes from the agony-column of a popular German magazine.[2] A distressed correspondent writes in with her problem: *Nach einem Verlobungshahr und drei Ehejahren siezen mich die Geschwister meines Mannes immer noch.* ('After an engagement lasting a year and three years of marriage my husband's brothers and sisters still address me as *V*'). She finds the situation more and more upsetting and wonders how the transition can now be achieved. The reply is that there is no definite rule regulating such matters (*Eine bestimmte Regel, nach der so etwas abzulaufen hat, gibt es nicht*); that everyone has been rather stubborn; and that it all ought to be sorted out over a drink (*bei der nächsten Flasche Wein*). It is only because the overall system permits, but does not prescribe, the transition from *V* to *T* in the situation in which the young woman in question found herself that the transition itself, or the failure to achieve it, can be of significance. Tolstoy, as we shall see, deliberately highlights and comments upon the transition that Levin achieves with Kitty: he makes explicit the fact that Levin takes the initiative, that Kitty approves but does not immediately reciprocate and indeed does not consistently use *T* to him until the wedding day.

Let us turn then to *Anna Karenina*. The text to which I shall be referring is that of the collected works published in Moscow in the early 1950s (Tolstoj 1953). This edition has the advantage for our purposes that it systematically translates in the footnotes all the words, phrases and sentences in other languages with which the text is sprinkled. The vast majority of these non-Russian words, phrases and sentences are in French. There are almost 150 bits of French in the text: ten of these contain a pronoun of address, and four of them are of particular interest in that a French *V*-form is translated by the editors with a Russian *T*-form – in one case, as we shall see, incorrectly.

None of the non-Russian text in *Anna Karenina* is more than a few words long. In this respect, *Anna Karenina* differs strikingly from *War and Peace*, in which whole letters and conversations are given in French. (Interestingly enough, Tolstoy had systematically translated these into Russian for the third edition of 1873. But the original French was restored for the fifth edition of 1886 and its successors by Countess Tolstoy and Strakhov: *cf* Troyat 1965:384. Tolstoy himself had by then lost interest in his earlier work.) Much of the conversation that is given in Russian in *Anna Karenina* is nonetheless intended to be understood as if it were in French. Sometimes Tolstoy tells us explicitly that either French or Russian is being used. But generally he does not; and we have to infer on the basis of internal evidence or situational appropriateness whether the Russian text is to be construed as representing French or not.

---

2 I am indebted to one of our visiting students, Renate Buchner (from the University of Bonn), who supplied me with the example in a sociolinguistics seminar (University of Sussex, Spring 1977).

One of the clues is the pronoun of address that is employed. For Tolstoy in his representation of French consistently uses the Russian *vy* as the conventional equivalent of the French *vous*; and, as we have already noted, the French *T*-form was not used as a pronoun of solidarity – not even by husbands and wives – in the circles to which Karenin, Oblonsky, Vronsky and Levin or Anna, Dolly and Kitty, belonged. It follows that in dialogues involving any of these – the principal characters – the presence of a *T*-form is a sure indication that Russian is being spoken. The presence of a *V*-form, however, does not of itself imply that the conversation is to be construed as being in French. Not all of these seven characters are on *T*-terms with one another. Furthermore, not only do transitions occur, at identifiable points, for Vronsky and Anna and for Levin and Kitty, but characters who are on *T*-terms with one another may switch to *V* in the course of a quarrel or estrangement. For example, at the very beginning of the book, when Dolly still feels estranged from her husband, Oblonsky, because of his infidelity, she addresses him as *V*, though he, as always, uses *T* to her. At a certain point she uses *T*, and Tolstoy draws our attention to the fact, and to the effect this has on Oblonsky. But she immediately reverts to *V* for the remainder of their period of estrangement (Pt 1, Ch 4).

Something of the complexity of the problem has now emerged. The complexity is further increased when we consider, as we shall do briefly, the question of translating the Russian text of *Anna Karenina* into English, on the one hand, and into French, on the other. We will leave the question of translation on one side for the present.

In his detailed account of Russian pronominal usage in the nineteenth century, which gives all the necessary background information, Friedrich (1966:216) points out that 'Tolstoy was abnormally aware of the pronominal symbolism of social differences, and was prone to interject passing comments on the usage of protagonists in his own novels'. Let us begin with a particularly striking example of this. It comes from Part 2, Chapter 22 – about a quarter of the way through the book. Anna is staying at the Karenins' summer villa at Krasnoe Selo, so that she can be near her lover, Vronsky, while he is taking part in the races. Vronsky comes to visit her; and he finds her alone. He addresses her as *V* and, as Tolstoy tells us, in French. She replies in Russian. We know this, not because we are told by Tolstoy that she does, but because she uses *T*. And her use of the *T*-form is marked in the text with a preceding dash to indicate her momentary hesitation. What precisely this hesitation signifies, we must infer for ourselves. It may be that Anna does not normally use *T* to Vronsky except in moments of intimacy (*cf* Pt 2, Ch 11) or still oscillates between *V* and *T*. It may be that she hesitates because she is afraid that her young son, Serëzha, may suddenly arrive and overhear them: and this is a contextually plausible inference. Whatever the reason for her hesitation the dash in the text highlights the use of the *T*-form: *Ja ne zhdala – tebja* ('I did not expect –

you'). But Vronsky continues to speak French, and Tolstoy tells us that this was what he always did, because it enabled him to avoid both the Russian *V*, which was impossibly cold for them, and the Russian *T*, which was too dangerous.

Tolstoy makes a similar comment about the difference between the Russian and the French *V*-forms at the point where Anna's husband, having decided not to divorce her, conveys his decision to her by letter and asks her to return to Petersburg. 'He wrote without using any form of address to her, and in French, using the pronoun *vous*, which does not have that note of coldness which it has in Russian' (Pt 3, Ch 14). We are not told on this occasion that Karenin deliberately uses French so that he can avoid, not only the cold *V*-form, but also the intimate *T*-form. But his use of French is of a piece with the almost bureaucratic formality of his letter, his significant failure to use a form of address at the beginning of his letter and the style of signature that he adopts: 'A. Karenin'. On the other hand, when Anna and Karenin are temporarily reconciled after her illness and recovery and Betsy comes to plead Vronsky's cause, having spoken to Anna in French in front of Betsy, Karenin repeats what he has just said in Russian, as soon as Betsy leaves. And naturally, in the circumstances and in his current state of mind, he uses *T*. Tolstoy comments: *When he spoke Russian to her and used* 'ty', *this* 'ty' *irritated Anna intolerably* (Pt 4, Ch 20).

There are other occasions when Tolstoy comments directly upon the difference between the French and Russian pronouns of address. But let us return to the scene at Krasnoe Selo, with Vronsky visiting Anna and Anna wondering whether to tell him that she is pregnant. Vronsky, it will be recalled, is speaking French and Anna is speaking Russian (Pt 2, Ch 22). Anna does tell Vronsky. His reaction, after a moment's consideration, is to urge upon her the necessity of putting an end to their life of deception. He makes his point in French: we know this because he continues to use *V*. She asks him how and then, either immediately or, more probably, after he has said that she must leave her husband and that, only if she does this, can their two lives be fully united, he switches briefly to Russian. The only indication of this is the *T*-form; and since there are two short utterances without any pronoun of address between the last of Vronsky's *V*-containing utterances and the first of his *T*-containing utterances, we cannot be sure exactly at what point his switch from French to Russian occurs. Anyway, when he sets about trying to convince her, we are told that he does so in his customary calm and determined tone (Pt 2, Ch 23). By implication, his previous two or three utterances were spoken in a more emotional tone of voice. It is consistent with his return to a more normal tone that he is again using the *V*-form and, therefore, since there is no question of estrangement, speaking French. And Anna, who feels shame and confusion at the mention of her husband and is vexed by Vronsky's insistence that they have got to resolve the situation, also switches at this point to *V*, presumably in French. She gets angry with him and he tries to calm her. Then comes another change of mood and, after her irony and anger, speaking, as we are told, in a sincere and tender tone of voice, she switches back to *T*: *Ja proshu tebja, Ja umoljaju tebja* . . . ('I beg you, I beseech you . . .'). And, this time, Vronsky responds immediately with *T*.

It is obviously impossible to go through many such passages in detail. I will take just one more involving Anna and Vronsky. This comes from Part 7, Chs 23–26, towards the end of the book. Anna and Vronsky have long been living together; and Anna uses *T* when she speaks Russian to Vronsky (and calls him Alexei) even in front of others, provided that they accept the situation, as Golenyščev, Vronsky's friend, did when she and Vronsky were in Italy (Pt 5, Ch 7) and as Dolly, her sister-in-law, did when she visited them in the country (Pt 6, Ch 17). Anna and Vronsky have quarrelled and Vronsky has gone out to dine with his bachelor friends. Such bits of their quarrel as are reported are marked by the use of *V*. But there is no way of telling from the text, and Tolstoy does not inform us, whether they have used French or Russian. As was mentioned earlier, whereas the use of *T* definitely indicates that it is Russian that is being spoken, the use of *V* does not of itself prove that the person in question is speaking French. People who are normally on *T*-terms in Russian might very well switch to *V*, but continue to speak Russian, in the course of a quarrel. However that may be, Anna has decided that she will mollify Vronsky when he comes back. She greets him 'with a guilty and timid expression on her face' and uses *T*. He also uses *T*. They soon start quarrelling again. He makes a scarcely veiled threat, which she challenges using *V* (*Čto vy chotite etim skazatj?*, 'What do you mean by that?'). He responds with a *V*-containing utterance, but switches back to *T*, as she is about to leave the room. He makes a concession about leaving Moscow for the country at impossibly short notice. She too switches back to *T* as she seeks, and obtains, reassurance. The following day they start quarrelling again, using *T* throughout. When he comes to her afterwards on some pretext or other, she speaks to him in French. They are now estranged, at least in Anna's mind, more definitely than ever before; and she relives in her memory the more hurtful moments of their most recent quarrel. Not only does she remember what Vronsky has actually said to her. She imagines, and puts into words, much else that she thinks he had really wanted to say; and, although, as we have seen, the quarrel was in fact conducted in *T*-containing utterances, Anna uses *V* in the utterances which she imagines Vronsky saying to her. This is consistent with her view of what his real feelings for her now must be.

The difference between this passage and the earlier one, also involving Anna and Vronsky, is that there is no reason to believe that any of the conversation, actual or imaginary, with the exception of one utterance by Anna, is in French. The same holds for another passage in which Anna's husband switches at a certain point from *T* to *V* in the course of a discussion with Anna's brother, Oblonsky. Oblonsky – 'Stiva as he was called in fashionable society': this is what Tolstoy tells us on the very first page of the novel – exudes bonhomie at all times, never takes offence and is on *T*-terms with all the principal characters. In fact, he provides us with one of the few exceptions in *Anna Karenina* to the generalization that French *T* was impossible for Russian aristocrats when they were addressing social equals: on an earlier occasion, in Part 4, Chapter 8, we are expressly told that he has spoken French, and yet his utterance contains three *T*-forms.[3] Since there is no other reason for Tolstoy to tell us that Oblonsky is speaking French, I feel sure that we are intended to note what for anyone else would be a solecism and say to ourselves, smiling 'That's just typical of Stiva'. The passage in which Karenin switches from *T* to *V* occurs much later (Pt 7, Ch 17). Oblonsky has come to see him on two unrelated matters: first, to get Karenin's support in his attempt to procure a very lucrative sinecure for himself; and, second, to persuade Karenin to give Anna (Oblonsky's sister) a divorce. During the first part of their conversation they both use *T*, even though Karenin is far from enthusiastic about giving Oblonsky his support for a post which, in Karenin's opinion, carries an unjustifiably high salary. As soon as Oblonsky mentions Anna, Karenin's expression changes: he switches to *V* and, significantly, refers to her, not as Anna, but as Anna Arkadjevna. We are not told that he has also switched languages; and it is fair to assume that he has not. There were two quite different and independent reasons for Karenin and Oblonsky to be on *T*-terms: as high-ranking civil servants of the same social standing and as brothers-in-law. During the first part of the conversation they are enacting the former role, and Karenin is comfortable enough in it. But as soon as Oblonsky adopts the role of brother-in-law, Karenin gives a clear indication, as he has said earlier in so many words, that the family-relationship that once existed between them has changed in character (Pt 4, Ch 8).

The passages that we have looked at where there is a switch from *T* to *V* without, apparently, there being any switch from Russian to French may be compared with the eight passages from other Russian works that Friedrich (1966) has analysed in terms of what he calls switching and breakthrough. There are many other instances in *Anna Karenina*. We also find recorded the occasion on which Levin first uses *T* to Kitty. She has just agreed to marry him. *I can't believe that you love me*, he says (Pt 4, Ch 15). She smiles at this use of the *T*-form; but she does not herself reciprocate for quite some time. In fact, during the period of their engagement, she alternates between *T* and *V* – on one occasion using both in juxtaposition, and then finally taking the plunge with *T* – until the very day they get married (Pt 5, Ch 2). This initial asymmetry between the man's and the woman's usage before marriage,

3 Another exception is Vronsky's use of *T* in French to Golenyščev (Pt 5, Ch 7). But then we are told that their use of French, rather absurd in the circumstances, is simply the automatic reaction of Russian aristocrats who wish to hide something from the servants.

especially when the woman was so much younger than the man, was quite normal; but Tolstoy deliberately draws our attention to it. Like much else in Tolstoy's account of Levin's relations with Kitty, it faithfully reflects, as we know from Tolstoy's diaries and Countess Tolstoy's reminiscences, details of Tolstoy's own relations with his young bride. We know that the young Countess Tolstoy, Sonia, hesitated to use T to her husband on their nuptial night, terrified as she was by the prospect of the ordeal of physical love that she had to face and about which she knew nothing other than what she had read in Tolstoy's diaries (*cf* Troyat 1965:310).

Reference has now been made, in more or less detail, to about a dozen places in *Anna Karenina* where the pronouns of address that are employed by the principal characters, with or without Tolstoy's own comments and whether they are using French or Russian, are of interest to us. There are of course very many other passages that might have been cited to illustrate the points that have been made; or to illustrate such other points as the consistent use of T to servants and the use by some serfs of T to their master. We have been concerned solely with the pronouns of address employed by the aristocracy to their social equals; and the instances that have been mentioned will suffice for the present purpose. We now take up the question of translation.

It was mentioned earlier that the modern edition of *Anna Karenina* that I have used gives footnote translations of all the non-Russian bits that occur in the text and that ten of these, being in French and containing a pronoun of address, are grist to our mill. Six of them involve a French V-form that is translated with a Russian V-form and four contain a French V-form that is translated by means of a Russian T-form. All that needs to be said about the former is that their translation presents no problem, since they are used between people who are on V-terms in Russian, anyway. The latter are more interesting, since they indicate clearly the editor's sensitivity to the differences between the French and the Russian T/V distinction. Let us take them one by one. I will quote the actual French. There is never more than a single short sentence or two involved and the sentences, being quoted in the original, exemplify nicely the kind of *mondain* remarks that tend to be inserted by Tolstoy in the middle of what is clearly genuine Russian, rather than Russian representing French.

When Vronsky goes to meet his mother at the railway station, she starts a sentence in Russian using T, but breaks off and finishes it in French, switching automatically to V: *Vous filez le parfait amour. Tant mieux, mon cher, tant mieux.* (Pt 1, Ch 18). It is also worth noticing, incidentally, the appellation: *mon cher*. There was quite a range of salon-style French terms of address to choose from; and, when Countess Lydia Ivanovna in her excitement calls Karenin 'mon ami' instead of 'Alexei Alexandrovič' in the presence of others, Tolstoy comments upon the fact (Pt 7, Ch 22). The second of the four French bits that we are now looking at is quite straightforward. It is when Dolly goes to see Anna in the country. Anna wants to tell Dolly everything that has happened and she switches from Russian, using *T*, to French, saying *Je ne vous ferai grâce de rien* and then back to Russian. The last two of these four bits of French occur in the conversation between Oblonsky and Karenin to which fairly detailed reference was made above; and they occur during the second part of the conversation, when Karenin has switched from *T* to *V*. Oblonsky says *Vos scrupules* . . ., an unfinished sentence, which is correctly translated by the editors with a Russian *T*-form. The fact that Oblonsky when speaking French to Karenin in this relatively strained situation conforms to the social norm is worth noting. Earlier, it will be recalled, when he was trying to round up a group of friends for dinner, he had used *T*, even in French, to Karenin; and Tolstoy had commented on this. After a moment's further conversation, Karenin says *Vous professez d'être un libre penseur*. This too is translated in the editorial footnote with a *T*-form; and, in my opinion, incorrectly. For Karenin, as we have seen, has now switched to *V*; and there is no reason to believe that he has simultaneously switched to French for the whole of this second part of the conversation. Of course, if he has switched to French (so that Oblonsky is speaking Russian and Karenin is speaking French) the translation is, in this respect at least, correct, because Tolstoy himself uses the Russian *V*-forms to stand for the French *V*-forms in the Russian that is intended to be read as French. And, if Karenin had used the very same sentence in the earlier part of the conversation, the editors would have been right to translate it as they have done. There could hardly be a more strikingly direct illustration of the stylistics of bilingualism and the context-dependence, though not so far the impossibility, of translation.

Editorial translations of the kind that occur in the footnotes of the modern edition of *Anna Karenina* are not only possible, but for the most part easy enough to handle, as far as the *T/V* distinctions of French and Russian are concerned. All we have to do is to ask ourselves which pronoun a bilingual Russian aristocrat would have used if he had been speaking Russian rather than French; and the text usually gives us the information that we require. When I inserted into my title the phrase 'the impossibility of translation' I was thinking primarily of the problem of translating *Anna Karenina* as a whole into, say, English or French. I submit that it is impossible to translate it satisfactorily into either language; and for interestingly different reasons.

The two most widely available English translations are those of Constance Garnett, first published in 1901 and republished in paperback in 1977 at the time of the BBC's television serialization of *Anna Karenina* (*cf* Garnett 1977), and of Rosemary Edmonds, first published in 1954 (*cf* Edmonds 1954). I have not read through either of these translations, but I have dipped into both of them, and in particular checked the passage to which reference has been made earlier. The results are instructive. Neither translation makes any attempt, of course, to mark the differential use of *T* and *V*, in either

English or French, systematically throughout the text. The only way in which this could have been done is by using *thou* for *T* and *you* for *V*; and appending an explanatory note in the preface or in a footnote at the first use of *T*. It is not difficult to imagine the incongruity of the English that would be produced by the systematic and consistent employment of what is for most people nowadays either an archaic or a rustic pronoun of address to translate the Russian *T*-form. So the wisest choice, undoubtedly, is the one that both translators have made. This means that one of the principal clues is removed which tell us whether French or Russian is being spoken; and some of the general flavour or atmosphere is lost. More important, there is no representation of the switch from *V* to *T* and back to *V* (and of the distancing that is effected by Anna's use of *V* in what she imagines Vronsky might have said to her) in the quarrel between Anna and Vronsky (Pt 7, Chs 23–6); or of Karenin's switch from *T* to *V* in his conversation with Oblonsky (Pt 7, Ch 17); or of Anna's use of *T* to Dolly, but of *V* to Kitty (Pt 7, Ch 28). In fact, there are indefinitely many places where the sensitive reader of the Russian text would, perhaps unconsciously, note and respond to the pronoun-selection that Tolstoy has made, or envisaged his characters making, at particular points; and all the information that is conveyed by the selection of *T* or *V* where the Russian system of the time permitted its users the choice between them is lost.

But there are also several places, as we have seen, where Tolstoy inserts his own comments about his characters' use of *T* or *V*. How do the two translators cope with such passages? The answer is that no single solution is adopted and that none of them is very successful. Curiously enough (perhaps because she felt, rightly, that it was such a significant instance of the choice of *T*), Constance Garnett does use *thou* at the point when Vronsky comes to see Anna in the country and she, speaking Russian to his French, hesitates before committing herself to her pronoun selection: *I did not expect . . . thee*, says Anna. But then she continues (where the Russian, of course, still has *T*) with *You startled me*. How many readers, I wonder, will take the point of that single occurrence of *thou*? And, if they do, will they think that Anna has immediately regretted her choice of *T* and switched back to *V*? Or that this is the only occasion when Anna uses *T* to Vronsky? The Rosemary Edmond's translation is at least consistent: *I did not expect . . . you* and *You startled me*. As for Tolstoy's comment about Vronsky's use of French: Constance Garnett says . . . *speaking French as he always did to avoid using the stiff Russian plural form, so impossibly frigid between them, and the dangerously intimate singular form*; and Rosemary Edmonds . . . *to avoid using the word 'you' which sounded so impossibly cold in Russian, or the dangerously intimate 'thou'*. Rosemary Edmonds is closer to the Russian text at this point. But it is the Constance Garnett translation which has Anna using the single, unexplained occurrence of *thou*! As for Tolstoy's comment on Karenin's letter to Anna, both translations are identical (except that

Rosemary Edmonds substitutes the English *you* for the French *vous*): *making use of the plural 'vous' which has not the same note of coldness as the corresponding Russian form* (Garnett 1977:280; Edmonds 1954:305). But when Tolstoy remarks on the effect that Karenin's *T*-form has on Anna, Constance Garnett expands the text, saying *using the Russian 'thou' of intimacy and affection* (Garnett 1977:414), rather than simply *and called him thou* (Edmonds 1954:449).

All these translations of Tolstoy's own comments about the use of *T* and *V* are reasonable enough, except that they bear no relation to the text in which they are embedded. Far less satisfactory is the device that both translators adopt, inexplicably, when Dolly switches to *T* and Oblonsky notices this, at the very beginning of the book: *She had called him 'Stiva'* say both translations (Garnett 1977:18, Edmonds 1954:24).[4] Although the use of the hypocoristic form of Oblonsky's first name serves the purpose well enough at this point, the device of introducing the first name into the conversation to signal the use of a Russian *T*-form cannot be generalized, partly because it is not always contextually appropriate to use it and partly because the selection between first name alone (in the hypocoristic form) and first name plus patronymic does not correlate exactly with the selection between *T* and *V*. And the device fails completely in my view when it is adopted by Constance Garnett (1977:483) to translate the passage in which Kitty uses *T* then *V* to Levin, and finally opts for *T* after her maid has left the room: *'Kostya! Konstantin Dmitrich!' (These latter days she used these names almost alternately). 'I didn't expect you'.* But the Rosemary Edmonds translation is worse. It changes the text and omits the point entirely *'How are you? How . . . Well, this is a surprise!'* (Edmonds 1954:470). To think that generations of readers of *Anna Karenina* will not know that Kitty hesitated between *T* and *V* until the day of their marriage or appreciate the significance of this fact! And to think that, whether they read the Constance Garnett or the Rosemary Edmonds translation they will have to make do with Levin's *I can't believe you love me, dear!* and the comment: *she smiled at that 'dear'* (Garnett 1977:396; Edmonds 1954:430)! I referred at the beginning of this paper to the significance of the transition from *V* to *T* and of the sudden thrill that the achievement of this transition can bring. Both translations fail conspicuously to convey the significance of this important *rite de passage*; and in their failure they no less conspicuously demonstrate the thesis that it is the purpose of this article to put forward and substantiate.

4 I have deliberately not gone into the question of names, or more generally of non-pronominal terms of address (and reference). Problems face the translator here too. For example, when Levin, addressing Karenin, hesitates because he has forgotten his name (Pt 4, Ch 9), it is not *Karenin* that he has forgotten – he uses this as a term of reference in the preceding text and the Russian *imja*, 'name', does not denote the family-name anyway. It is not possible for Levin to address Karenin, in the circumstances, other than by first name and patronymic. In comparable circumstances, for persons of that class and that period the French term of address would be *Monsieur* and the English *Karenin*.

[247]

Less space need be devoted to the question of translating *Anna Karenina* into French. The main point that I wish to make is that the reader of a French translation has to allow for the fact that sometimes the French *vous* is translating a genuine Russian *vy*, as it were, and sometimes a Russian *vy* which represents a French *vous* – but a French *vous* with the implications and presuppositions that it had a century ago for the members of a particular social class. And if the translation consistently uses the French *tu* for the Russian *ty* (as does the particular translation that I have to hand: Soloviev 1961), we end up with a non-French *T/V* opposition and incongruity between the passages which translate genuine Russian and the passages which translate French-representing Russian. In this respect, of course, the French reader is in a position which is the converse of that in which the Russian reader finds himself. Whereas the Russian reader has to read some of the Russian as if it were French the French reader has to read some of the French as if it were Russian; and there is no doubt that, as far as the representation of the *T/V* distinction is concerned, a French translation of *Anna Karenina* is less unsatisfactory than an English translation must be. It is after all possible for the French reader to note both the similarities and the differences between the Russian *ty/vy* and the French *tu/vous*, just as it was possible for Tolstoy and other bilingual Russians of his class to note and exploit these similarities and differences. The fact remains, however, that in order to appreciate the significance of some of the switches from *V* to *T* or more particularly from *T* to *V* in the text, the French reader will have to adjust, consciously or unconsciously, to a non-French system of oppositions. For example, Levin's first use of *T* to Kitty and her reluctance to use *T* to him in the presence of her maid transfer very readily into French. So too does Anna's deliberate use of *T* to Vronksy in front of Golenyščev; or her use of *T* to Dolly, but *V* to Kitty. But Karenin's switch from *T* to *V* in his conversation with Oblonsky and Anna's switch from *V* to *T*, and back, in the course of her quarrel with Vronsky do not transfer so readily. It is far less natural, I think, for people who have once achieved the transition to *T* in French to switch back again to *V* because they have quarrelled or are estranged. In this sense the French *T/V* distinction is less subject to what Friedrich (1966:239) calls 'breakthrough' than the Russian *T/V* distinction is – or, at least, was in Tolstoy's day.

It has been my intention, in this paper, to give some indication of the semantic load that can be borne by a simple grammatical distinction and of the way in which an author can deliberately exploit the differences between two language-systems, each of which is available, in particular situations, to the members of a particular speech-community.[5] As I said at the outset,

---

5 Many would say that what I am calling semantics is a matter of pragmatics. The question is, in part, terminological. What I wish to emphasize is that a proper control of the *T/V* opposition is as much a part of knowing the language as is a proper control of the descriptive meaning of words and constructions.

nothing that has been reported here will be new to anyone who knows Russian and French (and is familiar with the passages in *Anna Karenina* to which I have referred). And there are very many other grammatical or lexical distinctions that I might have chosen to illustrate the general point that I have been concerned to emphasize: that there may be semantic distinctions drawn by one language-system that either cannot be translated at all or can be only roughly and inadequately translated in terms of some other language-system. This point is familiar enough; and it was generally accepted by linguists in the hey-day of structuralism. And yet there is good reason to reaffirm it at the present time and to illustrate it with what I trust is both a comprehensible and a convincing example of its validity. For the structuralist viewpoint is no longer as fashionable as it once was; and linguists tend to be more interested in the similarities that there are among language-systems than they are in the differences. As we have seen, Tolstoy was well aware of the differences between Russian and French. So too, presumably, were the other members of the bilingual Russian aristocracy to which he belonged – as indeed anyone must be who knows both languages. Recent work in sociolinguistics has made it abundantly clear that some degree of bilingualism, or even multilingualism, is far from exceptional in speech-communities; and the use of one language rather than another on particular occasions is quite frequently determined by the kind of considerations that Tolstoy makes explicit in some of the passages that we have looked at. The fact that, although Tolstoy's novel deals with a bilingual community, he has chosen to represent the French dialogue in Russian is an additional complication, which has the effect that the reader is not always certain how to interpret particular utterances. From the point of view adopted in this article, the additional complexity introduced by the use of Russian to represent French serves to bring out in the text itself, both the similarities and the differences in the two language-systems.

BAD WORDS, GOOD WORDS, MISUSED WORDS
ARCHIBALD A. HILL

Purists condemn words and word-uses; linguists often defend them, and in so doing acquire the reputation of being totally – and immorally – permissive. In the belief that to formulate a more consistent and realistic rationale of even a small part of the criteria of usage may be useful and lead to understanding, I shall in what follows take up the semantic characteristics of good and bad words, with a brief excursus on related criteria of judgment.

As an example of the purist position on words semantically good or bad, I shall quote from 'Aristides,' writing in the department 'Life and Letters' of *The American Scholar* (Winter 1976–7, *pp* 20–30). His article is entitled 'The State of the Lingo.' Two criteria are given for the meaning of words. A word is bad if its meaning is too far from reality, and a word is bad if it has too little meaning. The type example of a word too far from reality is *lifestyle*. Of this, Aristides says –

> In its contemporary uses are implied a number of assumptions. Chief among these is an assumption about the absolute plasticity of character – change your lifestyle, change your life – that is simply not true; and the popularity of the word ... is testimony to how much people want to believe it.

I doubt, however, that a word based on a false assumption is necessarily bad. The word *unicorn* was certainly once based on a belief in the reality of such animals, but I have not heard of objections to the term.

[250]

Aristides' position is typical of those who believe that the meaning of a word is assigned before it appears in context, and that the assignment is made by the sum total of past uses. More naive persons believe that it is assigned by dictionaries, but I do not accuse Aristides of that particular naiveté. I can only guess at the contexts which led Aristides to his position, but it is at least clear that he has found the word in contexts he dislikes, and used by people he dislikes. A context he might well have met and disliked is a section of syndicated material commonly found in newspapers. The section is called *Life/Style* and seems to be devoted to current, fashionable behavior. The intellectual content of the section is not markedly high, and so might lead one who spells his intellectual status with a capital I, to dislike it, and feel superior to it. I do not believe, however, that plasticity of anything more than behavior is implied in this newspaper material, so that Aristides' condemnation is at best extreme, and at worst, a rationalization of an emotional attitude.

I believe, on the contrary, that most linguists would accept the statement that words mean only what fits the context in which they occur, and that meaning from other contexts is irrelevant. The position, as I have often said in print, has been most clearly formulated by Martin Joos, who states that of possible meanings for a word, the meaning that adds least to the totality of the context is best. The Joos statement is, in fact, an application of Occam's razor, the rule of simplicity.[1]

If we apply the Joos formulation to uses of *lifestyle*, the result is that meanings such as 'absolute plasticity of character' appear unnecessary. For instance on January 2 of 1977, I heard a commentator on TV say that Americans were extremely wasteful of energy, and that unless we changed our 'lifestyle', we would face disastrous scarcity. Surely the commentator was talking about change of observable and habitual behavior, and not about all the myriad things like memory, emotion, values, that make up essential character. The Aristidean position can have been reached only if the interpreter makes no effort to see how many possible meanings fit the individual context, and insists that all meanings are present every time a word is used.

The second category of condemned words, those with too little meaning, is represented by such words as *meaningful*. On page 24 Aristides quotes from a statement by Jimmy Carter, that he 'prays to make his life *meaningful*.' Aristides objects that Hitler's life and that of St Francis were both meaningful, and is thus led to say that 'What Carter means only God knows'. The conclusion clearly ignores two elements of the context. One is that Carter is praying, and the second is that he is speaking of himself. To think that in these circumstances Carter was asking that his life be like Hitler's is ludicrous. The word is clear, and means approximately 'producing tangible, good effects for the future'. It is only when the word is examined

1 See for instance, Hill 1976: xi and 142, and the bibliography there given.

in other contexts without regard to this one, that the word can be said to be meaningless.

But while I believe that Aristides' criteria for badness in words are false, I think it is important to state that some words are indeed bad. A word is bad if it is ambiguous to such a degree that it leads to misunderstanding. For me, the perfect example of such a word is *inflammable*, if it is applied to substances. As most dictionaries now recognize, *inflammable* can be confused with *non-combustible*, and so lead to accidents. I have on occasion heard objections to the use of the clearer form, *flammable*, by purists, in spite of dictionary statements that it is to be preferred as a label of warning.[2] One such purist stated to me that it would be better to educate speakers in the meanings of words than to use the clear, but unetymological label. The man who made the remark is a well-known scholar, but I refrain from giving his name, since he surely might regret a remark with most surprising implications.

Somewhat similar considerations apply to one of the most violently attacked of modern word-uses, that of *disinterested* to mean *uninterested*.[3] The approved meaning of the word is not by any means always clear, and in some contexts *disinterested* can be interpreted as either 'impartial' or 'bored.' Here is a hypothetical sentence which is ambiguous, unless one insists on only the approved meaning, rejecting the other on principle.

Bad art exhibitions can result from choices by disinterested judges, though good exhibitions can also result.

To make the meaning clear, it would be necessary to add a redundant reinforcement, as we often do, and say 'disinterested, impartial judges.'

It seems to me therefore that the usual form of advice to students of composition, 'Do not use *disinterested* to mean *uninterested*,' is inadequate. It ought to be something like this – 'Do not use *disinterested* unless the meaning 'impartial' is clear. Further, if you wish to avoid criticism from the extremely careful, never use *disinterested* to mean *uninterested*.'

Such advice, if followed, would considerably reduce the use of *disinterested*, and indeed, if users of the language become more sensitive to its ambiguity, the word might disappear. Such disappearance has often enough been observed in the history of language, thus establishing a principle that words

2 *The American Heritage Dictionary*, for instance, forthrightly says '*Flammable* is especially appropriate in technical writing and where the term serves expressly as a warning, since it is less subject to confusion than *inflammable*'.

3 *Heritage* says that the meaning 'bored' for *disinterested* is not acceptable to 93 per cent of the usage panel, 'though it is often thus employed'. The history of the term and the dislike for it are curious. The OED gives both the meaning 'bored' and 'impartial,' with 'bored' from 1612, and 'impartial' only from 1659. The meaning 'bored' is labelled '(?obs),' though this label is deleted in the *Supplements*, with quotations, mostly from journalism, to 1970. The prefix *dis-* with reversal of meaning is thoroughly established (*dishonest, disloyal*), so that there can be no etymological objection. Nor is an objection on the basis of obsoleteness justified. The only reason I can suggest is that the distinction in meaning between 'disinterested' and 'uninterested' was felt to be valuable, though there are plenty of other ways of making the distinction.

which dangerously overlap other words or meanings, disappear as a part of natural linguistic processes.[4] Nor need we fear that disappearance will result in impoverishment of the vocabulary, since new words continually appear.

While I think that ambiguous individual words are the only ones we can safely call bad in meaning, as soon as we pass to combinations of forms, we find that more criteria apply. I am assigning such combinations to the area of style, since I believe that style is essentially a matter of relations, not of entities.[5] Examples of bad combinations are easy enough to find, and I agree heartily with the style-watchers who condemn them. I disagree only with the always repeated statements that these bad examples debase and pollute the language. It is not the English language which such utterances debase, but English and American style. In contradiction of the statements about pollution of language, I would maintain as a general and incontrovertible principle that no instance of bad language-use affects in the slightest the possibility of good use of the words and structures of any language. Nor is good style the property of any one dialect – as the literary excellence of *Huck Finn* sufficiently proves.

On all levels, examples of bad style fall into a few general categories, of which the first is illogicality, resulting from incompatibility of meaning in the elements composing the construction. On the phrase level, a form which perfectly illustrates such incompatibility is a horror I saw quoted somewhere a few years ago – 'monocular binoculars'. On a slightly higher level are mixed metaphors, which are either illogical or produce ludicrous images. One such is a sentence I once inadvertently produced in an extemporaneous class lecture.

In that case, you will be in danger of falling tongue-tied between two stools.

Sometimes the fault consists in no more than unnecessary redundancy, like 'surrounded on all sides,' though a similar form recently cited by Edwin Newman on television is somewhat different. The form is 'surrounded on three sides'. The elements are incompatible at least etymologically, but it is curiously difficult to convey the meaning without using the condemned expression. A second class of less than satisfactory style usages consists in a statement of excessively wide, and therefore vague, meaning. An excellent example is again from Edwin Newman, this time from his book *Strictly Speaking* (Warner Books, 1977, *p* 21). Newman quotes from the California Highway Patrol, 'If you drink, exclude vehicle use'.

---

4 Leonard Bloomfield (1933:394–8) cites the classic example of the replacement of the descendant of Latin *gallus*, 'cock,' in just those regions of France where the descendant of *gattus*, 'cat,' had come to be homonymous with it, as the result of a sound change.

5 This definition slightly extends that given in Hill 1958:406. I there defined style as a matter of relationships between entities, characteristic of larger units than the sentence. While style is indeed a matter of whole discourses, I now feel that combinations of entities within the sentence, like nonce compounds and collocations, are also elements of style.

It should be pointed out that examples of bad stylistic formations are normally nonce-uses. Even here, when such a formation becomes established, there is no longer any reason to object to it. An example of an illogical phrase which, so far as I know, is never objected to is 'pierced ear-rings,' since it is the ears, not the ear-rings, which are pierced.[6] Thus, then, objection to bad style is really objection to bad stylistic processes rather than to bad formations.

A special case of language use which results in condemnation of style is the use of fillers, like the currently ubiquitous 'you know'. These fillers may be no more than the schwa-like vowel which is the characteristic hesitation-sound of English; they may be fully formed words like 'well'; they may be phrases like 'I guess', or the already quoted 'you know'. They have a curious distribution, since they do not occur with regularity solely at the phonological and grammatical joints in the sentence, often occurring just before the peaks of information instead. The sort of occurrence I have in mind is like the following – 'That tie looks – you know – EXPENSIVE.' These forms do not contribute to meaning at all, and are outside the semantic structure of the utterance. They do, however, perform a useful function. For the speaker, they give time for formulating the coming material, and for both speaker and hearer, they signal that the speaker will continue; the hearer's turn to reply has not come. A second curious fact about them is that if there are not too many fillers, the hearer tends not to notice them; he edits them out of his interpretation more or less automatically. If the speaker is less articulate than the hearer, however, so that the hearer formulates his interpretation more rapidly than the speaker formulates his utterance, the hearer is apt to be irritated, and object. Finally, of course, these fillers never occur in writing, and rarely in formal speech, where they are edited out. In formal speaking, however, they may leave traces even after disappearance. Pauses may be substituted for the fillers, as in the markedly short phrases characteristic of the delivery of President Carter. The only statement to add about meaningless fillers is that if anyone is so naive as to suppose that they might destroy the communicative function of language, he is frightened by a chimaera. There is no evidence that the information contained in speech ever lessens with use, no matter how bad the use may be.

If the two beliefs that individual words can be semantically bad, and that bad style pollutes the language, are false, one might well ask what harm the twin beliefs do. I believe they are harmful in that they obscure the good and bad qualities of writing and speaking, thus making the good qualities harder to produce. The two attitudes encourage an excessive attention to isolated forms, and conversely foster a tendency to overlook the importance of extended structure, symmetries, and images which make the larger virtues of good language use. I think all linguists would agree that there is no

6 I owe this example to a conversation with W. Nelson Francis, who points out that the phrase is the result of haplology, from 'pierced-ear ear-rings'.

external standard of logic or etymology which is the criterion of language forms. Moreoever, I would now maintain that the only external semantic criterion of bad individual forms is dangerous homonymity, a condition which language characteristically cures without language-watchers' attention.

What can we say about the typical objections to individual words, which whether justified or not, are very real? For instance, to speak of a 'bored, disinterested judge,' will undoubtedly produce an unfavorable reaction in some hearers or readers. There are several things to be said about such reactions. First of all, no matter what the rationalization may be, such a reaction is based on association. That is, the objector associates the word with a class of persons he dislikes, and feels superior to. The only exception to the associational basis of condemnation is the occasional nonce-confusion of words, which the speaker himself would probably recognize as a momentary mistake – for instance, the use of *aesthetic* where *ascetic* was intended.

But while recognition of the associational basis for dislike of individual words is important, it does not follow that speakers and writers should disregard all such objections. The late Albert H. Marckwardt was quite right in saying that attitudes towards words are a part of their history, and that the user of them has the right to know what the attitudes are, and who holds them (Marckwardt 1973:138).[7] The objections I should have to usage statements such as those given in the *Heritage Dictionary* are that (as Marckwardt said) the study is spotty rather than systematic, and that too often the usage notes are colored by rationalizations. Thus though I am here not quoting the *Heritage*, it would be quite proper to say that *kudos* should not be interpreted as a plural in academic or formal writing, but it would be improper to say that such a form is bad because it is an ignorant misinterpretation of a Greek noun ending. The reason for knowledge of attitudes towards words is that any speaker or writer necessarily wants to achieve the results he desires without antagonizing his audience. In consequence, a language user has good reason to want to know how his audience is going to react to the vocabulary he uses. Thus dictionaries might well refine the usage survey introduced in *Heritage*, by making it more systematic and extensive, by rigidly suppressing all rationalizations, and above all, by giving detailed information about what sorts of audiences words are fitted for, and what sorts of audiences would reject them. In fact, a good and workable definition of correctness in language-use is that it is that which produces the desired result. Anything that can be done by dictionaries, grammars, teachers, and scholars, to further correctness thus defined, is a high and worthy goal.

7 The Marckwardt essay is a thorough and penetrating critique of the *Heritage* usage panel. The essay should be read by all dictionary users.

LINGUISTIC RELATIVISM:
THE DIVORCE OF WORD FROM WORK
JAMES SLEDD

This essay originally began with an epigraph – Richard Wilbur a good deal scratched, but serviceable. The altered verses consisted of a relative clause introduced by *which* and describing a happy spot where 'word and work are one' – that is, where what one says and what one does are in creative harmony. The reader is correct in inferring that refusal of permission by the holder of the copyright made both my title and the following sentence incomprehensible without the present explanatory clumsiness: 'The inanimate relative which blocks escape from schizophrenia is the ambiguous political doctrine that all languages and all dialects are somehow equal, none better than any other.' Perhaps a penitent paragraph will now allow me to proceed intelligibly. As follows.

I have to argue that although many linguists TALK relativism (especially if they are also anthropologists), and although many popularizers have been tempted to swear in the words of their masters, just nobody – neither linguist nor popularizer – is a relativist in action. The contradiction has been tolerated in some quarters for really humane or at least innocently sentimental reasons, but in others because it tranquillizes both manipulators' victims and the linguistic conscience, which can continue to sleep quietly in the pretense that there is nothing either good or bad in language or in culture.

Luckily for sinful pedagogues, presumptuous universal judgments on the relative merits of languages and dialects are unnecessary. They should be replaced either by overtly political translations or by particular comparisons in which purpose and circumstance are also specified. Real choices are often not among languages and dialects at all, but among ends and means – means made available by speech-varieties presented without the speakers' choosing. On this topic – the likely effect of choosing one style of expression instead of another – sociolinguists ought to speak with eloquent understanding; but too frequently they offer good examples of bad writing.

It would be easy to gather a posy of recent statements of relativistic theory from the gardens of middlebrow linguistics and of pedagogy, but here one rose must smell as sweet as many:

> The scientific study of language has convinced most scholars that ALL languages, and correspondingly ALL dialects, are equally 'good' as linguistic systems. All varieties of a language are structured, complex, rule-governed systems which are wholly adequate for the needs of their speakers . . . In other words, value judgments about language are, from a linguistic point of view, completely arbitrary . . . there is no way in which one variety can be linguistically superior to another . . . It is also SOCIALLY wrong . . . to imply that particular social groups are less valuable than others (Trudgill 1974:20, 21, 65, 81).

To question so happy a consensus is to guarantee outraged rejoinders; but on serious examination it appears that the relativists' assertions are vague, that their theory and their practice are hard to reconcile, and that ritual repetition has not removed all doubt from the minds of relativists themselves.

Strictly, the equality they assert would be meaningless if their relativism were real, for if one man's meat is another man's poison, any man's judgments that merits are equal are necessarily without merit, quite as empty as contradictory judgments that they are not; and vagueness must certainly be acknowledged when residual prudence limits assertions to LINGUISTIC virtue, INHERENT merit, merit judged 'from the point of view of linguistic science', STRUCTURAL goodness, or the like. All the old questions about language and use, competence and performance, must now be worried again as disputants explain how a language (which exists only in men's minds) is usable for purposes for which in fact those same men cannot use it, and how the language itself is distinguishable from the disabling attitudes toward it.

But these hard questions are easy compared to the notorious contradiction between all relativisms and any action – here the contradiction between the belief that all languages and cultures are equal and the fixed intent to change people's cultures and languages. So one Eminence, after declaring that cultural and linguistic relativism must be part of a teacher's 'basic approach', immediately directs the teacher 'to consider means for adding new language

[257]

or cultural patterns to equip a child to participate in some new group or activity' (Galvan and Troike 1972:304). But if the child already has at his disposal the language which is his culture's perfect tool, by definition its perfection allows him any participation which his culture makes desirable, and his teacher appears as a relativist in theory but in practice an unreasoning tyrant. When the same linguist urges steps to counteract the danger that some other language might replace English as 'the leading language of international communication' (Troike 1977:2), percipient readers will take his relativism as seriously as devotees of *Animal Farm* take Jimmy Carter's promises.

A sense of these and other difficulties appears plainly in the work of the more responsible scholars inclined to relativism. In his useful introduction *Sociolinguistics*, Peter Trudgill considers the argument that just as 'there is no need for a child to learn a new dialect' because ex hypothesi he already has a perfectly good one, so 'There is no need for Spanish Basques to learn Spanish, because Basque is itself a perfectly good language'. Trudgill's conclusion destroys the belief that every language is its culture's perfect tool:

> The parallel does not quite work, because clearly there IS a need for Basques to learn Spanish, since they live in Spain and have to function as part of Spanish society. The argument, therefore, has to be taken one stage further: there would be no need for Basques to learn Spanish IF, as Basque nationalists advocate, they did not live in Spain, but were given their political independence and could form a nation-state of their own (Trudgill 1974:137).

I suspect that for relativists 'a culture' imagined as hermetically sealed and static may play somewhat the role that was played in Chomsky's *Aspects* by that 'ideal speaker-listener, in a completely homogeneous speech-community, who knows its language perfectly and is unaffected by ... grammatically irrelevant conditions' (Chomsky 1965:3): a language is its culture's perfect tool if we abstract from all the circumstances that make it less than perfect. The difference is that Chomsky makes his abstraction consciously for purposes of inquiry, while the assertion that a language is its culture's perfect tool confuses dream-kingdoms with realities for purposes of argument.

Another device for saving relativism by abandoning reality is the qualification that the equivalence claimed for all languages and dialects is a POTENTIAL equivalence. The qualification follows rightly from the anthropological assumption that man is one or from the Chomskyan belief that all men share one innate capacity for language, but the introduction of potentiality drains linguistic relativism of all significant content. Ingenious individuals have invented artificial languages which are notably simpler than the natural languages that provided their materials; and in such inventions as Esperanto and its modification Ido, one can trace changes both through 'normal processes of development' and by conscious, deliberate intervention (McQuown 1964:556–60). Since children of the speakers of an artificial language may come to speak it natively, all stages and versions between current Esperanto and the linguistic gleam in the eye of Zamenhof are POTENTIALLY equivalent to Vedic Sanskrit. Potential equivalence is as remote from actuality as hermetically sealed and static cultures are from Harlem.

Gillian Sankoff, writing excellently on political power and linguistic inequality in Papua New Guinea, is more direct in acknowledging some difficulties in relativism. 'Extreme linguistic relativism needs a good deal of qualification'; for language contact, prolonged bilingualism, and the use of pidgins and lingue franche 'seem to lead to certain types of reduction in surface complexities of the languages used' (Sankoff 1976:284–6). What Sankoff maintains, then, is not that she has studied all languages and devised a measure which shows that all are equal but only that 'there is no evidence' of their INEQUALITY in 'basic machinery' for the performance of just one of their many functions, the transmission of messages. Candidly she admits that because 'some languages are used in cultural contexts and for purposes for which other languages are not, . . . they are to some extent adapted or specialized to these purposes and contexts', especially by 'lexical proliferation and stylistic elaboration' (284). Sankoff refuses either to deny all inequalities among languages or to treat all linguistic differences as serious inequalities. She is right in both refusals.

The spectrum of opinion includes many writers, today and in the past, whose judgments of linguistic relativism would be considerably less favorable than Sankoff's restrained and limited objections. A list of men of letters who have NOT thought all languages and dialects equal would be much longer than a list of those who have, since men whose daily task is right linguistic choice are not easily convinced that linguistic choices are negligible; and to the men of letters one might variously add black militants, militant feminists, and such journalists and journals as the denigrators of Webster's *Third New International Dictionary*, the civil-tongued Edwin Newman, or *Time* magazine, which from the citadel of pure language in New York inquired, a few years ago, 'Can't Anyone Here Speak English?'[1] Linguistic relativism is not the doctrine of the literati or of the common man, and some few anthropologists and linguists might themselves be cited to prove that even the professional consensus is weakening now. It is fair to say that the doctrine is time-bound and dubious, a characteristic faith of the anthropology of the earlier twentieth century, and that a questioning

1 August 25, 1975.

pedagogue need not suppress his doubts on the grounds that expert opinion is unanimously against him.

But to insist that linguistics is value-laden, to say that not all languages and dialects are equal, is not to deny that all languages are alike in basic ways. They are, because all MEN are alike in their language-learning capacity (which however is insulted by the claim that its products are identical no matter what the circumstances); and the basic likeness includes the fact that all natural languages have complex phonological, grammatical, and semantic systems. All men have noses, too, and the wary pedagogue does not deny that his exists.

Nor does the insistence on differences among languages, dialects, and expressions commit the pedagogue to the belief that judgments of linguistic value are easily made. Foolish judgments are predictably commonplace, for the refusal of so many linguists to risk even informed and tentative judgment guarantees that unexamined dogmatism will prevail. The point is simply that a denial of relativism is not a commitment to foolish absolutes. Languages, dialects, and particular linguistic forms are not good or bad absolutely, in complete abstraction from users, uses, and attendant circumstances. Men would not create them if they met no needs at all; but some can meet some needs, some others, and though I shall now expand the argument against the relativist, the burden of proof remains on him, because he will not admit what all men show by their actions that they do in fact believe and what indeed is obvious to common sense. Even drunken Sir Toby knew what to expect when one gentleman thou'd another.

In expanding the anti-relativistic argument (which I would be presumptuous to call mine), it is important to emphasize again that 'the central idea of a value-free and truly objective social science is logically contradictory' (Scholte 1972:433). Most people who talk about their love of 'knowledge for its own sake' have too much sense to hit up a foundation for a grant to determine the total number of warts on the left hands of the white male citizens of Seattle; but the pretended relativism of the 'pure professional' with no 'moral center' but a well-paid job (Diamond 1972:422) can still create monsters – 'the cult of the expert', the 'mandarins' damned by Chomsky, the 'language engineers' who solemnly ask themselves whether they should try to eradicate the dialects of people that they dislike. The dreadful detachment of 'we' from 'they' comes natural for the pure professional. Though – or because – he contradicts himself by teaching the absolute value of cultural relativism, his easiest allegiance is to established power. If all values are relative, one boss is as good as another, and the affluent self-importance of engineering other people's language is not at all repugnant.

But the dominant pure professional among sociolinguists is unlikely to be persuaded by the argument that relativism may become toadyism. He is more accessible to distinctively linguistic arguments, one of which is provided by the current fashion for pidgins and creoles. There is wide agreement that pidgins are much simplified,[2] that pidgins sometimes become creoles, with expanded structures and uses, and that creoles may in turn be decreolized and may merge, then, with standard languages. From these agreements, a dilemma results for the linguistic relativist. If pidgins and creoles are not dismissed as irrelevant deviants but are accepted as real languages, then it is impossible to maintain that all languages are equal either structurally or functionally; while if pidgins and creoles in at least their earlier stages are NOT real languages, then the relativist must say at what point and by what changes of what features they BECOME real languages, the equals of all others. Similar arguments can be made, as I have suggested, for artificial languages, which can conceivably become natural, for the successively more complex grammars which children develop on their way to adult mastery, for dying languages whose surviving speakers either never learned them fully or have partially forgotten them, and so on. To dismiss such arguments as mere exhibitions of partial competence is only to name the difficulty which they present.

But the questioning pedagogue need not risk dubious battle about pidgins and creoles in order to argue that not all languages and dialects are equal. Even relativistic linguists commonly admit that real languages differ greatly in the degree of their lexical development, and sufficient differences in vocabulary can entail unequivocal differences in structure too. Halle and Keyser, for example, sum up

> the change that the Old English stress rules underwent as a result of the influx of Romance words ... A second word stress rule – the Romance Stress Rule ... – was added and a special subcategorization in the lexicon was provided which determined which of the two stress rules applied to a given word. All other rules remained as before (Halle and Keyser 1971:109).

A relativist would only be multiplying unfounded claims if he should answer that a particular complication at one point in a grammar is always so matched by a simplification at another that total complexity remains a constant for all languages at all times, and he would be abandoning the argument about relative complexity altogether if he should assume an agnostic stance before such conventional general statements as the following from Elizabeth Traugott:

> When we look at the kinds of differences that have occurred between grammar A at time X and grammar B at time Y, we will usually find that

---

2 To deny that pidgins are much simpler than natural languages reduces the argument about complexity to total inanity by demonstrating that in fact linguists can't even agree on what they mean by saying that languages are or are not equally complex; but most readers will not choose that horn of the dilemma.

these changes involve either simplification or elaboration, very rarely just the rearranging of materials already available (Traugott 1972:14).

Relativists who make all languages equal in merit as well as in complexity must now answer two further questions. First, are simplification and elaboration neutral, or do they cause differences in value? Second, if simplification and elaboration are neutral, why are the changes tolerated by the speakers in whose minds the changing languages exist? Satisfactory answers must deal with particular cases (like the development of the Modern English auxiliary system or the current adoption of *r*-ful speech by many *r*-less speakers of American English) and cannot be limited to indignant oratory about the impossibility of saying that Old English is worse than Middle English or that Modern English is better than either.

The reconciliation of the *r*-less to the *r*-ful is sometimes conscious. Another consciously directed linguistic change is the complex of processes involved in standardization. Standard languages need more registers to serve more purposes than folk speech does and therefore differ from folk speech in both syntax and vocabulary. If then one cites the further platitude that standard written languages interact with the everyday speech of those who read and write them, it is hard to see how folk speech and standard languages can fail to differ in complexity and in usefulness for different purposes. An attempt to translate *The Vanity of Human Wishes* into the Lancashire dialect of Tim Bobbin's Tummus and Meary will provoke laughter – and useful meditation on the possibility of perfect translation and the complete separability of content from expression.

Relativistic dogma looks equally questionable when one attempts to apply it to the many different kinds of plurilingual and pluridialectal speech-communities, from Sri Lanka to the Lowlands of Scotland. In such communities, two or more widely differing dialects or even languages are necessary for the purposes which single dialects may serve elsewhere. The relativist, however, must keep pretending that all languages and all dialects in ALL communities are equal in complexity of form and function and in merit. If he attempts to qualify his assertions, he risks reducing them to insignificance; while if he refuses qualification, he runs head-on into the attitudes and beliefs of real people in the real world, who know that they can't accomplish the same purposes with all the languages or dialects that they command.

A desperate rejoinder is still conceivable – namely, that linguistic science is indifferent to popular attitudes. But attitudes are judgments of value firm enough to govern the possibilities of action, and though the linguist who ignores literary traditions or questions of community, identity, and understanding may proudly call himself a scientist, the price of ignoring the foundations of human society is that society will ignore such linguists. As it should.

Linguistics today has no 'integral and concrete object' smaller than the universe as known to man, for everything which Bloomfield in his scholarly asceticism threw out of the science came crowding back in with Chomsky, Katz and Fodor, the generative semanticists, and the present generation of hyphenated interdisciplinarians: linguistics has become whatever goes on in departments of that name. But confessed English-teachers need not bother their heads about such high matters any more than they really need to bother about perfect intertranslatability and the separation of content from expression. Historical accident defines the tasks of English departments too, one of them being the real thought about linguistic values which linguistic relativism blocks. English-teachers who also call themselves linguists can wear either hat while studying the principles of choice among languages, varieties of languages, and particular synonymous expressions.

Those choices involve, of course, not only one's own speech and writing but also – and maybe more importantly – the demands for speech and writing that one makes on others. It is not enough to say, as some sociolinguists have, that one attempts and asks appropriateness. Social appropriateness as unique determinant makes conformity the only function or end of language, as if some men must in the nature of things be bosses and others must be bossed. But Standard English – middle-class white English – is not always well-chosen English. The bureaucrat appropriately uses a variety of the Standard, his pompous polysyllabism, to baffle, to conceal vacuity, and to escape responsibility. Some purposes in speaking are the opposites of others, as Hobbes pointed out in the *Leviathan*,[3] and any serious study of usage and demand requires analysis of the many ends of language besides decorous oppression.

The sociolinguistic exhortation to appropriateness and consequently upward mobility in the mainstream culture was phrased more openly by a Texas schoolteacher in a modern analogue to Christian faith. Her aim in teaching, she said, was to move up from steak to lobster and to draw her students after her. With that cupidinous criterion of choice, many sociograntsmen naturally write badly; but in a Festschrift for a polished writer and gentle spirit, I refrain from the exhibition of monstrosities. Thus charity forbids the use of a final and unanswerable argument against linguistic relativism.

---

3 See the fourth chapter, 'Of Speech'.

SUBJECTIVE APPRAISAL
OF PHONOLOGICAL VARIANTS
RAVEN I. McDAVID, Jr,
RAYMOND K. O'CAIN & LINDA L. BARNES

1

Many events have sharpened Randolph Quirk's natural powers as one of the keenest observers and ablest students of the English language to arise in Britain – his rearing as a Manxman, his travels and experiences, and his career at the University of London (for three generations the British center for serious study of the English language). If one must emphasize a single aspect of his protean career, it is his association with the study of usage and the attitudes speakers have towards usage. And in an age when rapid social change in Britain may have significant effects on the standard of English and attitudes towards it, his work takes on increasing significance. It is therefore appropriate that an essay in honor of Randolph Quirk should examine American evidence bearing on the relation between usage and attitudes.[1]

Britain – England at least – has been dominated by metropolitan London. Standard English in its written form was largely shaped by the Westminster Chancery (Fisher 1977); upper class London speech was the model for British Received Pronunciation, (but *cf* Abercrombie 1952–3). The prestige of RP still endures, along with a generous recognition of other pronunciations as acceptable in their place, as befits a society of orders and degrees, however its surface structure may change.

1 An earlier version of this paper was read 10 March 1978 at the Second Symposium on Language and Culture in South Carolina, Columbia, South Carolina.

[264]

The American situation has been different from the beginning. No one center – Boston, Philadelphia, or Charleston – dominated the life of the colonies; nor today is New York, Chicago, Miami, or Los Angeles – or any combination of them – uncritically accepted as a model. Nor has the United States had an ordered social structure; the class system has remained fluid, with wealth and formal education generally more important than inherent culture or family status (Shuy, Wolfram, and Riley 1967, Allen 1973–6; but *cf* O'Cain 1977). And Americans are characteristically more concerned about details of usage the English either accept or ignore as a matter of course.[2]

2

Students of English usage have long labored to make the point that the status of a linguistic form is not inherent, but is derivative of the status of its users. It must also be recognized that judgments about usage are not very reliable guides to actual usage (Marckwardt and Walcott 1938, Crisp 1971, Creswell 1975). To determine the facts of usage requires direct observation of the behavior of users of the language; to determine the status of a usage there must be an independent correlation of linguistic and non-linguistic facts (*cf* Fries 1940, Atwood 1953, Kurath and McDavid 1961).

There are several dimensions to the relationship between usage and judgments about usage. Given a corpus of usage judgments, it can be asked to what degree they conform to the facts of usage; given a body of facts about usage, one might explore the extent to which they evoke judgments. Moreover, the researcher should distinguish between overt judgments and covert judgments. Overt judgments, generally made about the usage of others rather than that of the speaker, are expressed opinions that a form is either modern or old-fashioned, correct or incorrect, associated with some regional or ethnic group, and the like. Covert judgments, on the other hand, are those made about the speaker's own behavior, and are reflected by the kinds of usage decisions the speaker makes under various conditions and in response to various notions of correctness.[3]

3

McDavid and O'Cain 1977 compared usage and judgments about usage from the perspective of how well a corpus of overt judgments reflected facts of regional and social distribution. The statements on usage were documented in 144 field records made in South Carolina for the Linguistic

2 One view of the contrast between the two nations can be found in the papers of Read (1973) and Quirk (1973).

3 The variety of overt judgments can be seen by an inspection of Kurath, Bloch *et al* 1939–43, Kurath, McDavid, O'Cain, and Dorrill 1978–, and Allen 1973–6. Covert judgments may be overt in form, *eg* the denial by an informant that he uses a particular form. And Ann Landers or Abigail Van Buren, advice columnists, agree that good manners dictate that overt judgments on language, as well as on other social matters, should be eschewed.

Atlas of the Middle and South Atlantic States. Singled out for comparison were 45 items that provoked the greatest number of judgments from 32 cultured informants. For further comparison the judgments of 112 non-cultured informants on the same items were also tabulated.[4]

Analysis of the subjective appraisals of usage revealed that the informants offered the greatest number of judgments on lexical items, the fewest judgments on grammatical items; judgments on phonological items approached but seldom equalled those on lexical items.[5] It was confirmed that there are individual differences in how freely opinions about usage were expressed; moreover, as the number of judgments by an informant increased, the judgments became more discriminating, but not necessarily more accurate. Not surprisingly there were both qualitative and quantitative differences in the ways informants from the two groups responded subjectively. What was surprising was that no differences in overall accuracy distinguished the informants from the two different cultural backgrounds when the judgments were compared to the social and regional distributions of the items.

4

For the present study we have taken a somewhat different perspective on the relationship of usage judgments to actual usage. First, we have chosen to search for judgments about the status of several groups of forms selected from McDavid 1952 for which the social distribution is especially striking.[6] Secondly, covert judgments as well as overt judgments have been taken into account.[7] And third, the judgments have been taken from 2325 informants

4 Informants were placed into one of three broad categories indicative of general cultural experience (see Kurath, Bloch *et al* 1939:44). The cultured (or cultivated) informants are those who by their recognized place in the social structure of their communities may be presumed to provide models of usage. The uncultured group includes the users of both folk speech and common or popular speech.

5 Analyzed were nineteen vocabulary items, each judged at least seven times; eighteen phonological items, each judged at least five times; and eight grammatical items, each judged at least four times.

6 In 1937 Bernard Bloch proposed the general pattern of differences among the varieties of American English: vocabulary differences, manifested in the choices of national, regional, or local terms, reflect differences in cultural experience; grammatical differences, as in the principal parts of verbs, reflect social differences; and phonological differences reflect regional differences.

While these distinctions are still generally valid, further research has recommended refinements. Atwood's (1953) study of grammatical evidence disclosed that there were regionally distributed grammatical forms, mostly in non-standard usage, *eg* the preterites *clim, clam, clome,* or *clum* against standard *climbed,* but also the standard preterites *dived* and *dove.*

As Atwood was completing his study, McDavid was beginning collaboration with Kurath on *The Pronunciation of English in the Atlantic States* (1961). McDavid discovered the other side of the coin, that there are social differences in pronunciation as well as regional ones.

7 Considered covert judgments were instances when a form recorded from spontaneous conversation differed from an elicited form, when a second form was given in response to a repeated question, or when the informant made a spontaneous self-correction. *Cf* Kurath, Bloch, *et al* 1939:45–8. If two or more forms were recorded under the same conditions they are presumably of equal status.

interviewed for four regional linguistic atlases.[8] Hypothesizing that variants with distinct social distributions would evoke a large number of both overt and covert judgments about usage, we examined the following:

1 postvocalic /r/ in *barn, beard*
2 /ɪu/, a New England archaism competing with /u/ and /ju/ as in *blew, grew, threw, new, tube, Tuesday, due(s)*
3 /ɵ/, a relic phoneme contrasting with /o/ in *coat, home, road, toad, toadstool, whole*
4 low-central /ɑ/ contrasting with low-back /ɔ/ as in *fog, hog, office, want*
5 reflexes of Middle English long o – /u/, /ʊ/, /ʌ/ in *gums, hoofs, roof, soot, took.*

In the following tabulations, the overt and covert judgments are summarized separately. For the latter, the figures indicate the number of times informants modified their responses towards the pronunciation designated.

The judgments on postvocalic /r/ give no hint of its social distribution. There were, incidentally, eight overt judgments on the vowels /ɛ/, /e/, and /æ/ in *beard*.

	OVERT		COVERT
barn	0	/r/	7
	0	/ə/	6
beard	0	/r/	0
	0	/ə/	2

There were no judgments, either overt or covert, for the vowel of *blew, grew,* or *threw*. For *new* the overt judgments indicated that both /ɪu/ and /ju/ were giving way to /u/. The covert judgments, on the other hand, point to /ju/ as the prestige form. There were also five incidental overt judgments on the lack of /r/ in *threw* (or *throwed*).

	OVERT		COVERT
new	0	/ɪu/	6
	12	/ju/	12
	5	/u/	8

The covert judgments for *tube* and *Tuesday* are likewise indicative of competition between /u/ and /ju/. A large majority of the overt judgments for *Tuesday* indicate that /tʃu/ is old-fashioned.

8 There were 409 informants for the *Linguistic Atlas of New England* (Kurath, Bloch, *et al* 1939–43), 1216 for the *Linguistic Atlas of the Middle and South Atlantic States* (Kurath, McDavid, O'Cain, and Dorrill 1978–), 208 for the *Linguistic Atlas of the Upper Midwest* (Allen 1973–6), and 492 for the Linguistic Atlas of the North-Central States. Permission of the American Council of Learned Societies to quote unpublished materials from the Middle and South Atlantic States and from the North-Central States is gratefully acknowledged. The National Endowment for the Humanities is supporting editorial work on the North-Central States at Chicago and on the Middle and South Atlantic States at South Carolina.

	OVERT		COVERT
tube	1	/ju/	3
	2	/u/	3
	2	/tʃu/	0

	OVERT		COVERT
Tuesday	4	/ɬu/	3
	11	/ju/	12
	2	/u/	11
	41	/tʃu/	2

For *due(s)* the overt judgments affirm, as for *tube* and *Tuesday*, that the initial affricate is old-fashioned. Though the overt judgments favor /u/, the covert judgments favor /ju/.

	OVERT		COVERT
due(s)	7	/ɬu/	1
	2	/ju/	8
	5	/u/	1
	15	/dʒu/	0

The overt judgments on New England 'short o' generally indicate that /o/ is modern, but sometimes affected. A large majority of the covert judgments are confirmatory.

	OVERT		COVERT
coat	6	/ɵ/	3
	13	/o/	6
home	3	/ɵ/	4
	0	/o/	5
road	2	/ɵ/	0
	1	/o/	11
toad	0	/ɵ/	0
	0	/o/	0
toadstool	1	/ɵ/	1
	0	/o/	3
whole	4	/ɵ/	6
	1	/o/	14

The overt judgments concerning the contrast of /ɑ/ and /ɔ/ are too few and too heterogeneous to indicate any consensus. The covert judgments are almost evenly divided.

	OVERT		COVERT
fog	7	/ɔ/	5
	0	/ɑ/	2

[268]

hog	5	/ɔ/	6
	2	/ɑ/	3
office	3	/ɔ/	6
	1	/ɑ/	2
want	0	/ɔ/	0
	0	/ɑ/	8

A large majority of nearly 500 overt judgments indicates that /ʌ/ in *hoofs, roof, soot,* and *took,* or /u ~ ʊ/ in *gums,* is old-fashioned. But in about half the judgments, /ʌ/ in *gums* and /ʊ/ in *roof* are also characterized as old-fashioned or heard, but not used. The covert judgments, far fewer in number, by and large confirm the newer forms. And there were a dozen incidental judgments on /f ~ v/ in *hoofs.*

	OVERT		COVERT
gums	112	/u/	0
	55	/ʊ/	0
	32	/ʌ/	1
hoofs	5	/u/	6
	4	/ʊ/	5
	37	/ʌ/	0
roof	2	/u/	16
	21	/ʊ/	26
	55	/ʌ/	2
soot	11	/u/	2
	14	/ʊ/	8
	157	/ʌ/	1
took	0	/u/	0
	1	/ʊ/	9
	24	/ʌ/	0

5

The five words illustrating the reflexes of Middle English long o give the clearest evidence of a relationship between social distribution and usage judgments. The forms that appear rarest (if ever) in standard usage receive the largest number of judgments, overt or covert: /u/ and /ʊ/ in *gums,* /ʌ/ in *hoofs, roof, soot, took.* For some of these, as one may see in Kurath and McDavid 1961, there may be an expression of a regional as well as a social judgment. This is most likely for *roof,* where both /u/ and /ʊ/ appear in cultivated speech but /ʌ/ only in folk speech. Not only were there large numbers of judgments for these words, but there was an identifiable majority opinion, which in turn was borne out by the covert judgments in a majority of instances. It is worth further exploration to see if informants tend to offer judgments about general linguistic properties of various sorts, rather than on a word by word basis.

We have observed already that in some instances judgments were offered on more than one trait of some words, *eg beard, hoofs, threw (throwed)*. Though morphological judgments were not tabulated, it may be the case that they override phonological matters, thus accounting for the lack of judgments on *threw, blew, grew*; notice too that *took* has fewer judgments than the other words in the same group and that its phonological development intersects with the way it is conjugated. Finally, the convergence of overt and covert judgments may be a group trait, as in the New England short o /ə/ words, the reflexes of Middle English long o, and the status of initial affricates in *due(s)* and *Tuesday*. On the other hand, while the overt judgments and the covert judgments are contradictory in several cases, it is again a group property of the words with /ɪu/, /ju/ and /u/ in competition.

The evidence examined by McDavid and O'Cain (1977), however, does not show any appreciable tendency for informants to concentrate their overt judgments on particular phonological sets. Indeed, the trend is to single out variants on a word by word basis.

It is clear that a research tool like the regional linguistic atlases of the United States and Canada does offer a perspective on the relationship between usage judgments and regional and social distributions. As these relationships are worked out for more and more words and features, and as matters like the regional and social distributions of the types of judgments are explored, we should gain further insight into a provocative aspect of human behavior.

REMARKS ON THE
TYPOLOGY OF MODERN ENGLISH
JOSEF VACHEK

It is well known that typological problems have always attracted the attention of students of English. Facing the commonplace fact that the grammatical system of Old English was of essentially synthetic, inflexional character, while that of Modern English is prevailingly analytical, strongly tending towards the isolating type, some scholars tried to classify this difference in evaluational terms. The best known of such attempts was undoubtedly that of Otto Jespersen (1894), who was convinced that the process leading from synthesis to analysis should be regarded as demonstrating progress in language. However, few theses of the great Anglicist scholar have been regarded as so controversial as this one. It has been rightly objected that the 'progressive' status of a system of a certain language does not at all depend on the means employed by its morphological level but exclusively on the presence or absence in this system of such means as are capable of expressing all the needs and wants felt, in the given period of time, as urgent by the users of that language (*cf* GCE:2 *ff*).

It will have been noticed that the formulation just adduced has been stated in functionalist terms. It indeed appears that only when formulated in these terms can problems of value in linguistic typology, and of typology in general, have any sense at all. One can even say that it was exactly the functionalist and structuralist approach to facts of language which revived the interest in typology by throwing some new light on its possibilities and by delimiting more exactly some of its basic aspects. Thus, *eg*, particular stress was laid by the Prague linguist Skalička (1935, 1958) on the fact, now universally admitted, that hardly any language can constitute a 'pure' linguistic type. In other words, since all languages appear to be more or less typologically 'mixed', one can classify a language as belonging to this or that type only in the sense that the features characterizing that type are dominant in it but by no means exclude the presence in it of some other features characterizing some other type or types. Thus, already in the early phase of the Prague linguistic school, Jakobson (1932) duly pointed out an essentially agglutinative morphemic make-up of the imperative mood in Modern Russian, a language which, admittedly, is basically inflexional. So much, then, for the typologically mixed character of most if not all languages.

But the functionalist and structuralist approach to problems of linguistic typology has also emphasized another important point: typological differences between languages are by no means confined to the make-up of their morphological levels. Indeed, the consequences of such morphological differences can also affect other levels of language, mainly the syntactic and lexical, but at times even the phonological. The fact that the fixation of the Modern English word-order in the sentence was due to the analyticization of English morphology had been known for a long series of decades. But there are also other interdependencies. In an earlier monograph (Vachek 1961) we hope to have demonstrated that the morphological reshaping of English from the synthetic to the analytical type was to become reflected also on the phonological level of language inasmuch as it was to become responsible for the reshaping and revaluation of the consonantal opposition of voice into that of tension. We also pointed out that perhaps even the reshaping of the quantitative opposition of contact (cf Jakobson and Halle 1956:24) may have been at least coinfluenced by the needs of the typologically changed grammatical system of English.

Another important contribution to a more adequate solution of some old typological problems was submitted, though indirectly, by the results of research obtained by modern structuralist and functionalist phonology. Already in the mid nineteen-thirties the Prague phonologists (eg Mathesius 1935:29) pointed out that the phonological system of language hardly ever constitutes an absolutely homogeneous structure but, as a rule, includes some subsystems whose items signal some specific function of the words containing them. The items of one such system, eg, are phonologically stamped as synchronic foreignisms, while another such subsystem signals a strong emotional colouring of its items. As concrete specimens of synchronic foreignisms may be adduced the Modern English diphthong [ɔɪ] and the Modern Czech consonant [g] (cf Vachek 1964a:78 ff; 1968:62 ff); well known phonological signals of emotion are the Modern French 'accent d'insistance' and the Modern Czech long vowel [ɔː].

The importance of this contribution to typological theory rests not only in the ascertainment of the heterogeneousness of the phonological system: it lies, above all, in the recognition that the said heterogeneousness is functionally motivated. As we tried to show in another paper (Vachek 1964*b*), one might almost speak of a kind of functional complementariness of the phonological regularities on the one hand, such as are found in the synchronically domestic, purely communicative and non-emotional stratum of the word-stock, and, on the other hand, of the deviations violating those regularities, deviations which are often met with in the synchronically foreign and/or emotionally coloured strata of that same word-stock. To put the point differently, the two strata of phonological facts must not be regarded as embodying mutually contradictory forces, but rather as embodying co-operative forces which, so to speak, join their efforts for one common purpose, that is to say, for an all-sided, all-comprehensive expression by the phonological system of all semantic and emotive shades of the content to be communicated by the users of the language.

The value of this 'multilevel approach' of the system of language was duly pointed out a decade ago by the American linguists Weinreich, Labov, and Herzog (1968). They most convincingly refute the official generativist and transformationalist conception of language; besides, they aptly emphasize the importance of the heterogeneous conception of language for the explanation of the motivation of changes in language. In all fairness, the Americans trace back the origin of the heterogeneous conception to two typical representatives of the Prague linguistic group, Mathesius and Jakobson, who formulated the main ideas of this conception already in the early nineteen-thirties. At the same time, of course, the Americans also recall the well-known paper on the 'co-existence of phonological systems' by Fries and Pike (1949), which, of course, was printed some fifteen years later than the pioneering theses of the Prague linguists. Still, it must be added here that even the three sharp-sighted American scholars, for all their penetrating observations on the importance of the heterogeneous character of the phonological system of language, have missed one important point. They have failed to lay due stress on the functional unity of that system, on what we called here above functional complementariness: in fact, it is this type of unity which is able to span, and even to make the best of, the formal differentiation of the elements composing the system. So much, then, for the importance of the multilevel approach in phonology.

If, however, one is to grasp the typological problems of Modern English in their entirety, one must realize that the observations of the Prague linguists concerning the principles of this multilevel approach (for this very term, see also Trnka 1964) and particularly of the functional complementariness closely connected with it, as commented on above for the phonological situation in language, are also valid for other language levels, not merely for the phonological level.

On the lexical level, of course, the matter has been known for many decades. Already in the first beginnings of this century Henry Bradley

(1904) and Karl Luick (1914) most eloquently pointed out the existence in Modern English of the two lexical strata, now often popularly called 'short words', common to any speaker of the language and denoting, as a rule, the realities of everyday life, and opposed to them, the 'long words', less common or even unintelligible to many speakers of the language and denoting more abstract extralingual realities. Similar differences can also be found on the syntactic level where the analogous distinction contrasts simpler and more complex syntactic structures. Even on the morphological level some differences of the kind may be discovered, though admittedly to a much lower degree, in the domain of nouns (see, *eg*, the formation of the plurals of specialized terms by Graeco-Latin endings, as in *bacilli, crises, phenomena*, etc). Still, there is at least one region in which the typological differentiation in English morphology appears to have been rather systematically carried through: it is in the domain of adjectives where the formation of the comparative and superlative degrees is differentiated in the short and long words of the category by using the synthetic or, respectively, analytical means for the purpose. These facts are, naturally, too well known to need further comment.

As already briefly pointed out, much less typologically differentiated in morphology are the Modern English substantive nouns, the vast majority of which follows the same, essentially analytical pattern of declension, whether they belong to the 'short' or to the 'long' category of the lexical stratum. However, in the domain of substantive nouns one can, after all, observe another important difference which is sometimes overlooked and which can again be formulated in typological terms. It concerns, naturally, not so much morphology but rather differences in the morphemic structures of the two categories of nouns. It indeed appears that the word-formative structure of substantive nouns is rather remarkably polarized in the items belonging to the two lexical strata. It has been universally known, that is to say, that the repertoire of affixes (both prefixes and suffixes) that can be utilized in the so-called short words of Modern English is distinctly smaller than in the long words; Jespersen (1909–49, VI) adduces 13 prefixes and 31 suffixes characterizing the domestic word-stock (without classifying them systematically, as we do here), while the corresponding figures for the foreign, mainly Romance and Graeco-Latin items are 57 and 71, respectively. This difference based on the data inventorized on the lexicographical basis can be supplemented by statistical data based on a random examination of coherent contexts: in the first 300 words of the present paper one finds only 19 words derived by domestic affixes, as opposed to 57 whose affixes are of foreign, mainly Graeco-Latin type.

Besides, it is commonly admitted that in the domain of the synchronically domestic lexical stratum a very favourite procedure resorted to for the purpose of naming is composition (the results of the procedure are, naturally, not merely compounds but also – probably more frequently – collocational word-groups, *cf* Mathesius 1975: 31 *ff*). On the other hand, the naming units found in the synchronically foreign lexical stratum are characterized prevailingly, as shown by the above figures, by the word-formative method of derivation – this is especially so with polysyllabic expressions coined according to Graeco-Latin models (such as *conformably, differentiation, electricity, extraordinary, informative, internationalism, terminology, transatlantic*, etc). It has often been overlooked that this important difference in the word-formative make-up characterizing the two lexical strata of Modern English is no less striking than the difference in the syllabic extent which is usually regarded as particularly typical of them (the traditional assessment of this supposedly main differential feature is clearly reflected by the very terminology, opposing the 'short' words to the 'long' ones).[1]

Incidentally, the difference in word-formative method is the more interesting in that it has obviously emerged in English only in the course of its historical development. Since Old English was still, as is commonly admitted, an essentially synthetic language, its prevailing method of word-formation was still that of derivation. Although, of course, composition as a word-formative procedure was not unknown in Old English (but, characteristically, was much more resorted to in poetry than in prose), there was hardly any trace of collocational word-groups which result so abundantly from the operation of that procedure in Modern English. Such groups, clearly, could only emerge in the language when the old synthetic inflexion was replaced by the new, analytical one, *ie* in Late Middle English and Early Modern English. Besides, the number of Latin loanwords in Old English was relatively small and those Latin loans which had been taken over as a rule did not represent clear derivative cases of the kind found in great quantities in the present-day language. Needless to say, under these circumstances no stylistic differentiation could have existed in Old English of the sort which one so abundantly finds in the modern language.

That stylistic differentiation deserves still more attention here. It is only too often overlooked that the heterogeneousness of the Modern English word-stock, split between the two strata of the 'short' and 'long' words, is closely allied with the typological split between the two word-formative

---

1 It should be noted here that our concern for the word-formative structure of the two opposed lexical strata of English clearly differentiates our approach from that of Barbara Strang (formulated in her most original and highly inspiring paper included in the present volume), who is concerned exclusively with problems of English monosyllables. Another fundamental difference between the two approaches is that while we characterize our two lexical strata in essentially synchronistic terms (*ie* as synchronically domestic versus synchronically foreign), following here the Prague tradition established more than four decades ago in Mathesius 1935, Strang conceives the domesticity of the English monosyllables discussed by her in exclusively etymological terms (see the note to her *Table* 4). She thus necessarily fails to see that what she calls post-Conquest English formations (such as zero derivations, shortenings, back-formations etc) constitute, at least for the greatest part, domesticated items of the vocabulary, and thus factual additions to the category of the 'short', *ie* synchronically domestic, lexical stratum of English. For the moment we must confine ourselves to this note, hoping to take up the involved issues in greater detail on some other occasion.

models, the prevailingly compositional and the prevailingly derivational. And what is even more important – and what has probably not yet been explicitly formulated – is again the fact that behind this heterogeneousness of form, correlated with a difference in the stylistic approach to one and the same extralingual reality, one has to recognize a higher kind of functional unity. Just as on the above-discussed phonological level, also on the 'higher' language levels the unity is again given by the totality of needs and wants which face the language users and impose upon them the difficult task of adequately coping with this many-sided totality. Seen in this light, the heterogeneousness of the formal typological differences becomes harmoniously unified into a functional unity of means differentiated according to the situation in which they are to be used. Let us recall again what was said here earlier about the functional complementariness of the phonological means available to the language user.

Incidentally, it should be noted that the statistical indices by which Greenberg (1954) most interestingly attempted to express the places of individual languages in his typological classification are unable to provide the necessary typological information for the very reason that those indices were worked out without due regard for the essentially different status of the two lexical strata discussed here.

In conclusion let us point out that not many language systems possess such a rich scale of ostensibly heterogeneous typological means which, however, are harmoniously unified for a common communicative purpose. Henry Bradley's (1904) and Otto Jespersen's (1905) statements stressing the ability of English to differentiate shades of meaning more efficiently than many other languages, statements pronounced more than seventy years ago, become thus confirmed by modern functionalist methods of typological research. And, let us add, the unequal richness of such typological means in different language systems may supply another important criterion of the typological classification of languages (and, possibly, establish an evaluative criterion of the functional efficiency of the compared language systems, a criterion more subtle and more reliable than those suggested by previous research).

THE ECOLOGY OF
THE ENGLISH MONOSYLLABLE
BARBARA M. H. STRANG

1

I am not aware that anyone has written in precisely the terms of my title before. In choosing it I am setting out to show that matters are different from what I had supposed, and I must start by trying to show, in the absence of previous studies, what my suppositions were and where they came from. Only rarely can I point to specific sources – for instance, to the way monosyllabic items have been used in arguments that certain forms of linguistic change are to be accounted for in terms of speakers' wishes to select from variants in such a way as to differentiate words.[1] More generally we find a tendency to imply, or to draw inferences from implications, in a way that seems to have created an ambience of assumptions – for instance, that monosyllables have a special place in determining the repertoire of distinctive sounds in a language, that it is clear to a native speaker what are the permitted syllable-types of his language, that in English considered specifically there is a tendency for monosyllables to be the older, *ie*, stabler, elements of vocabulary, the commonest elements of vocabulary, the most native elements of vocabulary. It would be tedious to trace how this ambience of assumptions has come into being or to test how widespread it is, but after trying my conclusions on varied audiences I am satisfied that there is a case for presenting the evidence against the assumptions, and that this evidence raises important general questions of an unpredictable sort.

1 See examples in Samuels 1972:143.

This investigation came into being serendipitously. Scanning the OED and its Supplements for material needed in two other connections, I was repeatedly struck by challenges to my assumptions, and decided to make a systematic collection of evidence relevant to the following questions:

(*a*) How many of the monosyllabic sound-patterns possible in English are actually realized?

(*b*) Is there any constraint on the number of homonymous monosyllables that can co-exist?

(*c*) Does graphic variation increase the number of monosyllabic homophones that can co-exist?

(*d*) Does high frequency or heavy or specialized functional load, normally assumed to correlate with functional diversification, inhibit the development of homophones, or kill off the less dominant existing ones?

(*e*) Is there evidence of selection through time in favour of variants that increase differentiation between monosyllabic items?

(*f*) Are monosyllables typically [i] old? [ii] native? [iii] common? [iv] long-lived? and [v] have they always had, in English at least, the same average life-span?

Reviewing the evidence so collected, I could not overlook the consideration that it raised numerous further questions of some significance.

In setting about the collection of evidence I soon found there were decisions to be made, some rationally, some arbitrarily. First, I restricted collection to single-morpheme monosyllables in order to avoid the huge increase in permitted patterns, with little return in interest, involved in including all the extra types brought under consideration by admission of -(e)s, -(e)d; doubtful cases, like the rare *Branks*, of uncertain morphemic structure, were excluded. Secondly, decisions had to be taken about just what should count as a monosyllable. The evidence of dictionary transcriptions of such items as *Bower, Briar* indicates uncertainty, and recent editions of Jones's *English Pronouncing Dictionary*[2] are to say the least, evasive on this point. In such cases I have included or excluded according to what seems to be the majority view, a policy which affects my totals but not the distributional patterns that emerge. That there is uncertainty is of some interest, however; the more so as I began to suspect, as I proceeded, that there may well be a natural class of lexical monosyllables and a slight mismatch between it and the class of phonological monosyllables.[3] These possibilities require further investigation.

Next, decisions had to be made about sampling. I hope it is unnecessary to say that I have formed an impression of evidence from the whole alphabet

2 See, for instance, the Editor's Preface (by A. C. Gimson), viii and Explanations, Sections xx and xxiii, 12, in the 1967 edition.

3 Briefly, certain ancient stem-extensions, of which typical modern forms are -*y*, -*le*, -*er*, seem to enter into patterns typical of monosyllables. I hope to return to this question on another occasion.

and from the whole range of phonological possibilities, an impression which satisfies me that my sample, though untypically clear and simple in structure, is broadly representative. But listing all the material and counting it according to all relevant measures would have been unmanageable for me and would have presented readers with such complex data that they could hardly have seen the wood for the trees. So I have restricted the detailed and quantified investigation to all syllable-onsets of a given type. The constraints on my choice were quite severe. A consonant-onset was needed because it exemplifies a wider range of syllable-types than a vowel-onset. An onset with a good match between graphic and phonological values was needed to keep the study within manageable compass. An onset within the graphic range A–G was needed because incipient answers to Question *f* suggested that there might have been a surprising change of direction in the present century, and this made the evidence of the 1972 OED Supplement essential. In effect, the choice was between B- and D-; B- was marginally more interesting because of its wider range of onsets.

Certain other decisions, too, were taken in the knowledge that my findings would tend in a certain direction, though they had still to be quantified. In broad terms, I was able to take decisions which would minimize the values of trends to be identified; thus, though distortion is inevitable, its effect is deflationary. The issues are as follows. First, it was clear that my historical perspective would have to be sufficient to enable me to contrast one 500-year period with another, and preferably the last 1,000 years with its predecessor; but many items which are now monosyllables were not so 1,000 years ago.[4] Nevertheless, present monosyllables are my basis. Secondly, it is pointless to consider ecological distribution except within the confines of a single speech-variety, which for practical purposes must be Standard English, but 1,000 years takes us back to a time when there was no variety corresponding to present-day Standard English. Nevertheless, all the evidence we have for the earlier period has been used, and like the first decision, this undervalues the changes identified. But the question of relevant variety is more complex than this. For as basis of the phonological analysis of the present-day material there is no practicable alternative to Received Pronunciation, the variety (or range of varieties) most systematically described by phonologists and transcribed by lexicographers. This has a historical identity even shorter than that of the standard variety in its lexical aspects. Moreover, dialectal items have wandered into and out of the lexical standard, and there is no record which makes clear, concerning every word that has declined into dialect, just when the loss of currency in standard occurred. The only practicable course is to accept inclusion in the OED as some evidence of currency in the literary language (which is not quite the same as either Standard English or Received

---

4 In many cases, however, the old second syllable represented a quantity which has been absorbed into the remaining syllable without change in the total 'weight' of the word (*eg, nama, name*).

Pronunciation), signalling items which the O E D regards as not standard.[5] We have also to remember that the fullness of the record varies from time to time, and that the O E D editors adopt a broader basis for the inclusion of twentieth-century than that of earlier items. Again, the effect of all these distortions is deflationary.

Finally, though the investigation is concerned with both graphic and phonological realizations, phonology is treated as the primary ecological level. However, over 1,000 years not only pronunciations but also phonological systems have changed. Sounds once distinctive have merged, and at least one unitary sound has split. In broad terms it makes sense to analyse according to present-day phonology, but this creates a difficulty about the placement of, say, items which became obsolete before the Great Vowel Shift. Least distortion is caused if we place such items under the values they probably would have had if they had survived, but there is a good deal of uncertainty, even guesswork, in the case of items rare, of unknown dialect-provenance, and unknown etymology and/or meaning. Such problematic items are placed at the end of their section in the phonological corpus and signalled with a query;[6] they have no significant effect on the analysis.

2

Having taken these policy decisions on the basis of an informal scanning of the evidence, I set about the systematic assembly and interpretation of the data. The first task was to make out an index card for each relevant O E D entry, selecting and discarding from the dictionary data in such a way as to bring ecologically relevant information into clear focus. The spelling-form(s), transcription and a summarized etymological note were necessary; meanings as such were unnecessary, though the presence of a distinctive meaning was essential to the identity of an item, and so to Question *b*. To answer Question *d* it appeared necessary to include an indication of how many different meanings were recorded under each entry. It was also essential to include, in broad terms, the 'life-span' of each item or sense; this was done by centuries.[7] In this way an alphabetical corpus of some 1,700 items was produced; anyone who is surprised at the size of this total has a partial (negative) answer to Question *f*iii. If monosyllables were typically common words (as common words are typically monosyllables), our untutored guesses about their numbers would be fairly correct. The material then had to be re-arranged in phonological order; this was done on a plan derived from Gimson's analysis of syllable-onsets and -closures (Gimson 1970:239–55), according to a method explained in the Appendix.

The object was not merely collection, but also dissection; I was concerned

5 For the notation see the *Explanations* at the beginning of the Appendix.
6 Thus the query relates to the validity of the placement, not to the genuineness of the item.
7 For the notation see the *Explanations* at the beginning of the Appendix.

to cut away whatever was obscuring the essential structure I hoped to lay bare. The translation from alphabetical to phonological order made possible a further step in this direction, for the first stage had already revealed two things, both negative. First, the number of heads and subheads for an item does not show any tendency to stand in inverse relation to the number of homophones co-existing in a given syllable-type. The negative cannot be proved, but a revealing example is syllable-type (1) /biː/ (all syllable-types mentioned in the text are listed in the Appendix). Further, there is no evidence that the three related factors of high frequency, heavy functional loading, and specialized grammatical use have any tendency, separately or jointly, to block the development of homophones, or to cause early loss or variation of such homophones, as has sometimes been suggested (Samuels 1972:143); *cf* again type (1) realizations 1–5, and type (90) /biːn/, realizations 542–7 (*been* is not counted because it is morphemically complex). So the answer to Question *d* is *no*. This is not to say that functional selection never operates against monosyllables. If I had based my sample on other onsets (those involving taboo-words) it would have emerged that there is selection where misinterpretation could cause embarrassment, though not where it would cause no more than confusion. It is possible that this reflects a property of the English rather than of language.

3

The first thing I wanted to read off from the phonological corpus was how the lexicon exploited the phonological potential. For this purpose the aliens, a group of about 30 items using non-English sounds or patterns, had to be put aside, leaving 1,662 relevant entries. There are seven major syllable-types (I–VII); within each we may note five points: how many patterns are *possible* (P), how many *possibilities* are *realized* (PR), how many lexically distinct *realizations* there are (R), what is the *ratio* between P and PR, and what is the *average* number of R per PR (*Table* 1).

In *Table* 1 the syllable-types are listed in an order broadly representing an intuitive notion of progression from simplest to most complex. It is hardly surprising that there proves to be a correlation between this ordering and progression from maximum to minimum exploitation, whether gauged by ratio or by average. The structure of the scale is remarkable in that the two extremes are realized: I has the highest conceivable realization-rate and VII(*b*) the lowest conceivable average. In between, however, there are some oddities. To me it is not intuitively clear which is simpler, CVC or CCV; the ratio favours one, the average the other (the same could be said of CCVC and CVCC, where a similar though less marked pattern is observable). All -VCCC structures are problematical, but the total absence of monomorphemic CVCCC, as contrasted with CCVCCC, raises the question: is this accidental, or etymological, or due to some preference for a measure of balance between onsets and closures?

Secondly it is striking that among the seven types only II allows us to say with certainty what the range of possibilities is, even in so thoroughly-described a variety as Received Pronunciation; permitted onsets and closures are relatively clear, but whether it makes sense to say that all of them can be combined, when in VII hardly any of these combinations occur, is far less certain.

Table I   How the possibilities are exploited

Syllable type	Syllable pattern	P*	PR list-numbers	Total	R list-numbers	Total	Ratio P:R	Average
I	CV	? 14	(1)–(14)	14	1–124	124	1:1	9.0
II	CVC	380	(15)–(182)	168	125–864	740	2·25:1	4.4
III	CCV	? 28/9	(183)–(202)	20	865–930	66	7:5	3.3
IV	CCVC	? 780	(203)–(348)	146	931–1366	436	5:3:1	2.4
V	CVCC	? 1121	(349)–(413)	65	1367–1565	199	17:1	3.0
VI	CCVCC	? 2301	(414)–(455)	42	1566–1658	93	55:1	2.2
VII (a)	CVCCC	?		0		0		
(b)	CCVCCC	?	(456)–(459)	4	1659–1662	4	?	1.0

*Types I CV and III CCV have queried totals because of the doubt about inclusion of -aɪə, -aʊə; types IV–VII have queried totals because, although the permitted onsets are clear and the permitted closures are clear, it is less certain what the total of overall permitted patterns is. If we say that every permitted onset can proceed, via every permitted vowel, to every permitted closure, the figure we come to is extravagantly high. In addition we violate some powerful tendencies which are not quite rules, *eg* concerning the types of cluster normally preceded by long vowels or diphthongs.

Thirdly, there might be a temptation to argue a general cybernetic cause for, or even to deduce a general cybernetic law from, the inverse relationship between complexity of syllable-structure and level of exploitation. But caution suggests that a combination of language-specific factors (of etymology and sound-change) may be a sufficient explanation.

Fourthly, at its peak the level of exploitation is higher than might be thought tolerable, yet this does not make for instability. Thus, under pattern (5) /bɜː/ we have realizations 35–53, including 9 nouns which are full hononyms, one arriving 14c, one 15c, two 16c, two 17c, three 18c, and all surviving at least till 19c. Patterns (6) /beɪ/, (53) /bʌt/, (54) /bʌk/ make the same points, sometimes even more forcibly. Far from supporting classic theories of functional selection, the evidence shows quite clearly that merger or fusion or semantic attraction are the favoured forms of response to disturbance, in so far as homonymy causes any disturbance. This is a topic deserving full-length investigation, but examples of fusion can be seen at (5) 41, 44; (6) 57; (53) 286, 287, 291, 295, 296; (54) 298, 300, 302.

Finally, the evidence suggests that there may be another kind of functional correlation, which I have not seen proposed before, and for which I do not venture an explanation. On the usual basis of calculation /ʌ/ is placed 5th in frequency out of the 20 vowel sounds, with 1.75% of occurrences (Gimson 1970:148, quoting Fry). However, its frequency in terms of numbers of distinct items in which it occurs is much higher; for instance, in this sample type II has /ʌ/ from 277–407 *ie* 130 realizations, whereas the other short vowels have far lower totals – /ɪ/ 59, /e/ 32, /æ/ 58, /ɒ/ 70, /ʊ/ 30; type V has /ʌ/ 56 against other totals of 22, 22, 14, 16, 2. Moreover, we can trace that this level of frequency has not always characterized /ʌ/ and its predecessor /ʊ/. In 15c the repertoire of items in /ʊ/ was type II 29, type V 9; in the 16 and 17c respectively for the /ʌ/ reflexes alone it was type II 58, 69; type V 19, 27; growth has continued (as the examples already referred to under (53), (54) indicate). The split of /ʊ/ into /ʌ/ and /ʊ/ has been for various reasons one of our most puzzling sound-changes. That it synchronizes with a more than doubling of lexical load (in this sample) can hardly be fortuitous. This suggests another topic for extended investigation.

4

On grammatical distribution little need be said. We expect nouns to predominate, and overwhelmingly they do. Verbs come next, joining nouns in a natural class set off from all the rest (*Table* 2). In *Table* 2 functions have to be distinguished from items because some items have more than one grammatical function (though OED's presentation minimizes the representation of this difference). Almost every Group II item occurs in Group I. What is of particular interest is the economy in the utilization of resources afforded by zero-derivation (ZD). The growth in productivity of this type of formation should be noted (*Table* 3). In *Table* 3 we may take centuries 1 and 2 together because of the poverty of the record in 2. Thereafter there is a constant sharp increase in numbers and proportion, with a century of peak change at 6, when the repertoire doubles and the percentage reaches a level from which it can climb only gently in face of other kinds of innovation. It is also striking that (apart from 2) the lowest growth-rate is in 10 (for which OED's principles of inclusion are broadest); this would be true even if the figures were grossed up to represent a full century instead of only 70 years. The slow-down cannot be explained by saying that saturation-point has been reached (*ie* nearly all possible ZDs have already been formed). The

Table 2   Grammatical distribution

	Number	Percentage of items	Percentage of functions
Group I *ns*	993	60	56.5
vs	577	35	33
Subtotal	1570	95	89.5
Group II *adjs*	128	8	7.5
advs	27		
preps	9	3.5	3
conjs	2		
ints	14		
Subtotal	180*	11.5	10.5

*The grand total amounts to more than 1662, and the second column to more than 100 per cent, because some single entries in OED are assigned to more than one form-class.

Table 3   The contribution of zero-derivation

Century	Items	Number ZD*	Percentage ZD
1	222	6	3
2	226	6	3
3	356	6+21−0=27	8
4	509	27+40−1=66	13
5	608	66+36−5=97	16
6	782	97+98−14=181	23
7	870	181+66−42=205	23
8	907	205+34−20=219	24
9	1000	219+84−50=253	25
10	1062	253+19−?7=265	25

*The figures added in each century represent the total of newly recorded formations: the figures deducted represent the total of old formations which were lost. The gross quantity of formation is much greater than the net increase, especially in 6.

population at risk is constantly renewed both because new formations of other types (including loans) are entering it, and because 'second-generation' ZD is quite common (as when *Buck sb.*[10] derives from *v.*[3], which in turn is from *sb.*[1]). We can hardly avoid concluding that within the general line of growth there have been two turning-points: an upward one in 6 and a downward one in 10. In terms of total productivity and of stability, we can see that 373 items have been added, of which 259 survive.

5

In Sections 3 and 4 we have already been led to trespass into the field now to concern us: patterns of heritage and change. In 1 probably 97% of items are from OE, though rather more than 3% may be new; but 50% of those that clearly go back to OE equally clearly go back to Common Germanic, *ie* are 1,000 years old (or more) by the time our corpus begins. This suggests a survival-rate not too different from that of the last 1,000 years (*Table* 4), but a very much lower productivity-rate. From our starting-point in 1 we can identify losses from the OE inherited stock, and gains and losses in innovations classified as loanstock, post-Conquest English formations (PCEF – including ZD, shortenings, back-formations, etc), and, later, unexplained and onomatopoeic items.

The overall trends can best be read off from the graphs. The rate of loss from the OE stock is remarkably steady, and on a curve very similar to the one we might postulate for the previous 1,000 years; but the rate of innovation is so much greater that the residue amounts to 14%, not 50%, of the total stock.

At the beginning of our period hardly anything is etymologically unexplained, and nothing that is recorded is onomotopoeic (the latter may well be due to the bias of the record, but the former hardly can); onomatopoeia creeps in in 4; by 9 the unexplained stock is as large as the OE, and now it is even larger. This is surely odd. Since the onomatopoeic classification is very loosely used in OED,[8] and the unexplained classification covers a good deal that may include an element of sound-symbolism,[9] there are grounds for taking these two types together (as in the graphs); in that case, they overtake the OE stock in 8. The last half-millennium is characterized by a rate of formation in the spectrum sound-symbolism-onomatopoeia-unexplained for which there is no precedent. The same seems to have been happening in neighbouring Germanic languages, but there is often no reason to believe one development to be the source of the other.

Overall, the *Table* and the graphs show that our present stock of monosyllables is not typically old, or native, or stable, any more than it is typically made up of common items. Nor have patterns of development been stable – a very high level of productivity and loss began in 6 and has now declined, and an outstanding characteristic of the last few centuries has been the large population of ephemera – many of them more than nonce-words or *hapax legomena*, but not secure enough to survive the turn of a century. Here are many changes not accounted for by the well-known trends in lexical development at the periods in question.

6

I would like to mention one further topic, on which I can report only in a rather nebulous way. I would describe it as the problem of identity and definition. To some extent this was foreshadowed by the earlier reference to a tendency towards merger, which could alternatively be described as loss of identity; this is something else requiring detailed investigation because it plays a surprisingly large part. Its counterpart, which is also remarkably common, is diversification, so that overlapping series of forms and functions are created, and in the absence of clear etymological explanation we can be left uncertain about how many different items we are dealing with, even in lexicographers' terms. From extensive relevant material I will select one range of examples, the series (182) to (192) *ie* BLV, under which OED records: BLEA /bliː/ (= bleat), var BLAY /bleɪ/; BLAH (imitative); BLORE *sb.* (app. related to BLOW, BLAST); BLORE *v.* (var. or parallel of BLARE); BLUR *v.* (= BLARE, BLORE); BLUR(R)E (*cf* BLUR, BLOW, BLORE); BLOW *v.*[1,2] (ran together in ME; also derivatives BLOW *sb*[2,3]); BLEAR *v.*[1] (*cf* BLUR); BLEAR *v.*[2] (*cf* BLARE); BLARE (*cf* BLEA); BLURE, BLOURE, BLOWRE *sb.* (f. BLOW, *cf* BLADDER). In this summary of OED's evidence I have grossly

8 *Cf eg* the etymological entries for *Blear v.*[2] *Bob a.*[3] and *v.*[3]

9 This element is accorded a particularly high rating by Marchand 1969:397–428. An earlier study by Smithers (1954) proposed to introduce the term *ideophone* into English for a class of items largely overlapping with those under consideration. I am grateful to my colleagues Dr R. N. Bailey and Mr P. J. Frankis for this reference, and more generally to them and other members of the Research Seminar of the Department of English Language in the University of Newcastle upon Tyne for constructive discussion of many points in an early version of this paper presented to that seminar. The analysis was completed just before the appearance of the H-N volume of the OED Supplement; it may well be that the selection of a B- sample somewhat overrepresents the 'ideophonic' element in the vocabulary as a whole.

Table 4   Heritage, innovation and loss

CENTURY

```
2 OE            224                              -2 = 222 (92% of total stock)
  Loanstock     3+4                                 =   7
  PCEF          8                                   =   8
  Unexplained   5+1                                 =   6
                                                    ___
                                                 243 (= +10% over
                                                    ___  preceding century)

3 OE            222                              -9 = 213 (60%)
  Loanstock     7+ up to 69 (NOTE)       =  76-4 =  72
  PCEF          8+    47                  =  55-3 =  52
  Unexplained   6+    18                  =  24-5 =  19
                                                 356 (= +47%)
                                                 ___

4 OE            213                               - 9 = 204 (40%)
  Loanstock     72+       76              = 148-10 = 138
  PCEF          52+ 68=120                  - 9 = 111
  Unexplained   19+ 35= 54                  - 3 =  51
  Onomatopoeic  0+  6=  6                   - 1 =   5
                                                 509 (+43%)
                                                 ___

5 OE            204                               - 9 = 195 (35%)
  Loanstock     138+ up to 50            = 188-22 = 166 (27%)
  PCEF          111+      71             = 182-18 = 164 (27%)
  Unexplained   51+       27             =  78- 5 =  73
  Onomatopoeic  5+        5                       =  10
                                                 608 (1 19%)
                                                 ___

6 OE            195                              -15 = 180 (23%)
  Loanstock     166+  67                = 233-32 = 201 (26%)
  PCEF          164+ 148                = 312-42 = 270 (34%)
  Unexplained   73+  49                 = 122-12 = 110
  Onomatopoeic  10+  16                 =  26- 5 =  21
                                                 ___
  Total gains       280    Losses    106   782 (28%)
                    ___                ___   ___
```

(NB: Of the 106 losses 63 were innovations in the same century)

```
7 OE            180                              -13 = 167 (20%)
  Loanstock     231+  51               = 282-26 = 256 (29%)
  PCEF          270+ 106               = 376-77 = 299 (34%)
  Unexplained   110+  39               = 149-25 = 124
  Onomatopoeic  21+   9                =  30- 6 =  24
                                                 ___
  Total gains       205    Losses    147   870 (+11%)
                    ___                ___   ___
```

(NB: Of the 147 losses 65 were innovations in the same century)

```
8 OE            167                               - 6 = 161 (18%)
  Loanstock     256+  24               = 280-15 = 265 (28%)
  PCEF          299+  64               = 363-36 = 327 (36%)
  Unexplained   124+  29               = 153-28 = 125
  Onomatopoeic  24+   7                =  31- 2 =  29
                                                 ___
  Total gains       124    Losses     87   907 (+4%)
                    ___                ___   ___
```

(NB: Of the 87 losses 31 were innovations in the same century)

[286]

9 OE	161		-14	$=147\ (15\%)$
Loanstock	$265+\ 70$		$=335-49$	$=286\ (29\%)$
PCEF	$327+146$		$=473-90$	$=383\ (38\%)$
Unexplained	$125+\ 41$		$=166-14$	$=152\ (15\%)$
Onomatopoeic	$29+\ \ 7$		$=\ 36-\ 4$	$=\ 32$
	—			
Total gains	264	*Losses*	171	1000 $(+10\%)$

(NB: Of the 171 losses 79 were innovations in the same century)

10 OE	147			$=147\ (14\%)$
Loanstock	$286+\ 11$		$=297-\ 4$	$=293\ (28\%)$
PCEF	$383+\ 45$		$=428-11$	$=417\ (40\%)$
Unexplained	$152+\ 12$		$=164-\ 4$	$=160\ (15\%)$
Onomatopaeic	$32+\ 14$		$=\ 46-\ 1$	$=\ 45$

1062 $(+\ 6\%$ over 70 years)

(NB: As we approach the present-day the estimation of losses becomes highly uncertain; totals for gains and losses are therefore omitted.)

NOTE Etymologies in OED are not always cut-and-dried, though some are firmed up by the *Oxford Dictionary of English Etymology*. In cases where the Dictionary editors express doubt (rather than incapacity to explain), I have assigned the item to the category highest on my listing – to OE, if that or a loan is possible; to the loanstock, if that or PCEF is possible, etc. This is in accordance with the principle of biasing all arbitrary decisions against the direction of my findings. It means that there is some enlargement of the upper figures at the expense of the lower figures for each century (especially the early ones). In practice the greatest impact is on the figures for loanstock, and this is signalled once for all by the indication that the total for 2 is 'up to 69'.

NOTE TO THE GRAPHS

The graphs represent a visual summary of the information in *Table* 4, and do not contain additional information. The post-Conquest centuries, coded 1–10, are marked at the bottom, from left to right, while the number of items classified by etymological type, the numbers for each type added above the OE line (*ie* represented cumulatively), are marked vertically from zero to 1100 (a total which accommodates the maximum co-occurring at one time). Graph 1 shows there is a post-Conquest heritage of over 200 items (about 12·5 per cent of the ultimate total), to which, at the outset must be added only minimal representation of other types of formation. The position appears to remain static for two centuries, which may well be no more than a reflection of the poverty of records at this period. In centuries 3–4 a fan-shape begins to open up, the sharpness of the angle perhaps again reflecting no more than delays in the recording of items. At first the steepest rate of growth is in loans, but in 7–10 they are overtaken by native formations (PCEF). At first, too, unexplained/onomatopoeic items are of negligible importance, but then numbers grow until in 9–10 they overhaul in size the OE stock. The figures in this graph show net growth, *ie* losses are subtracted from gains. In Graph 2, the figures for increases are gross, *ie* the amount of innovation rather than the level of overall change is shown; they are also non-cumulative, *ie* each of the three types of post-Conquest innovation is shown independently from a zero base. In this presentation, if we concentrate on the period 4–10 as being more reliably documented, we see a steady, parallel growth-rate in loans and unexplained/onomatopoeic items, whereas native formations (PCEF) show a sharp increase in 6, a steeper growth-rate thereafter, and an ultimate total almost double that of the other two combined. Graph 3 shows the loss rate up to 9, since it can hardly be calculated for 10. For the OE stock it is simply an inversion of the steadily falling line in Graph 1; for items of all types introduced after the Conquest it shows a rapid climb, overhauling the OE line in 3, and demonstrating the much higher level of ephemerality in these newer words (with nearly eight times the losses of the older words). The two lines are non-cumulative, and show that some 38 per cent of the total population has dropped out over 9 centuries.

[287]

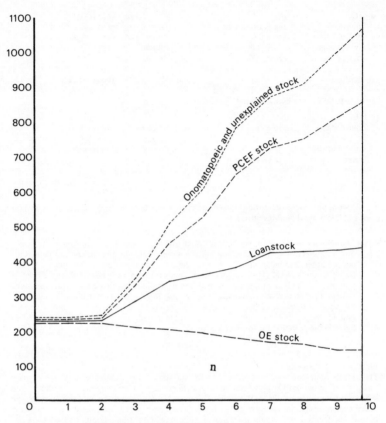

Graph I Cumulative net growth (or OE stock at base).

oversimplified by leaving out many homonyms, and I have no way of representing the multidimensional intersections. But the broad picture is clear: all possible realizations of BLV occur and are linked by a continuous series of overlapping functions. No doubt I have cheated by choosing a range of realizations obviously involving sound-symbolism, but this does not alter my suspicion that part of our present sense of the tidy separation of words is due to a cleaning-up operation in recent centuries, which may not be unconnected with the development of our lexicographical tradition, but which would not have been needed in earlier periods.

Leaving B- for a moment, we can see that the same recent centuries have produced a double counterpart to this phenomenon, if we take function as our starting-point and look at divergent realizations. This can be illustrated from two ranges of words describing horses' tails. There is a limited range

[288]

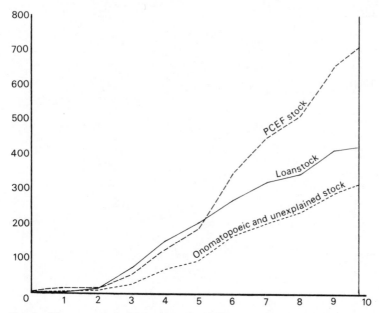

Graph 2 Non-cumulative gross increase in post-conquest items.

of things that can be varied in a horse's tail, and without going into details I will state my conviction that all the words in the following list designate very few differences, and most indicate what would now be called either a *bang* (-tail) (first recorded 1861) or a *switch* (-tail) (first recorded 1689); FLETCH (1704), FLICKY (1690), FLIG (1677), FLIGGY (1711), FLIP (1723), FLISK (1680), FRISK (1694); SWISH (1826), SWITCH (1689); WHISK (1679), WHISKED (1675). But some examples in the list lead in to a third apparent principle of variation, that of keeping more or less constant an implicit simile or metaphor, while exploiting phonologically and lexically distinct realizations (though sometimes there seems to be interference from both these levels). So we have horse-tails classified as BESOM (1695), BROOM (1616 'broome or brushing taile'), BRUSH (1675); BUSHED (1872), BUSHY (*c* 1613), SWEEP (1686), ?SWING (1681) (this is printed *swig*, which may not be the error OED takes it to be). The overlap in currency of many of these variants is particularly striking. It looks as if there is a tendency, most powerful in the seventeenth century, when these terms begin to be recorded, for series of loose transfers to take place, on a phonological or a semantic basis, the latter either literal or figurative in nature. Long ago people might have argued that this sort of instability is what is to be expected as the outcome of a long period of oral transmission, especially in a dialectally diversified speech-community. More recently scholars have preferred to

[289]

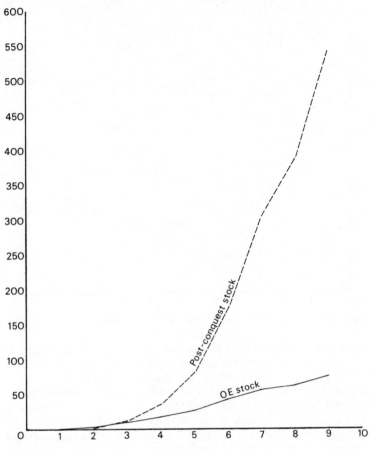

Graph 3 Losses.

stress the overwhelming evidence that non-literate societies are as linguistically stable as literate ones. Can it be that both views are right? It is, after all, reasonable to suppose that stability in oral transmission is chiefly associated with the elements acquired in early childhood and maintained by constant use; perhaps the transmission of technical terms, acquired later and used relatively infrequently, involves quite different mental operations. This is the last question I intend to pose on this occasion.

APPENDIX

I Explanations

(a) In the identification of distributions, periods are referred to as follows:

$I = 1000-1099$; $2 = 1100-1199$; $3 = 1200-1299$; $4 = 1300-1399$; $5 = 1400-1499$; $6 = 1500-1599$; $7 = 1600-1699$; $8 = 1700-1799$; $9 = 1800-1899$; $10 = 1900-c1970$.

Period 10 reaches to the closing date for collection by OED Supplement 1972, which is 1968 for A and progressively a little later up to G. Dates given by OED as *a* plus a century boundary are assigned to the previous century (*eg a*1100 = 1); dates given by OED as *c* plus a century boundary are assigned to the following century (*eg c*1100 = 2).

A + to the left of a 1 indicates that the item was recorded earlier, and therefore +1 serves for items of OE, Gmc and IE origin indifferently; a + to the right of a 10 indicates that the item is still in familiar use (showing no sign of obsolescence) at the time of writing (1975). Thus the maximum time-span is $+1-10+$. Discontinuity in the record is shown by a semi-colon between two sets of currency figures, thus $1-3$; $7-10+$.

L indicates that an item, though in OED, is or was of limited currency, whether dialectally or otherwise. There are three uses of L:

[i] unbracketed it indicates that an item was L throughout its recorded history, thus 7–8L.
[ii] bracketed it indicates that by the end, though not at the beginning, of its recorded history, an item was L, thus 4–9 (L).
[iii] bracketed with a preceding + it indicates that after the date of last recording the item is said by OED, without quotation, to have persisted in L currency, thus 6–8 (+L).

(b) In the classification of types of new formation, PCEF stands for *post-Conquest English formation*. The largest group within this class is ZD (formed by *zero-derivation*), but it also includes a few other types, such as abbreviations and clippings.

2. Selected Corpus

The sections of the analysis referred to in the text are reproduced below. The complete text is available on application to the Department of English Language, The University, Newcastle upon Tyne NE1 7RU, price 50p.

Possible syllable patterns are numbered in a bracketed sequence, *eg* (1); actual realizations in an unbracketed sequence, *eg* 1.

(1) biː 1 B 5−10+ [letter of alphabet]
2 BE *v.* +1−10+ [Com. Gmc.]
3 BEE[1] +1−10+ [Com. Gmc.]
4 BEE[2] +1−10+ [Com. Gmc.]
5 BEE[3] [letter of alphabet]

(5) bɜː 35 BIR *v.* +1−4 [Gmc.]
36 BIRR (*sb.*) 4−10+(L) [a ON.]
37 BIRR *v.* 6−9 (1) [f. *sb.*]
38 BUR, BURR *sb.* 4−10+ [app. ON.]
39 BUR *v.*[1]9 [f. *sb.*]
40 BUR *v.*[2]9−10L [f. *sb.* 5]
41 BURR, BUR *sb.*[1]5−10+ [Derivation unclear; II, III may be separate words. *Cf* BURROW *sb.* 5]
42 BURR, BUR *sb.*[2]6−9 [origin unknown]
43 BURR, BUR, *sb.*[3]6−10+ [Etymology uncertain]
44 BURR, BUR *sb.*[4]7−10+ [app. var. of BUR *sb.*]
45 BURR, BUR, BUR *sb.*[5]8−10+ [Origin uncertain]
46 BURR *sb.*[6]8−10+ [app. imitative]
47 BURR, BUR *sb.*[7]7−9 [a F; *cf* BURL *sb.*]
48 BURR, BUR *sb.*[8]8−9 [Hind.]
49 BURR *v.*[1]7 [f. *sb.*[1]]
50 BURR *v.*[2]9−10+ [f. *sb.*[1] 3]
51 BURR *v.*[3]8−10+ [f. *sb.*[6]]
52 BURR *v.*[4]9 f. [*sb.*[4]]
53 BYR. *v.*3−4 [var. of BIR *v.*]

(6) beɪ 54 BAY *sb.*[1]4−10+ [a OF.]
55 BAY *sb.*[2]4−10+ [a F.]
56 BAY *sb.*[3]4−10+ [a F.]
57 BAY *sb.*[4]4−10+ [Two words inextricably confused, both a OF.]
58 BAY *sb.*[5]5−10+ [Doubtful origin; *cf v.* 4]
59 BAY *sb.*[6]7−10+ [Short: *bez-antler.*]
60 BAY *sb.*[7]6−8 [a F. *Cf* BAIZE]
61 BAY *sb.*[8]6 [Uncertain origin; *cf* BECK]
62 BAY *a., sb.* 4−10+ [a F.]
63 BAY *v.*[1]4−10+ [Partly OF; partly *sb.*[4]]
64 BAY *v.*[2]7−9 [f. *sb.*[4]]
65 BAY *v.*[3]6 [a OF.]
66 BAY *v.*[4]6−10+ [source or derivative of *sb.*[5]]
67 BAY(E *v.*[5]6 [app. a pseudo-archaism]
68 BAY *v.*[6]10 [f. *sb.*[2]]

69 BEY *sb.* 6−10+ [a Osmanli. Also *byle.*]

(53) bʌt 277 BUT prep. conj. adv. +1−10+ [OE.]
278 BUT *sb.*[1]6−10+ [f. prep. etc]
279 BUT *sb.*[2]3 [*cf* PUT *v.*, OF. *bout*]
280 BUT *v.* 6−9 (+L) [f. *sb.*[1]]
281 BUTT *sb.*[1]3−10+ [Cogn. with Sw., Mod.G, Du; see HALIBUT]
282 BUTT *sb.*[2] 5−10+ [app. adopted 15c.; a common Rom. word]
283 BUTT *sb.*[3] 5−10+ [obscure; may be older than 15c if BUTTOCK (13c) is a diminutive of it]
284 BUTT *sb.*[4] 5−10+ [a F.]
285 BUTT *sb.*[5] 7(+L) [?a F.; *cf* BUTTE]
286 BUTT *sb.*[6] 5−10+ [Uncertain (for sense 3 *cf* BATTS)]
287 BUTT *sb.*[7] 7−10+ [?F. *bout*, ?a sense of BUTT *sb.* 3 or *v.*[2] II]
288 BUTT *sb.*[8] 6(+L) [?f. *v.*[1]4]
289 BUTT *sb.*[9] 7−10+ [f.*v.*[1] *cf* F]
290 BUTT *sb.*[10] 6−8; 9L [?a F *botte*]
291 BUTT *sb.*[11] 7−10+ [?a spec. use of *sb.*[3] 1 or 3]
292 BUTT *sb.*[12]6 [Unknown; *cf* BUCK *sb.*[4]]
293 BUTT *sb.*[13] 8−9L [no etym.]
294 BUTT *sb.*[14] 9−10+L [no etym.]
295 BUTT *v.*[1] 3−10+ [a OF; senses 3−4 influenced by *v.* 2; some questions cannot be assigned to a particular *v.*]
296 BUTT *v.*[2] 6−10+ [partly f. *sb.*[4] 1; partly aphetic]
297 BUTT *v.*[3] 8−9 [f. *sb.*[3]]
[BUTE has a 19c pronunciation belonging here]

(54) bʌk 298 BUCK *sb.*[1] +1−10+ [Orig. two words, indistinguishable in form after 11c]
299 BUCK *sb.*[2] 6−9 [Abbrev: -*wheat*, -*mast*]
300 BUCK *sb.*[3] 6−10+L [sense 2 belongs to *v.*[1]? as derivative; sense 1 of same orig. or f. OE. *cf* BOWK]
301 BUCK *sb.*[4] 7−10+ [no etym.]
302 BUCK *sb.*[5] 9−10+L [?var. of BOUK. Senses may not all belong here]
303 BUCK *sb.*[6] 7 [f.*v.*[2]]
304 BUCK *sb.*[7] 9L [Shortened f. Du.]
305 BUCK *sb.*[8] 9−10+L [Obscure]

306 BUCK *sb.*⁹ 9–10+L [Obscure]
307 BUCK *sb.*¹⁰ 9–10+ [f. *v.*³]
308 BUCK *sb.*¹¹ 9–10+ [a. Hind.
   Also *bukh*]
309 BUCK *a.*⁽¹⁾ 8L [*v.*¹ used attrib.]
310 BUCK *a.*² 10+L [Prob. f. *sb.*¹ 2]
311 BUCK *v.*¹ 4–9L [ME. f. *OE
   Also *bouk, bowk*, etc]
312 BUCK *v.*² 6–8 [f. *sb.*¹]
313 BUCK *v.*³ 9L [f. *sb.*¹]
314 BUCK *v.*⁴ 9–10+L [perh. f. *sb.*⁷]
315 BUCK *v.*⁵ 7–10+L [*Cf* Du.]
316 BUCK *v.*⁶ 8–10+ [?corruption
   of *butt*, assoc. with BUCK
   *sb.*¹]
317 BUCK *v.*⁷ 9–10+L [f. *sb.*¹ 2]

318 BUCK *v.*⁸ 9L [Obscure, but *cf*
   **sb.*⁹]
319 BUCK *v.*⁹ 9–10+L [f. *sb.*⁷]
320 BUCK *v.*¹⁰ 9–10+L [*cf* **sb.*¹¹
   Also *bukh* etc]
(90) bi:n 542 BEAN +1–10+ [Com. Cmc.
   Also *ben, been(e, bein, beyne*]
543 BEAN *v.* 10+L [f. *sb.*]
?544 BEANE, BEAYNE 4 [var. of
   BAIN]
?545 BEIN *a., adv.* 2–9L [Unknown.
   Also *been(e, bien*, etc]
?546 BEIN *v.* 5L [f. *a.*]
?547 BENE 1–6(+L) [OE. Also
   beane, ban.]

NOTE:
Two conventions in the above excerpts require explanation. Where a form-class identification carries a bracketed superscript *eg v.*⁽¹⁾ this means that OED did not use a superscript, but that the additional material in Supp calls for one, which may be used in cross-reference. * is used in accordance with Supp's convention, to identify entries not in OED; it does not, in this context, mean unattested.

REFERENCES

ABERCROMBIE, D. 1952–3. 'English accents.' *English Language Teaching* 7.113–23
AIJMER, K. 1977. 'Partiklarna ju och väl.' *Nysvenska studier* 57.205–16
AKMAJIAN, A., S. M. STEELE and T. WASOW. 1977. *The category AUX in universal grammar.* MS
AKMAJIAN, A., and T. WASOW. 1975. 'The constituent structure of VP and AUX and the position of the verb BE.' *Linguistic Analysis* 1.205–45
ALLEN, H. B. 1973–6. *Linguistic Atlas of the Upper Midwest.* Minneapolis: University of Minnesota Press
ALLEN, R. L. 1966. *The verb system in present-day American English.* The Hague: Mouton
ALLERTON, D. J. 1969. 'The sentence as a linguistic unit.' *Lingua* 22.27–46
ANDERSON, E. S. 1975. 'Cups and glasses: learning that boundaries are vague.' *Journal of Child Language* 2.79–103
ANDERSON, S. R. 1972. 'How to get even.' *Language* 48.893–906
   1978. 'Inflectional morphology.' MS, in *Language typology and syntactic field work,* ed by T. Shopen *et al*
ARISTOTLE. 1926. *Rhetoric,* translated by J. R. Freese. London: Heinemann; Cambridge, MA: Harvard University Press
ARNOLD, G. F., and O. M. TOOLEY. 1972. *Say it with rhythm, 3.* London: Longman
ATWOOD, E. B. 1953. *A survey of verb forms in the Eastern United States.* Ann Arbor: University of Michigan Press
BAILEY, C.-J., and R. W. SHUY (eds). 1973. *New ways of analyzing variation in English.* Washington, DC: Georgetown University Press
BAKER, C. L. 1971. 'Stress level and auxiliary behaviour in English.' *Linguistic Inquiry* 2.167–81
BALD, W.-D., and R. ILSON (eds) 1977. *Studies in English usage.* Frankfurt, Bern: Lang
BAR-HILLEL, Y. 1970. *Aspects of language.* Jerusalem: Magnes

[294]

BARRETT, R., and A. STENNER. 1971. 'On the myth of the exclusive "or".' *Mind* 79.116–21

BARTSCH, R. 1976. *The grammar of adverbials.* Amsterdam: North-Holland

BEEBE, R. D. 1976. *Frequencies of syntactic structures in Australian English.* Monash University dissertation

BENVENISTE, E. 1966. *Problèmes de linguistique générale.* Paris: Gallimard

BERMAN, A., and M. SZAMOSI. 1972. 'Observations on sentential stress.' *Language* 48.304–25

BIERWISCH, M. 1967. 'On certain problems of semantic representation.' *Foundations of Language* 5.153–84

BLOOMFIELD, L. 1933. *Language.* New York: Holt

BLOOMFIELD, M. W. 1970a. 'Episodic motivation and marvels in epic and romance.' *Essays and explorations: studies in ideas, language, and literature*, 97–128. Cambridge, MA: Harvard University Press

1970b. 'Generative grammar and the theory of literature.' *Actes du Xᵉ Congrès International des Linguistes.* III.57–65. Bucharest

BOLINGER, D. 1961a. 'Syntactic blends and other matters.' *Language* 37.366–81

1961b. *Generality, gradience, and the all-or-none.* The Hague: Mouton

1965. 'Linear modification.' *Forms of English*, 279–307. Cambridge, MA: Harvard University Press. [Originally in *PMLA* 1952, 1117–42]

1971. *The phrasal verb in English.* Cambridge, MA: Harvard University Press

1972a. *Degree words.* The Hague: Mouton

1972b. 'Accent is predictable (if you're a mind reader).' *Language* 48.633–44

1976. 'Meaning and memory.' *Forum Linguisticum* 1.1–14

1977a. 'Another glance at main clause phenomena.' *Language* 53.511–19

1977b. *Meaning and form.* London: Longman

BOWMAN, E. 1966. *The minor and fragmentary sentences of a corpus of spoken English.* The Hague: Mouton

BRADLEY, H. 1904. *The making of English.* London: Macmillan

BRAZIL, D. 1975. *Discourse intonation (Discourse analysis monograph 1).* Birmingham: University of Birmingham

BREMOND, C. 1973. 'Les bons récompensés et les méchants punis, morphologie du conte merveilleux français.' *Semiotique narrative et textuelle*, ed by C. Chabrol, 96–121. Paris: Larousse

BRESNAN, J. W. 1971. 'Sentence stress and syntactic transformations.' *Language* 47.257–81

1972. 'Stress and syntax: a reply.' *Language* 48.326–42

BROWN, G. 1977. *Listening to spoken English.* London: Longman

BROWN, R., and A. GILMAN. 1960. 'The pronouns of power and solidarity.' *Style in Language*, ed T. A. Sebeok. Cambridge, MA: MIT Press

BURTON, D. 1977. *Towards an analysis of casual conversation.* Birmingham: University of Birmingham (mimeographed)

BURTON-ROBERTS, N. 1976. 'On the generic indefinite article.' *Language* 52.427–48

CARTER, R. S. 1972. 'A class of "emphatic" sentences in English.' *Papers in linguistics* 5.402–20

CHOMSKY, N. 1965. *Aspects of the theory of syntax.* Cambridge, MA: MIT Press

1975. *Reflections on language.* New York: Pantheon

1977. *Essays on form and interpretation.* New York: Elsevier

1978. *On binding.* Cambridge, MA: MIT (mimeographed)

CHOMSKY, N, and H. LASNIK. 1977. 'Filters and control.' *Linguistic Inquiry* 8.425–504

CLARK, H. H. 1973. 'Space, time, semantics and the child.' *Cognitive development and the acquisition of language*, ed by T. E. Moore. New York: Academic Press

REFERENCES

CLOSE, R. A. 1977. 'Some observations on the meaning and function of verb phrases having future reference.' BALD, W.-D., and R. ILSON (eds)

COATES, J., and G. LEECH. forthcoming. 'The meanings of the modals in modern British and American English.' *York Papers in Linguistics*

CONTRERAS, H. 1976. *A theory of word order with special reference to Spanish.* Amsterdam: North-Holland

COULTHARD, M. 1977. *An introduction to discourse analysis.* London: Longman

COULTHARD, M., and D. BRAZIL. 1978. *Exchange structure (Discourse analysis monograph 5).* Birmingham: University of Birmingham

CRESWELL, T. J. 1975. *Usage in dictionaries and dictionaries of usage.* Alabama: University of Alabama Press

CRISP, R. D. 1971. *Changes in attitudes towards English usage.* Urbana, IL: University of Illinois dissertation

CRUSE, D. A. 1973. 'Some thoughts on agentivity.' *Journal of Linguistics* 9.11–24

CRYSTAL, D. 1966. 'Specification and English tenses.' *Journal of Linguistics* 6.1–34
1969. *Prosodic systems and intonation in English.* Cambridge: Cambridge University Press
1975. *The English tone of voice.* London: Arnold

CRYSTAL, D., and D. DAVY. 1969. *Investigating English style.* London: Longman
1975. *Advanced conversational English.* London: Longman

CRYSTAL, D., P. FLETCHER, and M. GARMAN. 1976. *The grammatical analysis of language disability.* London: Arnold

CUNNINGHAM, J. V. 1952. 'Influence of the *Romance of the Rose* on the Prologue to the *Canterbury Tales*.' *Modern Philology* 49.172–8

CURME, G. O. 1931. *Syntax.* New York: Heath

DAHL, O. 1974. 'Some suggestions for a logic of aspects.' *Göteborg contributions to the seventh international congress of slavists,* ed by G. Jacobsson, 21–35. Göteborg: Dept of Slavic Studies, University of Göteborg
1975. 'Review of VERKUYL 1972.' *Foundations of Language* 12.451–4

DANEŠ, F. 1957. *Intonace a věta ve spisovné češtině. [Sentence intonation in present-day standard Czech.]* Prague: Academia

DIAMOND, S. 1972. 'Anthropology in question.' *Reinventing anthropology,* ed by D. Hymes, 401–29. New York: Pantheon

DIK, S. C. 1968. *Coordination.* Amsterdam: North-Holland

DORFMAN, E. 1969. *The narreme in the medieval romance epic: an introduction to narrative structures.* Toronto: University of Toronto Press

DU BOIS, J. W. 1974. 'Syntax in mid-sentence.' *Berkeley studies in syntax and semantics I,* ed by C. Fillmore, G. Lakoff, and R. Lakoff, iii. Berkeley: Department of Linguistics, University of California, Berkeley

EDGREN, E. 1971. *Temporal clauses in English.* Uppsala: Almqvist and Wiksell

EDMONDS, R. 1954. *Anna Karenina.* Harmondsworth: Penguin

EHRMAN, M. 1966. *The meanings of the modals in present-day American English.* The Hague: Mouton

EMONDS, J. E. 1976. *A transformational approach to English syntax.* New York: Academic Press

EPSTEIN, E. L. 1978. *Language and style.* London: Methuen

EVERITT, B. 1974. *Cluster analysis.* London: Heinemann

FIENGO, R. 1977. 'On trace theory.' *Linguistic Inquiry* 8.35–62

FILLMORE, C. J., and D. J. LANGENDOEN (eds). 1971. *Studies in linguistic semantics.* New York: Holt

FIRBAS, J. 1968. 'On the prosodic features of the modern English finite verb as means of functional sentence perspective.' *Brno Studies in English* 7.11–48
1969. 'On the prosodic features of the modern English finite verb-object combination as means of FSP.' *Brno Studies in English* 8.49–59

1971. 'The concept of communicative dynamism in the theory of functional sentence perspective.' *Sborník prací filozofické fakulty brněnské univerzity* A 19.135–44

1974. 'Some aspects of the Czechoslovak approach to problems of functional sentence perspective.' *Papers on functional sentence perspective*, ed by F. Daneš, 11–37. Prague: Academia

1975. 'On the thematic and the non-thematic section of the sentence.' RINGBOM, H. *et al* (eds)

FIRBAS, J. and E. GOLKOVÁ. 1975. *An analytical bibliography of Czechoslovak studies in functional sentence perspective*. Brno: Brno University

FISHER, J. H. 1977. 'Chancery and the emergence of standard written English in the fifteenth century.' *Speculum* 52.870–99

FRANCIS, W. N. 1958. *The structure of American English*. New York: Ronald

1964. *A standard sample of present-day English for use with digital computers*. Providence: Brown University Press

FRASER, B. 1971. 'An analysis of "even" in English.' FILLMORE, C. J., and D. J. LANGENDOEN (eds)

1974. *The verb-particle combination in English*. Tokyo: Taikushan; 1979. New York: Academic Press

FREIDIN, R. 1978. 'Cyclicity and the theory of grammar.' *Linguistic Inquiry* 9.519–49

FRIEDMAN, N. 1955. 'Point of view in fiction: the development of a critical concept.' *Publications of the Modern Language Association of America* 70.1160–84

FRIEDRICH, P. 1966. 'Structural implications of Russian pronominal usage.' *Sociolinguistics*, ed W. Bright. The Hague: Mouton

FRIES, C. C. 1940. *American English grammar*. New York: Appleton, Century, and Crofts

1952. *The structure of English*. New York: Harcourt

FRIES, C. C. and K. L. PIKE. 1949. 'Coexistent phonemic systems.' *Language* 25.29–50

GALVAN, M. M., and R. C. TROIKE. 1972. 'The East Texas dialect project: a pattern for education.' *Language and cultural diversity in American education*, ed by R. D. Abrahams and R. C. Troike, 297–304. Englewood Cliffs, NJ: Prentice-Hall

GARNETT, C. 1977. *Anna Karenina*. London: Pan [First published, London: Heinemann, 1901]

GATES, J. E. 1977. 'The treatment of lexemes larger than the word in English dictionaries.' *Studies in lexicography as a science and as an art*, 37–54. Newark, DEL: Dept of Languages and Literature, University of Delaware (mimeographed)

GAZDAR, G. 1977. 'Univocal "or".' *The CLS book of squibs*, ed by S. E. Fox *et al.* 44–45. Chicago: Chicago Linguistic Society

GCE = QUIRK, R.; S. GREENBAUM; G. LEECH; and J. SVARTVIK. 1972. *A grammar of contemporary English*. London: Longman

GENETTE, G. 1972. *Figures III*. Paris: Seuil

GIMSON, A. C. 1970. *An introduction to the pronunciation of English*. 2nd edn. London: Arnold

GLEASON, H. A., JR. 1965. *Linguistics and English grammar*. New York: Holt

GOLKOVÁ, E. 1968. 'On the English infinitive of purpose in functional sentence perspective.' *Brno Studies in English* 7.119–28

GREENBAUM, S. 1974. 'Problems in the negation of modals.' *Moderna Språk* 68.245–55

(ed) 1977. *Acceptability in language*. The Hague: Mouton

GREENBERG, J. 1954. 'A quantitative approach to the morphological typology of languages'. *Method and perspective in anthropology*, ed by R. F. Spencer, 192–220. Minneapolis: University of Minnesota Press

GREENE, B. B., and G. M. RUBIN. 1971. *Automatic grammatical tagging of English*. Providence: Dept of Linguistics, Brown University

REFERENCES

GREENE, G. 1976. 'Main clause phenomena in subordinate clauses.' *Language* 52.382–97

GREIMAS, A. J., and J. COURTES. 1975–6. 'The cognitive dimension of narrative discourse.' *New Literary History* 7.433–47

GRICE, H. P. 1975. 'Logic and conversation.' *Syntax and semantics 3: speech acts*, ed by P. Cole and J. L. Morgan, 41–58. New York: Academic Press

HALLE, M., and S. J. KEYSER. 1971. *English stress*. New York: Harper and Row

HALLIDAY, M. A. K. 1967. *Intonation and grammar in British English*. The Hague: Mouton

1970*a*. 'Clause types and structural functions.' *New horizons in linguistics*, ed by J. Lyons, 140–65. Harmondsworth: Penguin

1970*b*. *A course in spoken English: intonation*. London: Oxford University Press

1975. *Learning how to mean*. London: Arnold

1976. *System and function in language*, ed by G. R. Kress. London: Oxford University Press

HALLIDAY, M. A. K. and R. HASAN. 1976. *Cohesion in English*. London: Longman

HANKAMER, J., and I. SAG. 1976. 'Deep and surface anaphora.' *Linguistic Inquiry* 7.391–428

HARTVIGSON, H. H. 1969. *On the intonation and position of the so-called sentence modifiers in present-day English*. Odense: Odense University Press

HELKE, M. 1971. *The grammar of English reflexives*. Cambridge, MA: MIT dissertation

HILL, A. A. 1958. *Introduction to linguistic structures: from sound to sentence in English*. New York: Harcourt Brace Jovanovich

1976. *Constituent and pattern in poetry*. Austin, Texas: University of Texas Press

HINES, C. P. 1977. '*Well . . .*'. *4th Lacus Forum*, ed by M. Paradis. New York: Hornbeam Press

HOOPER, J. B., and S. A. THOMPSON. 1973. 'On the applicability of root transformations.' *Linguistic Inquiry* 4.465–97

HORN, L. 1969. A presuppositional approach to *only* and *even*'. *Papers from the Fifth Regional Meeting, Chicago Linguistic Society*, ed by R. I. Binnick *et al*. Chicago: Chicago Linguistic Society

HOROVÁ, E. 1976. 'On the position and function of English local and temporal adverbials.' *Brno Studies in English* 12.93–124

HUDDLESTON, R. D. 1975. 'Homonymy in the English verbal paradigm.' *Lingua* 37.151–76

1976. 'Some theoretical issues in the description of the English verb.' *Lingua* 40.331–83

ISER, W. 1976. 'Der akt des Lesens: Theorie äesthetischer Wirkung.' *Uni-Taschenbücher 636*. Munich: Fink

1977. 'Interaction between text and reader.' [Paper delivered at the Tenth Triennial Congress of the International Association of University Professors of English, Poznan, Poland]

JACKENDOFF, R. S. 1972. *Semantic interpretation in generative grammar*. Cambridge MA: MIT Press

JACOBSON, S. 1964. *Adverbial positions in English*. Uppsala: A B Studentbok

1978. *On the use, meaning, and syntax of English preverbal adverbs*. Stockholm: Almqvist and Wiksell

JACOBSSON, B. 1977. 'Adverbs, prepositions, and conjunctions in English: a study in gradience.' *Studia Linguistica* 31.38–64

JAKOBSON, R. 1932. 'Zur Struktur des russischen Verbums. Charisteria Guilelmo Mathesio . . . oblata.' Prague: Linguistic Circle of Prague, 79–84. [Reprinted in *Selected Writings II*, 3–16. The Hague: Mouton]

1960. 'Comments.' *Style in language*, ed by T. A. Sebeok. Cambridge, MA: MIT Press

JAKOBSON, R., and M. HALLE. 1956. *Fundamentals of language*. The Hague: Mouton

JENKINS, L. 1972. *Modality in English syntax*. Bloomington, IN: Indiana University Linguistics Club

JESPERSEN, O. 1894. *Progress in language*. London: Sonnenschein; New York: Macmillan

1905. *Growth and structure of the English language*. Leipzig: Teubner

1909–49. *A modern English grammar I–VII*. Heidelberg: Karl Winter; Copenhagen: Elnor Munksgaard; and London: Allen and Unwin

1924. *The philosophy of grammar*. London: Allen and Unwin

JOHANNESSON, N.-L. 1976. *The English modal auxiliaries: a stratificational account*. Stockholm: Almqvist and Wiksell

JOHANNSON, S. (ed) 1979. 'Brown Corpus bibliography'. *ICAME News, No 2, 9–12*. Bergen: NAVF's EDB-senter for humanistisk forskning

JONES, D. 1967. *English pronouncing dictionary*, ed by A. C. Gimson. 13th edn. London: Dent

JONES, S., and J. MCH. SINCLAIR. 1974. 'English lexical collocations.' *Cahiers de lexicologie 24*. Paris: Didier-Larousse

KARLSEN, R. 1959. *Studies in the connection of clauses in current English: zero, ellipsis and explicit forms*. Bergen: Eides

KELLEY, E., and P. STONE. 1975. *Computer recognition of English word senses*. Amsterdam: North-Holland

KELLY, F. D. 1966. 'Sens and conjointure in the Chevalier de la Charette.' *Studies in French literature 2*. The Hague: Mouton

KEMPSON, R. M. 1975. *Presupposition and the delimitation of semantics*. Cambridge: Cambridge University Press

1977. *Semantic theory*. Cambridge: Cambridge University Press

1979. 'Presupposition, opacity and ambiguity.' *Syntax and semantics 11: presupposition*, ed by D. A. Dineen and C.-K. Oh. New York: Academic Press

KINGDON, R. 1958. *The groundwork of English intonation*. London: Longman

KLIMA, E. 1964. 'Negation in English.' *The structure of language*, ed by J. Fodor and J. Katz, 246–323. Englewood Cliffs, NJ: Prentice-Hall

KRUISINGA, E. 1908. 'De betekenis van het bijwoord *no*'. *De Drie Talen* 24.132–3

1931–2. *A handbook of present-day English*. Groningen: Noordhoff

KRUISINGA, E., and P. A. ERADES. 1953. *An English grammar*. Groningen: Noordhoff

KUČERA, H., and W. N. FRANCIS. 1967. *Computational analysis of present-day American English*. Providence: Brown University Press

KUČERA, H., et al 1970. *Student reports in computational linguistics*. Providence: Dept of Linguistics, Brown University

KURATH, H., B. BLOCH, et al 1939. *Handbook of the linguistic geography of New England*. Providence: American Council of Learned Societies. [2nd edn. 1973. New York: AMS Press]

KURATH, H., B. BLOCH, et al 1939–43. *Linguistic atlas of New England*. Providence: American Council of Learned Societies. [Reprinted 1972. New York: AMS Press]

KURATH, H. and R. I. MCDAVID, JR. 1961. *The pronunciation of English in the Atlantic states*. Ann Arbor: University of Michigan Press

KURATH, H., R. I. MCDAVID JR, R. K. O'CAIN, and G. T. DORRILL. 1978–. *Linguistic atlas of the Middle and South Atlantic states*. Chicago: University of Chicago Press

LABOV, W. 1970. 'The study of language in its social context.' *Studium Generale* 23.30–87.

1972. *Language in the inner city*. Philadelphia, PA: University of Pennsylvania Press

1973. 'The boundaries of words and their meanings.' BAILEY, C.-J., and R. W. SHUY (eds), 340–73

LADD, D. R., JR. 1977. *The function of the A-rise accent in English*. Bloomington, IN: Indiana University Linguistics Club

1979. 'Light and shadow: a study of the syntax and semantics of sentence accent in English.' *Contributions to grammatical studies: semantics and syntax,* ed by L. R. Waugh and F. van Coetsem, 93–131. Leiden: Brill

LADEFOGED, P. 1967. *Three areas of experimental phonetics.* London: Oxford University Press

LAKOFF, G. 1971. 'The role of deduction in grammar.' FILLMORE, C. J., and D. T. LANGENDOEN (eds)

LAKOFF, R. 1971. 'If's, and's, and but's about conjunction.' FILLMORE, C. J., and D. J. LANGENDOEN (eds)

1972. 'Language in context.' *Language* 48.907–27

1973. 'Questionable answers and answerable questions.' *Papers in linguistics in honor of Henry and Renée Kahane,* ed by B. Kachru *et al,* 453–67. Urbana, IL: University of Illinois

LAVER, J. 1970. 'The production of speech.' *New horizons in linguistics,* ed by J. Lyons, 53–75. Harmondsworth: Penguin

LEECH, G. 1969. *Towards a semantic description of English.* London: Longman

1971. *Meaning and the English verb.* London: Longman

LEECH, G., and J. SVARTVIK. 1975. *A communicative grammar of English.* London: Longman

LEHISTE, I. 1970. *Suprasegmentals.* Cambridge, MA: MIT Press

LEWIS, J. W. 1977. *People speaking.* London: Oxford University Press

LIMBER, J. 1976. 'Unravelling competence, performance, and pragmatics in the speech of young children.' *Journal of Child Language* 3.309–18

LIPSKI, J. M. 1976. 'Connectedness in poetry: toward a topological analysis of E. E. Cummings.' *Language and Style* 9.143–63

LONG, R. B. 1961. *The sentence and its parts.* Chicago: University of Chicago Press

1974. 'Problems in English grammar.' *TESOL Quarterly* 8.202–3

1975. 'Problems in English grammar.' *TESOL Quarterly* 9.89–94

LONGACRE, R. E. 1976. *An anatomy of speech notions.* Lisse: de Ridder

LUICK, K. 1914. *Historische Grammatik der englischen Sprache I.* Leipzig and Berlin: Tauchnitz

LUST, B. 1977. 'Conjunction reduction in child language.' *Journal of Child Language* 4.257–87

LYONS, J. 1968. *Introduction to theoretical linguistics.* Cambridge: Cambridge University Press

1977. *Semantics.* 2 vols. Cambridge: Cambridge University Press

MCCAWLEY, J. D. 1971. 'Tense and time reference in English.' FILLMORE, C. J., and D. T. LANGENDOEN (eds)

MCDAVID, R. I., JR. 1952. 'Some social differences in pronunciation.' *Language Learning* 4.102–16

MCDAVID, R. I., JR, and A. R. DUCKERT (eds) 1973. *Lexicography in English.* Annals of the New York Academy of Sciences 211

MCDAVID, R. I., JR, and R. K. O'CAIN. 1977. 'Prejudice and pride: linguistic acceptability in South Carolina.' GREENBAUM, S. (ed), 103–32

MCQUOWN, N. 1964. Review of *A planned auxiliary language,* by H. Jacob. *Language in culture and society,* ed by D. Hymes, 555–63. New York: Harper and Row

MACCARTHY, P. A. D. 1956. *English conversation reader.* London: Longman

MALINOWSKI, B. 1969. 'Supplement 1. The problem of meaning in primitive languages.' *The meaning of meaning,* by C. K. Ogden and I. A. Richards, 296–336. 10th edn. London: Routledge and Kegan Paul

MARCHAND, H. 1969. *The categories and types of present-day English word-formation.* 2nd edn. Munich: Beck

MARCKWARDT, A. H. 1973. 'Lexicographical method and the usage survey.' *Lexicography and dialect geography*, ed by H. Scholler and J. Reidy. *Zeitschrift fur Dialektologie und Linguistik, Neue Folge*, 9. Wiesbaden

MARCKWARDT, A. H., and F. WALCOTT. 1938. *Facts about current English usage*. New York: Appleton, Century, and Crofts

MARCOS MARIN, F. 1974. *Aproximación a la Gramatica Española*. 2nd edn. Madrid: Cincel

MATHESIUS, V. 1935. 'Zur synchronistischen Analyse fremden Sprachguts.' *Englische Studien* 70.21–35

1975. *A functional analysis of present day English on a general linguistic basis*. The Hague: Mouton

MENCKEN, H. L. 1936. *The American language*. 4th edn. New York: Knopf

MITTWOCH, A. 1977. *Equi or raising or both – another look at the root modals and at permissive allow*. MS

MORE, T. 1557. *Confutation of Tindale. The workes of Sir Thomas More Knight*. London: John Cawod, John Waley, and Richard Tottell

MORGAN, J. L. 1973. 'Sentence fragments and the notion "sentence".' *Issues in linguistics: papers in honor of Henry and Renée Kahane*, ed by B. Kachru *et al.* Urbana, IL: University of Illinois Press

MURILLO, L. A. 1975. *The golden dial: temporal configuration in 'Don Quixote'*. Oxford: Dolphin

MUSTANOJA, T. F. 1960. *A Middle English syntax*. Helsinki: Société Néophilologique

NYQVIST GOËS, A. 1974. *The stress system of English*. Stockholm: Almqvist and Wiksell

O'CAIN, R. K. 1977. 'A diachronic view of the speech of Charleston, South Carolina.' *Papers in language variation*, ed by D. L. Shores and C. P. Hines, 135–51. Alabama: University of Alabama

O'CONNOR, J. D. 1973. *Intonation of colloquial English*. 2nd edn. London: Longman

PALMER, F. R. 1965. *A linguistic study of the English verb*. London: Longman

1972. 'Noun-phrase and sentence: a problem in semantics/syntax.' *Transactions of the Philological Society* 20–43

1974. *The English verb*. London: Longman

1977. 'Modals and actuality.' *Journal of Linguistics* 13.1–23

1979. *Modality and the English modals*. London: Longman

PALMER, H. E., and F. G. BLANDFORD. 1969. *A grammar of spoken English*. 3rd edn, revised by R. Kingdon. Cambridge: Heffer

PERSSON, G. 1974. *Repetition in English. Part 1: sequential repetition*. Uppsala: Almqvist and Wiksell

PIKE, K. L., and E. G. PIKE. 1977. *Grammatical analysis*. Arlington, Texas: Summer Institute of Linguistics

POPE, E. 1973. 'Question-answering systems.' *Papers from the Ninth Regional Meeting, Chicago Linguistic Society*, ed by C. Corum *et al*, 482–92. Chicago: Chicago Linguistic Society

POPPER, K. R. 1972. *Objective knowledge*. London: Oxford University Press

POSTAL, P. M. 1974. *On raising*. Cambridge, MA: MIT Press

POUTSMA, H. 1928–9. *A grammar of late Modern English. Part 1*. Groningen: Noordhoff

PRINCE, G. 1973. *A grammar of stories: an introduction*. The Hague: Mouton

PULLUM, G. K., and D. WILSON. 1977. 'Autonomous syntax and the analysis of auxiliaries.' *Language* 53.741–88

QUINTILIAN. 1958. *Institutio oratore*, translated by H. E. Butler. London: Heinemann; Cambridge, MA: Harvard University Press

QUIRK, R. 1955. 'Colloquial English and communication.' *Studies in communication*, 169–80. London: Secker and Warburg

REFERENCES

1963. 'Poetic language and Old English metre.' *Early English and Norse studies* presented to Hugh Smith in honour of his sixtieth birthday, ed by A. Brown and P. Foote, 150–71. London: Methuen. [Reprinted in *Essays on the English language: medieval and modern*, 1968. London: Longman; Bloomington, IN: Indiana University Press]

1965. 'Descriptive statement and serial relationship.' *Language* 41.205–17

1968. 'The Survey of English Usage.' *Essays on the English language: medieval and modern*, 70–87. London: Longman; Bloomington, IN: Indiana University Press

1973. 'The social impact of dictionaries in the UK.' MCDAVID, R. I., JR, and A. R. DUCKERT (eds), 76–88

1974. 'Our knowledge of English.' *The linguist and the English language*, 164–76. London: Arnold

1978. 'Grammatical and pragmatic aspects of countability.' *Die Neueren Sprachen* 3.317–25

QUIRK, R., and S. GREENBAUM. 1973. *A university grammar of English*. London: Longman [=*A concise grammar of contemporary English*. New York: Harcourt Brace Jovanovich.]

QUIRK, R., and J. SVARTVIK. 1979. A corpus of modern English.' *Empirische Textwissenschaft: Aufbau und Auswertung von text-Corpora*, ed by H. Bergenholtz and B. Schaeder. 204–18. Königstein: Scriptor

QUIRK, R., J. SVARTVIK, A. P. DUCKWORTH, J. P. L. RUSIECKI, and A. J. T. COLIN. 1964. 'Studies in the correspondence of prosodic to grammatical features in English.' *Proceedings of the Ninth International Congress of Linguists* 679–91. The Hague: Mouton

READ, A. W. 1973. 'The social impact of dictionaries in the United States.' MCDAVID, R. I., JR, and A. R. DUCKERT (eds), 69–75

REINHART, T. 1976. *The syntactic domain of anaphora*. Cambridge, MA: MIT dissertation

RINGBOM, H. *et al* (eds) 1975. *Style and text*. Stockholm: Skriptor

ROE, P. 1977. *Scientific text (Discourse analysis monograph 4)*. Birmingham: University of Birmingham

ROSCH, E., and C. B. MERVIS. 1975. 'Family resemblances: studies in the internal structure of categories.' *Cognitive Psychology* 7.573–605

ROSS, J. R. 1973. 'A fake NP squish.' BAILEY, C.-J., and R. W. SHUY (eds), 1973

SACKS, H., E. A. SCHEGLOFF, and G. JEFFERSON. 1974. 'A simplest systematics for the organization of turn-taking.' *Language* 50.696–735

SAID, E. 1975. *Beginnings: intention and method*. New York: Basic Books

SAMUELS, M. L. 1972. *Linguistic evolution*. Cambridge: Cambridge University Press

SANKOFF, G. 1976. 'Political power and linguistic inequality in Papua New Guinea.' *Language and politics*, ed by W. M. O'Barr and J. F. O'Barr, 283–310. The Hague: Mouton

SAVAGE, H. 1928. 'The significance of the hunting scene in *Sir Gawain and the Green Knight*.' *Journal of English and Germanic Philology* 27.1–15

SCHEGLOFF, E. A. 1972. 'Notes on a conversational practice: formulating place.' *Studies in social interaction*, ed by D. Sudnow. New York: Free Press

SCHEGLOFF, E. A., and H. SACKS. 1973. 'Opening up closings.' *Semiotica* 8.289–327

SCHMERLING, S. F. 1976. 'Synonymy judgments as syntactic evidence.' *Texas Linguistic Forum* 4.118–31

SCHOLTE, B. 1972. 'Toward a reflexive and critical anthropology.' *Reinventing anthropology*, ed by D. Hymes, 430–57. New York: Pantheon

SHOPEN, T. 1971. 'Caught in the act.' *Papers from the Seventh Regional Meeting, Chicago Linguistic Society*, 254–63

SHUY, R. W., W. A. WOLFRAM, and W. K. RILEY. 1967. *Field techniques in an urban language survey*. Washington, DC: Center for Applied Linguistics

SINCLAIR, J.MCH. 1975. 'The linguistic basis of style. RINGBOM, H. *et al* (eds)
SINCLAIR, J.MCH., and R. M. COULTHARD. 1975. *Towards an analysis of discourse.* London: Oxford University Press
SKALIČKA, V. 1935. *Zur ungarischen Grammatik.* Prague: Carolina University of Prague
1958. 'O současném stavu typologie.' ['On the present state of typology.'] *Slovo a slovesnost* 19.224–32
SMABY, R. M. 1974. 'Subordinate clauses and asymmetry in English.' *Journal of Linguistics* 10.235–69
SMITH, B. H. 1968. *Poetic closure: a study of how poems end.* Chicago: University of Chicago Press
SMITHERS, G. V. 1954. 'Some English ideophones.' *Archivum Linguisticum* 6.73–111
SOLOVIEV, A. 1961. *Les oeuvres littéraires de Tolstoi,* vols 9–10. Lausanne: Éditions Recontre
STAROSTA, S. 1977. *Affix-hobbling.* MS
STEINBERG, M. 1974. 'What is exposition? An essay in temporal delimitation.' *The theory of the novel: new essays,* ed by K. Halperin, 25–70. London: Oxford University Press
STEVICK, P. 1966. 'The theory of fictional chapters.' *The Western Humanities Review* 20.231–41
STOCKWELL, R. P., P. SCHACHTER, and B. H. PARTEE. 1973. *The major syntactic structures of English.* New York: Holt, Rinehart, and Winston
STRANG, B. M. H. 1968. *Modern English structure.* 2nd edn. London: Arnold
SVARTVIK, J., and D. WRIGHT. 1977. 'The use of *ought* in teenage English.' GREENBAUM, S. (ed), 179–201
SVOBODA, A. 1968. 'The hierarchy of communicative units and fields as illustrated by English attributive constructions.' *Brno Studies in English* 7.49–101
THACKERAY, W. M. 1848. *The history of Pendennis.* London: Nelson
THOMASON, H. R., and R. C. STALNAKER. 1973. 'A semantic theory of adverbs.' *Linguistic Inquiry* 4.195–220
TODOROV, T. 1969. *Grammaire du Décameron.* The Hague: Mouton
TOLSTOJ, L. 1953. *Anna Karenina.* Moskva: Gos. Izdat
TRAUGOTT, E. C. 1972. *A history of English syntax.* New York: Holt, Rinehart and Winston
TRNKA, B. 1964. 'On the linguistic sign and the multilevel organization of language.' *Travaux Linguistiques de Prague* 1.33–40
TROIKE, R. C. 1977. 'The future of English.' *Linguistic Reporter* 19.8.2
TROYAT, H. 1965. *Tolstoi.* Paris: Fayard
TRUDGILL, P. 1974. *Sociolinguistics: an introduction.* Harmondsworth: Penguin
VACHEK, J. 1958. 'Some notes on the development of language seen as a system of systems.' *Proceedings of the Eighth International Congress of Linguists* 418–9. Oslo: Oslo University Press
1961. 'Some less familiar aspects of the analytical trend of English.' *Brno Studies in English* 3.9–78. [Reprinted in VACHEK, J. 1976, 310–85]
1964a. On peripheral phonemes of modern English.' *Brno Studies in English* 4.7–109. [Reprinted in VACHEK, J. 1976, 177–287]
1964b. 'Notes on gender in modern English.' *Sborník prací filozofické fakulty brněnské univerzity* A 12.189–94
1968. *Dynamika fonologického systému současné spisovné češtiny.* [*The dynamism of the phonological system of present-day standard Czech.*] Prague: Academia.
1976. *Selected writings in English and general linguistics.* Prague: Academia
VENDLER, Z. 1967. 'Verbs and times.' *Linguistics in philosophy,* 97–121. Ithaca, NY: Cornell University Press

REFERENCES

VERKUYL, H. J. 1972. *On the compositional nature of the aspects.* Dordrecht, Holland: Reidel

VISSER, F. T. 1963–. *An historical syntax of the English language.* Part 3, first half, 1969; Part 1, 1970. Leiden: Brill

WATERHOUSE, V. 1963. 'Independent and dependent sentences.' *International Journal of American Linguistics* 29.45–54. [Reprinted in *Structural Theory 1: Structuralist*, ed by F. W. Householder, Harmondsworth: Penguin, 1972]

WEINREICH, U., W. LABOV, and M. HERZOG. 1968. 'Empirical foundations for a theory of language change.' *Directions for historical linguistics*, ed by W. P. Lehmann, and Y. Malkiel. Austin: University of Texas Press

WEKKER, H. Chr. 1976. *The expression of future time in contemporary British English.* Amsterdam: North-Holland

WELLS, G. forthcoming. 'Learning and using the auxiliary verb in English.' *Language development: course reader for the Open University – E362: cognitive development: language and thinking from birth to adolescence*, ed by V. Lee. London: Croom and Helm

WILLIS, R. S., JR. 1953. *The phantom chapters of the Quijote.* New York: Columbia University Press

ZANDVOORT, R. W. 1969. (1975, 7th edn.). *A handbook of English grammar.* London: Longman

ZETTERSTEN, A. 1969. *A statistical study of the graphic system of present-day American English.* Lund: Studentlitteratur

ZIMMER, W. 1957. 'Die neuenglische Interjektion.' *Zeitschrift für Anglistik und Amerikanistik* 5.245–320

ZWICKY, A. M. 1970. 'Auxiliary reduction in English.' *Linguistic Inquiry* 1.323–36

ZWICKY, A. M., and J. SADOCK. 1975. 'Ambiguity tests and how to fail them.' *Syntax and semantics 4*, ed by J. Kimball, 1–36. New York: Academic Press